OBSERVATIONAL ASTRONOMY FOR AMATEURS

J. B. SIDGWICK
F.R.A.S.

SECOND EDITION
prepared by
Dr. GILBERT FIELDER

THIRD EDITION
prepared by
R. C. GAMBLE
B.SC., F.R.A.S.

DOVER PUBLICATIONS, INC.
NEW YORK

The publisher of this edition wishes to express his appreciation to Herbert A. Luft, who suggested republication and oversaw preparation of this reprint.

This Dover edition, first published in 1980, is an unabridged and unaltered republication of the third (1971) edition as published by Faber and Faber, London, except that an Appendix setting forth the table of contents to Sidgwick's companion volume, *Amateur Astronomer's Handbook*, has been omitted because of lack of space; and a new Supplemental Bibliography listing books published since 1955 (the date of the first edition) has been especially prepared for the present edition by Herbert A. Luft.

International Standard Book Number: 0-486-24033-9
Library of Congress Catalog Card Number: 80-66642

Manufactured in the United States of America
Dover Publications, Inc.
180 Varick Street
New York, N.Y. 10014

CONTENTS

CONTENTS

3. GENERAL NOTES ON PLANETARY OBSERVATION

4. MERCURY

5. VENUS

CONTENTS

CONTENTS

15

TABLE OF ABBREVIATIONS

The following commonly occurring abbreviations and symbols are used in the sense quoted unless the contrary is specified or is obvious from the context.

Å   Ångström unit $=10^{-8}$ cms

A.A.H.   *Amateur Astronomer's Handbook*

A.E.   *Astronomical* (or *American*) *Ephemeris*

AT   Apparent time

A.U.   Astronomical Unit

α Right Ascension

B   Latitude

B.   (followed by number): reference to Bibliography, section 20

B.A.A.   British Astronomical Association

Bibliographical abbreviations: see section 20

c/i   colour index

CM   central meridian

D   aperture of objective in ins

Dec   Declination

d/v   direct vision

δ Declination; or, diameter of the pupillary aperture of the eye

ET   Ephemeris Time

E/T   Equation of Time

F   focal length of objective

f   focal length of ocular; or, following

f/   focal ratio (F/D). $f/10$ is said to be a larger focal ratio and a smaller relative aperture (D/F) than, e.g. $f/5$

$\mathcal{J}$ equivalent focal length

GMAT   Greenwich Mean Astronomical Time

H   hour angle

HP   high power (of oculars)

HR   hourly rate

I   intensity (of radiation)

I.A.U.   International Astronomical Union

JD   Julian Date

L   longitude

LP	low power (of oculars)
LPV	long-period variable
λ	wavelength
M	magnification; or, integrated magnitude; or, absolute magnitude
M'	minimum useful magnification
M''	maximum useful magnification
M_r	minimum magnification for full resolution
m	apparent stellar magnitude
m_b	bolometric magnitude
m_p	photographic magnitude
m_v	visual or photovisual magnitude
MSL	mean sea level
MT	Mean Time (prefixed by L=Local, or G=Greenwich)
μ	refractive index; or, micron=10^{-4} cms
NCP	North Celestial Pole
NPS	North Polar Sequence
ν	constringence
OG	object glass
ω	deviation
p	preceding
p.a.	position angle
π	stellar parallax; or, transmission factor of an optical train
ϕ	latitude
R	theoretical resolution threshold
R'	empirical resolution threshold
r	angular radius of a given diffraction ring or interspace; or, angular separation of components of a double star
r'	linear radius of a given diffraction ring or interspace
RA	Right Ascension
SPV	short-period variable
ST	Sidereal Time (prefixed by L=Local, or G=Greenwich)
t	time; or, turbulence factor
UT	Universal Time
ZD	Zenith Distance
ZHR	zenithal hourly rate

EDITOR'S PREFACE TO THIRD EDITION

Since the second edition of this book appeared, in 1961, little revision to the text has been found necessary. As Dr. Fielder has said, in his preface to the second edition, a book of this kind does not change greatly with the passage of time. Careful attention has, however, been given to the data, which have been revised and brought up to date, and references to data from the *Nautical Almanack*, available only up to 1960, have been omitted.

R. C. GAMBLE, *Editor*

EDITOR'S PREFACE TO SECOND EDITION

A book of this kind does not change greatly with the passage of time yet progress in Solar System astronomy has been remarkably rapid, recently, and many revisions have been made in order to bring the text and the Bibliography up to date. A note must be given here about the new ephemerides now in use, which introduce **Ephemeris Time.**

Following upon recommendations of the International Astronomical Union, various changes have been made to the content of the *Nautical Almanac* and the tables for 1960 *et seq* will be published in London and Washington under the respective titles *The Astronomical Ephemeris* and *The American Ephemeris*. Although these titles are different, the contents will be identical, and, in this book, both publications will be referred to as '*A.E.*'

The changes which have been made have arisen because of the need for greater accuracy in the predictions of astronomical events. Predictions tabulated for years prior to 1960 were based on the rotation of the Earth. However, the Earth's axial angular velocity is not quite uniform and hence equal intervals of Universal Time (UT), based on the Earth's rotation, are not equal by absolute standards. In an attempt to overcome this difficulty, accurate predictions will in future be referred to a new time scale, called Ephemeris Time (ET), based on the orbital motions of the Earth and Moon calculated from gravitational theory. These calculated motions must be compared with positional observations made over an extended period, and ET may then be determined accurately from the relationship

$$ET = UT + \Delta T$$

only after the correction ΔT has been determined with the requisite accuracy.

18

At the time of writing (1960), ΔT has not been well-determined, and astronomers wishing to compare their observations—which should, as always, be referred to UT—with predictions given in ET may add the appropriate (at present, approximate) correction ΔT to the Universal Time. Values of ΔT are tabulated in the *A.E.* For 1960, for example, the correction is of the order of $+35$ seconds of time.

For completeness, the available *A.E.* data have been added, where appropriate, at the end of chapters in this book. The *N.A.* data have been retained and refer, of course, to years prior to 1960.

I should like to thank R. G. Andrews (Director of the Variable Star Section of the British Astronomical Association), J. Heywood (Director of The Radio and Electronics Section of the B.A.A.), and J. Paton (Director of the Aurora and Zodiacal Light Section of the B.A.A.) for answering questions which arose during the revision.

G. FIELDER, Editor

FOREWORD

This book is intended as a sequel or companion volume to my *Amateur Astronomer's Handbook*. The latter concerned itself with the instrumental and theoretical background of practical astronomy, and its plan and intention were those of a reference handbook. The present volume is devoted to the observational techniques employed in the various fields of amateur work. Though conceived as a single unit, the two books are individually self-contained and are independent of one another; cross-references between them have been kept to a minimum.*

In the Foreword to *A.A.H.* I stressed the value of the British Astronomical Association to all amateur astronomers in this country, and the importance to the practical telescope-user of joining one of its Observing Sections. The following Section Directors have read the relevant sections of this book in MS and have given me the benefit of their specialist knowledge in these fields: D. W. Dewhirst (Sun), H. P. Wilkins (Moon), H. McEwen (Mercury and Venus), A. F. O'D. Alexander (Jupiter), M. B. B. Heath (Saturn), James Paton (Aurorae), G. Merton (Comets), J. P. M. Prentice (Meteors), W. M. Lindley (Variable Stars), and W. H. Steavenson (Methods of Observation). To them I am deeply indebted, well realising how greatly the book has benefited from their generous expenditure of time and trouble on its behalf. Finally I should like to acknowledge my appreciation of the labours of Sarita Gordon, who drew the 230-odd diagrams for this book and for *Amateur Astronomer's Handbook*.

London,   J. B. SIDGWICK
June 1954.

---

* Where such occur, *Amateur Astronomer's Handbook* is referred to as *A.A.H.*

SECTION 1

SOLAR OBSERVATION

1.1 Introduction

It being generally true that the amateur is plagued by, above all else, limitation of light grasp, the Sun offers the outstanding advantages of large angular size combined with an abundance of light. It is therefore particularly suited to observation with small instruments, and is one of the few professionally-studied objects on which valuable work (as distinct from work which is primarily of interest to the observer) can be done with amateur equipment. In spectroscopy, particularly, it is the one field in the whole of astronomy where the amateur can really go to town.

Within reason, focal length is more important than aperture in a telescope designed for solar work exclusively. But because light grasp is no longer a factor to worry about, except in the negative sense, it is sometimes forgotten that the degree of resolution of solar detail that is obtained is still a function of D. For detailed solar observation, if it is to be undertaken regularly, an aperture of 6 to 9 ins should be considered the minimum; the main features—spots, faculae, and prominences—are well seen in a 3-in, but not in sufficient detail.

The usefulness of unsilvered mirrors, as a means of reducing light grasp without at the same time reducing resolution, is emphasised elsewhere. It should also be borne in mind that an inferior objective will perform just as badly on the Sun as on more difficult objects: all branches of observation demand objectives of the highest quality, and the Sun is no exception.

Solar observation is immensely facilitated, and its accuracy improved, by an equatorial mounting, especially if clock-driven. Visual observation by projection and the study of the chromosphere and prominences, in particular, are so difficult with an altazimuth that the equatorial may be regarded as virtually essential.

1.2 Observation by projection

The Sun is the only astronomical object bright enough to be observed in this way, and owing to the great concentration of heat in the exit

21

pupil it is the most satisfactory method of examining its general appearance. Even for the detailed examination of small areas under high magnification, it may be preferable to direct observation providing certain precautions are taken (see section 1.3), though the contrary view—that such detail as pores and the granulation of the photosphere are best seen by direct vision—has been held by many experienced observers.

The projected image is reversed laterally as compared with the visual or photographic images. A mirror therefore facilitates the comparison of projection drawings and photographs.

(i) Objective only:

Image scale being a function of F, a specially constructed Sun telescope (see section 1.15) is required to give an image of sufficient linear diameter in the focal plane. Taking the Sun's mean angular semi-diameter as 16′, the linear diameter of the primary image is given by

$$d = 0 \cdot 0094 F$$

An easily remembered form of this relationship is that the linear diameter of the Sun's focal plane image is 1·13 ins for every 10 ft focal length.

(ii) Objective and ocular:

For observation by projection with ordinary telescopes, therefore, an ocular must be used to give an image of observable linear size. The diameter, d, of the projected image is directly proportional to the focal length of the objective, and to the distance, s, of the screen from the ocular, and inversely proportional to the focal length of the ocular; putting M for the magnification (F/f), therefore,

$$d = k \cdot M \cdot s$$

where k is a constant. In the case of a ¼-in ocular (i.e. HP—× 180—with a 3-in refractor of normal f/ratio) and a projection box 8 ins long, the value of k is approximately 0·07. Thus the approximate diameters of the projected images produced under these circumstances by a f/15 3-in refractor and by a f/6 6-in reflector would be respectively 12½ ins and 10 ins.

For whole-disc studies, the highest magnification that includes the whole of the solar image in the field should be used. For detailed work, the highest magnification that the atmosphere will stand. Ordinary Huyghenians are best; cemented oculars cannot be used, since the concentration of heat would melt the balsam.

The applications of the projection method are twofold:

(a) Whole-disc record of the spots and more obvious faculae. In this work, great attention should be paid to the correct representation of their sizes, positions, and orientations, and none to the detail of their structure. Pores can often be brought to visibility by gently tapping the telescope tube so that the image vibrates for a second or two.

Recommended size and reticulation of the projection blank: diameter 6 ins; horizontal and vertical diameters divided into 12 primary

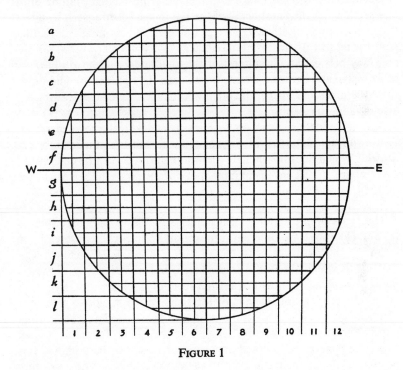

FIGURE 1

and 24 secondary parts, giving the smallest squares of the grid a side of 0·25 ins.

To facilitate the quick and correct identification of the positions of spots, the primary divisions may be lettered and numbered. It is essential that the grid be lightly and finely drawn (very sharp 2H pencil, e.g.), or small details such as pores will tend to be missed or even obscured. Some observers also mark in the grid diagonals. This certainly helps the correct delineation of the spot outlines, but has the disadvantage of cluttering up the blank and therefore tending to conceal small features.

Bristol board, or bromide photographic paper (unexposed, fixed, and washed) gives a good surface on which to draw the grid. Plaster of Paris, cast on plate glass and stripped off when set, has also been recommended as a projection surface.

(*b*) Laying down an accurately drawn and oriented outline of the umbra and penumbra of a spot or spot group, the detail to be filled in either by direct observation with a solar diagonal or from the projected image.

Unless the projected image is protected from daylight falling on it (see section 1.3) the finest detail of the HP image is better seen by direct vision than by projection. Drawing, however, is very much more difficult, owing to (*a*) alternating monocular and binocular vision, (*b*) discrepancy between the brightness of the alternately presented objects—solar image and drawing-board. If not even the outlines are laid down from the projected image, the orientation and scale of the drawing are also difficult to establish.

A suitable scale to work on is 18 ins to 24 ins to the solar diameter. A note of the diameter of the solar image must be made on every drawing which does not include the whole disc; this can be determined by comparing any convenient inter-spot distance with the same distance on the 6·in projection.

The types of projection-screen holder suitable to the conditions of (*a*) and (*b*) above are different (see section 1.3), but the observational technique in the two cases is the same. A gridded circle, identical with that on to which the image is projected, but more heavily drawn, is pinned to a drawing-board beneath a sheet of tracing-paper. By means of the underlying grid, details of the image, seen projected upon the identical grid of the projection card, are transferred to the tracing-paper. The screen is observed, as much of the detail of a facula or spot as can be memorised is noted in accurate relation to the grid, and this portion of the image transferred to the drawing-board. The procedure is slow—though practice speeds it up to a surprising degree—since accuracy is the vital consideration.

The screen carrying the projection blank is oriented by allowing the Sun's image to trail across it: it is rotated about the optical axis until the limb or a spot (preferably small and well defined) trails one of the horizontal grid lines. The image is then centred by the Dec slow motion, when the horizontal diameter will be the EW median line, and the N and S points of the image will be the ends of the diameter perpendicular to it.

With an equatorial the image, having once been oriented, remains so, though both the orientation and the coincidence of the image with the projection disc should be checked periodically during observation. With an altazimuth the orientation must be readjusted at intervals whose length depends upon the magnification employed and the distance of the Sun from the meridian; this must be discovered by trial.

The date, UT, seeing scale number, E and W points, and helio-graphic coordinates of the centre of the disc (from *B.A.A.H.* or *A.E.*) must be added to every drawing, whether of the whole disc or of a single spot or spot group.

1.3 Projection apparatus

(*a*) *For whole-disc observation with low magnification and small disc scale*

The problem is to construct a frame for the support of the projection

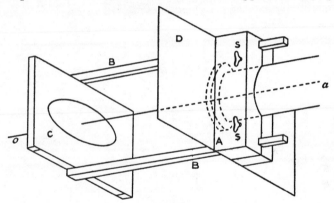

FIGURE 2

blank in a plane perpendicular to the optical axis, at such a distance (found by trial) from the highest-power ocular which includes the whole solar disc in the field as to give a solar image of the required size; the frame at the same time being rigid enough to maintain these adjustments and light enough to be attached to the drawtube without grossly upsetting the balance of the instrument and affecting its steadiness.

(*i*) The split hardwood collar *A* (Figure 2) is lined along its inner surfaces with felt, and clamped to the drawtube by means of the screws *S, S*. The image is oriented by rotating the drawtube. The bars *B, B* are clamped in a position parallel to the optical axis, *oa*, by the same tensioning screws. The framework *C*, which supports the projection card, is morticed and glued to the ends of these bars. Screen *D* excludes direct sunlight from the projected image; a circular screen with a central hole, to fit over the upper end of the telescope tube, achieves the same end and also helps to counteract the extra weight of the projection attachment. Adjustment of the size of the image is obtained by sliding the bars *B, B,* through the collar.

This design has the advantage that the distance of the screen from the ocular is variable, and that the image can therefore be made to fill the 6-in blank irrespective of the Sun's angular diameter.* It is, however,

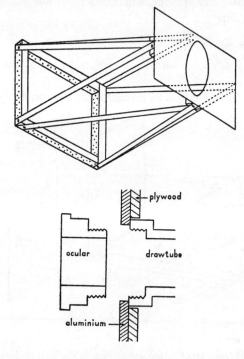

FIGURE 3

less steady than the design described below, and the accurate setting of plane of the projection perpendicular to the optical axis more difficult to obtain and maintain.

(*ii*) Sellers' open framework,† secured by the ocular. The front end of the framework (Figure 3) consists of a 4-in square aluminium sheet with a central hole just large enough for the threaded part of the ocular

---

* The Sun's angular diameter varies from 31′ 30″.8 to 32′ 35″.2 during the course of the year. At mean distance its diameter is 32′ 2″.36.

† B. 50 (reference to Bibliography, section 20).

to pass through it, and a 5-in square of plywood with a central hole just large enough to clear the drawtube collar; this is bolted to the aluminium sheet so that the two holes are concentric. Then when the collar is slipped through the hole in the aluminium rectangle and screwed into the drawtube, the combined aluminium and plywood sheet is clamped firmly between the ocular and the collar of the drawtube.

The framework is built up of aluminium slats on this forward end, as illustrated. Dimensions are omitted, since they depend on focal lengths of objective and ocular, and the correct distance of the projection screen from the ocular must be found by trial. The cross-pieces of the frame, supporting the projection card, are also omitted from the diagram. Orientation of the image is obtained by rotating the drawtube. Finally, the top, bottom, and one side of the framework are covered with black paper or cloth.

(b) *For observation of small areas of the solar disc, with high magnifications and large disc scale*

Owing to the dilution of the image with increased magnification, contrast will be reduced below the useful threshold unless daylight, as well as direct sunlight, is excluded from the image. The grid is therefore enclosed, and constitutes the rear wall of a nearly light-tight box.

To obtain the required distance from screen to ocular: let m' be the magnification of the ocular used for the projection of the 6-in image; let m be the magnification of the highest-power ocular available for the large-scale projection; let d' be the distance of the screen in the 6-in projection; then d, the required distance, is given by

$$d = \frac{nd'm'}{m}$$

where $n=3$ for an image scale of 18 ins to the solar diameter,

$n=4$ for an image scale of 24 ins to the solar diameter.

Make a plywood box of length d, and height and width equal to about one-quarter or one-third of the solar diameter—say 6 ins. The front wall of the box, by which it is attached to the telescope, is constructed as in para (a) (ii) above. The rear half of one side of the box is omitted, to allow examination of the image; the interior of the box should be given a matt black finish.

1.4 Determination of spot positions

To be of value, the determination of the positions of all spots visible on the solar surface must be carried out every day on which the Sun is visible. Even so, it is a field that is adequately covered by the professional observatories—the Greenwich photoheliographic record, supplemented by observations at the Cape, being a notable example. Such records are also worthless unless their accuracy is of a high order.* Working from a projected image is, after photography, undoubtedly the most satisfactory method; in the case of photographic records, the orientation of the image must be known.

The heliographic data that are required are P, B_o and L_o (see sections 1.20, 1.21).

1.4.1 Position angle and distance from the centre of the disc by direct observation: Simple and convenient, though not of a high order of accuracy. It requires an equatorial driven at the solar rate for ease of manipulation.

Orient the eyepiece so that a spot, or the solar limb, trails one of the horizontal webs of a Slade micrometer, thus setting the latter E and W. Bring the solar image concentric with the engraved circles and clamp the telescope. Count the number of squares, and estimate to 0·2 or 0·1 of a square, NS and EW from the centre of the grid to the spot. Suppose it lies x squares from the central EW web and y squares from the central NS web, and that the predetermined angular length of the side of each square is z. Then if θ' is the angle between the NS web and the line joining the centre of the spot and the centre of the disc, and ρ' the apparent angular distance of the spot from the centre of the disc,

$$\tan \theta' = \frac{y}{x}$$

$$\rho' = zx \,.\, \sec \theta'$$

and the position angle (always measured from the N point eastward) of the spot is:

θ' if the spot lies in the Nf quadrant,
$180 - \theta'$,,   ,,   Sf ,,
$180 + \theta'$,,   ,,   Sp ,,
$360 - \theta'$,,   ,,   Np ,,

By applying P to θ' we obtain θ, the position angle of the spot relative, not to the N point, but to the Sun's central meridian.

1.4.2 Position angle and distance from the disc centre by projection: Project the solar image on to a 6-in grid. Orient the latter so that the horizontal diameter coincides with the EW direction. Then θ', ρ' and θ can be derived as explained in section 1.4.1.

---

* Approximate determinations, which are useful for identification purposes, can be quickly made with a Stonyhurst disc (see section 1.4.3).

1.4.3 Heliographic coordinates: Stonyhurst discs: During the course of the year the value of B_o varies from approximately $+7°2$ to $-7°2$. Stonyhurst discs are constructed showing the heliographic appearance of the solar disc for the eight whole-degree values of B_o from $0°$ to $\pm7°$. Each disc is 6 ins in diameter; they were* made, by Messrs Casella, in two forms—on card for direct projection, and on transparencies for laying over drawings of the disc. The former are the more convenient to use, the drawing on tracing-paper that has been made from the projection disc merely being laid over the appropriate Stonyhurst disc.

Lay the tracing, with its marked EW diameter, over the Stonyhurst disc whose value of B_o is nearest to the value at the time of observation. By means of the $0°$–$30°$ protractors at either side of the disc, orient the drawing to the correct value of P: it follows from the rule of signs for P that if it is positive,

E end of horizontal diameter should be $P°$ above the zero mark on the protractor,

if P is negative,

E end of the horizontal diameter should be $P°$ below the zero mark on the protractor.

Read off from the disc the position of the spot E or W of the central meridian, and N and S of the equator. Call the former l and the latter b. l is positive if the spot is W of the meridian, negative if it is E; b is positive if the spot is N of the equator, negative if it is S.

The reduction then falls into two stages:

(*i*) Correction of the measured heliographic latitude for the difference between the latitude of the centre of the disc for which the Stonyhurst disc is constructed (B_d) and that at the time of observation (B_o).

(*ii*) Derivation of L, the spot's heliographic longitude, from the measured quantity l.

(*i*) If we write B for the heliographic latitude of the spot, then at the limb

$$B=b$$

at the centre of the disc,

$$B=b\pm(B_o-B_d)$$

and, generally, at a distance l E or W of the central meridian,

$$B=b\pm[\cos l(B_o-B_d)]$$

---

* B. 24. Unfortunately these are no longer being printed, and it is necessary to take photographic or manual copies of a set.

where the rule of signs is:

> if $B_o > B_d$: b positive, the sign of the last term is $+$,
>
> b negative, the sign of the last term is $-$,
>
> if $B_d > B_o$: b positive, the sign of the last term is $-$,
>
> b negative, the sign of the last term is $+$.

(*ii*) The value of L_o decreases at an average rate of 13°2 per 24 hours. Hence to obtain the value of L_o at the time of observation, a certain quantity must be subtracted from L_o at the preceding midnight (tabulated in *A.E.* or *B.A.A.H.* at 4-day intervals) or added to the value of L_o at the following midnight. The Table below will facilitate this correction:

Interval	Change in L_o	Interval	Change in L_o
1^{m}	0°01	50^{m}	0°46
2	0·02	55	0·50
3	0·03	1^{h}	0·55
4	0·04	2	1·10
5	0·05	3	1·65
10	0·09	4	2·20
15	0·14	5	2·75
20	0·18	6	3·30
25	0·23	7	3·85
30	0·28	8	4·40
35	0·32	9	4·95
40	0·37	10	5·50
45	0·41		

Having obtained the corrected value of L_o, L is derived from

$$L = L_o \pm l$$

A quicker method, in convenient logarithmic form, involves the measurement of θ, the spot's position angle, and r/R, its distance from the disc centre expressed as a decimal of the radius of the disc:

Derive an angle α, such that $\sin \alpha = r/R$.

Derive an angle N, such that $\tan N = \tan \alpha \cos (P - \theta)$, P, as before, being taken from *A.E.* or *B.A.A.H.*

If $L =$ heliographic longitude of the spot,

    $B =$ heliographic latitude of the spot,

    $L_o =$ heliographic longitude of the centre of the disc,

    $B_o =$ heliographic latitude of the centre of the disc,

Then $\tan (L - L_o) = \tan (P - \theta) \sec (B_o + N) \sin N$,

            $\tan B = \tan (B_o + N) \cos (L - L_o)$.

Stonyhurst discs are useful when referring to a particular spot in a written communication, since it is sufficient for its identification to read off the coordinates from the 'nearest' disc without any reduction for date.

1.4.4 Heliographic coordinates: Porter's disc: The spot's coordinates can be quickly and easily deduced from rectangular coordinates measured from a single Porter disc, which fulfils the function of the set of 8 Stonyhurst discs. Copies of this disc, together with instructions, are available to members of the B.A.A.; or the amateur can make his own copies from the prototype in B.47, and use them according to the instructions given under that reference. The disc is 6 ins in diameter, and the derived coordinates are correct to within a degree or two. The Porter disc undoubtedly provides the most convenient, if not the most accurate, method of deriving the heliographic coordinates of spots.

Two errata in the above-mentioned paper should be noted: (*a*) p. 63,

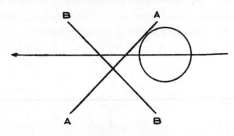

FIGURE 4

lines 3 and 4 from foot, transpose the words *clockwise* and *anticlockwise*, (*b*) p. 65, line 4 of *Example*, for *anticlockwise* read *clockwise*.

1.4.5 Heliographic coordinates: Carrington's method: While this method gives positions of a high order of accuracy, it may be doubted whether the laborious reduction is justified by the type of observations that the average amateur can make. However, since the method has never been described in any readily accessible general text,* details of it are given below.

The method can be operated either by cross-wire micrometer or by a projection card, marked with two mutually perpendicular lines, over which the solar image is trailed. In the latter case the adjustments to which attention must be paid are: cross-lines exactly perpendicular to one another, plane of the projection card perpendicular to the optical axis, and intersection of the lines located on the optical axis.

The image is allowed to trail across the micrometer webs or the cross

* It is described by Maunder in B. 36, 37.

on the projection card, such that its centre passes slightly above or below the intersection of the cross (Figure 4). Thus transits of the limb at the two webs will not be simultaneous. For the projection method it is convenient to use a 20-cm square of millimetre graph paper whose diagonals are clearly drawn in.

The observations consist of the timing of the transits of the E and W limbs and of the spot at each of the webs, A and B, to the nearest $0 \cdot 1$ secs. The mean should be taken of at least three sets of transits. An example of a convenient layout for the record in the case of a single spot is given below:

	Diagonal	Times of:			Mean time of transit	Interval between spot and disc centre	
		1st transit h m +	2nd transit h m +	3rd transit h m +			
		s	s	s		Over A	Over B
p limb	A				A_p		
	B				B_p		
spot	A				a	$a-A_c$	$b-B_c$
	B				b		
f limb	A				A_f		
	B				B_f		
solar centre	A				A_c		
	B				B_c		

A_c and B_c are derived from the transit times of the limbs:

$$A_c = \frac{A_p + A_f}{2}$$

$$B_c = \frac{B_p + B_f}{2}$$

The reduction falls into three stages:

(*i*) Derivation of position angle and distance from the centre of the disc, from the observational data.

(*ii*) Conversion of position angle and distance to heliographic co-ordinates.

(*iii*) Calculation of the area of the spot, if required (see section 1.5).

(*i*) Let $\theta=$ angle subtended at the centre of the disc by the line joining the spot and the N end of the solar axis,

$P=$ position angle of the N end of the solar axis,

$i=$ inclination of the Sun's path to the parallel of Declination passing through the centre of its disc.

P is taken from *A.E.* or *B.A.A.H.*; i from the Table on p. 32; θ is derived as follows:

$$\theta=\alpha+(\epsilon\pm i-P)$$

where

$$\tan \epsilon=\frac{A_f-A_p}{B_f-B_p}$$

$$\tan \alpha=\frac{a-A_c}{b-{}_{\mid}B_c} \cdot \frac{1}{\tan \epsilon}$$

The logarithmic forms, for convenience in computing, are

$$\log \tan \epsilon=\log (A_f-A_p)- \log (B_f-B_p)$$
$$\log \tan \alpha=[\log (a-A_c)-\log (b-B_c)]-\log \tan \epsilon$$

The use of 4-figure tables justifies working to the nearest $0°1$.

The true (heliocentric) angular distance ρ of the spot from the centre of the disc is taken from the Table on p. 32, using the value of r/R (the distance expressed as a decimal of R, the solar radius) given by

$$\frac{r}{R}=2 \sec \alpha \cdot \frac{b-B_c}{B_f-B_p}$$

or, more conveniently,

$$\log \left(\frac{r}{R}\right)=0{\cdot}3010+\log \sec \alpha+[\log (b-B_c)-\log (B_f-B_b)]$$

(*ii*) Let $B=$ heliographic latitude of the spot,

$B_o=$ heliographic latitude of the centre of the disc.

Then $\qquad \sin B=\cos \theta \cos B_o \sin \rho+\sin B_o \cos \rho$

Let $L=$ heliographic longitude of the spot,

$L_o=$ heliographic longitude of the centre of the disc,

$l=$ longitude of the spot measured from the central meridian.

Then $\qquad \sin l=\sin \theta \sin \rho \sec B$

and $\qquad\qquad L=L_o-l$

33

Inclination of the solar path to the Dec circle passing through the centre of its disc:

Date		i	Date	
Feb	25	$+0°06$	Apr	10
	5	$+0·05$	May	2
Jan	24	$+0·04$		16
	14	$+0·03$		27
	6	$+0·02$	Jun	5
Dec	30	$+0·01$		14
	21	$0·00$		22
	15	$-0·01$		30
	7	$-0·02$	Jul	9
Nov	29	$-0·03$		19
	19	$-0·04$		30
	7	$-0·05$	Aug	13
Oct	13	$-0·06$	Sep	8

Relationship between r/R and ρ:

r/R	ρ	r/R	ρ	r/R	ρ
0·100	5°7	0·730	46°7	0·910	65°3
0·200	11·5	0·740	47·5	0·920	66·7
0·300	17·4	0·750	48·4	0·930	68·2
0·350	20·4	0·760	49·3	0·940	69·8
0·400	23·5	0·770	50·2	0·950	71·6
0·450	26·6	0·780	51·1	0·960	73·5
0·500	29·9	0·790	52·0	0·970	75·7
0·525	31·5	0·800	52·9	0·980	78·3
0·550	33·2	0·810	53·9	0·990	81·6
0·575	34·9	0·820	54·9	0·991	82·0
0·600	36·7	0·830	55·9	0·992	82·5
0·620	38·1	0·840	56·9	0·993	82·9
0·640	39·6	0·850	58·0	0·994	83·5
0·660	41·1	0·860	59·1	0·995	84·1
0·680	42·9	0·870	60·2	0·996	84·6
0·700	44·3	0·880	61·4	0·997	85·3
0·710	45·1	0·890	62·6	0·998	86·1
0·720	45·9	0·900	63·9	0·999	87·2

1.5 Determination of spot areas

A graphical method of determining the areas of spots, whose accuracy is within the limits imposed by the projection method of recording the spot, is described by Sellers (B. 49).

It is based upon the fact that the area of a square on the surface of a sphere, whose side subtends 1° at the sphere's centre, is very nearly 49 millionths of the surface of the hemisphere. If each side of such a square is divided into 7 parts, and the square further subdivided, each secondary square will have an area of one-millionth of the area of the hemisphere.

On a scale of 24 ins to the diameter, an unforeshortened 1° square will have a side of 0·21 ins; the side of each secondary square will then be 0·03 ins, the drawing of which is quite practicable with a very sharp 2H pencil.

The procedure is to project the Sun's image on to a gridded circle 2 feet in diameter. Copy the outline of the spots, with the greatest accuracy possible, on to a similar gridded circle. On this superimpose a grid of 0·21-in primary and 0·03-in secondary divisions—it need only be a couple of inches or so across—drawn on tracing-paper. Count the secondary squares that are more than half covered by the umbra and penumbra (ignoring the remainder). This number will then be the area of the spot expressed in millionths of the solar hemisphere, uncorrected for foreshortening (ϕ).

If, for ease of drawing, a 2°-square grid is constructed (primary divisions 0·42 ins, secondary 0·06 ins), then ϕ will be four times the number of secondary squares. A still more time-saving simplification is to use 1-mm graph paper, in which case the number of squares counted must be multiplied by 1·72 to give the area in millionths of the Sun's hemisphere. In this case it would be the drawing of the spot that is made on a transparency.

To the area so derived a correction for foreshortening must be applied, unless the spot is at the centre of the disc. If the number of secondary squares of a 1° grid be ϕ, and the distance of the spot from the centre of the disc be r, the semidiameter of the disc being R, then the area corrected for foreshortening is given by

$$\Phi = \phi \sec \theta$$

where θ is an angle such that $\sin \theta = \dfrac{r}{R}$

Alternatively, Φ may be derived from direct measurement of the disc, using either the above expression and measuring θ, or

$$\Phi = \phi \cdot \frac{R}{x}$$

and measuring R and x. θ, R and x are the quantities shown overleaf.

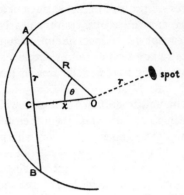

FIGURE 5

Given that the distance of the spot from the disc centre is r, from any point A on the circumference draw a chord AB, of length $2r$. The distance from O to the midpoint, C, of this chord is x, and the angle subtended at O by the semichord AC is θ.

The precision of the method does not justify taking θ to more than the first decimal place. Since the inaccuracy increases very rapidly with sec θ, the area of a spot cannot be derived with sufficient accuracy to make the measurement worthwhile if $\theta > 60°$ approximately, except for provisional estimates of spots newly appeared on the E limb.

To save playing with protractors and compasses, the value of sec θ may be taken from the Table below, where it is tabulated against r (expressed in inches, for a 6-in disc). Or these values of r may be used to construct concentric circles within a 6-in disc on tracing-paper; when this is laid over the disc drawing, the appropriate value of sec θ for the spot may be read off without further calculation or geometrical work.

r	sec θ	r	sec θ
0·42	1·01	1·80	1·25
0·59	1·02	1·92	1·30
0·72	1·03	2·02	1·35
0·82	1·04	2·10	1·40
0·91	1·05	2·17	1·45
0·99	1·06	2·24	1·50
1·07	1·07	2·34	1·60
1·13	1·08	2·43	1·70
1·19	1·09	2·50	1·80
1·25	1·10	2·55	1·90
1·48	1·15	2·60	2·00
1·66	1·20		

1.6 Direct visual observation

Adequate protection for the eye is the first consideration. The required intensity of the emergent pencil being in the region of 0·1 % to 0·01 % that of the incident radiation, reduction of aperture is useless; it is in any case undesirable owing to its reduction of the objective's resolving power. Available methods, which may be used singly or in combination, are (a) absorption, (b) fractional reflection at unsilvered surfaces, (c) polarisation. When the image is viewed by projection, it will be remembered, no reduction of the incident intensity is required.

The possibility of using suncaps alone is confined to the smallest apertures—say, below 3 ins. Even so, they tend to get extremely hot, forcing the eye back from the exit pupil, and may crack or even melt; they also cause loss of contrast, in which respect neutral tints are preferable to the extreme spectral colours, of which blue is the worst. They are constructed of plane parallel glass (the balsam and gelatin of an ordinary colour filter would immediately melt), of density from about 3·0 to 4·0 (percentage transmissions 0·1 and 0·01 respectively), and are mounted so as to fit over the eye lens of the ocular.

Alternatively, a neutral glass wedge may be used; this has the advantage that the intensity of the image can be adjusted to changing weather conditions and the altitude of the Sun.

At every unsilvered air/glass surface, the intensity of the reflected pencil is reduced to about 5% that of the incident. Hence, a single such reflection (e.g. solar diagonal) will have to be supplemented by a neutral filter of density about 2·0 to 2·5, or by further reduction of intensity by polarisation (see Table below). Two reflections will require a lighter filter (density in the region of 1·0 to 1·5), unless the Sun is already partially obscured by mist or cloud, when even a second unsilvered reflection may reduce the brightness of the image too much.

Solar eyepieces: percentage transmissions

		1st unsilvered reflection	2nd unsilvered reflection	3rd unsilvered reflection
		5·0	0·25	0·0125
Neutral filter Density=1·2	6·3	0·32	0·016	0·0008
Neutral filter Density=2·5	0·32	0·016	0·0008	0·00004

Three reflections will bring the intensity of the emergent pencil within the required range of 0·1–0·01%, and only a narrow margin of reduction by polarisation need be allowed, for conditions of maximum solar brilliancy. More than three unsilvered reflections will reduce the intensity below the required level under all conditions of observation. It should be remembered that an odd number of reflections reverses the image in one plane (L and R, or up and down), while an even number of reflections leaves the image as it is presented to the first reflecting surface.

Some solar diagonals employ a right-angled, first-surface prism.

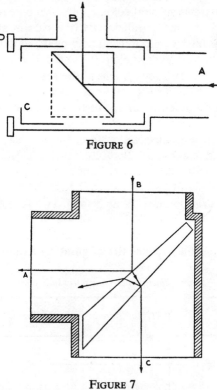

FIGURE 6

FIGURE 7

A: to ocular, *B*: to drawtube, *C*: open

Figure 6 shows a combined Sun and star diagonal of this sort. It fits into the drawtube at *A*; the ocular is at *B*. The prism is mounted in a sleeve *C* which slides into the body of the diagonal, being retained by the screw ring *D*. In the position shown by continuous lines, the prism turns the incident light through 90° by total internal reflection, and the diagonal can be used for stars. If *C* is removed, turned back to front, and replaced, the prism now occupies the position shown by broken lines; reflection is external, and the diagonal can be used (with a light neutral filter) on the Sun.

More satisfactory is the Herschel wedge (Figure 7), with its complete suppression of secondary reflections. It is a first-surface reflecting prism of small angle, and reflections from the rear surface are deflected from the field, as they would not be with a plane parallel mirror. It screws into the drawtube, and the ocular into it; it therefore involves a racking-in of the drawtube from the normal focus, in common with all

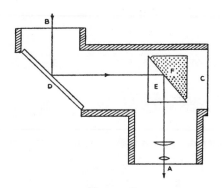

FIGURE 8

A: to eye, *B*: to drawtube, *C*: open, *D*: unsilvered plane reflector,
E: right-angled prism, *F*: liquid prism

diagonals. There being only one reflection, a suncap or other dimming device must be used with it.

The Colzi eyepiece utilises a liquid prism to reduce reflection at the surface of a glass prism (Figure 8). By filling *F* with a liquid whose refractive index is close to that of *E* (e.g. clove oil or vaseline oil), total reflection at the hypotenuse of *E* can be prevented, and any required degree of partial reflection obtained.

With the addition of a second unsilvered mirror (either Herschel wedge or black glass flat) the possibility of further reduction by polarisation is introduced (Figure 9). As a result of the double unsilvered reflection the intensity of the emergent beam will be reduced to 0·25% of the incident. If, further, β is Brewster's angle,* the ray XY will be completely plane-polarised, and rotation of the second wedge will reduce the intensity of its transmitted ray to zero when the plane XYB is perpendicular to AXY (i.e. the ray YB is perpendicular to the page).

* About 56°–58°, according to the refraction index of the glass. See further *A.A.H.*, section 21.3.4.

However, the periphery of the field will not be reduced in intensity by rotating the second wedge, since only the central rays will be incident at Brewster's angle, and away from the axis will be progressively incompletely polarised.

An elaboration of the above provides for a second pair of reflecting

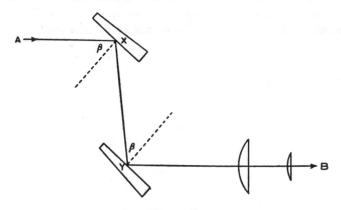

FIGURE 9
A: to drawtube, *B*: to eye

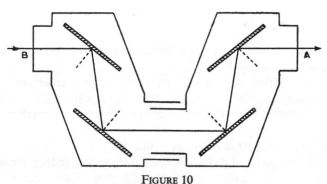

FIGURE 10
A: to ocular, *B*: to drawtube

surfaces (Figure 10): any degree of reduction is now obtainable by rotating the half of the body to which the ocular is attached, about the axis joining the two central mirrors. Since four unsilvered reflections would reduce the intensity of the image below the observing threshold, the first mirror is silvered. The disadvantage of this type of solar ocular, despite its great convenience in use, is its size and weight; also the

40

increased length of light path may necessitate the drawtube being racked in a greater distance than the makers of the telescope allowed for.

A different design, employing the same principle, is illustrated in Figure 11. The shaded half of the body screws into the drawtube; the unshaded part can be rotated about the axis XY. The prisms A and B are set at the polarisation angle; the secondary reflectors, C and D, are plane parallel discs of black glass. As shown in the figure, the transmission of the polariser would be something under 10%; when rotated through 90° from this position of maximum transmission, transmission would be reduced to zero.

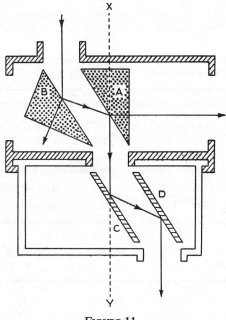

FIGURE 11

The problem can be tackled from the other end, in the case of reflectors, by the use of an unsilvered speculum. This also obviates the danger of distortion or cracking of the flat through excessive heating; it also allows the full aperture to be used, making available the maximum resolving power which the objective is capable of providing.

An unsilvered speculum carries the disadvantage that observation by projection is impossible. But the main drawback is the greatly increased trouble that is encountered from differential heating and expansion of the unsilvered, as compared with a silvered, speculum. This generally produces a gradual shortening—and often the ultimate destruction—of the focus. Opinions differ regarding the value of an open-backed cell.* The back of the mirror may be either polished or ground without materially affecting the clarity of the image. The only radical solution of the problem of differential heating is the employment of Pyrex for an unsilvered speculum.

If the flat is also unsilvered, little further reduction will be needed, and in the case of a partially obscured Sun the reduction will already be excessive. In this case a silvered flat is used in conjunction with a suncap, diagonal or polarising eyepiece (with silvered surfaces, if polarisation by reflection); the last is to be preferred because of the ready adjustment of the final intensity that it allows. Unsilvered flats must be of the wedge variety, a plane parallel flat giving trouble from secondary reflections in the field.

1.7 Instrumental: differential heating, etc

The thermal inequalities that can ruin definition in solar work occur within the speculum itself (in the case of a reflector)—and also in the flat—within the remainder of the instrument (particularly in the column of air enclosed by the tube of a reflector or refractor), and within the immediate surroundings of the instrument.

A thorough investigation of the relative effects in glass mirrors with and without a metallic first-surface film would be valuable: at the present time the advocates of unfilmed mirrors claim that the latter are superior because the heat absorption tends towards uniformity between first and second surfaces, whereas the heat absorption in a silvered or aluminised mirror is confined to the vicinity of its first surface; whilst those who prefer silvered or aluminised mirrors claim that their performance is superior because there is effectively no differential heating, the heat and light both being kept away from the body of the mirror by the high reflectivity of its first surface in both wavebands.

There is no doubt that if part of the glass mirror of a reflector is allowed to receive direct sunlight, while the rest of it is shaded by the top of the tube, definition will be ruined in a matter of seconds, owing to unequal heating and expansion, destruction of the figure, and loss of a single focal length. In any case, with a glass mirror, adjustments of the focus will have to be made during observation, particularly during the first 15 or 20 minutes.

The solution of the problem, in the case of reflectors, would certainly

---

* Cf. night observation, discussed in *A.A.H.*, section 10.4.

appear to be the use of a material of low thermal expansion—such as Pyrex or fused quartz—for all mirrors employed in solar work. The relative differential heating of a silvered (or aluminised) and of a plain surface would then be immaterial, since in neither case would the figure be affected. In the case of each of these materials the disadvantage for the amateur is expense. Fused quartz, though the worst in this respect, can nowadays be bought at a not prohibitive cost in the form of translucent discs with a thin transparent surface of sufficiently fine quality for working to an optically critical figure. Such specula give very fine performances when silvered or aluminised and are of proved excellence for such units as coelostat flats and Newtonian secondaries which are used at high angles of incidence, when even Pyrex introduces serious astigmatism.

Failing such near-perfect resolutions of the difficulty that an optical component forming an image of the Sun must necessarily be exposed to solar radiation, the performance of reflectors can be improved by blacking the interior of the tube; by using an open or lattice tube, or, if solid, providing it with numerous ventilation holes; and by using a tube of considerably larger diameter than that of the speculum, since air currents in the tube tend to stick to the outer parts.* Polishing the second surface of an unfilmed speculum will also improve definition by reducing scattered light.

Refractors, though they suffer less than reflectors from unequal heating of the objective, are more subject to thermal currents in the tube.

Shading the observing site is an important factor in the improvement of solar definition. Movable canvas screens can be used to prevent direct sunlight striking the mounting—and the tube itself, when not in use—and the immediate surroundings of the instrument. If it is mounted in an observing hut, a large degree of thermal insulation during the daytime can be obtained by spreading a false roof of canvas, stretched on a light wooden frame, a foot to eighteen inches above the true roof; the space between the two must be left open so that the air can circulate freely. All this has a direct bearing on the desirability of setting up a properly arranged solar observatory (see section 1.15).

It will often be found that the best definition occurs fairly early in the morning—despite the greater thickness of atmosphere through which the Sun is then observed—and also, rather surprisingly (unless it is only then that an improperly shaded instrument settles down to thermal equilibrium), towards sunset.

* For a fuller discussion of tube currents, see *A.A.H.*, section 11.2.

1.8 Telescopic work

The following short list is selected almost at random from the vast field of solar observation open to instruments of small or moderate aperture; a few hours spent in looking up the solar references in the literature of the last fifteen or twenty years will expand it a hundredfold. 1, 4, 6 and 7, below, require only a small aperture; the remainder demand some resolving power—6 ins at least is desirable, and if larger so much the better.

1. Mapping the spots daily (see section 1.4).

2. Drawing the detailed structure of spots. Attention should particularly be given to active spots and groups. Serial drawings of such spots, with sufficient aperture and magnification and on a large enough scale to show the fine detail, and made at intervals determined by the rate at which visible development is occurring, are of increasing value nowadays;* more and more spectrohelioscopes and spectroheliographs are coming into operation, and such drawings offer the possibility of correlating phenomena in monochromatic light with events visible in integrated light. The possibility of a repetition of the almost unique† Carrington-Hodgson observation of 1859 should also be kept in mind; the likeliest regions for a recurrence are complex spots at the height of their activity, and the remnants of great spots seen on a subsequent solar rotation.

Detail not otherwise visible is sometimes revealed by an extreme contraction of the field, with its consequent reduction of photospheric background and concentration of the observer's attention. This is most conveniently achieved by means of a Dawes diaphragm in the focal plane of a positive ocular.

Accuracy—a matter of patience and experience more than of skill as a draughtsman—is essential; time spent making casual sketches is time wasted. *All* drawings, of this or any other type, must be labelled with the UT to the nearest minute—if necessary, the UT of the start as well as of the completion of the drawing.

3. Besides the normal faculae there are two types that require special attention: (*a*) 'Dark faculae': vague, smudge-like markings, darker than the photosphere, about which very little is known and of which few observations have been recorded. They characterise the equatorial zone and are most readily seen near the centre of the disc; often contain a pore. Require moderate apertures (visible with 6 ins, but 9 ins is better). There is need for a considerable mass of observation of these

---

* See also section 1.9.

† For references to other observations of flares in integrated light, see B. 60.

objects, giving positions, appearance, and date and time of observation. (b) Polar faculae: occur within about 25° of the poles; fainter and smaller than the normal equatorial faculae; probably most numerous around spot minimum, but very little is known about them still. Best seen in large-scale projected images; recommended method of recording—dotted lines on a 6-in disc.

4. Ill-defined spots. Occasionally spots appear which are unaccountably vague and ill-defined; that this is not an instrumental or atmospheric effect is shown by the fact that they have been seen simultaneously with spots of normal appearance. Visible with a 3-in. Record position, date, and time of observation.

5. Pores. Charting might give results of value, if continued over a long enough period. Pores should always be watched since they are often the precursors of spots, and more information is wanted about the earliest stages of spot formation. Pores appear to be formed by the increased separation of the solar granulation ('rice grain'); the normal separation of individual granules—which can be seen satisfactorily in the projected image provided extraneous light is excluded—is about 2″. Gently tapping the projection frame, so that the image vibrates slightly, often reveals small pores that would otherwise be missed. Very precise focusing is also essential.

6. Scope for more work on the longitude distribution of spots (see e.g. B. 17), the correlation of longitude with other factors (such as size, longevity, type, the spot cycle, etc), and on the recurrence of spots in the same region of the solar surface. An example of the latter was provided by the great spot groups of February and July 1946: if the drift of the former is extrapolated to July it is found that the latter occurred in almost exactly the same position (latitude difference, 2°). It must be remembered that owing to the distribution of rotational velocity in zones, a given longitude loses its identity after 8 or 10 rotations.

7. Comparatively little study has been made of the laws governing the rate of growth and decay of spots, and of the correlations (if any) between this and factors such as spot type, latitude, spectrohelioscopic character, phase of the spot cycle, etc.

8. Scope for work on the rotation of spots. Pseudo-rotational effects which must be distinguished from true rotation spring from (inter alia) normal changes in the shape of the spot, changing orientation of the spot relative to the NS line (geocentric) during its passage across the disc, and the common tendency of the leader in a pair, whose axis is inclined to the equator, to gain in longitude on the trailer.

As examples of what the amateur can do without even putting his eye to the telescope may be mentioned Dr Alexander's work on the longitude distribution of spots (B. 17), including his discovery of a 400-day subcycle; and his analysis of the Greenwich photoheliographic results, throwing new light on the character of the 11-year cycle (B. 18).

1.9 Photography

Uniquely among celestial objects, the Sun offers the photographer a superabundance of light. The advantages that follow from this fact are notable: short exposures, no guiding, slow fine-grain emulsions, the opportunity to select moments of better-than-average seeing, and size of aperture only of importance in so far as resolution is concerned. The Sun alone offers scope for photography with a small altazimuth.

Reflectors and photovisuals can use any type of plate, the focus being determined either visually or photographically. With a visually corrected objective, on the other hand, the visual focus must be used with iso-, ortho-, or panchromatic plates and a yellow or orange filter. Whereas in the photography of most astronomical objects the increase of exposure necessitated by the suppression of the actinic wavelengths is a serious matter, in the case of the Sun it is of little importance.

Shutters must be capable of speeds up to about 1/500 sec, and if located near the focal plane of the objective must be constructed of metal, polished on the outer side and dull black on the plate side. But unless a separate telescope is available for viewing the image it is essential to use a reflex system with a focal plane shutter.

Filters should be as dense and monochromatic as is consistent with short exposures on the plates available. Glass filters (such as the Chance-Watson series) are less affected by heat than gelatin filters, but the general superiority and greater range of the latter make it worthwhile searching for a method of using them without damage: locating the filter far from the focus and near to the plate is ruled out by the fact that it would then have to be of nearly the same size as the plate itself; reducing the intensity of the image by diaphragming the objective is undesirable, since at any rate 5 ins aperture is required for adequate resolving power; if a compur shutter is used (which may be undesirable in itself—see above) the filter can of course be placed immediately behind the shutter; a solar diagonal can be used, with the filter at the camera end, though this produces image reversal; the filter may be slipped into place close to the eyepiece for the few seconds necessary to allow the exposure to be made, focusing being carried out by inspecting

the screen through the filter held in the hand. Of these various subter-
fuges, the last two are the most satisfactory.

Amplified images may be photographed by screwing the box of a
commercial camera, from which the lens has been removed, to stays
attached to the drawtube which can themselves slide in a second set of
stays fixed rigidly to the telescope tube. An astronomical ocular is used,
the camera box merely supplying the reflex mirror, shutter, and plate-
holder. For larger images than it is possible to accommodate in a
cheaply bought commercial camera (e.g. 6, 9 or 12 ins, or even larger,
at a distance of a foot or so from the ocular) it is better to construct a
multi-ply or aluminium box, square in section and tapered outward
from the ocular to the plate plane. If a space is left between the ocular
and the front of this box the changing of oculars and the approximate
centring of the image on the shutter (or hinged flap covering the hole
in the front of the box) are facilitated, and the dispersal of heat by convection is promoted, with consequent improvement of seeing.

It is impossible to lay down any rules regarding exposure times,
which depend upon the aperture, the degree of amplification, the plate
speed, filter density, and to some extent on the Sun's altitude (hence on
the time of day and season). An exposure-meter and a few trial plates
will quickly settle the matter. With small instruments and no exceptional conditions, the correct exposure will probably be found to lie
between 1/100 and 1/500 sec. In order to make an instrument 'slower'
without loss of resolution, it is better to reduce exposures, double up
filters, use slower plates, or increase magnification or projection distance,
rather than to reduce aperture.

Solar photography, as all other methods of observation, is much
facilitated if a long-focus horizontal Sun telescope is available. The
resolution of detail 1″ in diameter requires an aperture of only 5 ins.
The plate-scale of about 10″ per mm necessary to show this detail
requires, without amplification, a focal length of approximately 68 feet.
A 20-ft Sun telescope with a 4-in or 6-in objective (as described in
section 1.15) could therefore be extremely usefully employed. Such a
layout permits the use of a much heavier camera than could possibly
be attached to the telescope, it enormously simplifies the photography
of the projected image, and it allows any type of shutter to be used
under conditions where no vibration can be transmitted to the plate or
image. Owing to the shortness of the exposures, a siderostat is not
required (though anyone having gone to the trouble of laying out a
solar observatory would certainly have installed one for visual, spectrohelioscopic, or other purposes), a silvered or aluminised flat mounted

on a polar axis with Dec adjustment and RA slow-motion controls to the observing position being sufficient. Provision must be made for varying the position of the plate along the optical axis—over a range (increase) of about 0·001F—as the objective warms up.

Photography of the projected image offers the advantages of virtually unlimited enlargement of the image, increased exposure times involving less expensive shutters (though increased dependence on the atmosphere), and no auxiliary telescope necessary for viewing the image. Easy to arrange in a solar observatory, the precise relative adjustment of screen and camera is rather tricky when both are attached to an ordinary equatorial. The whole eye end of the telescope, including screen, camera, and observer's head, must then be covered by a light-proof hood. To avoid distortion of the image through foreshortening, the plate must be tilted in a plane perpendicular to that containing the optical axis and the line from the image centre to the plate centre, the angle of tilt being equal to that between the same two axes measured in the plane containing them. The image may be projected, as usual, on glossy Bristol board or direct on to a Stonyhurst disc. Providing the seeing is good and the focus precise, a quarter-plate photograph of a projected image 6 ins or so in diameter can be subsequently enlarged to show a great deal of spot detail, although, owing to some loss of definition in projection, this method is more suitable for whole-disc records.

Backed plates are essential in solar work. Under-exposed plates can always be intensified,* or they may be viewed on a ground-glass screen lit from below by a 150-watt lamp. Over-exposed plates need slow and very careful development. The bringing up of the relatively dark limb by dodging during the development is of little scientific value, though producing a 'picture' of greater verisimilitude.

It has already been emphasised several times that moments of minimum turbulence must be selected for the exposure of solar plates. For the recording of detail this often demands a lot of patience, and on some days is impossible of realisation. On the other hand, when turbulence is marked under magnification, and the recording of detail is impossible, fairly satisfactory whole-disc photographs may frequently be obtained. Turbulence, especially during the summer, is often comparatively slight when the Sun is low. Altitude, however, is a factor to be considered, since the Sun's actinic strength varies widely according to the length of the light-path in the atmosphere and the latter's water-vapour content. This is a less important consideration for the user of a visually corrected refractor than of a photovisual objective or reflector. A low Sun, or the

* See, e.g., *A.A.H.*, section 20.8.

presence of mist, must be countered either by longer exposures or, better, by a faster emulsion or a less dense filter. In so far as any general rule can be given, most satisfactory conditions are likely to be encountered around the middle of the day in winter and during the early morning or late afternoon in summer.

Whole-disc records of spot distribution are more quickly made with the camera than by eye and hand. Such work is largely a waste of time, however, being more than adequately dealt with by the 4-in and 9-in photoheliographs at Herstmonceux and by regular programmes at other observatories, notably the Cape. Furthermore a 3-in image (the largest that can be accommodated on a quarter-plate) is liable to miss the smaller pores (for which, see below, a 4-in image is the minimum); it is also too small for accurate measures of position to be made—these require 6-in images, plates for which become very expensive if used regularly.

There is, on the other hand, plenty of scope for the photographic recording of small pores, the detail of spot structure, and the changes of active groups at frequent intervals, with full aperture, high magnification, and stringent selection of the moment of exposure. There is nothing like a continuous record of spot detail (unlike spot distribution), and in recent years—when at any moment a vital correlation with spectroheliographic observations may be wanted—it has become increasingly important.

If the smallest pores are taken to be of the order of 1″ in diameter, apertures not less than about 5 ins are desirable. Taking the limit of photographic resolution as 0·002 ins, the plate-scale should not be less than about 3·7 ins to the solar diameter; in fact, it would normally be considerably greater than this, since amplification would in any case be required unless the focal length were of the order of 70 feet.

Orientation of the image can most conveniently be established by stretching a thread across the field close to the plate and orienting it EW by trailing the image.

Solar eclipses present perhaps the most fruitful opportunities for the solar photographer. According to the length of the exposures, and therefore to the phase of the eclipse, stationary short-focus cameras, clock-driven equatorials, or siderostat-fed long-focus telescopes may be used. Assuming that 0·002 ins is the limit of photographic resolution, we need be concerned with no movement of the image smaller than this during an exposure. Taking the Sun's angular motion as 15″ per second, the maximum permissible exposures with a stationary camera for various focal lengths are as follows:

Focal length		Maximum permissible angular displacement of image (″ arc)	Maximum permissible exposure (secs)
ft	*ins*		
	6	68·9	5·8
	12	35·2	2·4
	20	20·6	1·4
	30	13·8	0·9
3		11·5	0·8
4		8·6	0·6
9		3·8	0·25
12		2·9	0·19
20		1·7	0·11
40		0·86	0·06

Short-focus cameras on fixed mountings can thus be used to record the partial phases. Telescopes, as well as wide-angle cameras when photographing the outer corona, must be equatorially mounted and clock-driven. The partial phase can be recorded with a fixed camera making an exposure every 3 minutes (the images separated by approximately ¼°). During totality a considerably greater separation, or a series of singly exposed plates, is required to avoid overlapping of the images of the outer corona. Fixed wide-angle cameras of short F and small focal ratio can be used to record the inner corona with exposures of 1 sec or less, but to record the fainter outer regions the camera must be clock-driven for exposures of from 4 to, say, 20 secs. A variety of exposures is essential for showing the form of an object which, like the corona, has a considerable intensity gradient. The length of the middle exposure of the series can be estimated roughly beforehand by photographing terrestrial objects under poor illumination, e.g. low Sun or overcast sky. Some long exposures, of the order of 2^m at $f/15$, should be included to make sure of the outer regions. Hence a battery of cameras—each with its own operator if mounted separately—is desirable. If commercial shutters are not used, it is quicker to vary the effective exposures by means of aperture stops than by shutter speeds.* In any case, the programme must be thoroughly and repeatedly rehearsed, until each action becomes part of an automatic drill. Some short exposures should be included to show the prominences, which disappear in the glare of the corona when the exposure is long enough to record the latter adequately. The longest-focus cameras should be

* The relationship between relative aperture and exposure is detailed in *A.A.H.*, section 20.6.

used for short exposures with amplifying lenses to reveal the inner coronal structure and the prominences in greater detail.

Panchromatic plates, with or without filters, have been recommended when the totality zone is narrow and there is a lot of diffused sky-light; long dewcaps are also essential. Very light-tinted Crookes' glass might also be useful in conjunction with panchromatic plates, since it reduces the visual intensity by only about 5% while absorbing heavily the shorter wavelengths of the sky-light. Double-coated plates (a fast emulsion superimposed on a much slower one) have also been recommended. Panchromatic plates can be hypersensitised (increasing their sensitivity to the yellow region by as much as 25%) by immersing them in running water in the darkroom for an hour or so immediately before use.

The coronal spectrum can be photographed with the aid of a transmission grating mounted immediately in front of the objective with the engraved face towards the camera and the rulings vertical. The direct image and the first-order spectrum are then recorded on the one plate.

1.10 Solar spectroscopes

The various types of spectroscope suitable for amateur use are described in *A.A.H.*, section 19.

1.11 Spectroscopic observation of the disc

Quite modest equipment will show the main features of the Fraunhofer spectrum, but for anything more than sightseeing a certain amount of dispersion and aperture is required. Spectroscopic attachments to telescopes require careful focusing if they are to reveal all that they are capable of showing. The general procedure is: (*a*) Bring the Sun's image to a sharp focus on the slit jaws (a magnifying glass is a help). (*b*) Adjust the spectroscope eyepiece to the position giving greatest sharpness to the edges of the spectrum. (*c*) Bring the Fraunhofer lines to maximum clarity by collimator adjustments. This will to some extent destroy (*b*), but simultaneous adjustment of collimator and eyepiece will quickly find the best combination. (*d*) Finally, by means of the telescope focusing rack, make the fine adjustment of (*a*): set the slit centrally and radially across the limb and bring the edge of the spectrum produced by the solar limb to the sharpest focus.

A small-scale map of the main features of the solar spectrum is given in Figure 12; see also Table overleaf. More detailed maps are given in B. 57 and 58: Plate 33 of the former is a uniform-dispersion spectrum on a scale of about 3Å per mm and shows the most important

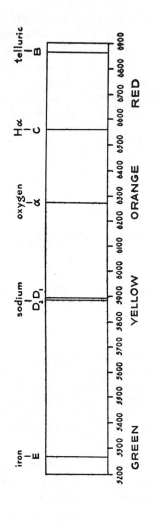

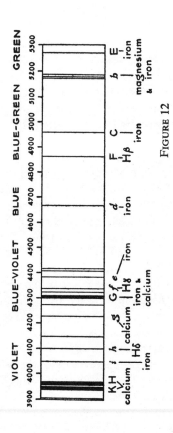

FIGURE 12

lines from 6900Å to 3900Å; Plate 34 represents a prismatic spectrum, from 6600Å to 3900Å, of total length 23·5 cms. Plates 9–16 of the latter reference cover the solar spectrum in great detail from 3900Å to 5400Å to a scale of 0·3 cms per Å. B. 348 (Appendix) tabulates the wavelengths of a number of the more important lines, including ones in the infrared and ultraviolet outside the above ranges. See also B. 48 (wavelengths of 20,000 lines from 2975Å–7331Å to 0·001Å; based on the D line of sodium; also relative intensities and identifications), B. 54 (revision of the preceding in the international system based on the red cadmium line, plus about 2000 lines up to 10,219Å, giving a total of 22,000 lines), B. 19, 20, 39.

Table of the more important Fraunhofer lines

Designation of line	Rowland Revised Wavelength (Å)	Origin
K	3933·68	calcium
H	3968·49	calcium
h ($H\delta$)	4101·75	hydrogen
g	4226·74	calcium
G	4307·91	iron, calcium
f ($H\gamma$)	4340·48	hydrogen
e	4383·56	iron
d	4668·16	iron
F ($H\beta$)	4861·34	hydrogen
c	4957·62	iron
b_4	$\begin{cases} 5167·33 \\ 5167·51 \end{cases}$	$\begin{cases} \text{magnesium} \\ \text{iron} \end{cases}$
b_3	5169·05	iron
b_2	5172·70	magnesium
b_1	5178·20	magnesium
E	5269·55	iron
D_3	5875·60	helium
D_2	5889·98	sodium
D_1	5895·94	sodium
α	6278·01	oxygen
C ($H\alpha$)	6562·82	hydrogen
B	6867–6881	oxygen

The main characteristics of spot spectra are also visible with a very simple grating or single-prism spectroscope attached to a small telescope. With the slit set EW, sweep across the disc with the Dec slow motion until the spot band appears along the length of the photospheric spectrum; with this setting of the slit the spot's spectrum will remain visible while the spot trails along the slit (assuming no clock drive) or, in the case of a driven equatorial, with the minimum of adjustment in RA.

The edges of the band should be clearly defined, and the distinction between the central umbral spectrum and the bordering penumbral spectrum well marked (Figure 13). Points to watch for are, in particular:

(a) Variations in the density of the band in different wavelengths.

(b) Differences in the normal widths of the photospheric lines where they cross the spot spectrum.

(c) Absence of lines in the spot spectrum from that of the photosphere.

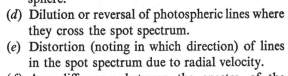

(d) Dilution or reversal of photospheric lines where they cross the spot spectrum.

(e) Distortion (noting in which direction) of lines in the spot spectrum due to radial velocity.

(f) Any differences between the spectra of the umbra and penumbra.

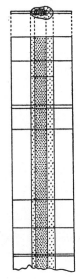

FIGURE 13

Records of observations of spot spectra must specify clearly the position of the slit relative to the solar image.

Flares—brilliant hydrogen outbursts in the chromosphere, which cannot properly be called eruptions since they have no radial velocity—require a spectrohelioscope for their full and detailed observation. They can, however, be to some extent observed by the open-slit method providing the spectroscope is of a dispersion giving sufficient dilution of the integrated light when the slit is widened. Even if this condition is not fulfilled, some useful results can be obtained by the regular observation of the $H\alpha$ and $H\beta$* lines when the slit is lying over spots—particularly those in active development. Any widening or reversals of these lines should be noted—together with the time (beginning and end), position, and approximate intensity—and an attempt made to widen the slit slightly. Reversals on the disc can be seen with quite small instruments, with a narrow slit. In either case there is scope for regular patrolling of the spots. The widening of the hydrogen lines may be most impressive when the flare is intense, having been known to exceed 20Å for short periods. Intense flares are of rare occurrence, however,

* Flares have, at one time or another, produced strong emissions in D_1, D_2, D_3, H, K, and the b group, as well as in the more usual $H\alpha$ and $H\beta$.

and typically last only a matter of minutes—exceptionally for several hours. All observations, however incomplete, are therefore of value, and may fill a gap in the spectrohelioscopic observations. Particularly required are observations of the early stages in the development of flares, and measures of area and intensity; but for these a spectroscope of considerable dispersion, if not a spectrohelioscope, is a *sine qua non*.

For a well-documented account of past observations of flares without a spectrohelioscope, see B. 41.

1.12 Spectroscopic observation of chromosphere and prominences

Apertures of 4 ins and upwards are useful in this field, though the prominences can, of course, be seen with less. The dispersion of the spectroscope needs to be greater than that which will merely show the Fraunhofer spectrum, or insufficient weakening of the integrated light will be encountered when the slit is opened; a spectroscope to be used for observation of the prominences should be able to separate clearly the D_1 and D_2 lines in the yellow ($\Delta\lambda=6$Å).

Given the requisite dispersion, increasing the magnification has the effect of increasing the apparent dimensions of the slit and hence of the prominence when the slit is opened. Given the dispersion, also (i.e. with a given spectroscope), a short-focus telescope has some advantage over one of longer F, since its primary image scale is smaller, whence a greater area of the prominence will be seen with any particular width of slit. The choice is between a larger fraction of the prominence being seen on a smaller scale, or a comparatively small part of it seen on a large scale; generally the former is preferable.

Owing to the fineness of the adjustment that holds the prominence visible, an equatorial accurately driven at the solar rate may be considered essential. With practice, the observation of prominences with an altazimuth, if it has good slow motions, is perfectly practicable. There are, however, enough unavoidable difficulties in the way of successful astronomical observation without indulging avoidable ones—and the cost of an equatorial (even of a clock-driven one) for instruments of moderate aperture is not nowadays prohibitive.

A prominence spectroscope* is one embodying the following features:

(*a*) Adequate dispersion.

(*b*) A prism or grating which is set permanently so that a prominent chromospheric line, usually $H\alpha$,† is central in the field.

* See also *A.A.H.*, section 19.

† $H\alpha$, $H\beta$, and D_3 (helium) are the most important prominence emissions visible to the eye.

(*c*) A slit which is offset from the optical axis of the telescope by an amount equal to $0 \cdot 0047F$ * (the mean semidiameter of the solar image in the focal plane), so that rotation of the spectroscope about the telescope's optical axis will cause the slit, once it has been set tangentially on the limb, to travel round it. Alternatively, the solar image may be rotated on the slit jaws by means of an image-rotator.†

If the slit is placed radially across the limb at a point where there is a prominence, the *H*α line will be seen (given very precise focus and excellent seeing‡) to have a fine, bright prolongation which projects beyond the edge of the spectrum by an amount depending on the height of the prominence. If the slit, while tangential to the limb and a few " of arc from it, lies centrally across a prominence, the centre of the *H*α will be reversed, while the rest of the field is dull; this is the slit position required for the observation of prominences. If the slit is slightly displaced towards the centre of the solar image from this position, so that it lies over the disc, the whole of the *H*α will be dark and the field bright; if displaced slightly too far outward from the solar limb, the *H*α will be dark and the rest of the field dim. If the slit is moved steadily outward from the limb position, the length of the hydrogen reversals will vary with the size and shape of the prominence, finally contracting to nothing as the slit moves off the prominence altogether. If the slit, while in the limb position, is opened slightly, each reversal will widen into a monochromatic image of the jagged profile of the chromosphere and the base of the prominence.

That the prominence should be visible when the widened slit is passing radiation which is only approximately monochromatic is explained by the fact that it is seen against a dark background. The loss of this contrast is, inevitably, directly proportional to the width of the slit—and, for a given slit width, inversely proportional to the dispersion. Thus it is that a prominence is invisible by the open-slit method when it is projected on the disc, since the glare from adjacent wavelengths is then prohibitive. It is the job of the spectrohelioscope to overcome this.

The observational procedure is therefore as follows:

(*i*) Focus the solar image on the slit jaws.

* The figures for maximum and minimum solar semidiameter are $0 \cdot 00459F$ and $0 \cdot 00474F$. Some slight readjustment of the slow motions will therefore nearly always be required while patrolling the limb.
† *A.A.H.*, section 8.11, describes different forms.
‡ Visibility of the chromosphere and prominences is also much reduced by even a trace of haze or 'whitening' of the blueness of the sky.

(*ii*) Bring the *H*α line to a sharp focus in the centre of the field; slit nearly closed.

(*iii*) Rotate the spectroscope till the slit is perpendicular to the Dec axis and tangential to the E limb (position angle 90°).

(*iv*) Rotate spectroscope clockwise,* so that the slit, maintaining its tangential orientation, travels round the limb through N (0°), W (270°), and S (180°) to E again. During this operation the image must be kept centrally in the field, which even with a clock drive will require touches on the slow motions.

(*v*) Whenever, during (*iv*), a bright, reversed 'notch' appears on the *H*α line, continue the rotation of the spectroscope until it is at the centre of the line and open the slit to reveal the prominence.

(*vi*) With the slit 'open', make final focusing adjustments with the drawtube rack.

Records of prominence observations should include:

Date and UT.

Position angle (the sleeve of the drawtube should be graduated to show the p.a. settings of the slit).

Height (" arc).

Brightness.

Drawing, with scale. (In the case of active prominences a series of drawings should be made, the directions of motion being indicated by arrows.)

Any associated distortions of spectral lines.

Heights and other dimensions of prominences can be measured by means of an accurately drawn scale, reduced photographically on a glass diaphragm—both the number of graduations and the amount of reduction depending on the specifications of the instrument with which it is to be used—and mounted in the focal plane of the positive ocular of the view telescope.

The scale can be calibrated as follows: Orient spectroscope and scale so that both lie EW; the scale is then projected normally across the width of the spectrum. Adjust the telescope in Dec so that the Sun is central in the field; then clamp it *p* the Sun without altering the Dec setting. As the Sun transits the slit the spectrum will transit the scale. Time the transits of the *p* and *f* edges of the spectrum at any particular scale graduation ($t_2 - t_1 = T$). Also time the transits of either edge of the

---

* If the spectroscope is mounted, not in the drawtube, but in a star diagonal, it must be rotated anticlockwise from 90° in order to follow the same sequence of position angles.

spectrum at two widely separated graduations, n divisions apart $(t_2' - t_1' = T')$. Let the Sun's angular semidiameter in $''$ arc be R (taken from the *N.A.* for nearest 0^h UT). Then θ, the angular value of a single division of the scale, is given by

$$\theta = \frac{RT'}{\frac{1}{2}nT} \quad '' \text{ arc.}$$

There is great scope for systematic work on the prominences with adequate instrumental means. Many aspects of the relationship between spots and the overlying chromosphere are still imperfectly understood, largely owing to the former being too foreshortened for effective study when near the limb. The laws governing the motions of prominences,* again, will not be elucidated without the accumulation of many more observational data.

Since 1922 the daily appearance of the limb in $H\alpha$, as well as annual prominence statistics, have been published for the I.A.U. by Arcetri Observatory. The unit of profile area of a prominence is defined as the area contained between a $1°$ arc (heliocentric) of the Sun's limb and a concentric arc situated $1''$ arc above it:

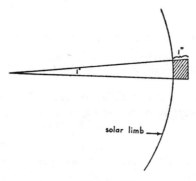

FIGURE 14

1.13 Eclipse observations

1.13.1 Partial:

1. Timing of contacts. The first is necessarily less accurate than the last if observed visually. Observe the chromosphere with a curved slit nearly closed (if a straight slit is used, any slight misorientation will result in the point of contact being missed) and note the obtrusion of the lunar limb into the $H\alpha$ reversal. A good drive is desirable—and at

* B.29, 51.

least an equatorial with good slow motions is almost essential—in order to keep the slit accurately coincident with the limb. Last contact can be observed by the same method.

2. If observing visually, note and record any outstanding irregularities on the Moon's limb.

3. Record visibility of the Moon outside eclipse, with times.

4. A continuous plot of the intensity of the solar radio-frequency radiation as the lunar limb crosses the disc may give valuable information regarding the source locations of the radiation.

1.13.2 Total:

(a) *Visual:* The following notes are rather a suggested programme for a team of observers than for a single observer, who could not hope to cover more than a fraction of the ground.

1. Timing of contacts: second and third contacts are given by the disappearance of the last Baily's bead (white, cf. the red prominences) and reappearance of the first. Record: method used; time to nearest 1^s0 or better; longitude, latitude, and height above MSL of the observing station.

2. Shadow bands: white sheet laid on ground, with vertical rods on flat bases to indicate their direction. Record: times of appearance (usually 0^m5 to 2^m before second contact and after third contact); direction of motion (stating whether true or magnetic bearings); speed (both this and their direction are independent of the motion of the Moon's shadow).

3. Baily's beads: caused by combined effects of irradiation and the serrated limb; visible for a few seconds before second contact and after third. Of no scientific interest apart from their indication of the times of the contacts.

4. Prominences. Record: colour (been described as whitish, pink, red, and yellow to the naked eye), identifying them by position angle from the N point of the disc.

5. Corona. Record: time of first visibility; extent and intensity; position and structure in relation to any prominences visible.

6. See section 1.13.1, paragraph 4.

7. Other phenomena: e.g. approach of the shadow (velocity up to 5000 m.p.h. if oblique to the Earth's surface—i.e. near sunset or sunrise), often visible in the sky, or overland if the viewpoint is well above the surrounding terrain; degree of darkening during totality (faintest stars visible).

8. Conditions. Record: temperature and barometer at intervals;

formation of dew, if any; direction and velocity of surface wind; wind deduced from movements of lower and upper clouds, if any.

(b) *Spectroscopic:* What work can be done is necessarily dictated by the equipment available. The following brief description shows what can be done with even a small slitless spectroscope. It should be so oriented that the length of the spectrum is normal to the line of cusps at the moment before totality.

1. Start observing about 10 minutes before totality.

2. Record time at which the curved Fraunhofer lines (arcs) become visible.

3. As the width of the continuous spectrum shrinks, bright arcs will be seen projecting beyond the continuous band.

4. Note if the prominent Fraunhofer arcs disappear simultaneously.

5. Instantaneous appearance of the flash spectrum at the E limb: second contact. Record time. The appearance and disappearance of the flash spectrum is an indicator of the moment of contact, which is sensitive to about $0^{s}.02$. Hence the possibility of a movie camera exposing 50 frames per second (normal speed, 24), with some method of synchronisation with radio time pulses. But to gain anything from such speeds, some form of sound-track time record would have to be used, and with typical amateur equipment synchronisation to the nearest 1^{s} would be nearer the limit possible (e.g. clock face reflected into the field of view).

6. Disappearances of the flash spectrum.

7. Disappearance of the chromospheric arcs and superimposed images of E limb prominences (during the short period of totality they will be complete rings).

8. Coronal rings (red and green, fainter than the chromospheric arcs or rings). Record: relative thickness and diameters of these rings; positions angles of any regions of abnormal intensity.

9. Appearance of chromospheric arcs at the W limb.

10. Appearance of flash spectrum at W limb.

11. Disappearance of flash spectrum and reappearance of continuous spectrum: third contact.

For the study of the coronal lines a spectroscope and view telescope of larger aperture, and correspondingly higher magnification, are desirable. For any detailed spectroscopic work, a slit spectroscope is, of course, necessary.

Maunder's 'Eclipse Suggestions' (B. 35), though written half a century ago, is still worth referring to. B. 55 is a more up-to-date treatment; see also B. 40.

Anyone interested in the computation of eclipses should refer to B. 26.

1.14 The radio astronomy of the Sun

Radio astronomical observations of the Sun are made at all wavelengths. In general four main types of instrument are used, the radiometer, the radio interferometer, the radio spectrograph, and the radio polarimeter. Observations with polarimeters yield information about magnetic fields when circular polarisation is observed. Amateurs in England have so far used interferometers in their expansion of 'low frequency radio astronomy' and radiometers for observations in the super high frequency region (centimetric wavelengths).

Three distinct types of radio noise are observed from the Sun: (i) noise from the quiet Sun, due to a thermal mechanism; (ii) a slowly varying component having a period of weeks or months and observed in the range 3 to 60 cm, and (iii) bursts and noise storms. There are five main spectral types of solar noise at present and other types are under discussion. As in visual astronomy there is an important call for continuous observations of the Sun on a number of wavelengths. There is a need for spectroscopic observations by amateurs. The bursts and noise storms are best observed with a radio spectroscope using rhombic aerials. In general the noise storms which last for periods of the orders of hours or days are associated with large sunspots, whilst the outbursts which only last for minutes are associated with flares. In neither case can it be said that all flares and all sunspots will be associated with radio noise, and the *visible* spots are not the sources of these emissions.

In the same way the terrestrial effects of intense solar activity are not necessarily related to the number of sunspots. Observations during the International Geophysical Year showed that there was greater solar and terrestrial activity associated with the Sun in September, 1957, than in the following month, when the sunspot number was actually greater.

The following terrestrial effects have been observed to accompany solar flares:

(a) *Magnetic crotchets*. A disturbance of the Earth's magnetic field usually occurs simultaneously with the peak of the flare. These magnetic crotchets, as they are called, are restricted to the sunlit side of the Earth and last for only a short time.

(b) *Radio communication fade outs*. Radio communications are considerably disturbed when flares are generated. Apparently a new layer of ionisation is formed on the sunlit side of the Earth—just below the E region—forming a new D region.

(*i*) Short waves: these are disturbed and undergo absorption. The period of strained conditions is confined to the sunlit side of the Earth and lasts only for a matter of hours.

(*ii*) Long-wave phase anomaly: The ionisation of the D region is shown up by the fact that the phase between the ground- and sky-waves at the receiver changes. Much work has been done on this problem at 18,000 m.

(*iii*) Magnetic storms, as distinct from crotchets, affect the F region of the ionosphere.

(*iv*) The newly-formed D layer tends to improve long-wave propagation conditions. It also has the effect of increasing the atmospheric noise level at the receiver; particularly in the tropics.

(*c*) *Solar corpuscular streams.* After about 26 hours from the occurrence of a large flare there are often violent magnetic storms and aurorae. These are thought to be due to the ejection of particles at a velocity of 1600 km/sec from the Sun.

(*i*) The Magnetic storms may last for several days and severely effect the F region of the ionosphere. Short-wave communications can be disrupted for several days.

(*ii*) Production of aurorae. (For a discussion of radio work on aurorae see **14.6**.)

(*d*) *Cosmic radio noise.* At a wavelength of 16 m it has been discovered that the newly-formed D region causes the radio emissions from the cosmic sources to be absorbed.

(*e*) *Radio noise from the Sun.* Many flares are accompanied by outbursts which last for from several minutes up to an hour. They are many times the intensity of the base level of the solar radio noise.

Bursts and flares which are prevalent at metre wavelengths cause great difficulties in observing thermal radio emissions from the Sun. For this reason the thermal emission from the chromosphere and the inner corona is generally observed on much shorter wavelengths.

(*f*) *Sudden ionospheric disturbances (S.I.D's).* Of the above features, the increase in ultraviolet radiation from the Sun which increases the ionisation in the D region of the ionosphere can be classified with those effects which produce sudden disturbances in the ionosphere (S.I.D's). The measurement of S.I.D's is of importance and one of the methods used is to observe the fading undergone by cosmic radio waves in the region of 11 m. This is then a measure of the absorption from which the increase in free electrons can be computed.

The S.I.D's which have been discussed are clearly the:

(a) Magnetic Crotchet
(b) Short-wave Radio Fade Out
(c) Long-wave Phase Anomaly
(d) Fading of Cosmic Radio Noise
(e) Sudden Enhancement of Atmospherics (S.E.A.)

Of these one of the most interesting is the S.E.A. since amateurs can build a simple receiver to observe S.E.A's and this can be useful in maintaining a flare patrol (see Ellison, *J.B.A.A.*, **69**, No. 3, 1959). This method is due to Bureau (R. Bureau, *Nature*, **139**, 110, 1937; see also *Proc. Phys. Soc.* B, **63**, 122, 1950, Les renforcements brusques des ondes très longues). He suggested that the radio waves generated by the lightning flashes of thunderstorms could be summed by a receiver operating on a wavelength of about 11 km. The D layer improves the reflecting properties of the long waves so that a receiver which is listening to thunderstorms which are generated from the tropics receives more noise from such storms when a solar flare occurs than it would otherwise. There is not however—and this is important—an increase in the number of atmospherics generated; it is only an increase in the integrated number which can be received. The apparatus required is simple, and can be built by the amateur, although a pen recording milliammeter is required. It is ideal for use in England, since the sky is often cloudy, and thus it provides an immediate comparison with other types of record. Further information can be obtained from the radio-electronics section of the B.A.A.

Amateurs of the B.A.A. are at present operating five phase-switching interferometers using large Corner V aerials. These are used for continuous observations of the Sun and are semi-steerable. One particular problem which is being examined is the extent of the outer solar corona. This is being achieved by observing the effects on the radio emissions coming from the Crab Nebula when the nebula is occulted by the corona. Observations can be made of the scattering, refraction, and absorption that the emission undergoes in the corona. An important feature of this work is that it is being carried out at frequencies near to the ionosphere's critical values. These are lower frequencies than have been used for this type of observation in England up to the present.

There is great scope for the amateur who wants only a simple aerial array in that a simple dipole array can be used to observe the Sun during the whole of its passage across the sky. Observations by amateurs working at different wavelengths would be of immense value in the studies of solar radio astronomy—more particularly since continuous

63

observations on a number of wavelengths have stopped at the Cambridge Observatories with the ending of the I.G.Y.

The literature devoted to radio astronomy is now vast (see, e.g. B. 334a, 336a, 343a, 345a). B. 43 is a useful reference on the subject of magnetic storms. Special references to solar radio work will be found in the bibliography.

1.15 Horizontal Sun telescope

The amateur who decides to specialise in solar work should consider very carefully the advantages of a permanent solar telescope, into which a stationary image is fed by a coelostat. The difficulties involved are mainly non-astronomical: (a) possession of a suitable room or hut, or the space in which to build one, (b) expense—which, however, can be considerably reduced if he is prepared to do as much of the constructional work as possible himself.

The advantages are imposing:

(a) A much longer focal length than can be employed in an ordinary telescope, giving with ease a solar image of, say, 2 ins diameter—which would be out of the question with a privately owned refractor or Newtonian.

(b) It permits the use of spectroscopes capable of doing justice to what even quite small apertures have to offer, when the object is the Sun. Spectroscopic attachments to a refractor or Newtonian must necessarily be light, and their dispersion small. No one who has ever seen the solar spectrum under wide dispersion (my own first view of it, at the focus of the Mt Wilson 150-ft tower telescope, was an unforgetable experience) will be prepared to go back to work with the type of spectroscope designed for attachment to small telescopes.

(c) Convenience of combining a direct-vision telescope, a solar-image projector, a camera, spectroscopes (prismatic or Littrow), and possibly a spectrohelioscope, mounted together under one roof in what is virtually a single instrument and instantly accessible and ready for use.

(d) Convenience of having the various instruments permanently mounted in comfortable observing positions.

(e) Convenience of the stationary image, obviating the necessity for a heavy and accurately driven equatorial, with continuously changing observing position.

(f) Comparative freedom from thermal currents, with a suitably designed installation.

(*g*) Finally, the unique scope that the Sun offers the amateur for valuable original research cannot be fully exploited with the ordinary telescope that is found in amateur hands.

Any number of different designs can be evolved, according to the nature and focal length of the objective and the ancillary instruments that are to be incorporated. The objective may be either an achromatic OG or a paraboloid. The specimen layout described below employs a 5-in achromatic and is based upon the recommendations of F. J. Sellers, who has himself built a Sun telescope of this type (Figure 15). See also B. 30.

The objective and the auxiliary instruments are housed in an oblong building oriented as nearly N and S as possible. (The scale given here is based upon a focal length of from 20 to 30 feet; a shorter but wider room could equally well be used.)

A: masonry pier carrying the coelostat,* which consists of two 5-in flats. The dotted area should be covered with a pent roof (no walls) to shade the window and the light-path from the coelostat into the hut; a sliding extension should be arranged so that the entire coelostat and pier are in shade when not being used; an additional shade, fixed to the pier itself, screens the collecting mirror from the Sun while in use. From the coelostat pier there should ideally be a clear view nearly to the horizon for 180° or more, centred on S.

O: objective (5-in achromatic), mounted on a NS slide so that its position is adjustable between *v* and *w* to allow the image to fall at any required distance from *C*.

B: light-proof tunnel surrounding the travel of the OG.

C: 5-in flat mounted with its centre on the optical axis of *O*. Its inclination is adjustable about a vertical axis, so that the reflected pencil may be turned towards *V*, *W*, *X* or *Y* as required.

V, W, X, Y, Z: masonry piers or stout timber benches (according to the nature of the floor and foundations) carrying the auxiliary instruments; the collimating axis of each must pass through the centre of *C*. *Y* carries the slit, grating, and ocular of a high-dispersion diffraction spectroscope; *Z* carries the collimating and image-forming paraboloids (see below). If a Hale spectro-helioscope is to be included in the equipment, this apparatus and arrangement is already halfway to it, while an easily made rearrangement of the piers would accommodate an Ellison

* *A.A.H.*, section 14.22.

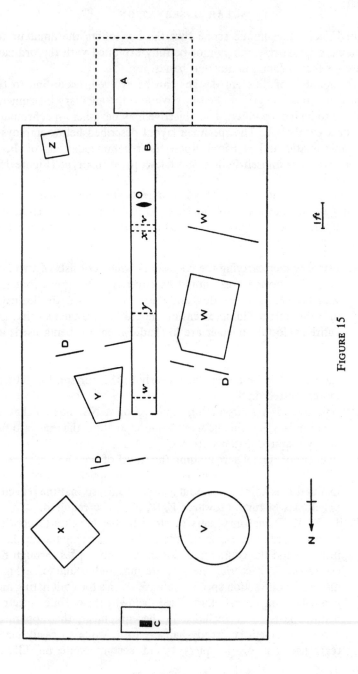

FIGURE 15

autocollimating spectrohelioscope.* *W* takes the mounting for a projection lens (an achromatic Barlow gives very good results); *W'* is a fixed projection screen. *V, X* can be used for mounting cameras, prismatic spectroscopes, etc.

D: movable screens with circular holes just large enough to allow the passage of the pencils.

Figure 16 shows in greater detail, and in elevation, a possible layout for the grating spectroscope:

G: slit on which the solar image is formed by the objective after reflection at *C*.

H: collimating paraboloid which reflects the light from the slit as a parallel pencil to *J*. The centre of *H* and of the slit must, of course, lie on an axis passing through the centre of *C*.

J: the grating (e.g. a 4-in replica)†; being mounted so that it is

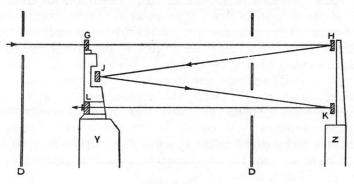

adjustable about a vertical axis, any region of the spectrum of any order can be reflected to *K*. The grating cell should also be mounted in such a way that the necessary adjustments to ensure that the rulings are vertical can be made easily.

K: second paraboloid, which brings the spectrum to a focus at

L: eyepiece or plate-holder.

If a parabolic mirror is used instead of an OG, the layout must be modified somewhat, though the principle remains the same. The flat, *C*, is replaced by the paraboloid, which is fed direct from the coelostat. Since tilting the mirror through wide angles (in order to bring the image

* *A.A.H.*, section 22.6.

† Replicas are not suitable for spectrohelioscopes, however (see *A.A.H.*, section 22.6).

to instruments situated, say, near the side walls of the hut) would introduce abaxial aberrations, the instrument piers must all be close to the optical axis of the objective. This introduces some practical difficulties, and for the amateur with limited resources the achromatic arrangement already described is probably more satisfactory.

When planning a horizontal Sun telescope and deciding on the sizes of the optical components, it must be remembered that allowance must be made for the extent of the field of view. Thus, for example, a 5-in coelostat mirror will not give full field illumination if the paraboloid, at a considerable distance from it, is only 5 ins in diameter. Either the paraboloid must be enlarged to accommodate a $\frac{1}{2}°$ expanding pencil from the coelostat, or else the size of the latter must be correspondingly increased.

The Snow Telescope at Mt Wilson is an example of a horizontal Sun telescope employing a paraboloid. In fact, two paraboloids are here available, so as to give a choice of image-scales without magnification by an ocular. The long-focus mirror ($F=143$ ft) is permanently mounted at the N end of the building; the short-focus objective ($F=60$ ft) is mounted between this and the coelostat in such a manner that it can be swung to one side when the long-focus mirror is in use; provision is made for inclining it slightly to the incident beam, and also for varying its position along the optical axis, so that the image can be brought to the various auxiliary instruments. Both objectives have an aperture of 24 ins; the coelostat and collecting mirrors have apertures of 30 ins and 24 ins respectively. The solar images produced by the objectives are 16 ins and 6·7 ins in diameter.

It is recommended that the two exterior mirrors should be rhodiumised, or at least aluminised. They should also be covered by a weatherproof housing, locked to the top of the pier, when not in use. Interior mirrors should be aluminised. All mirrors of Pyrex or fused quartz. The OG must be a first-class achromatic, and all flats figured to one-quarter of a wave.

Proper shading of the coelostat and the S end of the hut will do much to reduce thermal currents. Even so, it is difficult to free a horizontal telescope entirely from the effects of convection currents rising from the heated ground. (Hence the two later Sun telescopes at Mt Wilson are vertical tower telescopes.) The outside of the building should be painted white, and its surroundings planted with shrubs to protect the ground from the direct rays of the Sun. Image distortion and change of focus due to heating of the flats and mirrors are materially reduced by using Pyrex or fused quartz, but even so an alteration of focal length of as much as about 1.5% during observation must be expected. The films should be renewed as soon as their reflectivity begins to fall off, or distortion will result.

1.16 Sunspot numbers and other solar data

Also known as Wolf Numbers, Wolfer Numbers, Zurich Numbers, and Sunspot Relative-Numbers. An arbitrary index of the daily spotted-ness of the disc. First devised by Wolf at Zurich, and continued by Wolfer.

The Wolf Number, R, is arrived at by counting the number of disturbed areas (both groups and isolated single spots) g, and the total number of individual spots f, giving the former 10 times the weight of the latter, adding the two together, and multiplying by a coefficient k, whose value depends on the aperture of the instrument with which f and g were counted, and also on the care and experience of the observer:

$$R=k(f+10g)$$

The value of k is determined empirically: a long series of observations with a particular instrument by a particular observer are compared with the mass of data submitted to the Zurich clearing-house, and the coefficient selected which brings the two into best agreement. For a careful and experienced observer using the Zurich telescope ($D=10$ cms, $M=64$), $k=1.0$; for smaller instruments, k will be slightly larger than 1.0; for larger instruments, slightly smaller.

Thus if a standard instrument, properly employed, shows 2 spot groups, one containing 2 spots and the other 3, as well as 4 isolated spots, the Wolf Number for the day will be 69:

$$g=6 \text{ (i.e. } 2+4 \text{ disturbed regions)}$$
$$f=9 \text{ (i.e. } 2+3+4)$$
$$\therefore \quad R=1(9+60)$$
$$=69$$

Daily Wolf Numbers and monthly means are published quarterly in B. 59, which also includes for the three-monthly period:

(*i*) Chromospheric eruptions:

  date and time of observations and of maximum intensity,
  approximate coordinates,
  maximum width of $H\alpha$,
  maximum area,
  maximum intensity.

(*ii*) Active regions:

> rotation number,
> coordinates of centre,
> date of CM passage,
> age at CM passage,
> duration (solar rotations).

(*iii*) Diagram showing the hours during the three-monthly period during which the Sun was under spectrohelioscopic and spectroheliographic observation at the cooperating observatories.

(*iv*) Coronagraph measures of monochromatic (5303Å and 6374Å) coronal intensity at 5° intervals of position angle.

(*v*) Solar radio noise data.

(*vi*) Before 1945: character figures of calcium and hydrogen flocculi, on a scale from 0(complete absence) to 5 (maximum encountered at the peak period of solar activity).

(*vii*) Before 1939: character figures for the Sun's ultraviolet radiation.

Since 1947 the Swiss Federal Observatory at Zurich has been broadcasting the daily Wolf Numbers on the short-wave channels of the Swiss Broadcasting Corporation. With the exception of those to South America (in Spanish) the broadcasts are in English. They are given on the 4th and 5th of each month as follows:

Date	Time (UT)	Wavelength (m)			Destination
	h m				
	07 20	25·39,	25·28		Australia
	15 05	19·60,	16·87		Far East
4th	21 50	19·59			S. America
	22 30	25·28			N. America
	23 40	31·46,	25·28,	19·59	S. America
5th	01 40	31·46,	25·28,	19·59	N. America
	03 05	31·46,	25·28,	19·59	N. America

1.17 Classification of spot types

Cortie's classification,* based upon the telescopic appearance of the spot, is simple and reasonably comprehensive:

1. Group of one or more small spots.

---

* Also sometimes referred to as the Stonyhurst classification (B. 25).

2. Two-spot formations:
- (a) With the leader larger than the trailer.
- (b) With the trailer larger than the leader.
- (c) With both members of approximately equal size.

3. Train of spots:
- (a) With the principal spots well defined.
- (b) With none well defined (patchy penumbrae and irregular umbrae).

4. Single spots:
- (a) Round and regular.
- (b) Round and regular, with small attendant spots or pores.
- (c) Irregular.
- (d) Irregular, with train of small attendant spots.
- (e) Irregular, with small companions irregularly distributed.

5. Irregular group of larger spots.

An alternative classification, based upon the magnetic properties of the spot, has been developed at Mt Wilson:

α : Single spot, or group of same polarity; flocculi symmetrical.

αp: „   „   „   centre of group p centre of flocculi.

αf: „   „   „   centre of group f centre of flocculi.

β : Bipolar pair; leader and trailer of about equal size.

βp: „   leader larger than trailer.

βf: „   trailer larger than leader.

$\beta \gamma$:   „   leader and trailer accompanied by smaller spots of opposite polarity.

γ : Multipolar spots; rare, irregularly arranged spots of opposite polarity, not classifiable as β.

1.18 Classification of flares

Ellison has proposed the following rough classification of flares on a basis of size only:

Class 1: >100 $\leqslant 300$ millionths of the Sun's hemisphere.

„   2: >300 $\leqslant 750$ „   „   „

„   3: >750 „   „   „

This simple classification has not, however, been generally adopted, and the I.A.U. still (1953) recommends the older classification into four groups (1, 2, 3, 3+) based on a combination of area and brightness. Correct estimation of importance in these terms is unfortunately not easy, and requires considerable experience on the part of the observer.

1.19 Classification of prominence types

The classic classification is that of Pettit (B. 45), summarised below

I. Active prominences:

Ia: Interactive; involving exchanges between two prominences.

Ib: Common Active; material drawn down to a centre of attraction on the Sun's surface.

Ic: Coronal Active; centre of attraction so strong that material is drawn down from the upper levels of the Sun's atmosphere.

II. Eruptive prominences:

IIa: Quasi-eruptive; active, or active sunspot, prominence drawn bodily into a spot or centre of attraction.

IIb_1: Common eruptive ⎫ active, or active sunspot, prominence which rises to great distances (100,000 to 500,000 km) from the surface, and then disappears.

IIb_2: Eruptive arches ⎭

III. Sunspot prominences:

$IIIo$: Cap prominence; resembles a low cloud over the spot.

$IIIa$: Common coronal sunspot type; fan-like coronals converging on the spot.

$IIIb$: Looped coronal sunspot type; as $IIIa$, but the coronals strongly curved or even looped.

$IIIc$: Active sunspot type; similar to Ib pouring into the spot area.

$IIId_1$: Common surge; narrow filaments which rise, often to great heights, and then sink back along the same trajectory 'like an elastic band'.

$IIId_2$: Expanding surge; break into a spray, and begin to fade before sinking back into the spot.

$IIIe$: Ejection; small separate knots which are ejected and which do not return.

$IIIj$: Secondary eruption; spring from other sunspot prominences.

IIIg: Coronal clouds; form over a spot far above the chromo-spheric surface, and pour streamers down into it along curved trajectories.

IV. Tornado prominences:

$\left.\begin{array}{l}\text{IV}a: \text{ Columnar}\\ \text{IV}b: \text{ Skeleton}\end{array}\right\}$ rotating columns of material; disappear when the rotational velocity becomes excessive.

V. Quiescent prominences: lack external streamers; characteristic 'palisaded' structure.

VI. Coronal prominences: form above the surface and pour material down to centres of attraction; when occurring as groups over spot areas, these are equivalent to IIIa and IIIb.

1.20 B.A.A.H. data

(a) $\left.\begin{array}{l}\text{RA}\\ \text{Dec}\\ \text{Angular diameter}\\ P: \text{ Position angle of rotational axis}\\ B_o: \text{ Heliographic latitude of centre of disc}\\ L_o: \text{ Heliographic longitude of centre of disc}\\ \text{Time of transit every 4th day}\end{array}\right\}$ at mean noon at 4-day intervals.

(b) Dates of commencement of Carrington's (Greenwich Photo-Heliographic) series of synodic rotations

(c) Details of the year's eclipses

1.21 A.E. data

(a) $\left.\begin{array}{l}\text{Apparent RA}\\ \text{Apparent Dec}\\ \text{Semidiameter}\\ \text{Equation of Time}\\ \text{Longitude}\\ \text{Latitude}\\ \text{Radius Vector}\\ \text{Precession in longitude}\\ \text{Nutation in longitude}\\ \text{Apparent longitude}\\ \text{Horizontal parallax}\\ \text{Obliquity of Ecliptic}\end{array}\right\}$ at 0^h ET daily.

73

Apparent Sidereal Time
Mean Sidereal Time $\Big\}$ at 0^h U.T. daily.

Apparent time of Transit of F.P. of Aries
Mean time of Transit of F.P. of Aries $\Big\}$ daily.

(b) Equatorial Rectangular Coordinates (X, Y, Z)—at 0^h ET daily.

(c) Precessional constants.
Mean Elements at Epoch.

(d) Elements, Circumstances, Map, Path, and Besselian Elements of all solar eclipses.

(e) Ephemeris for Physical Observations:
   P: Position angle of rotational axis (measured
     E from N point of disc)
   B_o: Heliographic latitude of centre of disc $\Bigg\}$ at 0^h UT daily.
   L_o: Heliographic longitude of centre of disc
   Interpolation Table for L_o

(f) Rotation Numbers (Carrington's series)
     and dates of commencement $\Big\}$ throughout the current and the 8 preceding years.

(g) Time of Sunrise
     ,,   ,, Sunset $\Big\}$ at 5-daily intervals.
     ,,   ,, Astronomical Twilight
   in 13 latitudes from $0°$ to $+60°$.
   Tables for deriving the above for the Southern Hemisphere.

1.22 Solar data *

Semidiameter at unit distance: $16' 1''18 = 961''18$
Diameter: 864,000 miles = 1,391,000 km
Mass: $333,434\oplus$
Volume: $1,300,000\oplus$
Density: $0·26\oplus = 1·41 \times$ water
Mean superficial gravity: $28·0\oplus$
Stellar magnitude: -27
Rotation number: Carrington's series of synodic rotations (also known as the Greenwich Photo-Heliographic Series). Rotation No. 1300 began on 1950 Nov 12.43.

---

* The data in this section, and the corresponding sections under the various members of the Solar System that follow, are taken for the most part from *A.E.* and *B.A.A.H.*

LUNAR OBSERVATION

2.1 Amateur work

It is unnecessary to dilate on the reasons for the Moon being an admirable object for study with small instruments.

Amateur work is mainly devoted to the following topics, some of which have in the past been given much more attention than others:

(*a*) Cartography.
(*b*) Study of the rays.
(*c*) Lunar change.
(*d*) Colorimetric work.
(*e*) Theoretical work, and the statistical discussion of observations.
(*f*) Occultations.
(*g*) Eclipses.
(*h*) Work with thermocouples, photometers, and spectroscopes.
(*i*) Photographic work.

The specialist, choosing an instrument specifically for lunar observation, will not consider apertures smaller than 8 ins or so; the usefulness of the telescope decreases as the aperture is decreased from this figure, but is still far from exhausted at 3 ins. For lunar, as for planetary, work aperture is above all others the instrumental desideratum (see also section 3.3).

Magnification must in general be suited to the type of observation. For valuable work on the detail of the lunar surface, instrument and atmosphere should be capable of permitting the use of $\times 400$ to $\times 500$ at least.

Glare, which if unreduced may obscure the finer detail altogether, can be overcome in various ways: (*a*) increasing magnification: limited by atmospheric turbulence, restriction of field, etc; (*b*) reducing aperture: consequent loss of resolving power; (*c*) neutral filter: the best of these three methods; (*d*) daytime observation: at first and third Quarters a polarising filter is useful for reducing the intensity of the background sky-light, whose maximum polarisation occurs along a great circle 90°

from the Sun, while the sunlight reflected from the Moon is, on the average, polarised very little. (B. 99a).

In this field of observation it is impossible to overrate the importance of *any* technique (whether instrumental dodge or the organisation of the observations) to render the data as objective and impersonal, and as internally consistent and also comparable with those of other observers, as possible.

2.2 Cartography

Following the recent photographic surveys of the entire lunar surface to a resolution of 10 km or better by the U.S. *Orbiter* series of spacecraft, there is no longer any useful contribution which telescopic observation can make in the field of lunar cartography. The volume of new observational data provided by the *Orbiter* photographs is so large, however, that sufficiently careful and detailed study will be fruitful in the field of cataloguing and mapping the surface features.

2.3 The lunar rays

Visibility of the rays varies inversely as the size of the angle at the Moon between the Sun and the observer; neither the Sun nor the Earth being 'overhead' from a particular locality on the Moon's surface is itself sufficient. Some, however, are visible at as little as 20° from the terminator.

The rays provide great scope for work, since there is not yet adequate observational data to test rival theories as to their origin and nature (e.g. Vand, B. 110). Whether or not superficial granulation or pitting can account for the observed features of the ray systems is another problem that can only be solved through the accumulation of many more observations than are at present available.

Owing to their ill-defined appearance, and the lack of simultaneity between their best visibility (far from the terminator) and that of other surface features (near the terminator), there is not yet in existence an adequate map of even the more prominent rays.

Statistical discussion of the characteristics of their distribution— e.g. occurrence on high or low ground, broken or smooth ground, on slopes facing towards and away from* the centre of the system, discontinuities, curved arcs,† avoidance of surface features,‡ etc—might

---

* E.g. the Tycho ray on the western slopes of the Altais.

† E.g. Copernican rays in the vicinity of Pytheas, Pytheas G, and Bessarion D.

‡ E.g. Tycho rays in the vicinity of Clavius, Bullialdus, Scheiner, and Longomontanus.

be very fruitful. Also that of their appearance in different regions—complexity or otherwise of their structure, variations of width, etc; more reliable data are wanted concerning the intercommunication of different ray systems; the smaller ray systems; the radiation of rays from points other than the crater centre—or, if aligned upon the centre, only becoming visible at some distance from the centre; the association of rays with lines of craterlets. Finally, there is a great need for an accurate photometric study of the rays in all parts of the disc.

2.4 Lunar change

Serial observations are alone of value, and increase in value as the number of lunations covered by the series increases. Thus a general picture of the nature of the variation throughout a single lunation may emerge, as well as of possible variations at equivalent epochs in different lunations. It is essential that the material be extensive enough to eliminate personal visual idiosyncrasies.

It is impossible in theory, and often difficult in practice, to distinguish between changes of tone and changes of form (i.e. physical changes), since the latter can only be perceived in terms of the former unless the shadow provides a clue. No truly physical changes (of which Linné is the classical example) have been substantiated, although there have been innumerable suspected instances (see B. 89, 96, the latter having a useful bibliography).

It is not yet established to what extent recurring tonal changes are objective, and to what extent dependent upon differing solar altitude. The majority of examples (the 'variable spots') fall into one or other of four categories: (*i*) those reaching maximum brightness between local noon and Full, (*ii*) those reaching minimum brightness between local noon and Full, (*iii*) those brightening continuously throughout the day, (*iv*) those darkening continuously throughout the day. In some cases it has been shown by the use of restricted fields that what had previously been accepted as a change in one area is in reality a contrast effect from changes of illumination in a contiguous area (Plato's floor being an instance). Polarising filters might also assist in distinguishing real from apparent tonal variations.

Many examples of non-periodic change, mostly concerning the visibility of small detail, have been reported. Much work will still be required to ascertain to what extent such variations are objective.

The observational material is not at present adequate for a thorough discussion of causation: whether nature of surface combined with angle of vision and angle of illumination can eliminate 'vegetation'.

(Pickering's insect 'plats', in the Eratosthenes region, are not nowadays considered seriously. Indeed, Pickering's explanations in general need neither be accepted nor be allowed to detract from the value of the mass of observational material itself, which no subsequent worker can afford to ignore; see B. 97, 103).

Recommended observational method: for each spot or area under observation, select a number of adjacent or nearby areas of varied tones, rather in the manner of a variable star observer selecting comparison stars. There must be a prior investigation of these areas to ascertain whether, and if so in what manner, their tone varies with the phase angle.

Alternative method: an attempted objective scale of 5 or 10 steps, one limit and the median point being represented by shadows and the mare tone respectively.

2.4.1 Transient Lunar Phenomena: Happenings other than the above, ephemeral or instantaneous, and quite unpredictable, for which an eye should always be kept open, are:

(a) Localised or temporary 'obscurations'. That these are reported especially in the region near the terminator suggests that they may be dependent on grazing illumination or sudden temperature change. Suggested explanations: penumbrae of lunar shadows, broken ground, dilution of shadow by reflected light, clouds of dust blown up by gases from beneath the surface. See B. 99c, 99e, and, e.g. B. 114, 121.

(b) Red 'glows'. Local reddish colorations of the lunar surface such as might be caused by vulcanological activity. At best small in area and pale of hue, therefore visually best detected using a rotating system of red and blue filters to cause any region departing significantly from a neutral colour to appear to fluctuate in brightness. See B. 99d.

(c) 'Flashes': Possibly meteorites striking the lunar surface in shadow or on the dark segment of the disc. There are a few recorded instances only.

2.5 Colorimetric work

Though the Moon presents a pretty uniformly monochromatic appearance, browns, greens, and purplish tints do occur, as well as various tones of grey. A preliminary description of areas with most marked tints and variations of tint in 15 formations is given by Haas in B. 95.

Usual method of observation has been to use the grey tint of a mare, at a uniform distance from the terminator, as a standard of reference.

This is inevitably unsatisfactory, allowing personal idiosyncrasies to run riot, as well as being intrinsically imprecise. The employment of colour filters to exaggerate or suppress tints seems to extend most chances of a useful technique, but much work is still needed in its development. There is scope here for the accumulation of a mass of observational data, prior to which no satisfactory discussion can be made.

Records should include: date, time, longitude of terminator (or, Sun's colongitude), atmospheric clarity, Moon's altitude, aperture and type of instrument, magnification, filter (if any, and giving the bandwidth whenever possible), method of comparison used.

Considerable work has been done, especially in America, on the colours of lunar shadows. With small apertures these invariably appear jet black, but with larger instruments a brownish tint can often be seen or imagined. Very faint at best, it is probably psychological—due to irradiation or the effect of contrast. But more work, as objective as possible, is needed. 'Coloured shadows' have been suspected in the case of (*inter alia*) Eudoxus, Klaproth, Petavius, Phocydides, Pythagoras, Stevinus, Victa, Zuchius.

The bluish, phosphorescent-appearing glow which has been reported from some shadows—particularly from the inner terraces and central mountain of Aristarchus soon after sunset—should also be mentioned. Suggested explanations include: reflection from sunlit surroundings; twilight (least likely); broken ground, the projections catching the Sun (limited application); some form of electronic re-emission (correlation required with the sunspot cycle). It is now fairly certain (Kosyrev, B. 99b) that Aristarchus exhibits luminescence.

2.6 Statistical discussion

How powerful an instrument desk-work can be is shown by Young's recent statistical discussions of the diameters and distribution of lunar craters, throwing new light on their possible origin and past history (B. 118). Also MacDonald's series of papers in *J.B.A.A* during the early 1930's (B. 100).

Though in many fields of lunar observation the crying need is for more data, there is nevertheless much scope for work of this nature, e.g. bearing on such questions as the meteoric or internal origin of the craters, relative ages of different areas of the crust, nature of the rays, etc. Statistical data of various types are being recorded, by members of the Lunar Section of the B.A.A., on special photographic charts.

2.7 Occultations

Grossly under-observed by amateurs, considering their great value, the simplicity of the equipment, the ease with which the observations are made, and the small fraction of the available observing time that they occupy. They should be part of the regular programme of every serious observer.

Errors between the observed and calculated position of the Moon —occultations providing one of the most convenient and accurate methods of determining the Moon's position—may be due to a number of factors, error in mean longitude being the chief; the detection of these errors is a vital check on lunar theory. From the reduced observations of occultations can be derived the parallactic inequality, solar parallax, mass of the Moon, and other quantities.

Observations are useless unless made available.

All objects within 6°5 of the ecliptic are liable to be occulted; these include the planets (Mercury and Pluto only sometimes), Regulus, Spica, Pollux, Aldebaran and Antares (mag 1), β Tau, γ Gem, β and δ Sco, η Oph and σ Sgr (mag 2), the Pleiades and the Hyades.

Occultations tend to recur under similar conditions after a period of 6798^d (18^{y}6), the time taken by the Moon's nodes to complete one revolution, though conditions may be reproduced more accurately after 6798$\pm$27^d.

The length of time (z) over which a given star may be subject to successive monthly occultations depends upon its latitude. Assuming mean conditions, it is given, in days, by

$$\frac{z}{3\!\cdot\!17724}=x-y$$

where x, y are such that

$$\sin x=\frac{\tan (b+1°\ 12'\ 36'')}{\tan 5°\ 9'}$$

$$\sin y=\frac{\tan (b-1°\ 12'\ 36'')}{\tan 5°\ 9'}$$

where b=star's latitude,
    1° 12′ 36″=Moon's mean semidiameter plus parallax,
    5° 9′=mean inclination of Moon's orbit,
    3·17724=mean daily motion of the nodes.

When b=0°, z (minimum) = 512^d (c. 20 successive occultations).

       b=3° 56′, z (maximum) =2193^d (c. 80 successive occultations).

$b = 5°9'$ (max), z $= 1517^d$ (c. 57 successive occultations).

The maximum time during which a star can be under occultation is
$1^h 54^m$, the following conditions being observed:

(a) Occultation diametral, i.e. star, centre of Moon's disc, and
observer in line at mid-occultation.
(b) Moon at apogee (minimum angular diameter, but also minimum
velocity).
(c) Observer situated at equator (maximum displacement in same
direction as the Moon, owing to the Earth's rotation).
(d) Moon on meridian at mid-occultation (maximum parallax in
RA).

For a more detailed account of the conditions of occultations, see
B. 111.

2.7.1 Equipment and preparation for observation: A small refractor,
mounted anyhow (since the telescope is most conveniently kept stationary), is perfectly adequate. Use moderate magnification and full
aperture, and see that the observing position is perfectly comfortable
and relaxed.

Some minutes before the occultation, time the Moon's drift across
the field diameter. At half this time before the predicted time of occultation, set the telescope so that the star is at the *f* edge of the field. The
occultation is then likely to occur at or near the centre of the field,
which both aids observation and provides some degree of warning.
This procedure is risky, however, if the observing station is far (say,
more than 150 miles) from the tabulated station, and is impossible in
the case of stars fainter than mag 7·5, whose occultations are not predicted. *B.A.A.H.* and *A.E.* predictions are normally accurate to within
0^m3, but may be inaccurate by $\pm 0^m5$ or, exceptionally, $\pm 1^m$.

With a clock-driven equatorial, some degree of preparedness for the
disappearance or reappearance is given by an accurately set wrist-
watch or clock visible from the telescope.

Predictions given in the *A.E.* and *B.A.A.H.* include coefficients for
deriving the approximate time of disappearance or reappearance at
any observing station other than those tabulated (see section 2.13).

A.E. gives predictions of all dark-limb disappearances down to
mag 7·5, bright-limb disappearances of the brighter stars, reappearances
in the case of brighter stars only, daylight occultations of stars of mag 1
or brighter, and all planetary occultations.

2.7.2 Timing: Accuracy required: generally speaking, owing to the irregularity of the limb (which may introduce discrepancies of the order of 0^s5) timing to the nearest 1^s0—which fixes the position of the Moon to within something like half a mile—is sufficient, providing there is an adequate number of widely spaced observers. If, however, it is known that the observation has been made with greater accuracy than this, the fact should certainly be recorded: estimation to 0^s1 is perfectly practicable with a stopwatch, though the error is likely to be considerably larger than this—probably more like 0^s5. For methods of timing observations, see, further, *A.A.H.*, section 28.18.

2.7.3 Observational record: The essential data required for the reduction of the observation are:

1. Designation of star (catalogue number); in the case of unpredicted occultation, sufficient data to ensure its correct identification.
2. Date.
3. Derived time of occultation.
4. Longitude and latitude (to nearest $0'2$ at least; better, to $0'1$), and height above MSL, of the observing station.

Additional data which should if possible be included are:

5. Atmospheric clarity.
6. Stellar mag.
7. Phase: Disappearance or Reappearance.
8. Whether at dark or bright limb; if latter, whether earthshine; if eclipsed.
9. Method employed.
10. Assigned weight, estimated accuracy, or degree of confidence.
11. Estimated personal equation, and whether its correction is incorporated in the derived time.
12. Any anomalous appearances: gradual or step disappearance,* pausing on limb, projection over the limb, etc.

It is worth while tabulating the data—watch time, clock time, clock correction, watch correction (if any), personal equation, etc—neatly and logically in the Observing Book, to reduce the chances of arithmetical errors, such as the loss or gain of a whole number of seconds or minutes, the application of corrections with the wrong sign, etc.

2.7.4 Graze occultations: These are particularly interesting to observe, for the reason that until the last moment one is often uncertain whether an occultation is going to occur at all. Even greater readiness than

---

* As is possible in the case of a close double.

usual is required in operating the timing device, in order to reduce lag to a minimum.

A.E. predicts graze occultations for Greenwich and Edinburgh (*inter alia*). Occultations predicted as visible from one and not from the other should always be watched from stations in England and Wales.

Reports should include:

longitude and latitude of observing station,
instrumental details,
whether or not an occultation occurred,
whether passage behind lunar mountains was observed.

2.7.5 Personal equation: *A.A.H.*, section 25, presents a general account of personal equation, and emphasises its dependence upon a variety of factors—notably the observational method employed.

In the particular case of occultation observations, the more important factors influencing personal equation are:

(*a*) disappearance or reappearance,
(*b*) method: eye-and-ear, chronograph, or stopwatch,
(*c*) bright limb, dark limb, or dark limb in earthshine,
(*d*) brightness of the star.

(*a*) Reappearances, as compared with disappearances, are subject to a large systematic lag, irrespective of (*b*), (*c*) or (*d*), which makes their observation less valuable than that of disappearances; they are also more subject to random scatter. 2000 experimental observations by a single observer gave $0^s.10$ and $0^s.18$ as the average equation for disappearances and reappearances respectively. This would indicate that the extreme view—that reappearances are never worth observing—is not tenable.

(*b*) Experimental observations indicate that the chronograph method involves the largest but most uniform equation; the eye-and-ear method, the smallest equation but the greatest variations from the mean. That is, the chronograph is more subject to systematic error, the eye-and-ear method to accidental error. Available figures for the stopwatch are inconclusive; one observer found a constant lag of $0^s.5 \pm 0^s.1$ with an artificial star. The total lag in this case is compounded of the observer's personality and possible starting and stopping errors in the watch itself. Consequently the observer's equation must be redetermined if a new watch is brought into use. The results of various series of experimental observations of dark-limb disappearances, probably fairly representative of the equations of experienced observers generally, are quoted below:

	Mean	Limits	
Chronometer (mean of 10 observers) . .	0^{s}305	−0·1	−0·46
Eye-and-Ear („ 4 „) . .	0·08	−0·03	+0·09
Stopwatch („ 2 „) . .	0·055	−0·04	−0·07

(c) In observations of disappearances, the minimum equation is encountered at the dark limb illuminated by earthshine; at the invisible dark limb it is larger; and largest at the bright limb. The reason is probably that the greater the degree of warning received, the more the attention is focused on the muscular response rather than on the reception of the stimulus.* The following figures refer to 210 experimental observations with chronograph by two observers:

At visible dark limb	0^{s}25	0^{s}29
At invisible dark limb	0·29	0·32
At bright limb (favourable conditions)	0·33	0·32
At bright limb (excessive glare)		±2−3 secs

(d) A small magnitude equation, inversely proportional to the brightness of the star, occurs in occultation observations. The following figures refer to three series of experimental observations, (i) by an observer using the eye-and-ear method, (ii) and (iii) by two observers using chronograph:

	Magnitude	Mean equation
(i)	2·0–5·4	+0^{s}003
	5·9–7·0	0·035
	7·5–8·5	0·085
(ii)	4–5	−0·40
	6	0·47
	7	0·49
	8–9	0·59
(iii)	0–5	−0·35
	5–7	0·47
	7–10	0·65

Every observer intending to include occultations in his regular programme should determine his own personal equation under the different conditions described above. This can be done approximately (since

* See, further, A.A.H., section 25.

neglecting the factor of limb nature) by observing a switch-controlled artificial star which is extinguished by an assistant working within sight or earshot of a clock.

2.7.6 Prediction: Owing to the comprehensive data given in *B.A.A.H.* and *A.E.* (see sections 2.13, 2.14) it is not usually necessary for the amateur to undertake his own predictions. Nevertheless, the following notes on simple methods may be of interest:

1. Rigge's graphical method (B. 104) quickly yields results which are accurate enough for the practical purpose of not missing the occultation.

2. Comrie's semi-graphical method, involving 3-figure work, also quickly gives results with a maximum probable error of the order of 1^m (B. 91).

3. The parallax tables given in *B.A.A.H.*, 1929—designed for the reduction of the Moon's apparent position from its geocentric coordinates as given in the *A.E.*, thus facilitating the identification of stars involved in unpredicted occultations—can also be used for approximate predictions of occultations.

2.7.7 Reduction: Observations may be submitted (to the Director of the Computing Section of the B.A.A. or to H.M. Nautical Almanac Office, Herstmonceux Castle, Sussex) as they stand, or in a partly or completely reduced state. In all these cases they should be submitted not less frequently than quarterly, and not later than six months after the quarter in which they were made.

N.A. (1950 and other recent years) describes a method whereby the observer may, if he wishes, carry out the preliminary stages of the reduction himself, the final stages of all observations being carried out centrally (at the *N.A.* Office). This scheme has replaced the one described in B. 106, which was in operation up to 1943. This was a modification, due to Comrie, of Innes' method (B. 99), which involved the separation of the quantities dependent upon the observer's position and the precise moment of his observation from those solely concerning the positions of the Moon and star; this made possible the compilation (and publication in the *N.A.*) of Reduction Elements, whose use greatly reduced the labour involved in the work. The publication of Reduction Elements was suspended in 1942, however, and this method is no longer available. B. 106 should nevertheless be consulted by anyone interested in the reduction of occultation observations.

For the reduction of occultations of stars reference should also be made to B. 92, 93, 105; the employment of rectangular coordinates in this method by Davidson is also a considerable labour-saver, compared with the older methods. Like Comrie's method, however, it is designed for machine work rather than for logs.

2.8 Eclipses

Points to watch for include:

(*a*) Naked eye:

> Definition of edge of shadow.
> Colour and density of shadow throughout the eclipse.

(*b*) Telescopic:

> Times of contacts.
> Definition of edge of umbra (very variable and unpredictable); any irregularities in outline; width of 'edge' (region of noticeable density gradient).
> Edge of shadow of uniform colour; whether same as inner region of umbra.
> Visibility of limb and of surface features in different parts of the shadow:
>> (*i*) record of selected areas from bright to dark right through the passage of the shadow,
>> (*ii*) any anomalies noticed elsewhere.
>
> Any variation of density or colour between first and second half of the eclipse.

(*c*) Thermocouple observations.*

(*d*) Comparative visibility with different colour filters.

(*e*) Photographic record.

Besides details of the above, the record should include:

> Longitude, latitude, and height above MSL of the observing station.
> Atmospheric conditions, including details of any lunar halo.
> Aperture and magnification (if not the same throughout, specify fully).

Other notes:

> Use UT, to nearest 0^m1.
> Distinguish between celestial and selenographic cardinal points, if used.

* See also *A.A.H.*, sections 21.6, 21.7.

Use the faintest practicable red light for note-making. The visibility of the penumbra, when this alone lies on the lunar surface, can often be increased by the use of a neutral filter to reduce glare.

2.9 Photography

Satisfactory 'general views' of the Moon can be obtained with a small refractor and amplification of about ×60 with an ordinary Huyghenian, giving a plate-scale of about 4 ins per degree. With subsequent enlargement such plates provide useful photographic maps of selected regions. Tracings taken from these large-scale photographs can be used as accurately surveyed blanks to form a basis for drawings and detailed studies made at the telescope visually. This is, indeed, the most useful application of photography to the observation of the Moon with small instruments.

Photographs of the eclipsed Moon tend to be misleading owing to the photographic weakness of the radiation reflected from the eclipsed terrain. 5^m at $f/6 \cdot 5$ with moderately fast plates is not out of the way. There is, however, little of value that can be achieved by the photographic recording of lunar eclipses.

Stellar occultations can be observed photographically by guiding on the Moon so that the star trails. Examination of the trail at the Moon's limb with a microphotometer might be undertaken by anyone with the necessary equipment, with a view to discovering whether any trace of absorption in a lunar atmosphere can be detected—though this would be rather more than a forlorn hope.

Reduction of the effects of turbulence by the reduction of exposure times to the minimum is an extremely important factor of success in the photography of the amplified lunar image. Small focal ratios are therefore indicated. On the other hand, large aperture, though suffering more from turbulence than a small one, is required in the interests of resolution. 6 ins is perhaps a fair compromise between these conflicting demands. The guide telescope should have, beside long F, as large an aperture as possible: its increased sensitivity to turbulence will then aid the choosing of the best moment of exposure.

Photography of the unamplified image at the telescopic focus means subsequent enlargement; the focal image of the Moon in a $f/15$ 3-in, for example, is only about half an inch in diameter. This necessity indicates the use of the longest available F, very careful focusing, the slowest plate compatible with a short enough exposure to avoid the worst effects of turbulence, and a fine-grain developer.

Amplification of the primary image by an astronomical ocular,

Barlow or other negative lens, or even the original lens of a commercial camera, is generally preferable to relying wholly upon enlargement in the darkroom.*

Exposures depend too much upon focal ratio, plate speed, degree of amplification, filter density, and lunar altitude, phase and distance, for any general rules to be stated. Trial and error is the only sure method, but as a rough preliminary guide it may be said that the prime focal image at $f/12$ to $f/15$ will probably require from $1/20^s$ to 1^s without a filter, 5^s to 10^s or even longer with a filter; and a moderately amplified image at $f/8$ an exposure of the order of 1^s or less, at $f/15$ from 1^s to 5^s, which may have to be increased to 20^s or so when a filter is used.

Approximate equivalent exposures at different lunar phases are as follows:

Age	$3\frac{1}{2}^d$	7^d	14^d	21^d	$24\frac{1}{2}^d$
Exposure factor	12	4	1	4	12

When the Moon is in apogee, the perigee exposure needs to be increased by a factor of about $1\cdot25$. The region of the disc in which maximum detail is required to be shown also has a bearing on the exposure. At Full the brightness of the disc is relatively uniform, but at other times the limb is markedly brighter than the terminator. Therefore somewhat longer exposures are required if the terminator is the area of interest (the limb being over-exposed) than when the limb is (the terminator then being under-exposed). In connexion with exposure times, reference may also be made to B. 103a.

Owing to the Moon's eastward motion lunar rate differs from sidereal rate. For exact following in RA, the clock needs to be retarded very slightly to counteract this eastward motion, which amounts on the average to about $0\cdot023$ diameters per minute. At accurate sidereal rate an amplified image of diameter 2 ins cannot be exposed for more than about $2^s\!\cdot5$ (corresponding to a linear displacement of the image on the plate of approximately $0\cdot002$ ins). The Moon's motion in Dec amounts to about $0\cdot0092$ diameters per minute at maximum and zero at minimum, the latter occurring when the moon is in greatest N or S Dec. From these figures the maximum permissible exposure with a given equipment, driven at sidereal rate, can be calculated.

Fast plates are required to reduce exposures, and therefore atmospheric interference, to a minimum; slow plates, on the other hand, are required for minimum graininess if they are to be enlarged subsequently. Generally, it is better to under- than to over-expose; the plate can then be intensified in the development, which is another reason for pre-

* See, further, *A.A.H.*, section 20.11.

ferring a fast plate. Fine-grain developers should be used, and the plates must, of course, be backed.

2.10 Phase

The position of the lunar terminator is the most important single factor in the observation of the Moon; it is closely followed by libration and altitude, referred to in the next two sections.

The position of the terminator at a given time is specified in terms of selenographic longitude, which is reckoned E and W from the central meridian. The approximate longitude of the terminator throughout the lunation may be read from Figure 17. Or it may be derived from the

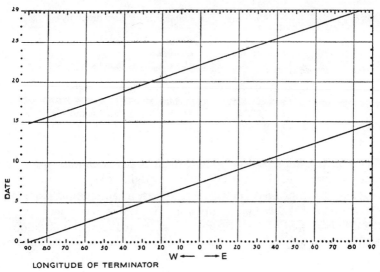

FIGURE 17

Longitude of the lunar terminator throughout the month

Sun's selenographic colongitude, whose daily value is tabulated in *A.E.*:

Sun's colongitude C	Longitude of terminator	
0°– 90°	C°	East
90°–180°	(180°–C)	West
180°–270°	(C–180°)	East
270°–360°	(360°–C)	West

Taking 29^d 12^h 44^m as the mean length of the lunation, a particular phase observed at night in a given lunation (lunation 0) will fall in daylight in the next lunation (lunation 1) and in subsequent odd-numbered lunations; in each even-numbered lunation from 2 onwards it will recur roughly $1\frac{1}{2}$ hrs later. In a period of 15 lunations the day-occurring phase will again have worked round to the time of observation in lunation 0. Thus:

Lunation	Time of occurrence of a certain phase	
0	$0^h\ 0^m$ GMT:	midnight
1	12.44:	daytime
2	1.28:	about 1^h5 later than lunation 0
3	14.12:	daytime
4	2.56:	about 1^h5 later than lunation 2
5	15.40:	daytime
6	4.24:	about 1^h5 later than lunation 4
7	17.8	daytime
8	5.52:	about 1^h5 later than lunation 6
9	18.36:	daytime
10	7.20:	about 1^h5 later than lunation 8
11	20.4:	evening
12	8.48:	about 1^h5 later than lunation 10
13	21.32:	evening
14	10.16:	about 1^h5 later than lunation 12
15	23.0:	about the same time as lunation 0

Hence phases are repeated at approximately the same time in the 2nd and 15th lunations, 59^d and 443^d after the original observation.

It must be emphasised, however, that phase means nothing more than the position of the terminator upon the visible disc. The appearance of the disc is altered, though the phase may be the same, by libration as well as by the varying inclination of the line of cusps with the terminator.

2.11 Libration

The second most important factor in lunar observation. It not only alters the inclination of the terrestrial observer's line of sight to every part of the visible lunar surface, but in addition is of paramount importance in the observation of the limb regions. In this work, full advantage must be taken of libration, which is continuously exposing a different region of the limb.

Libration in longitude—which can cause a maximum displacement of the disc's mean centre of 7° 45′ (selenographic) in either direction—is the combined effect of uniform rotation and non-uniform revolution. Libration in latitude—which may displace the mean centre by 6° 44′ on either side of the observed centre—is due to the non-coincidence of the equatorial and orbital planes. The mean centre may therefore be displaced by as much as 10° 16′ on either side of the observed centre, owing to combined libration in longitude and latitude. Libration thus alters the appearance of the disc considerably—at extreme libration in longitude, e.g. Mare Crisium is almost on the limb—and is responsible for revealing about 60% of the lunar surface to us at one time or another. Diurnal libration, due to the displacement of the observer's viewpoint arising from the Earth's rotation, may amount to nearly 1° in addition to physical libration.

The following two tables show how libration is related to the displacement of the mean centre of the disc, to the shape of the lunar meridian, to the visibility of the limb, and to the optimum observing conditions for objects near the limb in different regions:

Libration	Displacement of mean centre of disc	Meridian convex towards	Exposed limb
Longit. +	E	E	W
−	W	W	E
Latit. +	S	S ⎤ equator	N
−	N	N ⎦	S

Region of disc	Optimum conditions of libration	
	Libration in Longit. (or Selenographic Longit. of Sun)	Libration in Latit. (or Selenographic Latit. of Sun)
N hemisphere	0	+
S hemisphere	0	−
E hemisphere	−	0
W hemisphere	+	0
NE quadrant	−	+
NW quadrant	+	+
SE quadrant	−	−
SW quadrant	+	−

Dates of maximum libration in longitude and latitude are given in *B.A.A.H.*; *A.E.* tabulates the displacement of the mean centre in longitude and latitude (to 0°01) for every day of the year; the most exposed region of the limb, given the Earth's selenographic longitude and latitude (from *A.E.*), can be read off Figure 18.

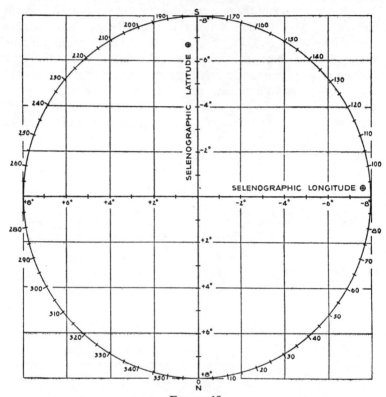

FIGURE 18

LIBRATION CHART

For the required date, take the Earth's selenographic longitude and latitude; plot the corresponding point against the axes. Connect the origin of the axes with this point and produce the line to intersect the circle. This point of intersection indicates the position angle of the region of the Moon's limb most favourably placed for observation. (Modified from R. E. Diggles, *J.B.A.A.*, **44,** No. 4, 144)

2.12 Altitude

The Moon's altitude at different phases varies with the time of year. Figure 19 representing the mean altitude of the Moon in its four phases throughout the year, as seen from a station in the Midlands, reveals the following relationship between phase, altitude, and season:

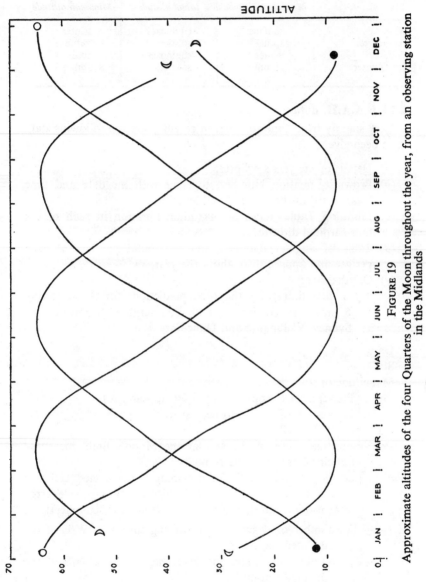

ALTITUDE

0| JAN | FEB | MAR | APR | MAY | JUN | JUL | AUG | SEP | OCT | NOV | DEC |

FIGURE 19

Approximate altitudes of the four Quarters of the Moon throughout the year, from an observing station
in the Midlands

	Maximum altitude	Mean altitude	Minimum altitude
New	summer	equinoxes	winter
1st Quarter	spring	solstices	autumn
Full	winter	equinoxes	summer
3rd Quarter	autumn	solstices	spring

2.13 B.A.A.H. data

Vary slightly from time to time; in recent years the following data have been given:

(a) Details of the year's eclipses.

(b) Brown's Lunation Number, together with the date and time (nearest 1^m) of the phases of all lunations.

(c) Libration Table: dates of maximum libration in each of the four cardinal directions.

(d) Table of angular diameter and horizontal parallax at each perigee and apogee throughout the year.

(e) Occultations:

> Selection from the *N.A.* predictions for the following 6 stations: Greenwich and Edinburgh, Melbourne and Sydney, Wellington and Dunedin:

Date

Star

Magnitude of star

Ph: Phase, i.e. D(isappearance) or R(eappearance)

          Elongation of Moon, to nearest whole degree

UT: of the D or R

P: position angle of the star at the Moon's limb, measured anticlockwise from the N point

a ⎱ coefficients (in ^{m} UT) for obtaining the corrected UT at a

   ⎰ station other than that tabulated (with a probable error

b ⎰ $<2^m$ if the separation of the two stations is <300 miles):

If $\pm\Delta\lambda$=number of degrees the observing station is W/E of the tabulated station

      $\pm\Delta\phi$=number of degrees the observing station is N/S of the tabulated station

        T=corrected time for observer's station

         T_o=tabulated UT

then $T=T_o+a(\pm\Delta\lambda)+b(\pm\Delta\phi)$

In early years *B.A.A.H.* used a different method of correcting for the difference in longitude and latitude between the observer's and the tabulated station. Instead of *a* and *b*, were tabulated

A_{max}
Δt: difference in secs from the time at the tabulated station for a displacement of 1 mile in the direction A_{max}

If T=corrected time for the observer's station
T_o=tabulated time (GMT)
D=distance (miles) of observer's station from tabulated station
A=direction of the observer's station from the tabulated station

then $$T=T_o+D.\Delta t(A-A_{max})$$

(*f*) Sun's selenographic colongitude for each midnight throughout the year.

2.14 A.E. data

(*a*) Mean Equator, Orbit, Longitude, and Elongation:

i: inclination of Moon's mean equator to Earth's true equator

Δ: distance, measured in the Moon's mean equator, from its ascending node on the Earth's true equinox to its ascending node on the ecliptic

Ω': distance, measured in the Earth's true equator, from the true equinox to the ascending node of the Moon's mean equator

Γ': mean longitude of the Moon's perigee, measured in the ecliptic from the mean equinox to the mean ascending node of the Moon's orbit, and thence in the Moon's orbit

Ω: longitude of the mean ascending node on the ecliptic, measured from the mean equinox

Mean Longitude: of the Moon, measured in the ecliptic from the mean equinox to the mean ascending node of the Moon's orbit, and thence in the orbit

D: Mean Elongation

at 10^d intervals.

95

(*b*) Apparent longitude ⎫
     Apparent latitude ⎬ at 0^h and 12^h ET
     Semidiameter   ⎪
     Horizontal parallax ⎭

Ephemeris transit of every upper and lower culmination.

(*c*) Apparent RA ⎫ at intervals of 1^h ET
     Apparent Dec ⎭

(*d*) Phases: date and time (to 1^{m}0) of beginning of every phase throughout the year.

(*e*) Perigee and Apogee: date and time (to 1^{h}0) of every one throughout the year.

(*f*) Elements and circumstances of the year's eclipses.

(*g*) Occultation times (nearest 1^{h}0) of planets and bright stars. Areas of visibility of occultations.

(*h*) Ephemeris for physical observations (for 0^{h}UT every day of the year):

> Age.
> Earth's selenographic longitude:=that of the centre of the disc seen from the centre of the Earth, measured in the plane of the Moon's equator from the lunar radius passing through the mean centre of the visible disc (+westward, −eastward).
> Earth's selenographic latitude:=that of the centre of the disc seen from the centre of the Earth, measured from the Moon's equator (+northward, −southward).
> Physical libration in longitude:+/−, W/E limb exposed.
> Physical libration in latitude: +/−, N/S limb exposed.
> Sun's selenographic colongitude: i.e. 90°−Sun's selenographic longitude.
> Sun's selenographic latitude.
> Position angle of Moon's axis: angle between the central meridian and the Dec circle through the centre of the visible disc.
> Position angle of bright limb: angle between the N point of the disc and the mid-point of the illuminated limb, measured eastwards.
> Fraction illuminated: i.e. fraction of the area of the whole disc which is illuminated=illuminated fraction of the diameter perpendicular to the line of cusps.

96

(*i*) LMT of Moonrise and Moonset daily on the Greenwich meridian at equator and 12 different latitudes in each hemisphere.

2.15 Lunar data

Mean distance from Earth: 0·002571 A.U.=238,840 miles.

Sidereal period: $27^{d}\!\cdot\!321661$.

Synodic period: 29^{d} 12^{h} 44^{m} $2^{s}8$.

Eccentricity: 0·05490.

Stellar magnitude of Full Moon at mean distance: $-12·5$.

Semidiameter at unit distance: $2''40$.

Semidiameter at mean distance: $932''58$.

Diameter: 2160 miles=3476 km.

Mass: $1/81·271\oplus=0·0123\oplus=3·674\times10^{-8}\odot$.

Volume: $0·0203\oplus$.

Density: $0·60\oplus=3·34\times$ water.

Mean superficial gravity: $0·16\oplus$.

Lunation number: Brown's series of lunation numbers, starting at 1923 Jan 16. Convenient reference system for all lunar observations. Lunation No 346 began at 1950 Dec 9^{d} 9^{h} 28^{m}.

SECTION 3

GENERAL NOTES ON PLANETARY OBSERVATION

3.1 Introduction

Planetary observation is at the same time one of the most popular branches of amateur work and one of the most exacting. The usefulness of larger than moderate apertures is much reduced by the atmospheric factor, which suits the amateur's purse; but the dividends paid by visual acuity are correspondingly high. The training of the eye and the mind to the particular requirements of planetary observation—such as the perception of infinitesimal tonal contrasts—is also a condition for extracting full value from the performance of the instrument.

The amateur intending to specialise in planetary observation is recommended to spend some time on the observation of drawings under similar conditions to those of the observation of the planet itself, and on the experimental investigation of his acuity by means of test drawings of 'planetary' detail observed from a distance both with and without the telescope. The advantage of being able subsequently to study close-up what he has just been observing under conditions similar to those obtaining in the actual observation of the planet will teach him more about visual acuity, thresholds of perception, and the observation and mis-observation of planetary detail than any amount of reading on the subject. Hargreaves' Presidential Address to the B.A.A. in 1944 (B. 3) should be read by all new planetary observers. See also *A.A.H.*, sections 2.6, 24.6.

3.2 Some requirements of planetary observation

(*a*) Experience, which is equivalent to the training of the eye, especially in the direction of sensitivity to detail near the threshold of size and contrast.

(*b*) Systematic observation: a homogeneous mass of observations, made over a large number of apparitions, is invaluable.

(*c*) Maximum possible reliability of all recorded detail, as regards

98

shape, size, position, and intensity. All detail that is 'glimpsed', or otherwise uncertainly observed, must always be specifically recorded as such, and no drawing should exaggerate the clarity, definiteness, or certainty of any observed feature.

(d) Full instrumental details, a statement of the condition of the seeing, and the time at which the main outlines of every drawing were laid down must accompany all records.

(e) The 'working up' at a later time of more or less 'rough' notes made at the telescope is not a satisfactory practice. Factual accuracy, not the production of works of art, is the correct aim.

3.3 Instrumental

As regards aperture, there are two schools of thought. W. H. Pickering advocated moderate apertures for planetary work, i.e. from 12 to 15 ins, maintaining that owing to atmospheric factors, instruments of this size will show finer detail than larger telescopes on nine nights out of ten; even under the very favourable conditions in Jamaica, nothing was to be gained, in his opinion, by using more than 20 ins even on nights of the most superlative seeing. In support of this view he instances the fact that at the 1924 opposition of Mars he observed with 11 ins in Jamaica all that was visible with the Lick 36-in refractor. Owing to the comparatively poor seeing at Lick, however, it is possible that in both cases more would have been seen with apertures of about 20 ins. Jarry-Desloges, working under excellent conditions in Algeria, agreed with this general conclusion, reckoning that for planetary work 8–14 ins were superior to 20 ins on 95–98 nights out of 100.

Antoniadi disagreed with this, maintaining that increased light grasp (making accessible fainter tone and tint gradations) and resolution (making accessible finer structure in the image) will probably combine to beat the performance of a smaller telescope on average nights, will certainly do so on the best nights, and even on really bad nights can take advantage of the moments of improved seeing that occur intermittently.

H. P. Wilkins similarly emphasises the advantages of large apertures for planetary (as for lunar) work: with the Meudon 33-in, for example, he was able to detect a mass of detail within lunar formations which his own 15¼-in showed as comparatively flat and featureless even under superior magnification.

In section 1.3 of *A.A.H.*, which deals with the apparent brightness of extended (i.e. non-stellar) images, it is shown that

$$\frac{\text{telescopic brightness}}{\text{naked-eye brightness}} = \left(\frac{M'}{M}\right)^2$$

where M' is the minimum useful magnification,* and M (the magnification used) must be higher than M_r (the resolving magnification†) and should in fact be as much higher as the increasing dilution of the image and reduction of contrast will allow. But $\dfrac{\text{telescopic brightness}}{\text{naked-eye brightness}}$ is a function of aperture, and hence the same image brightness is given by a large aperture using a magnification M as by a smaller aperture using a lower magnification than M: e.g. by a 10-in using $\times 800$ as by a 3-in using $\times 240$. At the same time the larger aperture offers the further advantages of increased resolution and images of more than 3 times the angular size.

Planetary observations worth recording can be made with a 4-in, though the desirable minimum is 1 or 2 ins larger than this. With 6 ins, full participation in the observing programmes of the Planetary Sections of the B.A.A. is possible; for regular work on the inner planets rather more aperture is desirable—say, 8 ins as the useful minimum— though spasmodic valuable observations can of course be made with smaller instruments. Summarily: for regular planetary work in this country less than 5 ins provides insufficient resolving power, while more than 12 ins or so is commonly rendered nugatory by the atmosphere.

Where aperture, without limit, has the undoubted advantage is in photographic work.

Regarding type of instrument, it is generally agreed that for critical definition of an extended image a refractor is superior to a reflector of equal aperture and optical excellence, owing to the different structure of the diffraction pattern in the two instruments.‡ The difference, however, is at least partially due to the difference in focal ratio, since a refractor at $f/20$ will be found superior to one at $f/15$, of equal aperture, where the delineation of fine detail is concerned. Where money is no object, the prospective planetary observer will invest in a refractor; where it is, he will be well advised to decide in favour of the larger reflector that the same outlay will secure.

Lowell's extreme view that for planetary work reflectors are virtually useless is not confirmed by the experience and records of innumerable amateurs. It is true, however, that the usefulness of a reflector for this type of work does not increase in direct proportion to aperture.

For serious work a clock-driven equatorial may be regarded as

---

* About $4D$ (i.e. $4 \times$ the aperture in inches).
† About $13D$ at least.
‡ See *A.A.H.*, sections 2.2, 2.3, 2.6, 23.

essential, although less convenient equipment *can* be used if the observer is prepared to put up with it.

Finally, it cannot be too often emphasised that all work involving critical definition demands objectives of the finest quality. A poorly figured speculum or an inferior OG will certainly fail to reveal detail that should be visible with the aperture concerned, and may even contribute spurious effects of its own.

3.4 Magnification

With given aperture, brightness of an extended image varies inversely with the magnification employed; given M, it varies directly as D. In planetary observation it is excess rather than lack of light that is, generally speaking, the embarrassment, and the value of aperture (up to the limit imposed by the atmosphere) lies primarily in its resolving power.

So far as generalisations can be made, glare is likely to appear as a factor tending to submerge fine detail present in the focal plane image when the magnification is reduced below about $20D$. Reduction of image brightness without reducing its resolution can be obtained by such means as neutral filters, partial reflection, polarising eyepieces, etc.

Saturn often appears to stand magnification better than either Mars or Jupiter. Mars, owing to its comparatively small disc, requires always the maximum M that the atmosphere will allow; it is comparatively seldom that the seeing will allow M as high as $50D$ or $60D$. The small disc of Uranus also necessitates use of the highest M possible. Venus naturally demands a rather wide range of M, and with small and moderate apertures can often be observed in the daytime with as much as $45D$ to $50D$. The magnification of Mercury's image is limited by want of illumination, unless D is considerable; amateur instruments will stand about $30D$ as the maximum that is normally useful.

In this connexion it is of interest to learn what sort of magnifications are employable with instruments outside the amateur range. Barnard considered that $40D$–$50D$ was much too high for planetary work with the Lick 36-in refractor: $20D$–$30D$ was nearer the mark, and in the case of Jupiter as little as $10D$–$15D$. Fine Martian and Jovian detail was invariably better seen with a magnification of $10D$ than $14D$, while only the coarsest detail was visible with $28D$. The latter was found suitable for the observation of Jupiter's satellites and some of the larger asteroids. Saturn, though benefiting more from magnification than its inner neighbours, was still seen better with $14D$ than $28D$.

The following figures summarise the discussion: they provide no more than a very rough indication of the sort of magnifications per inch aperture that will be found suitable for small (4 ins and less) and moderate (5–12 ins) apertures on nine nights out of ten. The corresponding figures for the Lick 36-in are added for comparison:

	Mars	Jupiter	Jupiter's satellites	Saturn	Uranus
Small apertures	40	40	60	50	60
Moderate apertures	15–30	15–30	35–45	30–40	35–45
Large apertures	10–15	10–15	30	20–30	30

Denning, who used a $12\frac{1}{2}$-in reflector for many years, concluded that for planetary work about $25D$ was the most frequently applicable, $35D$ being superior only on rare occasions of superlative seeing.

Many observers who have had long experience of planetary work with a variety of instruments—Denning and Ellison among them—have been of the opinion that, with amateur instruments generally, from ×200 to ×400 is the best planetary magnification range, more or less irrespective of aperture; more than ×400 involves considerable aperture, whilst even ×200 requires reasonably good seeing.

W. H. Pickering's often repeated dictum that ×400 is the minimum M with which original work can be carried out on the Moon and planets need not be taken too seriously, in the face of voluminous evidence to the contrary.

3.5 Oculars for planetary work

Of the characteristics exhibited by different designs of ocular,* the most important in planetary work are:

(a) Critical definition over a small field: for HP planetary (and lunar) work generally.

(b) Freedom from scattered light: especially in the observation of contiguous areas of greatly contrasted tone, and—even more important —for the visibility of small tonal contrasts near the threshold of visibility.

Providing that the focal ratio is reasonably small (as in the case of normally-constructed refractors and Cassegrains), ordinary Huyghenians give a satisfactory performance: they must be of first-class quality, however. Achromatic Ramsdens are generally preferable to a combination of Huyghenian and Barlow lens for Newtonians.

* Discussed in *A.A.H.*, section 8.1.

Superlatively fine definition being the main prerequisite of the success-ful observation of planetary surfaces, suitably corrected oculars are absolutely essential with instruments of small focal ratio. Orthoscopics, monocentrics, aplanatics, and Gifford eyepieces are generally the most suitable. Orthoscopics and monocentrics, each with their own advocates, are as good as any, with little to choose between them. Solid and cemented types conform well with the condition laid down in (b) above.

3.6 Colour observations

The estimations of colour are an important item in planetary obser-vation. Long-term changes of tint, even if suspected, are virtually impossible to establish by existing techniques, owing to the absence of an objective standard against which to compare the estimates of differ-ent observers, or even those of the same observer made at different times. Colorimetry, in fact, is the most subjective branch of planetary work (cf. meridian transits, for instance).

Contributing to the unsatisfactory nature of colour observations are the following factors, *inter alia*:

(a) Difficulty of determining the personal equation for colour, and uncertainty as to whether it is subject to short-term and/or long-term variations. Most eyes have some degree of colour peculiarity (the two eyes of a single observer are not even necessarily the same), which can only be detected and estimated by comparison with simultaneous esti-mates of identical objects by other observers.

(b) The impossibility of treating the records of different observers as comparable, i.e. of being confident that discrepancies in the recorded observations indicate objective changes of tint, rather than different personal equations.

(c) The vague, unsaturated character of planetary (and lunar) tints generally.

(d) Factors affecting the colour estimates of the observer, the omission of which from the observational record further reduces the latter's value:

(i) Magnification: as M increases, the depth of all tints decreases. This effect starts to be operative at as little as $15D$ or $20D$, indicating the value of fairly large apertures for colour work.

(ii) Colour characteristics of the instrument. No colour estimates made with a refractor can be trusted implicitly; not only is secondary colour certainly present, but its evaluation is practi-cally impossible. Reflectors, and achromatic eyepieces, are a *sine qua non* of satisfactory colorimetric work.

(*iii*) Relative darkness of the background, and atmospheric dispersion: high cloud, haze, and twilight modify tints as well as tones. Records should therefore state explicitly (α) whether the observation was made in daylight, twilight (within 2^h of the Sun on the horizon), or night, (β) altitude of object, (γ) atmospheric clarity in terms of the magnitude of the faintest zenithal star visible, or of the faintest star in the vicinity of the planet if the overall transparency is obviously not uniform.

How much false colour, due to atmospheric and instrumental dispersion, can be introduced into the image is illustrated by the following observational facts. The upper part of the image of a planet near the horizon will be tinted red, the lower part blue, owing to atmospheric dispersion. The colour introduced by a non-achromatic Ramsden varies from red at the centre of the field to blue at the periphery. Hence if the planetary image is placed in the upper half of the field, the two colour gradients will cancel each other, resulting in a more nearly colourless image. Definition may be improved in this way, but it is not difficult to appreciate that under conditions of this sort, objective estimates of colour are quite impossible. Colour estimates should always be made at or near culmination, and are worthless if the object is within 20° or so of the horizon.

Suggestions for colour observers:

(*a*) Continuous series of observations with a single telescope and magnification are required.

(*b*) Elimination of the personal equation might possibly be approximated to by the cooperation of a number of observers, working under identical conditions.

(*c*) Theoretically, every shade of colour is identifiable by the use of filters. In practice, the isolation of small patches of planetary colour by juggling with a large number of filters is out of the question. If, however, a filter is used, its number and/or name must of course be recorded.

(*d*) The record of each observation must, in view of the foregoing, be supplemented by the following data:

> magnification employed,
> date and time of observation,
> state of the atmosphere,
> altitude of the object,
> filter (if any).

(*e*) Other things being equal, large apertures have the advantage over small, owing to the greater brightness of their images.

3.7 Radiometric observations

The measurement of planetary radiation requires apertures outside the range that the amateur can normally command—ideally not less than 30 ins. Reflectors are essential, since glass is opaque to the long-wave radiation re-emitted by the planetary surface after absorption. This re-emitted energy—constituting 56% of the total radiation of Mars, and 86% of that of the Moon—is almost completely absorbed by 0·1 mm of glass. Photoelectric cell windows have therefore to be made of rock salt, fluorite, or some similar material. *A.A.H.*, p. 451 may be referred to for the transmission curve of the atmosphere (whose absorption of these wavelengths is caused mainly by water vapour, carbon dioxide, oxygen, and ozone), and also for those of 0·165 mm of glass, 4 mm of fluorite, and 4 mm of rock salt.

Anyone interested in such work should refer to B. 134, 135, 142

3.8 Photography

The planets—unlike the Sun or Moon—are not objects of which successful photographs can be fluked with bow-and-arrow methods and, perhaps, rather unsuitable equipment. The observation of planetary detail is essentially a visual rather than a photographic field. The independent photographic confirmation of drawings and visual observations would certainly be always welcome; unfortunately, however, the details requiring such confirmation are usually those near the threshold of vision, which the camera is incapable of recording.

The characteristics of planetary images which are of particular concern to the photographer are their small angular diameter and their faintness. The first necessitates the use of the maximum available F: the plate, therefore, must be exposed at the telescopic focus, and even then amplification is necessary; for without it, even when the focal length is several feet, the images are so small that all detail is lost in the emulsion diffusion and subsequent enlargement is useless. The second characteristic—faintness—which is increased by the necessity of using an amplifying lens, involves the use of the fastest plates possible, as small a focal ratio as possible (which, in conjunction with long F to give the requisite primary-image scale, means large D), and exposures of at least some seconds, demanding good atmospheric conditions. At least moderate aperture (ideally not less than about 6 ins) is also demanded in the interests of resolution.

The minimum amplification required for a given planetary disc with a given equipment can be deduced from equation (*a*), *A.A.H.*, section 3.1,* and the factors controlling subsequent enlargement (*A.A.H.*, section 20.11). The maximum amplification that can be usefully employed on a given occasion is limited by the current atmospheric turbulence. With over-magnification the length of the exposure required allows turbulence to blur the image, obscuring detail; while with under-magnification, as we have seen, detail is submerged in the photographic diffusion, and is therefore inaccessible even with subsequent enlargement to the point where the grain becomes visible. For a given atmospheric condition, the brighter the image the more it will stand amplification, and a rough guide to the order of amplification M for moderate apertures and good seeing is given by

$$M = n \cdot \frac{D}{F}$$

where the value of n lies between 60 and 100. Experience, however, is in the long run the only reliable guide. The same is true of exposures and development, and details of all these should be included in the record of each plate exposed, as a guide to future procedure. Regarding development, the natural tendency to force contrast should be avoided, since in the exaggeration of the main features the fainter detail is lost altogether.

It is worthwhile experimenting with different filters, since the elimination of the shorter wavelengths (panchromatic plates being used) always improves the definition of the image when the photographic seeing is good enough to justify the increased exposures. Photographs taken with a reflector and a range of so-called spectrum filters (short-band transmission) might produce interesting results.

The guide telescope should of course be used at full aperture, with a HP ocular to facilitate the choice of the moment to expose. If there is no separate guide telescope it is essential to arrange a quick change-over of the camera section (plate-holder, shutter, and amplifying lens) for the visual section (drawtube and ocular). Under these circumstances an extremely accurate drive is essential. Exposures, fortunately, will be fairly short—this already being dictated by the necessity of reducing the effects of turbulence. For the same reason fast emulsions are preferable to slower, fine-grain emulsions, which again indicates the use of

$$* \; h = \frac{\theta F}{k}$$

where h=linear diameter of primary image (ins), F=focal length of objective (ins), θ=angular diameter of object, k=57·3 when θ is expressed in degrees, or 206,265 when in " arc.

a large F and relatively large primary image, in preference to the subsequent enlargement of a smaller image. Useful data on exposure times will be found in B. 103a.

3.9 Position of the ecliptic

The planets—as also the Moon, Zodiacal Light and Band, and Gegenschein—being confined to the zodiac, the varying altitude and inclination of the ecliptic are of practical interest to the observer.

Since the ecliptic intersects the equator at the equinoxes, its point of midnight culmination has an altitude of 37° for an observer in 53° N latitude (the Midlands) at the end of March and September. Its greatest and least altitudes are reached at the winter solstice ($60\frac{1}{2}°$) and the summer solstice ($13\frac{1}{2}°$) respectively. Hence winter oppositions of the outer planets are, in general, more favourably placed in the sky than those occurring during the summer.

At the spring equinox, that section of the ecliptic lying to the east of the Sun is inclined to the horizon at a larger angle than that lying to the west; at the autumn equinox this relationship is reversed. The relevance of these facts to the observation of the Zodiacal Light is obvious.

3.10 Sequence of apparitions

Outer planets:

As evening star: Opposition→E Quadrature→Conjunction.
As morning star: Conjunction→W Quadrature→Opposition.

Inner planets:

As evening star: Superior Conjunction→E Elong.→Inf. Conjunction.
As morning star: Inferior Conjunction→W Elong.→Sup. Conjunction.

3.11 Data concerning the planets

B.A.A.H. gives the following general information about the planets each year, in addition to the specific data listed in sections 4–11:

(a) Graphical representation of the planets' visibility throughout the year, from which the times of rising and setting can be derived for stations in all parts of the British Isles.

(b) Scale drawings showing the changing appearances (phase and angular diameter) of the planets throughout the year.

(c) Elements of the planetary orbits.

(d) Dimensions of the Sun, Moon, and planets.

(e) Table of satellite data.

The *A.E.* contains a great deal of information which is vital to the planetary observer (also listed in sections 4–11).

The invaluable *Planetary Co-ordinates* (B. 13a) is likewise an essential companion to planetary observation.

The Annual Reports and Interim Reports of the various Observing Sections of the B.A.A. (published in *J.B.A.A.*) provide an almost uninterrupted review of planetary features and occurrences during the past half-century or so.

SECTION 4

MERCURY

4.1 Apparitions

The following intervals between successive phenomena are approximate:

$$
\begin{array}{l}
\text{morning}\left\{\begin{array}{l}\text{Inf. conjunction} \\ \text{W elongation} \\ \text{Sup. conjunction}\end{array}\right. \\
\text{evening}\left.\begin{array}{l}\text{E elongation} \\ \text{Inf. conjunction}\end{array}\right\}
\end{array}
$$

Inf. conjunction	} 4 weeks (spring)—2 weeks (autumn)
W elongation	} 7 weeks (winter)—3½ weeks (summer)
E elongation	} 7 weeks (autumn)—3½ weeks (spring)
Inf. conjunction	} 4 weeks (summer)—2 weeks (winter)

Elongations are always less than 28°—sometimes considerably so. In the N hemisphere, most favourable elongations E occur in the spring, most favourable elongations W in the autumn, since the planet is then at greatest altitude. In unfavourable years it happens that the spring and autumn elongations are small ones.

Mercury is observable telescopically for about 6 weeks at W elongation and 5 weeks at E elongation, during which time its angular diameter varies from about 5″ to 9″, and phase from nearly Full to a thick crescent. Its true brightness, as measured in stellar magnitudes, reaches a maximum around superior conjunction. At such times, however, it is so near the Sun as to be unobservable, and it appears brightest to the eye when seen against a darker sky at and near elongations.

4.2 Surface features

These are for the most part near the threshold of vision, and their observation and recording are correspondingly susceptible to personal visual idiosyncrasies. They consist of apparently permanent dusky markings, which, however, are of very variable visibility; and of whitish areas which characterise the limb regions and change from day to day. There are in addition anomalous appearances of the disc itself: unequal cusps, undue thickening of the crescent phase, etc.

The Reports of the Mercury and Venus Section of the B.A.A. form an admirable introduction to the subject; see also B. 4, 125; B. 4, in particular, is a storehouse of information for all planetary observers. Charts of Mercury's surface features will be found in B. 4, 122–124, 127, 128.

4.3 Observational technique

Since the contrast in Mercury's markings is poor, low magnifications are indicated, provided they do not entail excessive glare. Glare will obscure faint markings more effectively than the reduced contrast dependent upon increased magnification. Hence the necessity of always observing Mercury (as also Venus) against a twilight or daylight sky. Observation by daylight also ensures a reasonable altitude above the horizon. McEwen has found × 135– × 160 a satisfactory range of magnification with a 5-in refractor.

The chief difficulties encountered in the observation of Mercury are the shortness of the apparitions, the smallness of the disc, and the planet's angular proximity to the Sun.

All drawings should be marked with the date, time (GMAT or UT), type of instrument, aperture, magnification, and approximate altitude. A convenient scale for blanks is from 3 to 5 mm per " arc.

4.4 Finding by daylight

(a) With circles, taking RA and Dec from Almanac.

(b) When E of the Sun, take the difference between its Dec and that of the Sun from the Almanac. From known diameter of LP field, depress or elevate the telescope that amount from the Sun's centre; in the case of an altazimuth, let the Sun trail a web, and then depress or elevate the telescope in a direction perpendicular to the web. After an interval equal to the difference in RA between Mercury and Sun, the planet should be in the LP field; if not, very little sweeping will locate it.

(c) Starting from the Moon, on the day when the Almanac shows it and Mercury as being in conjunction, sweep in the direction and for the distance given.

When using either of the last two methods a wide-field finder (covering, say, 8° to 10°) is extremely helpful.

4.5 Solar transits

The remaining transits of Mercury to occur this century are as follows :

1970 May 9^d 8^h	1973 Nov 10^d 11^h	1986 Nov 13^d 4^h
1993 Nov 6^d 4^h	1999 Nov 15^d 21^h	

(approximate times of mid-transit)

4.6 B.A.A.H. data

(a) Dates of elongations and conjunctions.

(b) RA
Dec
Phase (% of diameter normal to line
of cusps which is illuminated)
Elongation (° arc)
Distance
} at 5-day intervals throughout the apparitions

4.7 A.E. data

(a) Heliocentric longitude
Heliocentric latitude
Radius vector
Orbital longitude
Daily motion
} at 0^h ET daily throughout the year.

(b) RA
Dec
Semidiameter
Horizontal parallax
Distance from Earth
Ephemeris Transit time
} at 0^h ET daily throughout the year.

(c) k: ratio of illuminated to total area of the disc
i: Earth's elongation from Sun, as seen from
Mercury
θ: angle between line of cusps and meridian
L: brightness of disc: amount of light received from
a disc of Mercury's albedo, of radius 1″, at unit
distance from Sun, and illuminated by the Sun
as Mercury's mean disc is illuminated
Stellar magnitude
} at 5-day intervals throughout the year.

(d) Elongations
Magnitudes
} at 0^h UT at 5-day intervals.

(e) Dates of conjunctions, elongations, stationary points, and of conjunctions with other members of the Solar System.

(f) Mean elements of orbit.
Mean anomalies (at 10-day intervals).

4.8 Data

Mean solar distance: 0·387099 A.U. = 3·60 × 10^7 miles.
Perihelion distance: 2·9 × 10^7 miles.

Aphelion distance: $4\cdot3\times10^7$ miles.

Sidereal period: $0\cdot24085$ tropical years.

Mean synodic period: $115\cdot88$ days.

Sidereal mean daily motion: $4°09$.

Mean orbital velocity: $29\cdot7$ m/s.

Axial rotation period: $59\cdot4$ days.

e: $0\cdot2056244$ ($+0\cdot0000002$) ⎫

i: $\quad 7°\ 0'\ 13''7$ ($+0''1$) ⎪

Ω: $47°\ 44'\ 18''9$ ($+42''7$) ⎬ Epoch 1950, Jan $1\cdot5$ UT

$\tilde{\omega}$: $76°\ 40'\ 39''0$ ($+56''0$) ⎪ (annual variations in brackets).

L: $33°\ 10'\ 6''07$ ($+53°43'\ 3''47$) ⎭

Angular diameter at unit distance: $6''68$.

Angular diameter at mean inferior conjunction: $10''90$.

Linear diameter: 4800 km$=3000$ miles$=0\cdot38\oplus$.

Mass: $1\cdot111\times10^{-7}\odot=0\cdot037\oplus$.

Volume: $0\cdot055\oplus$.

Density: $3\cdot73\times$water$=0\cdot68\oplus$.

Superficial gravity: $0\cdot26\oplus$.

Mag at maximum brightness: about $-1\cdot8$.

SECTION 5

VENUS

5.1 Apparitions

The following intervals between successive phenomena are approximate:

$$
\begin{array}{ll}
\text{morning} & \left\{\begin{array}{l}\text{Inf. conjunction} \\ \text{W elongation} \\ \text{Sup. conjunction}\end{array}\right. \\
\text{evening} & \left\{\begin{array}{l}\text{E elongation} \\ \text{Inf. conjunction}\end{array}\right.
\end{array}
\begin{array}{l}
\left.\rule{0pt}{8pt}\right\}\ 10\ \text{weeks} \\
\left.\rule{0pt}{8pt}\right\}\ 31\ \text{weeks} \\
\left.\rule{0pt}{8pt}\right\}\ 31\ \text{weeks} \\
\left.\rule{0pt}{8pt}\right\}\ 10\ \text{weeks}
\end{array}
$$

Elongations are never larger than about 47°. Venus is at maximum altitude (in the N hemisphere) at E elongations in the spring, when it may remain above the horizon till midnight. These particularly favourable apparitions recur at intervals of 8 years (=13 Venus's years) from 1948.

Venus is observable for about 7 months at each elongation. It has been seen with the naked eye when only 5° from the Sun at superior conjunction (position taken from Almanac, found with binoculars, Sun then hidden by gable, and picked up with naked eye). Another recorded instance is of its naked-eye visibility 35^d after superior conjunction, when 9° from the Sun. It can be followed right through inferior conjunction when this occurs midway between the nodes: then up to 9° from the Sun, measured along the same hour circle, the crescent less than 1″ wide being visible with binoculars.

Maximum brightness occurs about 35 days after E elongation and 35 days before W elongation.

5.2 Surface features

The following are some of the points to look for:

(a) Irregularities in the cusps: widening or blunting; unequal sizes.

(b) Terminator shading present or absent; uniform from N to S, or varying in intensity; extent; depth of tone; colour; any lighter spots or areas within the shaded zone.

113

(c) Any irregularities in the terminator itself.

(d) Any difference between the observed form of the terminator and that which would be expected from the known phase.

(e) Visibility or otherwise of the unilluminated section of the disc; brightness compared with the day sky.

(f) Vague greyish areas; extent, colour, intensity.

(g) Any relatively clearly defined markings should be recorded with the greatest possible precision, since they may throw light upon the problem of the rotation period.

(h) Width, brightness, and colour of the aureole.

See further B. 129–130a.

5.3 Observational technique

For the detection of surface features the most favourable combination of large angular diameter and large phase occurs about midway between W elongation and superior conjunction, and again between superior conjunction and E elongation, when the planet's angular diameter is about 15″ and its phase gibbous.

The apparition for observational purposes, however, may be taken as extending from a little before W elongation to as near superior conjunction as the proximity of Venus to the Sun and its own decreasing diameter allow; and again from as soon after superior conjunction as the planet is observable, until the narrowing of the crescent makes observation worthless after E elongation.

At maximum brightness, glare will submerge the soft and uncontrasted detail of Venus's surface unless it is reduced in some way—such as:

(a) Observation in daylight.

(b) Ocular diaphragm or reduction of the objective's aperture.

(c) Herschel wedge, or other Sun diagonal.

(d) Neutral or colour filter (Wratten K1 and K2 have been used with success).

(e) The presence of haze or high cloud often improves definition, probably by reducing glare.

Given observational precautions on the lines indicated above, faint markings, the darkening towards the terminator, and irregularities in the outline of the terminator may be seen with as little as 3 ins aperture. $50D$ or $60D$ can often be used when the planet is high in the sky.

Systematic observation of Venus calls for a sort of dogged perseverance. The value of negative observations should not be underrated.

Blanks for drawings should not be made too large, or there will be a tendency to elaborate the probably very small amount of detail that is actually seen. All drawings should be marked with the date, UT or GMAT, instrument (including details of any accessories), magnification, and approximate altitude of the planet at the time.

All observers of Venus are well advised to familiarise themselves with a useful paper on observational methods by P. Moore (B. 130b).

5.4 Finding by daylight

See sections 4.4, 5.1.

5.5 Solar transits

Of little practical interest at the present time: the next four transits occur on

2004 June 7
2012 June 5 } descending node

2117 December 10
2125 December 8 } ascending node

The last two transits occurred on 1882 December 6 and 1874 December 8.

5.6 B.A.A.H. data

(*a*) Dates of elongations, conjunctions, and greatest brightness.

(*b*) RA
Dec
Phase
Mag   } at 10-day intervals throughout the apparitions.
Angular diameter
Distance
Elongation

5.7 A.E. data

(*a*) Heliocentric longitude
Heliocentric latitude
Radius vector
Orbital longitude   } at 0^h ET on alternate days throughout the year.
Orbital latitude
Daily motion

115

(b) RA
Dec
Semidiameter
Horizontal parallax
Distance from Earth
Ephemeris Transit-time
} at 0ʰ ET daily throughout the year.

(c) k
i
θ
L
} (see section 4.7)
Stellar magnitude
} at 5-day intervals throughout the year.

(d) Dates of conjunctions, elongations, stationary points, and greatest brilliance, and of conjunctions with other members of the Solar System.

(e) Mean elements of orbit.

Mean anomalies (at 10-day intervals throughout the year).

5.8 Data

Mean solar distance: 0·723331 A.U.=6·72 × 10⁷ miles.
Perihelion distance: 6·67 × 10⁷ miles.
Aphelion distance: 6·76 × 10⁷ miles.
Sidereal period: 0·61521 tropical years.
Mean synodic period: 583·92 days.
Sidereal mean daily motion: 1°60.
Mean orbital velocity: 21·7 m/s.
Axial rotation period: 244·3 days.

e: 0·0067968 (−0·0000005)
i: 3° 23′ 38″9 (+0″04)
Ω: 76° 13′ 46″8 (+32″4)
$\tilde{\omega}$: 130° 52′ 3″3 (+50″6)
L: 81° 34′ 19″20 (−135° 12′ 30″3)
} Epoch 1950, Jan 1·5 UT (annual variations in brackets).

Angular diameter at unit distance: 16″82.
Angular diameter at mean inferior conjunction: 60″80.
Linear diameter: 12,200 km=7600 miles=0·96⊕.
Mass: 2·478 × 10⁻⁶☉=0·826⊕.
Volume: 0·876⊕.
Density: 5·21 × water=0·94⊕.
Superficial gravity: 0·90⊕.
Mag at maximum brightness: about −4·4.

SECTION 6

MARS

6.1 Apparitions

Conjunctions and oppositions occur, usually, in alternate years: near perihelion, oppositions recur at intervals of about 800^d, near aphelion at intervals of about 765^d, the mean interval from opposition to opposition being 780^d. Thus each opposition occurs, on the average, 7 weeks later in the year than its predecessor.

Most favourable oppositions are those occurring at perihelion, in August (longitude of perihelion being 333°). These recur at intervals of 15 and 17 years (7 and 8 synodic periods), and are less frequent than aphelic oppositions (February) in the ratio 2 : 3. Oppositions of Mars fall into two series, each lasting about 8 years. During one, each successive opposition is more distant than the last; during the other, each is nearer than its predecessor. Disregarding the factor of Declination, the most favourable for observation is the last opposition of the latter series.

Unfortunately for northern observers, Mars is always in S Dec at perihelic oppositions—Mars's perihelion lying in Aquarius—and the opposition following is more favourable for observers in Britain, the slightly reduced angular diameter being more than recompensed by the increased altitude.

Oppositions occurring during the early months of the year are unfavourable, since Mars is then near aphelion and its distance from the Earth is nearly twice that at a perihelic opposition. Favourable oppositions occur during the latter half of August and the early part of September.

The period during which Mars can be reasonably satisfactorily observed is limited to some 6 weeks on either side of opposition, and the practical advantage of perihelic oppositions lies less in the increased angular diameter of the disc than in the extended period over which observation is possible. The disjointed nature of the records of Martian observation (limited to about 3 months in every 26) is behind the continued lack of solution of so many problems connected with the planet.

The Martian S hemisphere is always turned towards the Earth at perihelic oppositions, the N at aphelic; British observers thus observe the northern hemisphere of Mars more favourably than the southern.

Angular diameter at aphelic opposition: about 14″,
,,   ,,   at perihelic opposition: about 25″,
,,   ,,   at mean opposition: about 17″·9.

At average oppositions, 1″ is subtended by a linear distance of from 200 to 300 miles at the Martian surface; even at perihelic opposition it is always more than 175 miles.

Declination limits: $\pm 25\frac{1}{2}°$ approximately. Observation is handicapped when the altitude of Mars is less than 30° or 40°; i.e. Mars in S Dec is not observable to full advantage from the British Isles.

Magnitude limits: at favourable opposition: about −2·8,
at conjunction: about +2·0.

6.2 Instrumental

Valuable results can be obtained by an experienced observer with a 5-in; this is the absolute minimum, however, for anyone intending to study Mars seriously—8 to 10 ins would be better. Nothing less than 5 ins will show anything of value, though providing good 'views' of the planet. A 3-in, for example, will at a favourable opposition show the main features such as the M. Acidalium and Syrtis, and even some of the more prominent canali such as Thoth and Nilosyrtis.

If the aperture exceeds about 12 ins, the atmosphere will seldom allow the full aperture to be used. It frequently happens that a 5-in will show everything visible with unlimited increase of D: it is only during the periods or moments of improved seeing that the larger aperture's performance will be able to demonstrate its superiority.

Direct comparisons of performance on different occasions have revealed an 8-in refractor showing more than a 36-in reflector; an 11-in refractor surpassing a $12\frac{1}{2}$-in reflector; canali invisible in the Greenwich 28-in stopped to 20 ins, but visible in an 8-in by T. E. R. Phillips; apertures less than 20 ins showing more than the Yerkes 40-in stopped to 30 ins.

For the amateur intending the serious observation of Mars, therefore, an aperture between 5 ins and 12 ins is recommended: a refractor if money is no object, otherwise a reflector. An equatorial mount is a necessity, and mechanical drive virtually so.

Mars does not generally stand very high magnification. $40D$–$50D$ is usually the useful maximum that can be used with smaller instruments, this requiring better than average seeing. Faint detail can often be seen better with something in the region of $30D$–$40D$.

Accuracy of focus becomes increasingly important as the magnification is increased. It is often helpful to focus on the limb or the polar cap, rather than on surface detail.

6.3 Longitude of the Central Meridian

The longitude of the CM at 0^h UT daily is given in *A.E.* The successive appearances of the Martian surface are dependent upon the following facts:

Rotation period$=24^h$ 37^m $22^s.654$.
Same longitude transits the CM $37^m.4$ later each night.
The longitude system passes the CM at the rate of $350^\circ.89202$ per day,

$$=30^\circ \text{ in } 2^h \text{ } 3^m.1,$$
$$=1^\circ \text{ in } 4^m.1,$$
$$=14^\circ.62 \text{ per hour,}$$

from which it follows that:

(*a*) A given area of the Martian surface will be alternately observable on the meridian at some time during the night for about a fortnight, and either invisible or only observable off the CM for about three weeks.

(*b*) If the time at which a given longitude is on the CM be taken as *t*, then its time of CM transit *n* days later is given by $t+t'$. Values of t' are tabulated below:

n	t′	n	t′	n	t′	n	t′
1	0^h 37^m	11	6^h 50^m	21	13^h 3^m	31	19^h 16^m
2	1 15	12	7 28	22	13 41	32	19 54
3	1 52	13	8 5	23	14 18	33	20 31
4	2 29	14	8 42	24	14 55	34	21 8
5	3 6	15	9 20	25	15 33	35	21 46
6	3 44	16	9 57	26	16 10	36	22 23
7	4 21	17	10 34	27	16 47	37	23 0
8	4 58	18	11 11	28	17 24	38	23 37
9	5 36	19	11 49	29	18 2	39	0 15
10	6 13	20	12 26	30	18 39		

(*c*) The correlation and comparison of a mass of observational material obtained throughout an apparition is facilitated if all drawings are made at such times that the longitude of the CM is a multiple of 30. The times at which this condition is satisfied are obtained by adding the intervals given in the subjoined Table to the time of transit of the zero meridian, given in *A.E.* for every day of the year:

Longitude	Interval	Longitude	Interval	Longitude	Interval
30°	2^h 3^m1	150°	10^h 15^m6	270°	18^h 28^m0
60	4 6·2	180	12 18·7	300	20 31·1
90	6 9·4	210	14 21·8	330	22 34·2
120	8 12·5	240	16 24·9	360	24 37·4

It is advisable to begin the drawing about 5 mins before the time at which the required longitude reaches the CM; the main outlines will then be laid down in more or less their correct relation to the limb.

The observations for the whole apparition can be planned in advance. Using a pro forma similar to that shown below, T_o, the times of transit of the zero meridian, for successive dates, are inserted from the *A.E.* The remaining columns are then filled in by means of the Table above.

Date	T_0	T_{30}	T_{60}	T_{90}	. . .	T_{330}

Those suitable for observation can be entered in ink, and the remainder either in pencil or else omitted.

(*d*) The longitude of the CM at any time *t* is given by

$$CM_t = rt + l$$

where r = change of longitude per hour (14°62),
   t = the required UT,
   l = longitude of the CM at 0^h UT (from *A.E.*).

Similarly, the longitude of the CM of any drawing is given by

$$CM = r(t_2 - t_1) + l$$

where t_1 = UT of beginning the main outlines of the drawing,
   t_2 = UT of completing the main outlines of the drawing.

This calculation is simplified by the subjoined Table, which gives the change of longitude of the CM in intervals of terrestrial time:

Mins \ Hrs	0	1	2	3	4	5	6
0	0°00	14°62	29°24	43°86	58°48	73°10	87°72
1	0·24	14·86	29·48	44·10	58·72	73·34	87·96
2	0·49	15·11	29·73	44·35	58·97	73·59	88·21
3	0·73	15·35	29·97	44·59	59·21	73·83	88·45
4	0·97	15·59	30·21	44·83	59·45	74·07	88·69
5	1·22	15·84	30·46	45·08	59·70	74·32	88·94
6	1·46	16·08	30·70	45·32	59·94	74·56	89·18
7	1·71	16·33	30·95	45·57	60·19	74·81	89·43
8	1·95	16·57	31·19	45·81	60·43	75·05	89·67
9	2·19	16·81	31·43	46·05	60·67	75·29	89·91
10	2·44	17·06	31·68	46·30	60·92	75·54	90·16
15	3·66	18·28	32·90	47·52	62·14	76·76	91·38
20	4·87	19·49	34·11	48·73	63·35	77·97	92·59
25	6·09	20·71	35·33	49·95	64·57	79·19	93·81
30	7·31	21·93	36·55	51·17	65·79	80·41	95·03
35	8·53	23·15	37·77	52·39	67·01	81·63	96·25
40	9·75	24·37	38·99	53·61	68·23	82·85	97·47
45	10·97	25·59	40·21	54·83	69·45	84·07	98·69
50	12·18	26·80	41·42	56·04	70·66	85·28	99·90
55	13·40	28·02	42·64	57·26	71·88	86·50	101·12

These values are based on the assumption of uniform rotation at the rate of 14°62 per hour. In fact this is the mean value, the limits being 14°60 and 14°64;* the maximum inaccuracy incurred by the use of the Table is 0°5 in the derived longitude of the CM, or 2^m in the time of meridian transit.

6.4 Drawings

6.4.1 Preparing the blanks: Blanks should be prepared beforehand. Convenient size for the moderate apertures suitable for Martian observation under normal seeing conditions is about 2 ins to the diameter at the time of opposition. The detail visible when Mars is far from opposition does not justify so large a drawing, and a better plan is to prepare a series of blanks, covering the whole apparition, to a

* The variation being the result of the changing terrestrial viewpoint, relative to Mars.

scale of 0·1 ins per ″ arc, or 3 mm per ″ arc. The construction of such small blanks, with considerable defect of illumination, is difficult, and a good plan is to draw them 4 times larger than scale and reduce them photographically.

The necessary data may be derived from *B.A.A.H.* (see section 6.8) or *A.E.* (see section 6.9):

	B.A.A.H.	*A.E.*
Angular diameter	10^d intervals	2^d intervals
P: p.a. of the N pole, measured E from the N point of the disc	10^d intervals	2^d intervals
Q: p.a. of point of greatest defect of illumination	10^d intervals	2^d intervals
Phase: Ph (expressed as %)	10^d intervals	—
q (angular value of greatest defect of illumination)	—	2^d intervals

For use on dates when Ph is 95 or larger, the blank may be drawn circular, but if Ph is less than 95 the figure of the Martian disc departs sufficiently from the circular to necessitate the following construction being carried out.

For the sake of example, it will be supposed that the following figures are extracted by interpolation from *B.A.A.H.* for the date and time corresponding to the required CM longitude:

$$\text{Angular diameter: } 7''8$$
$$P: \qquad\quad 26°$$
$$Q: \qquad\quad 293°$$
$$\text{Ph:} \qquad\quad 90$$

(whence greatest defect of illumination $=\frac{1}{10}\times 7''8$, or $q=0''78$).

Draw the circle *cpd* to a scale of 10″ per inch (Figure 20 (*a*)).
Draw the diameter *NS* to define the N and S points of the disc.
Draw the phase diameter *pd*, such that $\angle NOd = Q = 293°$.
The line of cusps is then *cc′*, perpendicular to *pd*.
Locate *t* on *pd*, such that $pt = 0·9\ pd$,

or $\qquad\qquad\qquad\qquad td = q = 0·078$ ins

The central two-thirds of the terminator can be drawn through *t* with compasses centred on *pd* and set to radius *r*, where $r=yR,$

R being the radius of the disc (0·39 ins),

y being a factor related to Ph in the manner shown below:

Ph	y	Ph	y	Ph	y	Ph	y
100	1·000	96	1·065	92	1·130	88	1·215
99	1·015	95	1·080	91	1·150	87	1·240
98	1·030	94	1·100	90	1·170	86	1·265
97	1·050	93	1·115	89	1·190	85	1·300

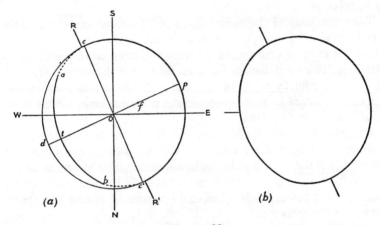

FIGURE 20

Construction of a Martian blank for date 81^d before opposition.
(2 × scale)

In this case, Ph=90.

Hence $y=1\cdot17$.

Hence $r=1\cdot17\times0\cdot39=0\cdot456$ ins.

Thus the centre of the circle, an arc of which is to be drawn through
    t, is the point f, where $ft=0\cdot46$ ins.

With centre f, and radius ft, draw the arc atb.

Complete the terminator by connecting up a and b with the cusps
    freehand.

Finally, lay out the diameter RR', such that $\angle NOR'=P=26°$, and
    mark in the projections of this diameter beyond the limb; also the
    WE axis through O perpendicular to NS.

The completed blank, devoid of construction lines, is then as shown in
Figure 20(b).

123

An alternative method—employing q, and avoiding the use of the protractor—is described in B. 143 (No. 22).

6.4.2 Orientation and execution: The correct orientation of the drawing is a matter of great importance. With blanks constructed as described in section 6.4.1 no particular difficulty will be encountered. Even without a micrometer, the direction in the image corresponding to the WE axis can be established by trailing; given a position micrometer (even a rough home-made scale will do), the web can be laid along the axis of rotation, also marked on the blank. Orientation by means of the polar cap, as an indicator of the position of the axis, or by means of the estimated point of greatest defect of illumination, is not to be relied on.

The correctness of the main outlines is of greater importance than niceties of shading, tone, and linear detail on the threshold of visibility. Therefore extreme care should be given to laying down the outlines, first of the polar cap, then of the main features in the central region of the disc, and finally of those near the limb. Beware of a systematic tendency (suffered by some observers) to place markings too far N or S, or E or W, on the blank.

The main features of the Martian surface are now thoroughly known, and the recording of the variations in their appearance constitutes the main body of the work possible with instruments of moderate aperture. Points for particular attention are variations in their size, shape, intensity, and colour; their occasional obscuration or even disappearance; and the occurrence of whitish areas at the limb and terminator, which fade and finally disappear as they approach the central meridian.

The main outlines completed, the finer detail is inserted. Only when the positions of the visible features are securely laid down should 'shading' be started. Its aim is to indicate the relative, not necessarily the absolute, intensities of the features whose outlines have been drawn. A change back to a LP ocular will often reveal tonal gradations within areas that appear uniform under high magnification. Written notes in amplification of the drawn features, intensities, etc, are often useful.

Finally, record the main colours of the image.

It is wise to omit all features and details that cannot be held steadily; at least, some distinctive form of notation should be used for details that are only glimpsed. It is a waste of time straining after microscopic detail with moderate apertures; there is plenty of macroscopic variation from opposition to opposition which is detectable with such equipment. It is better to be assured that in each drawing the shapes, sizes, relative positions, and relative tonal intensities of the main features are correctly stated.

The whole drawing should not take more than about half an hour; even so, rotation will have altered the appearance of the disc to a noticeable extent. It is always preferable to finish the drawing at the telescope, rather than to work it up from memory or from sketches: the dangers of the latter procedure are the tendency to 'finish' the drawing (i.e. to work it up to an extent sanctioned neither by memory nor, probably, by the eye in the first place) and the impossibility of comparing the drawing with the image for confirmation.

It should be possible to get one drawing per clear night throughout the apparition; two per night, as widely spaced as the planet's altitude will allow, are better. This routine is particularly desirable during the relatively scarce favourable oppositions.

Draw the same region night after night (see section 6.3), calling these drawings series A1. At a different time of night, and also as this region disappears from the observable part of the disc, make nightly drawings of successively visible regions (series B1, C1, D1, etc). On the reappearance of the first region, several weeks later, a new series of drawings (A2) is made; followed in due course by B2, C2, etc; and so on throughout the apparition. Any differences between a later and an earlier drawing of the same CM should be specifically noted, indicating whether the discrepancy is thought to be unintentional (inaccurate drawing), due to variation in the seeing, or accepted by the observer as objective.

At the end of the apparition a map of the whole Martian surface can, if it is thought worth while, be synthesised from the 30°-spaced series of drawings.

6.4.3 Auxiliary data: The following data should finally be appended to each drawing:

(a) Date.
(b) Time (GMAT) of beginning of main outlines (t_1).
(c) Time of completion of main outlines (t_2).
(d) Time of completion of drawing.
(e) Longitude of CM at the predecided time—which should be within a few minutes of t_2—to nearest degree (see section 6.3).
(f) Latitude of centre of disc (D_E from *A.E.*).
(g) Type and aperture of telescope.
(h) Magnification.
(i) Seeing.

125

Additional information which may be added later includes:

(j) Longitude of Sun, as seen from Mars (L_S from *A.E.*).

(k) Angular diameter of the disc.

(l) Declination of Sun, as seen from Mars (D_S from *A.E..*).

(m) Observer's name (if drawing is to be submitted to a central pool, such as the B.A.A. Mars Section).

6.5 Surface features

The following brief and miscellaneous notes should be supplemented by B. 4, 131, 143, etc. Maps of the Martian surface are to be found in, among others, B. 132, 133, 138, 143 (No. 15), 145.

(a) Canali: length (their visible extremities being carefully 'marked' with reference to other features); breadth (uniform or varying); straight, curved, continuous or broken; sharply or ill defined.

The canali are most favourably observed at aphelion oppositions, when Mars is in N Dec and its N hemisphere is turned towards the Earth.

(b) Polar caps: to be distinguished from the whitish polar areas; irregularities in the outline; detached areas or temporary protrusions; apparent projection beyond the limb; general changes in shape and size.

(c) Clouds: most commonly indicated by the partial or total obscuration of some well-known feature, or localised areas of abnormally light tone; occasionally seen as clouds, usually whitish, very rarely yellowish.

Records as nearly continuous as possible are needed: reobserve at intervals throughout the night when first seen, and check whether still visible the following night; record position, extent, duration, colour, intensity, and movements.

Whitish patches seen at the limb, which can often be followed well on to the disc: size, p.a., intensity, times of appearance (or first observation) and disappearance.

(d) Areas in which changes have been observed in the past, e.g. the Hyscus—Mare Sirenum region, the p side of Syrtis Major, Lacus Solis, etc. A mass of data is still required concerning long-term variations: ideally these demand observation under uniform conditions (so that the drawings are comparable) spread over a long series of oppositions.

6.6 Positional work

Estimations or measurements of the position of Martian surface features fall under the following main heads:

(*a*) determinations of longitude,
(*b*) determinations of latitude,
(*c*) to assist in drawing,
(*d*) determination of angular sizes,
(*e*) to assist in the orientation of the image.

(*a*) By timing transits of the CM. Such work, fundamental in the observation of Jupiter, has comparatively little scope as applied to Mars. Except during a few weeks at opposition it is difficult to judge the position of the CM accurately, owing to the large defect of illumination, and also to the fact that the mid-point of the terminator does not necessarily lie on the equator. Furthermore, there are no equatorial belts perpendicular to the axis (as in the case of Jupiter) to assist the eye. Measurements of drawings are also unsatisfactory, owing to the magnitude of the accidental errors; while the measurement of photographs necessitates the use of larger apertures than are usually found in amateur hands.

The bifilar micrometer can be used to take measures from the limb (not the terminator); but the most satisfactory method is to use a single-web position micrometer to define the CM, the web being set to the p.a. of the axis (from *A.E.*) and then superimposed upon the image so that it bisects the polar cap.

(*b*) By the direct measurement of drawings or photographs (but see (*a*) above), or by means of a filar micrometer; this ideally requires considerable aperture, however. Alternatively, the distance of the object from the N and S poles (expressed as a fraction of the polar diameter) may be estimated visually when on the CM. The Tilt being known, the latitude can then be derived.

(*c*) By determining the p.a. of fundamental points in the main visible surface features. The value of the micrometer in this role is doubtful. Given the patience requisite for the training of the eye in the accurate appreciation of relative positions, visual estimation is as accurate, unless large apertures are available.

(*d*) Owing to the systematic errors in micrometrical work, visual estimations of the absolute size of features is generally preferable. The micrometer can nevertheless be of use in the measurement of change of size; frequent measures of the diameter of the polar cap (major and minor axes), for instance, would be of value, and probably more consistent than a series of visual estimations. Another disadvantage of the micrometer, except for the measurement of major features, is that the appearance of the clearly defined web across the image is liable to make fine and poorly contrasted detail vanish altogether.

(*e*) See section 6.4.2.

6.7 Intensity and colour

The relative intensities of different areas simultaneously visible are very much more easily observed, recorded, and discussed with a reasonable degree of certainty than those of a single area at different times.

Tonal differences can be indicated either by shading or by a numerical scale; or by a combination of both methods, the main areas being laid down with pencil tone, and smaller variations being indicated by means of some arbitrary scale. For example:

> 1: exceptionally dark
> 3: normal tone of the green areas
> 6: normal tone of the reddish areas
> 8: tone of clouds at the limb
> 10: tone of polar caps at their brightest

Colour is more difficult to observe and record than tone, and requires larger apertures (since brighter image). With moderate apertures, few distinctions of colour will be noted, apart from the prevailing reddish- and bluish-grey of the 'deserts' and maria (within which are variations of tone rather than of colour), whitish spots (including the polar caps), and the greyish areas at the limb.

W. H. Pickering's suggested numerical scale for colours is liable to introduce confusion if a numerical scale is also used to record tonal intensities, besides being awkward to memorise. Some such modification of his colour scale as the following may be found useful for anotating drawings:

> w   : white
> ww : pale grey
> www: darker grey
> b   : white, with faintest blue tint
> bb : pale blue
> bbb : sky blue
> g   : pale green
> gg   : darker green
> y   : pale yellow
> yy   : darker yellow

128

yyy : yellow ochre
ry : orange
rry : deep orange
r : red

Careful choice of the optimum magnification is needed when making colour estimations. Generally speaking, too low a magnification yields a disc so small that no colour distinctions of any value can be seen at all; while over-magnification dilutes the image to such an extent that faint differences within the orange-red range are suppressed, and varieties of green and blue merge into a uniform greenish-grey.

The production of coloured drawings (e.g. with pastels, water-colours, etc.) at the telescope is not recommended. It encourages the pursuit of prettiness and 'finish' rather than objective accuracy, and results do not justify the time and trouble spent in overcoming the difficulties of matching colours in the dark.

See also section 3.6.

6.8 B.A.A.H data

RA
Dec
Magnitude
Angular diameter
P: p.a. of N pole measured E from N point of disc
Q: p.a. of point of greatest defect of illumination
Phase
Tilt: of the N pole towards or away from the Earth
Distance

at 10-day intervals throughout the apparition.

Longitude of central meridian at 0^h UT daily throughout the year.

6.9 A.E. data

(a) RA
Dec
Semidiameter
Horizontal parallax
Distance from Earth
Ephemeris Transit time

at 0^h ET on each day of the year.

(b) Heliocentric longitude
Heliocentric latitude
Radius vector
Orbital longitude
Orbital latitude
Daily motion
} at 0^h ET at 4-daily intervals throughout the year.

(c) Physical ephemeris:
Light-time (i.e. distance in 'light minutes')
Stellar magnitude
Position angle of axis of rotation (measured E from the N point of the disc)
$A_E + 180°$ (where A_E = areocentric RA of the Earth)
D_E (areocentric Dec of the Earth: latitude of centre of disc) = 'Tilt' in *B.A.A.H.*
$A_S - A_E$ (where A_S = areocentric RA of Sun)
D_S (areocentric Dec of Sun)
L_S (areocentric longitude of Sun)
$k \left(\dfrac{\text{illuminated area of disc}}{\text{total area of disc}} \right)$
i (elongation of Earth from Sun, as seen from Mars)
Defect of illumination
Position angle of defect (measured from the N point of the disc)
} for alternate days throughout the year.

Longitude of CM of geometric disc at 0^h UT
of Transit of zero meridian
} for every day of the year.

(d) Dates of conjunction, opposition, stationary points, and of conjunctions with other members of the Solar System.

(e) Mean elements of orbit.
Mean anomalies (at 10-daily intervals throughout the year).
Rotation elements.

(f) Elongations and Magnitudes for 0^h UT at 10-daily intervals.

6.10 Data

Mean solar distance: 1·523688 A.U. = 1·415 × 10^8 miles.
Perihelion distance: 1·285 × 10^8 miles.
Aphelion distance: 1·545 × 10^8 miles.
Sidereal period: 1·88089 tropical years.
Mean synodic period: 779·94 days.

Sidereal mean daily motion: 0°.52.
Mean orbital velocity: 15·0 m/s.
Axial rotation period: 24^h 37^m 22^{s}654.

e: 0·0933589 (+0·0000009)
i: 1° 51′ 0″0 (±0)
Ω: 49° 10′ 18″9 (+27″7)
$\tilde{\omega}$: 335° 8′ 18″9 (+1′ 6″2)
L: 144° 20′ 7″08 (−168° 42′ 50″52)

Epoch 1950, Jan 1·5 UT (annual variations in brackets).

Angular diameter at unit distance: 9″36.
Angular diameter at mean opposition distance: 17″88.
Linear diameter: 6800 km=4200 miles=0·53⊕
Mass: 3·232×10^{-7}⊙=0·108⊕.
Volume: 0·151⊕.
Density: 3·94×water=0·71⊕.
Superficial gravity: 0·38⊕.
Mag at maximum brightness: −2·8.

6.11 Satellite data

	I Phobos	II Deimos
Stellar mag at mean opposition distance	11·6	12·8
Mean distance from centre of Mars:		
A.U.	0·000062725	0·00015695
at mean opposn. dist.	24″7	1′ 1″8
Sidereal period	0^{d}3189103	1^{d}26244064
	=7^h 39^m 13^{s}85	=30^h 17^m 54^{s}87
Synodic period	7^h 39^m 26^{s}65	1^d 6^h 21^m 15^{s}68
Eccentricity	0·0170	0·0031
Discoverer	Hall	Hall

SECTION 7

JUPITER

7.1 Apparitions

Oppositions occur about one month later each year, the mean synodic period being 398^{d}88. Declination limits are approximately 25° N and S. Owing to the impossibility of wholly satisfactory observation when the planet is in S Dec, systematic observation is impossible in this country for about one-third of the revolution period (4 years in every 12).

The conditions regarding the visibility or otherwise of the same region of the surface on successive nights are given in the following Table. If a spot transits the CM at time t on night 0, then, throughout the following fortnight, assuming a rotation period of 9^h 55^m:

Column (3) gives the times $\pm t$ of the transits of the same spot over the CM each night,

Column (4) gives the time interval that the spot is W or E of the CM at the same time t each night,

Column (5) gives the longitude difference between the spot and the CM at the same time t each night.

For example, if a spot is observed to transit the CM at 16^h 30^m GMAT on January 6, then the conditions for observing the spot on January 14 are as follows: it will transit the CM at 16^h 30^m+6^h 20^m and 16^h 30^m−3^h 35^m=22^h 50^m and 12^h 55^m (col. 3), the latter alone being observable; at 16^h 30^m it will be 3^h 35^m (col. 4) or 130° (col. 5) west of the CM.

The chances of making repeat observations of the same region on or near the CM depend upon the length of the period during which Jupiter is observable each night (i.e. upon its Dec) and upon the time (early or late) during this period that the initial observation was made. Thus a spot observed early during the period of Jupiter's visibility on night 0 might be reobserved on nights 1, 2, 4, 6, 7 (rotations 3, 5, 10, 15, 17), etc; if late in the night, on nights 1, 3, 5, 6, 7 (rotations 2, 7, 12, 14, 16), etc; if approximately half-way between rising and setting, on

132

nights 2, 3, 5, 7 (rotations 5, 7, 12, 17), etc. In other words, reobservation of a given region cannot be hoped for more frequently than at, generally, every other rotation, with gaps of as long as 5 rotations.

(1) Night	(2) Rotation	(3) Times of CM transit ±t	(4) Time interval W/E (+/−) CM at time t	(5) Longitude difference between spot and CM at time t
1	2	-4^h 10^m	$+4^h$ 10^m	151°
	3	$+5$ 45		
2	4	-8 20		
	5	$+1$ 35	-1 35	57
3	7	-2 35	$+2$ 35	94
	8	$+7$ 20		
	9	-6 45		
	10	$+3$ 10	-3 10	115
5	12	-1 0	$+1$ 0	36
	13	$+8$ 55		
6	14	-5 10		
	15	$+4$ 45	-4 45	172
7	16	-9 20		
	17	$+0$ 35	-0 35	21
8	19	-3 35	$+3$ 35	130
	20	$+6$ 20		
9	21	-7 45		
	22	$+2$ 10	-2 10	79
10	24	-2 0	$+2$ 0	71
	25	$+7$ 55		
11	26	-6 10		
	27	$+3$ 45	-3 45	136
12	29	-0 25	$+0$ 25	15
	30	$+9$ 30		
13	31	-4 35	$+4$ 35	166
	32	$+5$ 20		
14	33	-8 45		
	34	$+1$ 10	-1 10	42

7.2 Amateur work

Jupiter is, with variable stars, probably the favourite observational field with amateurs. The variety of its phenomena recommends it, and its angular size and brightness allow valuable work to be done with small instruments; neither an equatorial nor a driving clock is essential, though both are a convenience and will result in a larger number of individual observations being made. CM transit observations can be undertaken with even a 3-in, but for regular work a 5-in refractor or 6-in reflector are the minimum desirable equipment. Transit measurements can be made as accurately with a 4-in as with an 8-in, providing the spot is clearly seen, but there will be fewer of them.

The various branches of Jovian observation are:
(a) Longitude determinations by timing the CM transits of the features, either optically or by radio.
(b) Micrometer measures for the determination of latitude.
(c) General appearance of the disc.
(d) Colour and intensity observations.
(e) Photographic (see section 3.8).
(f) Satellite phenomena.
(g) Radio work.
(h) Other work.

7.3 Determination of longitude

The most powerful technique for unmasking the secrets of Jupiter's atmosphere that has yet been developed, and the main item in the programme of regular observers of the planet. It has the advantages of speed (the timing of the CM transits of 50–100 spots is often the work of a single session at the telescope); accuracy; producing quantitative data, with consequent ease and effectiveness of subsequent discussion; and finally, it goes straight to the core of the problem of conditions in the Jovian atmosphere.

Changes in the appearance of the visible surface are due primarily to the operation of the longitudinal currents: each latitude has its own 'normal' rate of drift, though the correlation of latitude with rotation period follows no known law (cf. the Sun); neither are the boundaries in latitude of the currents by any means fixed or permanent. The change of difference of longitude of adjacent spots or groups of spots belonging to different currents can be extremely rapid. From the observed times of transit the rotation periods of the various currents are derived, and such measures, when collated and reduced, provide all our

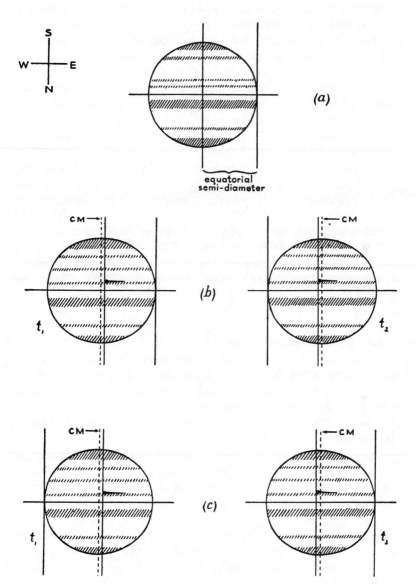

FIGURE 21

knowledge of these periods, as well as of the variations of rotational velocity within a given current.

The observations themselves may be made by radio, by visual estimation of the position of the CM, or by filar micrometer. In the latter case alternative procedures may be adopted:

(a) The webs are set to an angular separation equal to the equatorial semidiameter of the planet, and then superimposed on the image so that they are perpendicular to the belts (or, more accurately, set to the p.a. of the axis as given in *A.E.*), one web being kept tangential to the limb (Figure 21(a)).

(b) A method achieving greater accuracy by eliminating errors due to irradiation: the webs are set to a separation slightly smaller than the planet's equatorial semidiameter (Figure 21(b)). With the micrometer oriented to the p.a. of the axis (or with the horizontal web parallel to the belts, if the micrometer has no position circle) and one web tangential to the E limb, the time of transit of the spot at the other web is noted (t_1); then with the second web on the W limb, the time of transit at the first web is noted (t_2). The time of transit over the CM is then given by

$$t_1 + \frac{(t_2 - t_1)}{2}$$

(c) Alternatively, with the webs set at rather more than the planet's semidiameter apart (Figure 21(c)), the tangential web is set first on the W limb and subsequently on the E. These methods are least accurate when Jupiter is near quadrature, since similar settings at the illuminated and at the defective limb (markedly darkened) are more difficult than at two equally bright limbs.

In fact, however, the method of direct eye estimation of the time (to the nearest minute) of CM transit, without the help of a micrometer, is universally resorted to. The advantage of the micrometer—that it offers greater accuracy in a single measure—is outweighed by the following considerations:

(a) Owing to the greater speed of the eye method, a larger number of transits can be obtained in a given period of observation; when seeing is good, identifiable transits occur at the rate of 20 or 30 an hour with adequate apertures.

(b) Conversely, spots frequently come up to the CM in such rapid succession that only visual observation would obtain the transit times: there would simply be no time to readjust the webs on all of them, for it must be remembered that each recorded transit has to be supplemented with notes of the spot's position in latitude, shape, and intensity or colour, sufficient for its subsequent identification.

(c) Owing to Jupiter's high rotational speed, the eye can with practice become astonishingly accurate in its estimation of the moment at which CM transit occurs: one investigation of the accuracy of the method showed that practised observers agree consistently within 2^m, even though they may feel uncertain of the precise instant of transit by as much as 5^m; while errors of the order of 5^m are rare. The almost invariable tendency is to anticipate the transit, and once the sign and amount of the systematic error are determined (by comparisons with other observers, for example) a correction for personal equation can be applied. Though systematic, these personal errors are not necessarily permanent: it is not uncommon to find that their sign is reversed when Jupiter passes opposition (and the other limb then becomes defective), and that the right and left eyes have quite distinct systematic errors.

(d) The error in the derived rotation period becomes negligible when based on observations spread over a number of rotations, even though an individual transit may carry an uncertainty of from 2^m to 5^m. Rotation periods are not normally derived for features whose duration is less than about a month;* a total error of 5^m in the observations would produce an error in the derived period of only about $\pm 5^s$, and this error would decrease in proportion to the length of the interval between the first and last observations.

(e) The close juxtaposition in the field of an incisively defined web and an extremely ill-defined or poorly contrasted feature tends to suppress the latter altogether.

(f) The impossibility of repeating the micrometer measure, and the difficulty of keeping the limb web accurately tangential while the attention is directed to the meridian web (owing to their considerable angular separation).

(g) Visual determinations do not require a clock-driven equatorial.

Where there is scope for the micrometer is in the investigation of short-term variations of drift within a single current, since a single estimation by eye may give an error in the derived longitude of $\pm 3°$ or more. That such variations occur is well established, but little work has been done in this direction.

The observations should be recorded in the Observing Book in vertical columns:

* Features surviving from one apparition to the next are comparatively rare; those lasting longer than one revolution period—e.g. the Red Spot and the South Tropical Disturbance—very much more so.

Date. . . . .

(1)	(2)	(3)	(4) Longitude	
Serial No.	Description of feature	Transit time	λ_1	λ_2
1091	p end v.d. spot N edge NEB_N	11^h 34^m	—	177
1092	elong. proj. S edge STB	11 36	—	178
1093	consp. streak connecting NEB comps.	11 41	8	182
1094	ft. w. spot f RS	11 44	—	184

Column (1): serial numbers running consecutively throughout the apparition.

Column (2): as brief as is consistent with the certain identification of the feature. Recognised abbreviations (the observer can, and probably will, employ many more of his own devising) which are useful in this connexion are:

N	North
S	South
p	preceding
f	following
d.	dark
w.	white
v.	very
proj.	projection
comp.	component
elong.	elongation/elongated
consp.	conspicuous
indef.	indefinite/ill-defined
ft.	faint
RS	Red Spot
RSH	Hollow of the Red Spot
EZ	Equatorial Zone
SEB	South Equatorial Belt
SEB_N	North Component of the SEB
SEB_S	South Component of the SEB
NEB	North Equatorial Belt
NEB_N	North Component of the NEB

NEB$_S$	South Component of the NEB
S.Trop.Z.	South Tropical Zone
N.Trop.Z.	North Tropical Zone
STB	South Temperate Belt
NTB	North Temperate Belt
STZ	South Temperate Zone
NTZ	North Temperate Zone
SSTB	South South Temperate Belt
SSSTB	Southern component of SSTB (when the latter is divided into distinguishable components)
NNTB	North North Temperate Belt
NNNTB	Northern component of NNTB (when split into two)
SSTZ	South South Temperate Zone
NNTZ	North North Temperate Zone
SPR	South Polar Regions
NPR	North Polar Regions

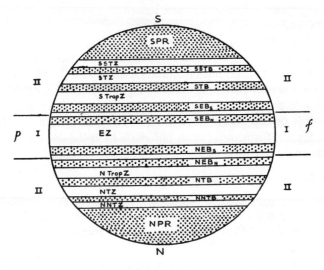

FIGURE 22

Column (3): To the nearest minute GMAT. Any clock or watch can be used that does not gain or lose more than 1 minute in 4 or 5 hours.

Column (4): The derived longitudes in Systems I or II respectively. Derived from *B.A.A.H.* or *A.E.* at the end of each observational session. Required data are:

  (a) Longitude (*L*) of the CM at 0^h UT preceding or following the observation, in System I (between SEB_N and NEB_S) or II (N of NEB_S and S of SEB_N).

(b) Rate of change of L at intervals of MT in each System, from which the change of L (ΔL) during the interval between 0^h UT and the time of observation is derived.

Then the required longitude of the spot is

$$\lambda = L \pm \Delta L$$

according as to whether the observation was made after or before 0^h UT. If $\Delta L > 360°$, add 360° to L; if the derived $\lambda > 360°$, reduce it by 360°; if in doubt as to which System the spot belongs to, enter up both λ_1, and λ_2.

Spots, though commonest in the equatorial and tropical regions, have been observed and measured right up to the edges of the SPR and NPR. Timed transits of the RS (p end, centre, and f end) are also extremely valuable, since its drift in longitude is considerable, and it is most desirable that as complete a record of its movements should be kept in the future as has been in the past.

In this work cooperation and the pooling of results are essential, so as to avoid gaps in the record of the apparition due to bad weather; a wide spread of observers in longitude is also desirable. More observers are always required, and the ranks of the Jupiter Section of the B.A.A. are open to anyone intending to take up systematic observing.

Records of CM transit observations should be sent to the Director of the Section fortnightly; other observations at the end of, or at intervals during, each apparition.

7.4 Determination of latitude

The changes of latitude of Jupiter's surface features are neither so large nor so rapid as their changes of longitude. Determinations of latitude need therefore be made much less frequently than those of longitude.

Figure 23 represents a median section through the body of Jupiter, taken in the plane which contains the line of sight from the terrestrial observer to its centre, O; P and E mark one pole and the equator respectively; PCE is thus a section of the Central Meridian; C is the centre of the apparent disc; P', where $P'O$ is normal to the tangent to the disc parallel to OC, is the N or S point of the apparent disc; X is a point on the CM whose latitude is required.

Two quantities have to be established by observation, the means of a number of micrometer measures being taken:

p', the polar semidiameter of the apparent disc (if the value of 1 turn of the micrometer screw is known, p' may be equated with the polar semidiameter—from *A.E.*—with negligible error in the final result).

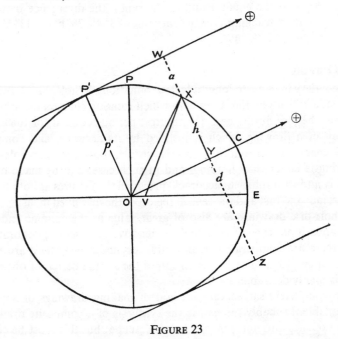

FIGURE 23

h, the angular distance of X north or south of the centre of the disc; it is derived by measuring XW (a) and XZ (d), the distance of X from each end of the CM,

whence $\qquad\qquad h = \tfrac{1}{2}(d-a)$

Then $\quad b = \angle XOE =$ the required zenocentric latitude of X,

$\left.\begin{matrix} h \\ p' \end{matrix}\right\}$ by observation,

$D_E = \angle COE$ (from *A.E.*),

$\phi = 21° 2'33$ (from $\sin \phi = 0\cdot3590$, the eccentricity of the Jovian ellipsoid),

$\theta\;$ is such that $\sin \theta = h/p'$,

$B\;$ is such that $\tan B = \sec \phi \tan D_E$,

and $\qquad\qquad \tan b = \cos \phi \tan (\theta + B)$

also b', the zenographic latitude of X, is given by

141

$$\tan b' = \sec \phi \tan (\theta + B)$$

where $b' = \angle XVE$, VX being normal to the tangent at X.

D, B, b, b' and θ are taken as positive if measured N from the equator, negative if measured S.

$b = b'$ at the equator and at the poles, the divergence between them reaching a maximum value of $3° 48' 38''$ at $b = 43° 5' 41''$, $b' = 46° 45' 19''$.

7.5 Drawings

Secondary in value to longitude determinations. Whole-disc drawings are made difficult by the speed with which rotation changes the appearance of the disc during even the shortest period required for the completion of a drawing which is justified by its accuracy and comprehensiveness. If very little detail is visible, however, a whole-disc drawing is better than nothing, and in such cases can be made quite quickly and with sufficient accuracy, provided the features at both limbs are attended to first and the central region of the disc filled in last.

Whole-disc drawings are also of great value at the extreme ends of each apparition; even though made under adverse observing conditions, and therefore comparatively unreliable or undetailed, they are well worth attempting, since any extension of the annual period of observation is highly desirable.

No completely satisfactory method of making drawings of Jupiter is available. Probably the best is the synthesis of a composite drawing from sketches and notes made at the telescope; but this must be compiled *immediately* after the observations are concluded, and a note as to its method of production always added to it. The consciously directed training of the visual memory is recommended.

Blanks of the correct degree of oblateness must be used; a suitable scale is about 2 ins to the equatorial diameter. The proportion of the lengths of the polar to the equatorial diameters is as 14 : 15, giving an eccentricity of about 0·359. Suitable diameters would therefore be 1·96 ins and 2·10 ins; with the usual cotton-loop-and-pins method of constructing an ellipse, the pins would then be 0·75 ins apart, and the length of the cotton (equal to the major axis of the ellipse) 2·1 ins. Since so small an ellipse is difficult to construct accurately, it is recommended that a prototype blank be drawn, 5 times larger than the required size (major axis 10·5 ins, distance between foci 3·77 ins, minor axis 9·8 ins) and reduced photographically. The blanks actually used at the telescope can be traced or otherwise transferred from this reduced prototype.

Detailed drawings of individual areas, designed to reveal the nature of the changes to which they are subject, are both more valuable and easier to produce than whole-disc drawings. A convenient method of setting out the record is to make a scale of longitudes across the head of a large sheet of cartridge paper (the size of the scale depending upon the size of the area under review), and to make the drawings at each successive observed transit vertically below one another down the page, with a scale of dates and times at one side. Drifts in longitude can be revealed by taking a transit observation at the time each drawing is made.

7.6 Colour estimates

See also section 3.6.

There is great scope for colorimetric observations of Jupiter providing they are reliable, and despite the technical difficulties it is work that is well within the reach of amateurs. As an example of what can be done by observers without previous experience, and using modest equipment, the observations during 1951 of a B.A.A. member with a 6-in reflector, $\times 240$, may be mentioned. Confining his attention to the SEB_N and STB, he was able to establish the facts that their colours varied from brown to grey in different longitudes, and that the 'warm' and 'cool' sections of the belts were not static in longitude but (in the case of the SEB_N) were drifting eastward at a rate of approximately $28°$ per 30^d. The observations were mostly made without prior knowledge of the longitude of the CM, and were confined to nights when the atmospheric conditions were favourable.

What is required in this field, above all else, is a long series of strictly comparable observations, made with full precautions to guard against the intrusion of spurious colour effects. In this way it will ultimately be possible to clear up the present rather confused and tentative conclusions regarding suspected long-term colour variations in the equatorial regions: see B. 152, 163–166; also B. 146, 159 dealing with the colour of the polar regions.

7.7 Satellites

7.7.1 Work: According to the equipment available:

(a) Shape of disc, and markings.
(b) Photometry: rotations; improved accuracy of variation periods; confirmation and measurement of suspected variations.
(c) Micrometer measures of the discs.
(d) Micrometer or photographic measures of position.
(e) Spectrography.

(*f*) Transit, eclipse, and occultation phenomena.

(*g*) Search for new satellites.

Of these, (*b*), (*d*), and (*f*) are possible with average amateur equipment; (*a*) and (*c*) require at least moderate apertures; while (*e*) and (*g*) require really large instruments and are out of amateur hands.

7.7.2 Description: See also section 7.15.

I: Would be visible to the naked eye but for the proximity of the planet; no markings visible with 10 ins of aperture; described as yellowish by the Pic du Midi observers (1941),* but greyish in transit; limb shading may give it an elliptical appearance when seen with moderate apertures; diameter (Pickering and Michelson), 1″03.

II: Would be visible to the naked eye but for the proximity of the planet; no markings visible with a 10-in; very light tint, making it difficult to see when in transit against a zone; diameter (Pickering and Michelson), 0″94.

III: Would be visible to the naked eye but for the proximity of Jupiter; elliptical appearance of the disc more marked than in the case of the other satellites—4 ins probably the minimum aperture, with abnormally good seeing; apparent ellipticity varies with position in orbit; a dark belt has been seen with as little as 6 ins; 'polar caps' with a 12-in, ×550; markings best seen when in transit, owing to reduced glare when against a light-toned background; yellowish, and very dark in transit; diameter (Pickering and Michelson), 1″40.

IV: Would be visible to the naked eye if not close to Jupiter; markings reported at various times, but require more than 10 ins aperture; described as dull chestnut colour by the Pic du Midi observers; diameter (Pickering and Michelson), 1″30.

7.7.3 Phenomena:

(*a*) *Transits:* Satellites and their shadows move in front of Jupiter from E (*f*) to W (*p*).

Before opposition: shadow precedes satellite, therefore falling on the disc before the transit begins.

After opposition: shadow follows satellite, therefore still being on the disc after the transit has ended.

The interval between the transit of satellite and shadow varies with the distance of the satellite from the planet and the time interval between the transit and opposition. It may be as long as several hours, often

---

* B. 151.

making the identification of shadow transits difficult, when nearer conjunction than opposition. IV may avoid transit altogether, passing above or below the planet.

(b) *Occultations and eclipses:* Satellites move on the far side of Jupiter from W (p) to E (f).

From opposition to conjunction: satellites are occulted at p limb, reappearing from eclipse on the f side of the planet.

From conjunction to opposition: satellites enter eclipse before reaching the p limb, reappearing from occultation at the f limb.

I: Both entry into and exit from the same eclipse can never be observed owing to the satellite's nearness to the planet: it always passes from occultation into eclipse, or from eclipse to occultation. Duration of combined eclipse and occultation, about $2\frac{1}{4}^h$.

II: Usually either entry into or exit from eclipse is alone observed, not both. Duration, about $2\frac{3}{4}^h$.

III: Entry into and exit from eclipse can both be observed, except near opposition. Duration varies within wide limits, average about $3\frac{1}{4}^h$.

IV: Immersion and emersion also individually visible, except near opposition. Duration varies within wide limits, average about 4^h. On the other hand, it may avoid the planet's shadow altogether; indeed, for two 3-year periods in every 12 years there are no phenomena for IV.

The satellites are not instantaneously extinguished on immersion, though the disappearance is rapid in the case of I and II.

(c) *Mutual eclipses and occultations of satellites:* These can only occur when the Earth is near the plane of the orbits, i.e. for a few months every 5–6 years. Important for the correction of their orbits, and interesting to observe if the requisite large aperture is available.

(d) *Jupiter without satellites:* It occasionally happens that all four major satellites are simultaneously absent from the visible sky, being in transit (T), eclipse (E), or occultation (O). The future occasions up to A.D. 2000 when this will occur are listed below:*

Date	Duration	I	II	III	IV
1961 Sep 27	1^h3	OE	T	T	E
1966 Jun 27	0·8	OE	T	T	T
1980 Apr 9	1·1	T	O	O	E
1980 Apr 9	0·9	T	OE	E	E
1990 Jun 15	1·5	OE	T	O	E
1991 Jan 2	1·2	T	OE	O	E
1997 Aug 27	0·5	O	T	OE	E

* From B.149.

(e) *General:* I, II, and III can never be experiencing the same pheno-
menon simultaneously, although any two of them may. This follows
from the fact that their respective mean daily motions are related in
such a manner that

$$n_I - 3n_{II} + 2n_{III} = 0$$

Jupiter's satellite phenomena are not merely interesting to witness,
but are of considerable practical importance, for accurately timed
observations are the data by whose means our knowledge of the satellite
orbits is improved.

See also sections 7.11, 7.12.

7.8 Radio work

Radio emissions from Jupiter have been received in the long wavelength part of the radio spectrum. (Wavelengths of the order 16 m and
13 m have shown intensive radiation whilst those of 7·5 m and 3·5 m
have shown radiation of singularly small intensity.) The radiation from
the planet is very intermittent. When it was discovered by Burke and
Franklin on 13 m it was apparently observable on one day in every
three. However there have been long periods since then (of the order of
months) when no radiations have been received from the planet.

The spectrum appears to have a very definite peak in the long-wave
region of 16 and 13 m. A number of theories have been put forward to
account for the peculiar type of emission that is received. It appears to
have the characteristics of a terrestrial thunderstorm but has a power
many thousands of times greater than that which occurs in such a
thunderstorm. This had led to theories that the emission is caused by
electrical discharges similar to those at the Earth's surface. Barrow and
Gardner and Shain have suggested that the radiation originates in a
plasma oscillation in an ionospheric layer surrounding the planet: it is
from this type of theory that the spectral curve described above may be
deduced. The test of this theory demands the accurate location of the
sources causing the emission. At the moment it is only possible to
determine their longitudes; the determination of latitudes requires considerably more knowledge of the radiation, and observations on several
different wavelengths in this region should be made together with
observations to examine the amount of circular polarisation.

Amateurs having sites in open country can easily build the aerial
arrays that are required. Even though they may be of the order of 100 ft
by 100 ft, they are simple to erect. The receiving apparatus is also very
simple. The observations mentioned above would enable the critical

frequency of Jupiter's ionosphere to be determined, and this could lead to the determination of its refractive index and critical angle and, hence, its ionosphere. Amateurs in this country are at present erecting an array for observations on 15 m.

The importance of amateur observations lies not only in determining the spectrum but in the fact that the bursts of noise from Jupiter are very irregular (quite apart from the fact that they sometimes disappear for months).

The Earth's ionosphere imposes difficulties of observation by limiting the angle at which radio observers can work. Another difficulty is that the observations are made in the communications band and it is very difficult to find free regions. The best way to approach this problem is to observe on a number of wavelengths for a week or more before deciding to erect an aerial system. One can then ascertain whether the wavelength is relatively clear from interference. Yet another problem is set by thunderstorms—these can interfere with the record and make it difficult to interpret *weak* jovian bursts. In all cases care has to be taken to ensure that the noise bursts are not originating in the terrestrial atmosphere. This does necessitate practice in observing.

The previous remarks refer to non-thermal radiation. Thermal radiation has been detected from Jupiter using a 3·18 cm maser. This type of apparatus is quite beyond the pocket of the amateur. The apparent black-body temperature of the planet based on the mean diameter of the visible disc is 165°K, with some 10% error. Over a period of time the apparent black-body temperature does not appear to vary with rotation. (See B. 145a.)

Drift curves at 10·3 cms have also been obtained. The measured average black-body temperature of all the observations is 580°K. No correlation has been found between the variations in the apparent black-body temperature and the planet's rotation. (See B. 151a.)

7.9 Other work

A notable example of what the enterprising amateur can achieve is provided by D. W. Millar's discovery, while collating 40 years' *Mem. B.A.A.*s, of a previously unsuspected and currently unexplained relationship between the latitude and rotation periods of belts that are not even contiguous; see B. 154. And it is only necessary to glance through the literature that has accumulated around the perplexing S.Trop.Z 'Circulating Current' to appreciate that Jupiter still holds much of interest for the visual observer; see B. 157, 169.

Other examples of areas of which observations abound in the literature and which for one reason or another have been intensively studied in the past include the Red Spot, possibly periodic (1919/20, 1928/29, 1938, 1943, and 1949) outbursts of spot formation and general activity in the SEB, similar suspected activity on the N edge of the NNTB, the S.Trop.Disturbance, etc. See, *inter alia*, B. 153, 155–157. B. 147, containing fully illustrated histories of the RS, S.Trop.Disturbance, Circulating Current, and SEB outbursts, should also be referred to for detailed descriptions of these features.

There is also room for a great deal more work on the detailed movements and behaviour of the spots, and of their interactions when passing closely to one another—as happens with spots situated near the edges of adjoining currents or longitude drifts, whose relative motion is often rapid: it has been noticed, for instance, that a bridge of lighter-toned material often joins such spots at about the time that their separation is minimal, beyond which bare fact little is known.

7.10 Daylight observation

The observation of Jupiter in the daylight sky has two advantages, though ideally it requires at least moderate aperture. In the first place it lengthens the annual period of observability, thus reducing the gaps in the observational record; and secondly, definition is often improved and higher magnifications possible. To be effective, however, the intensity of the field must be reduced. This can either be effected by means of filters (orange or deep red—Wratten K2 has been found satisfactory) or polaroid. The latter is most effective at and around quadrature, since maximum polarisation of sky-light occurs in a great circle 90° from the Sun, while reflected Jovian sunlight is unpolarised.

7.11 B.A.A.H. data

(a) RA, Dec, Mag, Polar and Equatorial diameters, and Distance: at 10-day intervals throughout the apparition.

(b) Longitude of the CM in System I (equatorial) and II (polar) at specified times throughout the apparition.

(c) Table of Change of Longitude at intervals of MT in the two Systems. (For more extended Table, see *A.E.*)

(d) Phenomena of Satellites I–IV throughout the apparition, in tabular form:
  times of beginning and end of eclipses,
  times of disappearance and reappearance from occultation,
  times of entry into and exit from transit,
  times of beginning and end of shadow transits,

148

eclipse coordinates,
configuration table.

7.12 A.E. data

(a) RA
Dec
Polar semidiameter
Horizontal parallax
Distance from Earth
Ephemeris Transit-time
$\Big\}$ at 0^h ET on each day of the year.

(b) Heliocentric longitude
Heliocentric latitude
Radius vector
Orbital longitude
Daily motion
$\Big\}$ at 0^h ET at 10-daily intervals.

(c) Physical ephemeris:

Light-time (i.e. distance in 'light minutes')

Stellar Mag

Position angle of axis of rotation (measured E from the N point of the disc)

$A_E + 180°$ (where A_E = zenocentric RA of the Earth)

D_E (zenocentric Dec of the Earth = latitude of centre of disc)

$A_S + 180°$ (where A_S = zenocentric RA of the Sun)

D_S (zenocentric Dec of Sun)

Equatorial diameter (angular)

Polar diameter (angular)

i (elongation of Earth from Sun, as seen from Jupiter)

Angular value of greatest defect of illumination

Position angle of point of greatest defect of illumination (measured from N point of disc)

Longitude of CM (Systems I and II) at 0^h UT

Correction for phase (correction + longitude of CM = longitude of the meridian bisecting the illuminated disc)

$\Big\}$ at 4-daily intervals throughout the year.

149

(d) Longitude of CM (Systems I and II) of the illuminated disc at
0^h UT daily throughout the apparition.

(e) Table of movement of the CM (Systems I and II) at 5-min intervals
from 0^m to 12^h.

(f) Diagram of orbits of satellites I–V at date of opposition.

(g) Mean synodic periods of satellites I–VII, and sidereal periods of
satellites VIII–XII.

(h) GMT of every 20th greatest elongation (E and W) of V.

(i) Table of multiples (1–20) of mean synodic period of V.

(j) Differential coordinates of satellites VI and VII (difference of
RA and Dec between Jupiter and the satellite at 0^h UT at 4-day intervals throughout the apparition).

(k) Diagram of configuration of Jupiter and I–IV at a stated time
daily throughout the apparition.

Table of times at which all the satellite phenomena occur.

Diagrams showing the position relative to Jupiter's disc at which
I–IV enter and leave shadow during eclipses.

Rectangular coordinates of the points of immersion of I–IV into, and
emersion from, the shadow at every eclipse.

(l) Dates of conjunction, opposition, stationary point, and of conjunctions with other members of the Solar System.

(m) Osculating elements of orbit and mean anomalies, all at 40-day
intervals.

Rotation elements.

(n) Elongations and Magnitudes for 0^h UT at 10-daily intervals.

7.13 Data

Mean solar distance: 5·202803 A.U.$=4·833 \times 10^8$ miles.
Perihelion distance: $4·598 \times 10^8$ miles.
Aphelion distance: $5·068 \times 10^8$ miles.
Sidereal period: 11·86223 tropical years.
Mean synodic period: 398·88 days.
Sidereal mean daily motion: 0°08.
Mean orbital velocity: 8·1 m/s.
Axial rotation period: System I: 9^h 50^m 30^{s}003.
System II: 9^h 55^m 40^{s}632.
Radio sources: 9^h 55^m 28^{s}8.

e: 0·0484190 (+0·0000016)
i: 1° 18′ 21″3 (−0″2)
Ω: 99° 56′ 36″0 (+36″4)
$\tilde{\omega}$: 13° 31′ 1″5 (+58″0)
L: 316° 9′ 33″57 (+30° 20′ 32″07)

Epoch 1950, Jan 1·5 UT (annual variations in brackets).

Angular diameter at unit distance: e 196″94, p 183″82.
Angular diameter at mean opposition distance: e 46″86, p 43″74.
Linear diameter e 142,700 km=88,700 miles=11·2⊕.
          p 133,200 km=82,800 miles=10·4⊕.
Mass: $9·55 \times 10^{-4}$⊙=318·4⊕.
Volume: 1312⊕.
Density: 1·34×water=0·24⊕.
Mean superficial gravity: 2·655⊕.
Mag at maximum brightness: −2·5.

7.14 Satellite data

	I Io	II Europa	III Ganymede	IV Callisto	V	VI	VII	VIII	IX	X	XI	XII
Mean distance from Jupiter: at mean opposition distance	2' 18".4	3' 40".2	5' 51".2	10' 17".7	59".2	1° 2' 40"	1° 4' 13"	2° 8' 35"	2° 9'	1° 3' 16"	2° 3' 24"	c. 2°
A.U.	0·00281956	0·00448620	0·00715590	0·0125865	0·001207	0·076605	0·078516	0·15720	0·158	0·077334	0·1508336	c. 0·148
miles	262,000	416,000	664,000	1,168,000	112,500	7,115,000	7,290,000	14,600,000	15,000,000	7,193,000	14,030,000	c. 13,000,000
Sidereal period: days	1·76913780	3·55118108	7·15455312	16·68901805	0·49817923	250·62	260·07	738·9	745	254·21	692·5	?
days, hours, minutes	1. 18. 27½	3. 13. 13½	7.3.42½	16.16.32	0.11.57½	250.14.40	260.1.24	738.21.30	745.---	254.5.0	692.12.--	
Mean synodic period (d, h, m, s)	1.18.28.35·95	3.13.17.53·74	7.3.59.35·86	16.18.5.6·92	0.11.57.27·6	266.0.--	276.16.--	631·2d	636d	270·01d	597d	?
Orbital eccentricity	small and variable	s. and v.	s. and v.	s. and v.	—	0·1550	0·2073	0·38	0·248	0·14051	0·20678	?
Diameter (miles)	2,100	1,860	3,270	3,140				11-17				
Mass: $\times 10^{-5}$ Jupiter	4·5	2·5	8·0	4·5								
$\times 10^{-9} \odot$	4·294	2·421	7·627	4·300								
Stellar magnitude (at mean opposition distance)	5·3-5·8 mean 5·5	5·7-6·4 mean 6·1	4·9-5·3 mean 5·1	6·1-6·4 mean 6·2	13 or fainter ? var.	14·7	17·5-18·0 (photog.)	17·0 (photog.)	18·6 (photog.)	19	19	18·3
Discoverer	Galileo/ Mayer 1610	Galileo/ Mayer 1610	Galileo/ Mayer 1610	Galileo/ Mayer 1610	Barnard 1892	Perrine 1904	Perrine 1905	Melotte 1908	Nicholson 1914	Nicholson 1938	Nicholson 1938	Nicholson 1951

VIII, IX, XI, and XII are retrograde.
VI-X, and XII have highly inclined orbits.

SATURN

8.1 Apparitions

Opposition occurs about 2 weeks later each year, the mean synodic period being 378^{d}09.

Dec limits: about 26° N and S.

As regards the reappearance of a given region, reobservation is possible at the 5th, 7th, 12th and 14th rotations, when a given longitude will be in the same position on the disc within about 3^h of the time of the initial observation.

The equatorial plane containing the rings is inclined to the orbital plane at about 27°. Twice, therefore, in the planet's sidereal period of 29·46 years, the Earth and the Sun will be 27° 'above' or 'below' the plane of the rings, and 7·5 years later the rings will be viewed edge-on.

8.2 Instrumental

For regular work on Saturn, and the recording of observations of value, not less than 5 ins aperture is effective; if more than 10 ins, so much the better. The visibility of the projections on the N edge of the SEB (1943) with a 5½-in shows that at times smaller apertures than this can contribute useful observations; but apertures less than about 5 ins, though giving excellent views of the ring system, lack the resolving power to show significant detail.

For photographic work, see section 3.8.

8.3 Longitude determinations

Our knowledge of the rotation periods in different latitudes, and of the manner in which they are related, is still very inadequate owing to the rare occurrence of features having sharp enough definition to give good transit measures. No opportunity must be missed of timing the CM transit of any sufficiently well defined spot (the edges of the equatorial belts seem particularly prone to spot production) or other

153

features that may appear. Any such appearance, with the observed or estimated time of CM transit, should also be reported to the Director of the Saturn Section of the B.A.A. by telegram, so that other observers can be warned. The larger apertures naturally have the advantage, though spots visible with a 5-in have been recorded.

8.4 Latitude determinations

Of any features that appear, and, regularly, of the edges of the belts; those especially required by the Saturn Section are:

centre of the EZ,
edges of the SEB and NEB,
edges of the SP Band and the NP Band,
edge of the SP area and of the NP area,
centre of Ring C against the globe.

Moderate apertures and a micrometer are desirable; the measurement of drawings, however carefully made, involves a wider margin of uncertainty than direct measurement of the image; this is to some extent mitigated if the drawings or measures of a large number of observers are available for meaning and smoothing (hence the value of a clearing house, such as the Saturn Section).

The latitude of a surface feature is derived as follows:

$h=$its angular distance N $(+)$ or S $(-)$ of the centre of the disc; the quantities given by observation are a, b, its distances from the two ends of the CM, whence

$$h=\tfrac{1}{2}(a-b)$$

$r=$polar semidiameter (from $N.A.$),
$B=$saturnicentric latitude of the Earth (from $A.E.$),
B' is such that $\tan B'=1\cdot12 \tan B$,
B'' is such that $\sin (B''-B')=h/r$.

Then the saturnicentric latitude, b, of the feature is given by

$$\tan b=\frac{\tan B''}{1\cdot12}$$

and its saturnigraphic latitude, b', is derived from

$$\log \tan b'=\log \tan b+2 \log 1.12$$

8.5 Surface features

The importance of missing no opportunity of making longitude determinations of any surface feature has already been stressed. Reports of spots observed should always include estimated time of

CM transit. Any changes in the general appearance of the belts, even though they may be useless for transit observations, should nevertheless be recorded with the greatest care.

Whole-disc drawings should preferably be made, and it is essential that the blanks be prepared beforehand; observing time is saved, greater accuracy is achieved, and a more consistent and therefore comparable set of records obtained. In constructing the blanks, the relevant dimensions need not be taken to a high degree of accuracy, and a single prototype will furnish blanks that will be available for several weeks. The following data are required:

Globe: p: polar semidiameter (from *N.A.*),

           e: equatorial semidiameter ($e = 1 \cdot 12p$),

           Phase may be disregarded, since even at quadrature Ph is not less than about 99·7, but the globe should never be represented by a circular disc.

Rings: P: p.a. of N semi-minor axis of the rings (from *A.E.*),

           a_A: major axis of outer edge of Ring A (from *A.E.*),

           b_A: minor axis of outer edge of Ring A (from *A.E.*),

           a'_A: major axis of inner edge of Ring A ($= 0 \cdot 88a_A$),

           b'_A: minor axis of inner edge of Ring A ($= 0 \cdot 88b_A$),

           a_B: major axis of outer edge of Ring B ($= 0 \cdot 86a_A$),

           b_B: minor axis of outer edge of Ring B ($= 0 \cdot 86b_A$),

           a'_B: major axis of inner edge of Ring B ($= 0 \cdot 66a_A$),

           b'_B: minor axis of inner edge of Ring B ($= 0 \cdot 66b_A$),

           a'_C: major axis of inner edge of Ring C ($= 0 \cdot 55a_A$),

           b'_C: minor axis of inner edge of Ring C ($= 0 \cdot 55b_A$).

When the rings are not wide open it will be found unnecessary to compute all the above values, at any rate of the minor axis, owing to the exaggerated foreshortening: a_A and b_A, a'_A, a_B, a'_B, a'_C and b'_C will suffice.

The best scale to use depends upon the aperture; $a_A = 4$ ins is the recommended order of size. Partial drawings, to record the finer detail of any unusual feature, should be made on a larger scale and should be accompanied by a whole-disc drawing made at the same time. Each drawing (on a separate sheet) should be supplemented by the observer's name, aperture, magnification, date, and GMAT.

8.6 The rings

(*a*) Micrometer measures. Occasional apparent eccentricity of globe in relation to the rings.

(b) Degree of visibility and appearance of the rings near the times at which plane passes through the Earth (seen edge-on), through the Sun (illuminated edge-on)—as happens every 15 years approximately—and when the Sun and the Earth are on opposite sides of the ring plane (unilluminated side turned to the observer). Visibility on the two sides of the globe often unequal.

(c) Appearance and width of ring shadow on the globe.

(d) Appearance of globe shadow on the rings; the often-observed 'crotchet' in the outline of the shadow where it crosses Cassini's Division is probably an optical and/or instrumental effect; a white spot in the same position (often reported, particularly a few months on either side of opposition), concave shadow profiles, and other anomalies probably arise from similar causes.

(e) Markings or variations of tone on the rings.

(f) Divisions in the ansae (other than Cassini's) have often been suspected; but considerable aperture and moments of perfect seeing are needed for such observations to be of value. Any micrometer measures of such divisions are most valuable; failing this, estimate the position (expressed as a fraction of the ring width) by eye or from drawings.

(g) Variations of visibility of Ring C, or irregularities in its outline.

(h) Suspected existence of a faint ring outside Ring A.

8.7 Occultations

All occultations of stars by planets are of great interest and value for the light they may throw upon the density and extent of the atmosphere; in the case of Saturn they are doubly important for the similar information they can give regarding the ring system.

Each period of observation should begin with a quick survey of the sky slightly ahead of the planet (i.e. in the direction of its apparent orbital motion), and should it appear that any star is heading for occultation this should be given priority over all else, since they are rare occurrences. The record should show the times of the star's arrival at the edges of the ring system and at the planet's limb; for every change in the star's brightness or colour the time, its position, and the nature of the fluctuation should be recorded; also whether or not the disappearance at the limb was instantaneous, and if not, the length of the interval during which fading was observed.

8.8 Satellites

See also sections 7.7, 8.14.

There is great scope for accurate photometric work on Saturn's satellites, none of whose amplitudes or even mean magnitudes is well determined; the variation of III and IV is not even established beyond doubt.

I: Difficult, owing to nearness to the planet; mag about 12·0.

II: Also always a difficult object, though less so than I; mag about 11·7, variable.

III: Visible with a 4-in, when far from the planet; mean mag about 10·6; suspected amplitude 0·25–0·5 mag; maximum at elongations, and W possibly brighter than E.

IV: Visible with a 4-in, when far from the planet; mean mag about 10·7; suspected amplitude 0·25–0·5 mag; maximum at elongations, and E possibly brighter than W.

The mean daily motions of these 4 satellites are related in such a manner that

$$5n_I - 10n_{II} + n_{III} + 4n_{IV} = 0$$

V: Visible with $2\frac{1}{2}$-in; easy with $3\frac{1}{2}$-in when at elongation; mag ? 9–10; possible amplitude of about 0·5 mag.

VI: Glimpsed with $1\frac{1}{2}$-in when near elongation; well seen with 2-in; mag 8·0–8·6 approximately; maximum between W elongation and superior conjunction.

VII: Difficult; mag about 15·0.

VIII: Largest amplitude of all the satellites: ? 9·5–11·0; maximum at W elongation, when visible with a 3-in.

IX: Difficult owing to its faintness and distance from the planet.

X: Not within the scope of the amateur observer. Mag about 14, close to edge of ring system.

Thus quite modest apertures can show a number of the satellites; but for accurate photometric work considerably more aperture is required than the bare minimum which allows them to be glimpsed when at maximum. Observational difficulties are considerable: (a) intrinsic faintness combined with proximity to the brilliant planet, (b) small amplitudes, (c) visibility affected by degree of opening of the rings, (d) visibility affected by their distance from Saturn, (e) lack of comparison objects.

It is advisable always to mask the planet and rings by an adjustable obstruction in the ocular; otherwise, the times of disappearance of the rings are the most favourable for satellite observations. Regarding (e) there are several alternatives: (i) field stars, when suitable ones are available, (ii) using VI (mag 8·3) as the comparison object, (iii) making relative inter-comparisons of two or more satellites; even the order of brightness, with no attempt at absolute values or even relative values in terms of magnitudes or steps, is preferable to nothing, (*iv*) photometer projecting an artificial star into the field.

Records of brightness estimates should always include the following supporting data:

time of observation,
p.a. of satellite from planet's centre,*
angular elongation from the planet,
whether or not an occulting bar was used,
identity of comparison object.

8.9 Colour and intensity estimations

See also section 3.6.

Objective variations of colour have been suspected (Ring C, for example) but are extremely difficult to substantiate.

The recording of the relative intensities of the different regions of the globe and the rings is an important part of the regular observer's work, and should be carried out frequently so that good means may be obtained. Ring C, again, should be given particularly careful attention; similarly the polar regions, for which a far greater quantity of observations is required.

Recommended scale of intensities, by means of which to annotate rough sketches of the main regions, is based on the brightness of Ring B just inside Cassini's Division in the ansae (scale no. 1; fractions being employed for anything brighter than this), and the tone of the planet's shadow on the rings or the sky background (scale no. 10).

8.10 Submission of records

The apparition's observations should be submitted to the Director of the Saturn Section at the end of each annual apparition, or immediately after June 30, whichever is the sooner. Anything of an unusual nature should be reported immediately, so that the full observing strength of the Section can be brought to bear.

Opposite is reproduced the printed pro-forma issued to members for reporting their observations in a convenient form for subsequent analysis and discussion.

* Note that the East point (i.e. p.a. 90°) is not the same thing as eastern elongation.

OBSERVER:..

Instrument(s)............................. *Year of Observations*..........................

ESTIMATES OF   { INTENSITY
(*Cross out those which do not* { COLOUR
apply).   { LATITUDES OF EDGES OF BELTS
   { SATELLITE MAGNITUDES

Month											
Day											
G.M.A.T.											
Inst. & Power											
Conditions											
Definition											
Class											
FEATURE											

8.11 B.A.A.H. data

   (*a*) RA
       Dec
       Magnitude
       Polar diameter
       Major axis of ring system   at 20-day intervals throughout
       Minor axis of ring system   the apparition.
       Saturnicentric latitude of Earth
          referred to ring plane
       Distance
   (*b*) Satellite data
   (*c*) Dimensions (linear, and angular at unit distance and mean
       opposition distance) of the ring system.

8.12 A.E. data

(a) RA
  Dec
  Polar semidiameter
  Horizontal parallax
  Distance from Earth
  Ephemeris Transit time

  at 0^h ET daily throughout the year.

(b) Heliocentric longitude
  Heliocentric latitude
  Radius vector
  Orbital longitude
  Daily motion

  at 0^h ET at 10-daily intervals throughout the year.

(c) Physical ephemeris:
  Light-time (i.e. distance in 'light minutes')
  Stellar magnitude
  Equatorial diameter
  Polar diameter
  i (elongation of Earth from Sun, as seen from Saturn)
  Angular value of greatest defect of illumination
  Position angle of point of greatest defect of illumination

  at 4-daily intervals throughout the year.

(d) Elements for determining the geocentric position and appearance of Saturn's rings:
  Major axis of outer edge of Ring A
  Minor axis of outer edge of Ring A
  U: geocentric longitude of Saturn ($U+180°$ =saturnicentric longitude of Earth)
  B: saturnicentric latitude of the Earth
  P: p.a. of the N semi-minor axis of rings
  U': heliocentric longitude of Saturn
  B': saturnicentric latitude of Sun
  P': p.a. of N semi-minor axis of rings, measured from the latitude circle through Saturn's centre

  at 4-daily intervals throughout the year.

(e) Map of the apparent orbits of the 7 inner satellites at date of opposition.

(f) L: mean longitude in orbit, for satellites I–VIII ⎫

M: mean anomaly, for satellites I, II, IV–VIII │ at 5-daily

θ: longitude of ascending node, for satellites I, III, ⎰ intervals

V–VII ⎱ through-

γ: inclination of orbit to ring plane, for satellite VII │ out

Sin γ for satellites V, VI, VII ⎭ the year.

(g) e: orbital eccentricity of VII ⎱ at 5-daily intervals

a: major axis of orbit of VII ⎰ throughout the year.

(h) UT of greatest E elongations of I–V throughout the apparition.

(i) UT of elongations and conjunctions of VI–VIII throughout the apparition.

(j) Differential coordinates of VII–IX (difference of RA and Dec between Saturn and the satellite) at 2-day intervals throughout the apparition.

(k) Tables for $p_1+p_2=$ position angle of satellite, measured from N point towards E, and $\dfrac{F}{\varDelta}$. a=apparent angular distance from Saturn, for satellites I–VIII throughout the year.

(l) Dates of conjunction, opposition, stationary points, and of conjunctions with other members of the Solar System.

(m) Osculating elements of orbit and mean anomalies, at 40-day intervals.

(n) Elongations and Magnitudes for 0^h UT at 10-daily intervals.

8.13 Data

Mean solar distance: 9·538843 A.U.=$8·861 \times 10^8$ miles.

Perihelion distance: $8·346 \times 10^8$ miles.

Aphelion distance: $9·376 \times 10^8$ miles.

Sidereal period: 29·45772 tropical years.

Mean synodic period: 378·092 days.

Sidereal mean daily motion: $0°03$.

Mean orbital velocity: 6·0 m/s.

Axial rotation period (equatorial): 10^h 14^m.

Probably the best figures to date are those derived from the 1936–37 spectrographic programme at Lick:

Latitude	:	27°	42°	57°
$\dfrac{\text{Rotation period}}{\text{Equatorial period}}$	:	1·06	1·08	1·11

The value for the equatorial period agreed within 2% with that obtained visually.

e: 0·0557164 (−0·0000035) ⎤
i:　　2° 29′ 25″2 (−0″1) ⎥
Ω:　113° 13′ 12″6 (+31″4) ⎥ Epoch 1950, Jan 1·5 UT
ϖ:　92° 4′ 6″6 (+1 10″5) ⎥ (annual variations in brackets).
L: 158° 18′ 12″89 (+12° 13′ 36″2) ⎦

Angular diameter at unit distance: e 166″66, p 149″14.
Angular diameter at mean opposition distance: e 19″52, p 17″46.
Linear diameter: e 120,800 km=75,100 miles=9·5⊕.
　　　　　　　p 108,100 km=67,200 miles=8·5⊕.
Mass: $2·856 \times 10^{-4}$⊙=95·2⊕.
Volume: 763⊕.
Density: 0·69×water=0·12⊕.
Mean superficial gravity: 1·14⊕.
Mag at maximum brightness: −0·2.
Ring system:

		Diameter	Ratio
	miles	at mean opposition distance (″ arc)	
Ring A ⎰outer	169,300	43·96	1·0000
⎱inner	149,000	38·69	0·8801
Ring B ⎰outer	145,500	37·80	0·8599
⎱inner	112,600	29·24	0·6650
Ring C inner	92,000	24·12	0·5486
Saturn equatorial	75,100	19·52	0·4440

Inclination of plane of rings to ecliptic: 28°068.
Ω: 168°815 (1950 Jan 0) + 0°014 annually.

8.14 Satellite data

	I Minas	II Enceladus	III Tethys	IV Dione	V Rhea	VI Titan*	VII Hyperion	VIII Iapetus	IX Phoebe†	X Janus
Mean distance from Saturn: at mean opposition distance — A.U. — miles	30".0 0·0012401 115,000	38".4 0·0015909 148,000	47".6 0·0019694 183,000	1' 0".9 0·0025226 235,000	1' 25".1 0·0035226 328,000	3' 17".3 0·0081660 759,000	3' 59".0 0·0098929 923,000	9' 34".9 0·0237976 2,213,000	34' 52" 0·086593 8,053,000	25".5 0·00106 99,000
Sidereal Period (days)	0·9424219	1·3702178	1·8878025	2·7369159	4·5175026	15·945452	21·276665	79·33082	550·45	0·7490
Mean daily motion	381°.9	262°.7	190°.7	131°.5	79°.7	22°.6	16°.9	4°.5	39°.25	480°.0
Inclination of orbit to ring plane	1° 31'	0° 1'.4	1° 5'.6	0° 1'.4	0° 21'	0° 20'	0° 10'.4	14° 32'.7	150° 3'.7	0°
Mean Synodic Period: d.h.m.s. — d.h.	0.22.37.12·4 0.22·6	1.8.53.21·9 1.8·9	1.21.18.54·8 1.21·3	2.17.42.9·7 2.17·7	4.12.27.56·2 4.12·5	15.23.15.25 15.23·3	21.7.39.6 21.7·6	79.22.4.56 79.22·1	523.15.36.– 523.15·6	0.17.59.– 0.18·0
Orbital eccentricity	0·0201	0·0044	0·0000	0·0022	0·0010	0·0290	0·104	0·0283	0·1633	0·0
Diameter (miles)	400	400	600	600	900	3000	200	600	100	200
Mass: ×10⁶ Saturn — ×10¹⁰ ⊕	0·07 0·201	0·12 0·351	1·14 3·268	1·76 5·028	4·04 11·56	241 688·8	0·54 1·558	1·7 5·0	— —	— —
Stellar magnitude (at mean opposition distance)	12·1	11·7	10·6	10·7	10·0	8·3	14·5	10·8	14	14
Discoverer	Herschel	Herschel	Cassini	Cassini	Cassini	Huyghens	Bond	Cassini	Pickering	Dollfus

* The only satellite in the Solar System known to have an atmosphere—methane (Kuiper, 1944).

† retrograde.

SECTION 9

URANUS

9.1 General

Opposition occurs about 4 days later each year. Dec limits about 24° N and S.

With a mean opposition mag of about 5·5, and a diameter of nearly 4″, Uranus is easily enough located once its approximate position is known. It offers no scope for amateur work, however, no details being visible except faint belts; these require at least 10 ins aperture.

9.2 Satellites

I, II: Beyond the reach of most amateur instruments, requiring apertures of the order of 18–20 ins even when an occulting bar in the ocular is used.

III, IV: Should be seen without much difficulty with an 8-in; been frequently glimpsed with 6-in, though this is not easy. Isaac Ward's astonishing feat of glimpsing them with only 4·3 ins aperture is not likely to be surpassed, or even approached.

V: Discovered photographically by Kuiper on 1948 Feb 16, using the Cassegrain focus of the McDonald 82-in reflector; orbit lies in same plane as the other four satellites.

See also sections 7.7, 9.5.

9.3 B.A.A.H. data

Star chart showing path throughout the year.
Stellar Magnitude.

9.4 A.E. data

(a) RA
    Dec
    Semidiameter
    Horizontal parallax   } at 0ʰ ET daily throughout the year.
    Distance from Earth
    Ephemeris Transit time

164

(b) Heliocentric longitude
   Heliocentric latitude
   Radius vector   at 0^h ET at 40-day intervals
   Orbital longitude   throughout the year.
   Daily motion

(c) Diagram of the apparent orbits of satellites I–IV at date of opposition.

(d) UT of greatest N elongation of satellites I–V.

(e) Tables for p_1+p_2=position angle of satellite, measured from N point towards E, and $F.\dfrac{a}{\varDelta}$=apparent angular distance from Uranus, for satellites I–IV throughout the year.

(f) Dates of conjunction, opposition, stationary points, and of conjunctions with other members of the Solar System.

(g) Sidereal periods of satellites I–V.

(h) Osculating elements of orbit and mean anomalies, at 40-day intervals.

(i) Elongations for 0^h UT at 10-daily intervals. Magnitude at opposition.

9.5 Data

Mean solar distance: 19·190978 A.U.＝1·783×10⁹ miles.
Perihelion distance: 1·699×10⁹ miles.
Aphelion distance: 1·867×10⁹ miles.
Sidereal period: 84·01529 tropical years.
Mean synodic period: 369·66 days.
Sidereal mean daily motion: 0°01.
Mean orbital velocity: 4·2 m/s.
Axial rotation period: c. 10^{h}8.

e: 0·0471842 (+0·0000027)
i: 0° 46′ 22″8 (+0″1)   Epoch 1950, Jan 1·5 UT
Ω: 73° 44′ 23″7 (+18″0)   (annual variations in
$\tilde{\omega}$. 169° 51′ 6″1 (+58″2)   brackets).
L: 98° 18′ 31″03 (+4° 17′ 46″13)

Angular diameter at unit distance: 68″56.
Angular diameter at mean opposition distance: 3″76.
Linear diameter: 49,700 km＝30,900 miles＝3·9⊕.
Mass: 4·37×10⁻⁵＝14·6⊕.
Volume: 59⊕.
Density: 1·36×water＝0·25⊕.

Mean superficial gravity: 0·96⊕.
Mag at maximum brightness: 5·7.

9.6 Satellite data

	I Ariel	II Umbriel	III Titania	IV Oberon	V Miranda*
Mean distance from Uranus: at mean opposition distance A.U. miles	14″5 0·0012820 119,000	20″2 0·0017859 166,000	33″2 0·0029303 272,000	44″4 0·0039187 364,000	9″3 0·0008 74,000
Sidereal Period : days days, hours	2·520383 2.12·489	4·144183 4.3·460	8·705876 8.16·941	13·463262 13.11·118	33h 56m
Mean Synodic Period (d.h.m.s.)	2.12.29.40	4.3.28.25	8.17.0.0	13.11.15.36	—
Stellar magnitude (at mean opposition distance)	?13–14	16–17	? 13–14	14	17
Discoverer	Lassell	Lassell	Herschel	Herschel	Kuiper

* data approximate.

SECTION 10

NEPTUNE

10.1 Apparitions

Opposition occurs about 2 days later each year. Declination limits, about ±25°.

10.2 Telescopic appearance

Opinions differ as to the minimum aperture that will show the disc (diameter 2″5 at mean opposition distance), and certainly the decision 'a disc or not a disc' when the object is at the threshold is one which is overwhelmingly influenced by such factors as the seeing and the experience of the observer.

It has been claimed to have been glimpsed with a 3-in; doubtful with a 4-in. Given good conditions, its appearance is certainly non-stellar with any aperture over 6 ins using adequate magnification, but under most circumstances the disc is probably invisible with about 5 ins or less, except when assisted by the eye of faith, since a magnification of about ×500 is the minimum desirable.

The best way of detecting its non-stellar character is to accustom the eye to the appearance of an accurately focused nearby star of about the same magnitude, and then switch the telescope quickly on to the planet.

Its opposition magnitude being about 7·7, it can be seen with only about ½ in aperture.

10.3 Satellites

I: Triton (retrograde and highly inclined) has been seen with a 6-in, though an inexperienced observer will probably require at least 8 ins; here again the absence of atmospheric turbulence is almost the deciding factor. If the body of the planet is hidden by an ocular bar, and the position of the satellite ascertained beforehand, it may be glimpsed with 5 ins, and should theoretically be visible with little more than 3 ins. In any case, it is a slightly easier object than the outer satellites of Uranus.

167

II: Nereid: discovered in 1949 May 1 by Kuiper with a 40-min exposure at the Cassegrain focus of the McDonald 82-in reflector, stopped down to 66 ins ($f/5$); it was then mag 17, and situated about 200″ from the planet. Period about 2 years; distance from Neptune about 2 million miles; orbit inclined at about 5° or 6° to the ecliptic; its magnitude implies a diameter in the neighbourhood of 200 miles, making assumptions regarding its albedo.

10.4 B.A.A.H data

Star chart showing path throughout the year.
Stellar Magnitude.

10.5 A.E. data

(a) RA
    Dec
    Semidiameter
    Horizontal parallax } at 0^h ET daily throughout the year.
    Distance from Earth
    Ephemeris Transit time

(b) Heliocentric longitude
    Heliocentric latitude
    Radius vector } at 0^h ET at 40-day intervals throughout the year.
    Orbital longitude
    Daily motion

(c) Tables for p_1+p_2=position angle of satellite I, measured from N point towards E, and $F.\dfrac{a}{\varDelta}$=apparent angular distance from Neptune of satellite I throughout the year.

(d) Dates of conjunction, opposition, stationary points, and of conjunctions with other members of the Solar System.

(e) UT of greatest E elongations of satellite I.

(f) Sidereal periods of satellites I and II.

(g) Diagram of apparent orbit of satellite I at date of opposition.

(h) Osculating elements of orbit and mean anomalies, at 40-day intervals.

(i) Elongations for 0^h UT at 10-daily intervals.
    Magnitude at opposition.

10.6 Data

Mean solar distance: 30·070672 A.U.$=2·793 \times 10^9$ miles.
Perihelion distance: $2·769 \times 10^9$ miles.
Aphelion distance: $2·817 \times 10^9$ miles.
Sidereal period: 164·78829 tropical years.
Mean synodic period: 367·49 days.
Sidereal mean daily motion: 0°006.
Mean orbital velocity: 3·4 m/s.
Axial rotation period
   spectroscopic: $15^h\ 40^m$
   photometric (half-period): 8^h —

e: 0·0085682 (+0·0000007)
i: 1° 46′ 28″1 (−0″4)
Ω: 131° 13′ 42″3 (+39″6)   Epoch 1950, Jan 1·5 UT
$\tilde{\omega}$: 44° 9′ 31″0 (+29″4)   (annual variations in brackets).
L: 194° 57′ 8″81 (+2° 11′ 49″4)

Angular diameter at unit distance: 73″12.
Angular diameter at mean opposition distance: 2″52.
Linear diameter: 53,000 km=33,000 miles=4·2⊕.
Mass: $5·177 \times 10^{-5}$=17·3⊕.
Volume: 72⊕.
Density: 1·32 × water=0·24⊕.
Mean superficial gravity: 1·00⊕.
Mag at maximum brightness: 7·6.

10.7 Satellite I data

Mean distance from Neptune: 0·0023635 A.U.
   at mean opposition distance: 16″8.
Sidereal period: $5^d876833 = 5^d\ 21^h044$.
Synodic period: $5^d\ 21^h\ 3^m\ 27^s$.
Mass: $3·448 \times 10^{-3}\ \Psi = 1·8 \times 10^{-8} \odot$.
Stellar mag at mean opposition distance: 13.
Discoverer: Lassell.

SECTION 11

PLUTO

11.1 General

At present passing through Coma Berenices from Leo towards Virgo at a mean rate of 1°5 per annum. Declination limits about ±40°, but for many years to come it will be in the equatorial regions.

Its magnitude at opposition is 14·87. It therefore requires 8½ ins aperture or more. With sufficient aperture, or photographically, it can be identified by means of the ephemerides in the *A.E.* or the list of guide stars in *B.A.A.H.*

11.2 B.A.A.H. data

RA and Dec throughout the year.
Stellar Magnitude.
List of guide stars.

11.3 A.E. data

(*a*) RA (astrometric)
    Dec (astrometric)
    Horizontal parallax   } at 4-day intervals throughout the year.
    Distance from Earth
    Ephemeris Transit time

(*b*) Heliocentric longitude
    Heliocentric latitude
    Radius vector   } at 0^h ET at 80-day intervals through-
    Orbital longitude   out the year.
    Daily motion

(*c*) Dates of conjunction, opposition, stationary points, and of conjunctions with other members of the Solar System.

(*d*) Osculating elements of orbit and mean anomalies, at 80-day intervals.

170

(e) Elongations for 0^h UT at 10-daily intervals.
Magnitude at opposition.

11.4 Data

Mean solar distance: 39·45743 A.U.$=3·666\times10^9$ miles.
Perihelion distance: $2,766\times10^9$ miles.
Aphelion distance: $4·566\times10^9$ miles.
Sidereal period: 248·4 tropical years.
Mean synodic period: 366·74 days.
Sidereal mean daily motion: $0°004$
Mean orbital velocity: 2·9 m/s.
Axial rotation period: 6·39 days.

e: 0·24852 ($\pm0·0$)
i: 17° 8′ 34″1 ($-0″2$)
Ω: 109° 38′ 1″4 ($+49″0$)
$\tilde{\omega}$: 223° 31′ 20″8 ($+50″3$)
L: 165° 36′ 9″2 ($+1° 27′ 59″1$)

Epoch 1950, Jan 1·5 UT (annual variations in brackets).

Linear diameter: 5,900 km$\pm$260 km ($=3,670$ miles$=0·46\oplus$) (Kuiper, 1950). Less than 6,800 km (Halliday, Hardie, Franz, and Priser, 1966, occultation method.)
Mass: approx. $0·1\oplus$.

SECTION 12

ASTEROIDS

12.1 General

Apart from the interest of tracking down and identifying the brighter asteroids, and as objects for photography, they offer little scope for amateur observation. Discovery is now carried on entirely by photography, and it is safe to say that none within the reach of small apertures (say, brighter than mag 12) remains undetected.

Vesta (4), the brightest, reaches mag 6 at opposition and is therefore at times just visible to the naked eye. Its brightness is variable, and there is perhaps scope for systematic magnitude estimations or photometric measures carried out over a long period.

Among the 25-odd which are brighter than mag 10 at opposition may be mentioned: Ceres (1), opposition mag 7·8; Pallas (2), mag 9·2; Juno (3), mag 9·4; Chaldaea (313), mag 9·0; Ilmatar (385), mag 9·7. Telescopically they are characteristically yellowish and indistinguishable from stars.

Work on their spectra has been carried out by Bobrovnikoff (B. 190), who succeeded in photographing twelve with the Lick 36-in refractor. He found that all absorptions in the photographic region were of solar origin; no emissions were detected. Divergences between the continuous elements of the spectra and that of the Sun were interpreted as rotational effects. The energy distributions of the continuous backgrounds were reminiscent of those of comets near perihelion; variation in that of Vesta indicated a rotation period of $5^h 55^m$, in good accordance with the visually derived period.

The clearing house for all asteroidal news and information is the Astronomisches Rechen-Institut at Heidelberg, which is responsible for collating observations, investigating claims of new discoveries, allocating numbers when such claims are substantiated. Cincinatti and Leningrad Observatories are responsible for ephemerides. Orbits and other data are published periodically in the *Astronomische Nachrichten*. B.191, a monumental compendium summarising all available data for the first 1091 numbered asteroids, is indispensable for workers in this field. Ephemerides of the first four asteroids, Ceres, Pallas, Juno and Vesta, are published in *A.E.*, and asteroid data also appear in B.A.A.H. (Minor Planets).

About 1600 asteroids are today named and numbered. Each year sees the addition of 30 or 40 genuine discoveries, as well as many rediscoveries.

12.2 Photography

The trails of the brighter asteroids can be photographed with short-focus equipment by guiding on a star in their vicinity; alternatively they themselves can be guided on, in which case the stars will trail. Guiding on any star near the ecliptic for from 2^h to 4^h, using a wide-angle (e.g. portrait) lens, will sooner or later reveal asteroid trails.

The camera requisites are wide angle and speed. The photographic intensity of a trailed asteroidal image follows a different law from that of either a point or an extended image. Being, instantaneously, a point image its brightness is a function of D^2, but since it is in motion across the plate, with displacement a function of F, its intensity also varies inversely as F. Hence the photographic intensity of the trail is a function of D^2/F. The lens requirement is therefore a large value of D for a given F, or a small value of F for a given D. Portrait lenses fulfil this requirement, and in fact many of Max Wolf's discoveries were made with a portrait lens of $5\frac{1}{4}$ ins aperture and exposures of 2^h.

12.3 B.A.A.H. data

For Ceres, Pallas, Juno, Vesta:

(*a*) Date of opposition.

(*b*) RA ⎤ at 10-day intervals throughout
   Dec ⎬ the apparition.
   Horizontal parallax ⎦

(*c*) Magnitude table.

For other asteroids reaching magnitudes brighter than about $+10$ during the year:

(*a*) Date of opposition.
   Magnitude at opposition.

(*b*) RA ⎤ at 10-day intervals throughout
   Dec ⎦ the apparition.

12.4 A.E. data

For Ceres, Pallas, Juno, Vesta:

(a) RA (astrometric, and apparent – astrometric)⎫
    Dec (astrometric, and apparent – astrometric) ⎪ at 0ʰ ET daily
    Horizontal parallax ⎬ throughout the
    Distance from Earth ⎪ apparition.
    Ephemeris Transit time ⎭
    Photographic magnitude at selected dates.

(b) Stellar magnitude at 40-day intervals throughout the year.

(c) Dates of conjunction, opposition, stationary points, and of conjunctions with other members of the Solar System.

12.5 Data

Ceres

Mean solar distance: $2 \cdot 767$ A.U.$= 2 \cdot 572 \times 10^8$ miles$=$
    $4 \cdot 139 \times 10^8$ km.
Sidereal period: $1 \cdot 681$ tropical years.
Axial rotation period: $9^h\ 5^m$.
Diameter: 700 km.
Mass: 60×10^{22} gm.
e: $0 \cdot 079$.
i: $10^\circ\!\!.6$.

Pallas

Mean solar distance: $2 \cdot 767$ A.U.$= 2 \cdot 572 \times 10^8$ miles$=$
    $4 \cdot 139 \times 10^8$ km.
Sidereal period: $1 \cdot 684$ tropical years.
Axial rotation period: not known.
Diameter: 460 km.
Mass: 18×10^{22} gm.
e: $0 \cdot 235$.
i: $34^\circ\!\!.8$.

Juno

Mean solar distance: $2 \cdot 670$ A.U.$= 2 \cdot 482 \times 10^8$ miles$=$
    $3 \cdot 994 \times 10^8$ km.
Sidereal period: $1 \cdot 594$ tropical years.
Axial rotation period: $7^h\ 13^m$.
Diameter: 220 km.
Mass: 2×10^{22} gm.
e: $0 \cdot 256$.
i: $13^\circ\!\!.0$.

Vesta

Mean solar distance: 2·361 A.U. = 2·195 × 10^8 miles = 3·532 × 10^8 km.

Sidereal period: 1·325 tropical years.

Axial rotation period: 5^h 20^m.

Diameter: 380 km.

Mass: 10 × 10^{22} gm.

e: 0·088.

i: 7°.1.

ZODIACAL LIGHT, GEGENSCHEIN AND ZODIACAL BAND

13.1 Introduction

Since one of the Observing Sections of the B.A.A. is devoted, at any rate partially, to the observation of the Zodiacal Light and the associated phenomena, it may seem invidious to suggest that such work is, in this country, a waste of time. It is nevertheless true that in the latitudes of Great Britain the Zodiacal objects appear as mere wan ghosts of their true selves, and that to observe them under anything approaching satisfactory conditions it is necessary to approach at least to within 35° of the equator. It is arguable that none of the numerous unsolved problems connected with these objects is soluble by observations made outside the tropics, and certainly it is true that half a century's observations made in this country (the majority of them being no more than bare statements of visibility) have produced no significant increase in our knowledge of their nature or even behaviour.

13.2 Appearance and nature

The Zodiacal Light consists of two cones, apparently centred on the Sun, and lying in or near the ecliptic. The apices of the cones are commonly 60° to 90° from the Sun in this country; 100° or 110° in the tropics. In the tropics, too, they are visible to within about 20° of the Sun, while the evening cone remains visible at least to the end of the first lunar quarter.

The brightness of the cones is commonly referred to that of some part of the Galaxy, but this can be misleading if the latter is near the horizon and meaningless unless the particular region of the Galaxy is specified. Thus in the tropics the brightest parts of the cones are frequently brighter than the densest regions of the Milky Way in Sagittarius, as seen there; in this country, also, they are as bright as, or brighter than, the Sagittarius region as seen here, when they are observed under

176

optimum conditions. But that is not to say that the Zodiacal Light appears as bright in England as in the tropics. However, the brightness of the Light varies.

The Gegenschein, situated at or near the anti-solar point, is very much fainter than the cones, though normally brighter than the Zodiacal Band, when both are visible. Its characteristic shape is oval rather than circular, its axes being in the proportion 2 : 1 roughly. In this country it is typically about $10° \times 20°$ in extent, though in the tropics it may be seen to extend over at least $30°$.

The Zodiacal Band is a very faint, parallel-sided extension of the apex of the visible cone (sometimes visible as 'wings' on either side of the Gegenschein), about $5°$ to $10°$ wide; its intensity falls off on either side of its median line, and also from the cone to about $135°$ from the Sun, whence it increases again until the Band merges with the Gegenschein at $180°$ from the Sun. In this country it is never brighter than about $\frac{1}{8}$G in Monoceros (usually much less), and even in the tropics is a difficult object near the threshold of vision.

The Light may be explained in terms of a disc of dust and some electrons in the plane of the Earth's orbit, centred on the Sun, and physically connected with the corona.

Slipher found the auroral lines to be strengthened, suggesting some sort of excitation. Hoffmeister, however, in 1939, failed to agree with this conclusion, finding the spectrum of the Light to consist of the normal night-sky spectrum with superimposed solar spectrum. He also secured (with a 17^h exposure) a photograph of the Gegenschein spectrum, with the same result. He concluded that both shine by reflected sunlight only.

The same conclusion is suggested by the results of photography with different filters. It has been calculated that the observed intensity could be reproduced by particles 2 metres in diameter spaced 1000 miles apart. Very high altitude investigations have been performed by Blackwell and he has concluded (B. 191a) that the Light is due mainly to the scattering of sunlight from interplanetary dust particles.

13.3 Observational conditions

In our latitudes the evening cone is best seen during the moonless periods from February to April, the morning cone during the moonless periods from August to October. It is at these times that the ecliptic makes its greatest angle with the W and E horizon respectively: during the summer and winter the ecliptic, in our latitudes, is inclined at about $40°$ to the horizon at sunset and sunrise; in the spring the angle at the W horizon is larger than this in the evening, and smaller at the E in the morning; in the autumn these conditions are reversed. In the tropics both cones are well seen throughout the year.

The cones should be looked for about 2^h after sunset or before sunrise, when the Sun is some 20° vertically below the horizon. The requisite local conditions are absence of cloud above the horizon concerned, absence of twilight, absence of artificial lights (i.e. the effective observation of the Zodiacal Light is restricted to country districts—even in the wartime blackout the pollution of urban atmospheres was a hindrance), a minimum of 10 minutes' dark adaptation of the eyes, and a dim red light for recording the observations. Given these conditions the Light is frequently visible to normal eyesight in this country, though the Gegenschein—and, still more, the Zodiacal Band—requires exceptional eyesight, and cannot be effectively observed outside the tropics. During the war, both were indeed regularly observed as far N as Cumberland, but mere visibility yields little information of value. The Gegenschein can only be seen during moonless periods when it is projected on a relatively starless region of the sky; the other conditions must be even more rigidly observed than in the case of the Light. During December and January it is rendered invisible by the Milky Way; during February and March it is well placed in Leo; passing into Virgo it becomes too low for effective observation in these latitudes, though occupying relatively starless regions in Aquarius and Pisces during the summer and early autumn; during the autumn, conditions again become favourable, with the Gegenschein in Aries and Taurus.

The Gegenschein is best located as follows: determine its approximate position on a star atlas, 180° from the Sun. Then let the dark-adapted eye wander at random over the area. If spotted, concentrate first on its position, then upon its shape and extent, resting the eyes frequently and avoiding prolonged staring.

13.4 Work, and further data required

As has already been remarked, it is probable that none of the many unsolved problems connected with the Zodiacal phenomena is capable of solution by observations made in this country. Examination of the mass of observational material that has accumulated during the last fifty years forces upon one the conclusion that in this field, where the observing conditions are of paramount importance, English observers provide more information about these conditions than about the objective nature of the object they are observing.

It is, for example, quite impossible to detect objective variations in the brightness or extent of the Light when the observing conditions impose very much wider variations on its brightness and extent as observed. The outstanding need is of observational data that are objective, accurate, and strictly comparable. This is just what, regarding the first desideratum at least, the British observer cannot provide.

The main points at issue, and upon which further data are required, are:

13.4.1 Brightness: Is there any systematic difference of brightness between the two cones?

The brightness of the Zodiacal Light has been observed to increase by a factor of about 2 following a very large solar flare (B. 197a). At present there seems to be some, but not conclusive, evidence that both long-period variations—up to several months—and sudden fluctuations occur; the former are difficult to disentangle from seasonal meteorological causes; the latter—characteristically a sudden increase of brightness, followed by a slower fading over several nights—is more likely to be objective.

What is the luminosity distribution within the cones themselves? How does the brightness fall off from base to apex, and from central axis to edges?

Are reported 'ripples' and 'flickerings' of intensity (travelling along the cones with a period of a few seconds) objective? If so, are they related to auroral pulsations? Or due to some such factor as fatigue, or related to the glimpsing of an object near to the visual threshold?

There is a great need for a long series of objective and comparable photometric observations of the Light and the associated phenomena. Bousfield's photometric work in Queensland (B. 192) has shown what can be done, given suitable observing conditions.

Photometric observations should always be made with the Sun at the same vertical distance below the horizon, to ensure consistency. If recording the brightness cf. the Milky Way, always specify the region that is being used as standard. Three photometric methods suggest themselves: visual estimations, compared with the Galaxy; instrumental;* elongation of the apex as a criterion of brightness—this, if valid, would at least be more precise than visual estimations.

13.4.2 Colour: It has at times been suspected that the evening cone is of a 'warmer' tint than the morning. Few records exist, however, owing to the difficulty of the observation. But it seems to be established

---

* *A.A.H.*, section 21.3.9, describes a very simple photometer which is suitable for work of this nature.

that the Zodiacal Light is of longer wavelength than the Milky Way, being of a definitely yellowish tint.

13.4.3 Position: The axis of symmetry of the Light is very close to the ecliptic. Blackwell (B. 191a) believes that the plane of the Light is closer to the average plane of the planetary orbits than it is to the ecliptic. Observations of position relative to the ecliptic are important, though decisive observations will probably come from observers in the subtropics, where the ecliptic can be perpendicular to the horizon.

It is not established whether or not the Zodiacal Band adheres to the ecliptic. Bousfield (Queensland) puts it in a plane inclined to the ecliptic, though a different one from that derived by Hoffmeister, which coincided with the orbital plane of Jupiter.

More data are also required concerning the position of the Gegenschein relative to the ecliptic.

13.4.4 Extent: Can the elongation of the apices of the cones be correlated with the sunspot cycle? As a result of a discussion of all published observations of the Light from 1668 to 1939 Thom (B. 198) discovered an apparent, and as yet unconfirmed, correlation between the visible extent of the cones and the solar cycle, their size being maximal during or just before every second spot maximum; the suspected correlation is therefore with the 22-year period of the Sun's magnetic activity rather than with the spot cycle.

Can the elongation of the apices be correlated with the time of year —if so, is it independent of terrestrial meteorology? Thom also unearthed apparent maxima during January and June.

Can the width of the cones (which is variable by about 100%) be correlated with the time of year?

Are the observed variations of size of the Gegenschein objective? There is some evidence that it is more elongated at the solstices than at the equinoxes.

13.5 Observational records

It is convenient to keep both an Observing Book and a Permanent Record. In the latter the data recorded at the time of observation are entered in a slightly modified form, more suitable for discussion, at the conclusion of each period of observation.

For routine observation the following data should be included:

13.5.1 General:
Date.
Location of observing site.

Time (UT).

Interval±sunset/sunrise.

Atmospheric clarity: either by minimum visible magnitude or by simple verbal description.

Moon: age, and interval from setting or rising.

Artificial lights.

Length of dark adaptation: should be not less than 10 mins, 20 mins being better before observation of the Gegenschein or Zodiacal Band.

13.5.2 Zodiacal Light: The ill-defined quality of its boundaries as seen in this country does not usually justify the making of a chart of its position, or the specification of the whole boundary. It will suffice to give:

Position of apex, expressed as an angular distance from Sun (see also section 13.6).

Angular width at horizon i.e. azimuth difference of points on the horizon where the boundaries of the cone, if produced downward, would intersect it.

Brightness cf. Milky Way in Cygnus or Gemini (e.g. 2G, ½G, etc), the comparison region being specified.

In the Permanent Record the Position of the Apex is converted to Distance of Apex from Sun (if this has not been recorded direct), the RA and Dec obtained by observation being converted to Longitude, and the Sun's longitude being taken from the *A.E.* Further data, which should be recorded if the visibility of the Light justifies them, are:

Deviation of the Apex from the ecliptic.

Relative definiteness of the N and S boundaries.

Notes on the intensity distribution within the cone.

Coordinates or bearing of the intersection of the axis of the cone and the horizon.

13.5.3 Gegenschein:

Position: drawn on a tracing of the naked-eye stars in the region.

Maximum and minimum diameters and their orientation.

Brightness.

Whether any connexion with the Zodiacal Band is detectable.

In the Permanent Record are added:

Distance of the centre N/S of the ecliptic.

Coordinates of the centre.

13.5.4 Zodiacal Band:

Position.

Angular width at specified points.

Brightness.

If visible on both sides of the Milky Way, where the latter crosses it.

In the Permanent Record the Position as expressed with reference to the stars in the Observing Book is converted to RA and Dec. Also added is:

Distance N/S of the ecliptic at specified points.

Records should be submitted to the Section Director as soon as they are made.

13.6 Methods of recording position and extent of the Light

1. Location of the apex, or of sufficient points along its boundary, with reference to the stars, to enable the coordinates of the apex or the whole outline of the cone to be later plotted on a tracing from a star chart. A method somewhat similar to that employed for describing the position of a meteor path can be used. For example:

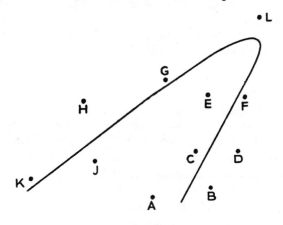

FIGURE 24

Position of apex would be specified as: $L \frac{1}{4} F$.

Position of whole cone would be specified as: $A \frac{1}{2} B$,
$$C \frac{1}{4} D,$$
$$E \frac{3}{4} F,$$
$$L \frac{1}{4} F,$$
$$G,$$
$$H \frac{2}{3} J,$$
inside (i.e. $< 3°$) K.

182

2. Location of the apex, or of sufficient points to define the whole cone, in terms of altitudes and azimuths, with the time of observation.

3. Graphical: Make tracings of a 60°-wide zodiacal zone, including all stars brighter than mag 4 or 5, but omitting all reference lines and systems of coordinates. Use these tracings for drawing in the outline of the Light, etc, if possible also its axis and some isophotic contours, and the horizon; this can conveniently be done on a ground-glass sheet covering a box containing a red light just bright enough for the tracing to be seen. If the stars are marked in ink and the observations recorded in pencil, the same tracings may be used over and over again; the Permanent Record is traced off at the conclusion of each observation, half a dozen of the brighter stars being included for purposes of orientation. This permanent tracing can then be laid over the original chart and the position of the ecliptic drawn in.

13.7 Instrumental

For routine observation of the Zodiacal Light all that is required is: a clearly graduated rule (1 inch at arm's length subtends about $2°5*$), a watch, a red desk light, a star atlas, and the *Astronomical Ephemeris*.

Photography: see section 13.8.

Photometry: Comparability and objectivity of the data are the vital considerations in assessing heterogeneous observational material, and these are largely lacking in existing records. Instrumental photometry eliminates to a large extent the effects of the variable sensitivity of the individual eye, as well as of the diverse sensitivities of different eyes; there remains the necessity for some form of control to allow for the application of the unavoidable correction for variable atmospheric transparency. One photometer suitable for Zodiacal work is described in *A.A.H.*, section 21.3.9. Another consists simply of an optical wedge with a coarse wire mounted across the diaphragm of a negative ocular. The telescope is directed at a starless field on the axis of the Light and the scale is read when the wire is just visible against the background; a second reading is taken with the telescope directed to another part of the sky at the same altitude. In each case (as, indeed, always) the mean of a series of readings is taken, the wedge being moved right away from its previous position between each setting. See also B. 196.

13.8 Photography

The difficulties presented by the Zodiacal Light as a photographic object are due, in general terms, to its faintness, but more specifically to

* See *A.A.H.*, section 36, for methods of estimating angular distances.

its combination of angular extent and low contrast. A fast lens and ultra-rapid plates are prerequisites of success, and since with such equipment fogging supervenes rather rapidly, plates should only be exposed under the most favourable circumstances: no trace of twilight, no Moon, very clear atmosphere. Regarding the last-named, it must be admitted that the British Isles are not the ideal situation for a prospective Zodiacal Light photographer. Other obvious precautions to take when exposing plates under conditions which favour fogging are to keep the lens clean, highly polished, and scrupulously free from dust; to reject any lens containing striae or air bubbles; and to reduce reflections within the camera to a minimum by means of suitably placed baffles and a dull black finish. The telescope on which the camera is mounted should be guided on a star, and under no circumstances must the exposure be continued beyond the point (discovered by trial) at which fogging becomes perceptible.

A wide-angle lens, providing good definition and equal illumination to the edges of its field, is required for an object with the angular extent of the Light; on the other hand a focal ratio of about $f/2$—and it should not be larger, or exposures will be prohibitively prolonged—makes this condition difficult of fulfilment, marked falling-off of the intensity towards the edge of the plate tending to exaggerate the contrast between the Zodiacal Light and the sky background. One way out of this difficulty, suggested by W. H. Steavenson, is to use two lenses simultaneously, each being directed at the edge of the Zodiacal cone rather than at its centre; the two plates can later be combined to form a single picture of the Light. Another subterfuge is to expose on the same guide star on successive nights, using a slower lens covering a wider field. A third method, suggested by Douglass (B.194), relies upon the fact that large areas of low contrast are more effectively recorded by a number of relatively short simultaneous exposures—in which, when combined, the faint contrast of each is intensified—than by a single long exposure. Thus a battery of three cameras on a single mounting, used simultaneously to give a succession of 2, 3 or 4 exposures, will provide 6, 9 or 12 negatives of the Light on a single occasion—a more satisfactory result than that of the second method described. These negatives are then superimposed, care being taken that they are accurately registered, for the printing. Exposures employed by Douglass with a $f/2$ lens ranged from 8^m to 20^m.

Still another way of tackling the problem of the combination of speed with wide field is described by Coleman in B.193. In front of the plate is fixed a mask bearing a transverse slit; this slit is arranged to lie at right angles to the ecliptic, and the plate is driven by clockwork in the direction parallel to the ecliptic. Successive narrow bands of the Light are therefore exposed, and a composite image built up on the plate. A $f/2$ lens was used.

Finally, anyone possessing a Schmidt camera would find it well worth his while to attempt the photography of the Zodiacal Light.

SECTION 14

AURORAE

14.1 General

The number of aurorae observed varies with both longitude and latitude of the observing station. High latitudes are more favoured than low; the correlation with longitude is rather more complex. Maximum auroral activity occurs about 2 years after sunspot maximum. In England the most favoured direction for the appearance of aurorae is NNW (350° true). Watch should be kept on every clear night during the moonless periods.

Aurorae are best observed with the naked eye, though photography is valuable for the exact recording of positions (see also section 14.5). Photographic stations in Norway and Scotland are collaborating in the simultaneous photographing of homogeneous arcs (which sometimes remain quiescent with little change of position for long periods) with a view to determining their true heights and geographical positions from mid-Atlantic to western Russia. B.A.A. members assist in this work by drawing the positions of arcs on special star charts at the specified times of exposure (every quarter-hour from 2000 UT onward —2000, 2015, 2030, etc). See also B. 203.

A small pocket spectroscope (which, with slit open, is capable of showing the characteristic green auroral line) is useful for establishing the auroral nature, or otherwise, of suspected sky glows.

The regular observation of aurorae requires no expensive equipment; what it does demand is an observing station in the country, well removed from artificial lights and urban 'smog', and with as nearly a 100% unobstructed horizon as possible. Though observers in the south see aurorae less frequently than those in the north, southerly stations are important in investigations of great aurorae and in latitude surveys of auroral frequency. Southern stations also have an advantage over northern during the summer months owing to the shortness of the northern nights.

If an assistant is available he should sit within earshot of the observer in a lighted room with a watch in front of him, recording the observations as they are called out and adding the time to each. If the observer is working alone, or if he is using star charts for the record, he will need to provide himself with a very subdued red light.

There is also scope for the amateur radio enthusiast in studying aurorae (see **14.6**).

14.2 Classes of display

Auroral displays are classified as:

(*a*) Normal: Limited to the region of the horizon—most usually arcs centred upon the magnetic north point; streamers and low-altitude curtains may also occur. Colour usually a uniform yellowish green.

(*b*) Notable: Displays involving at least half the sky hemisphere; or high-altitude arcs of marked green or red tints and covering a wide area of sky.

(*c*) Great: Involving all, or the greater part, of the sky; often a zenithal corona and large or flashing curtains; areas of very bright colour.

14.3 Auroral forms

The commoner auroral forms, together with their recognised abbreviations, are:

Glows (G): Segmental glows, near the N horizon, are typically the first forms to appear in a display; structureless, greenish yellow; often associated with arcs of the same colour.

Arcs (A): May occur singly, or several side by side; complete or broken; with or without rays; movements, if any, usually slow; greenish:

  HA: homogeneous arcs (i.e. arcs without ray structure); lower edge sharply defined, upper edge diffuse.

  RA: rayed arcs (i.e. arcs with ray structure).

  PA: pulsating arcs.

Bands (B): More diffuse and irregular than arcs:

  HB: homogeneous bands (i.e. lacking ray structure).

  RB: rayed bands (i.e. bands with ray structure); often known as curtains. One of the finest forms; usually yellowish green, may be whitish or red.

Draperies (D): Curtains composed of abnormally long rays.

Rays (R): Also known as streamers. Occur singly or in groups, parallel or radiating from an arc; often very long, narrow, and of uniform brightness; greenish yellow or red; movements typically slow.

Coronae (C): Radiating systems of rays converging at the zenith.

Surfaces (S) and Diffuse surfaces (DS): patches of auroral light without distinct boundaries, in clear sky, and well up from the horizon; often formed by the disintegration of an arc; no ray structure.

Pulsating surfaces (PS): Similar to DS except for their pulsating brightness.

Flaming, or Flashes (F): Succession of very rapidly moving sheets of bluish light, giving the impression of flashes shooting upward from the horizon towards the zenith.

Ghost arcs: Faint bands or arcs which sometimes survive for a while after the main display has faded; may occur in any part of the sky, and often move before fading.

It should be noted that colour in all auroral forms appears only when the luminosity exceeds the threshold of colour perception; all weak forms therefore appear a grey-white colour though actually they are usually greenish.

14.4 Records

The simplest form of observational record is made on the proforma reproduced below. It is used in the survey on which the B.A.A. is at present engaged. The aim of this survey is the eventual production of an auroral frequency map of the area covered—the last such map having been constructed as long ago as 1872, by Fritz. The cooperation of navigators of night-flying aircraft of the R.A.F. and civil air lines, and of observers in ships, has also been arranged.

EDINBURGH UNIVERSITY:
BALFOUR STEWART AURORAL LABORATORY

LAND OBSERVER'S REPORT · · · · · · · · · · · · · · · · · · NIGHTLY OBSERVATIONS

Year:	Month:	Geomagnetic Coordinates	
Station:		Longitude:	Latitude:
Observer:			

Night	Periods	Observing Conditions	Auroral Forms, Elevations, etc
1–2			
2–3			
3–4			
4–5			

The columns are entered as follows (note that negative information is valuable):

The geomagnetic latitude and longitude of the station are notified to an observer along with the first supply of report sheets.

Column headed 'PERIODS': Time or period of observation. UT in the conventional 4-figure notation. If an aurora is observed later on an evening when the absence of aurorae has already been noted, make two entries $\substack{0 \\ \times}$ (see below), with the time of each. N.O.M.=no observation made.

Column headed 'OBSERVING CONDITIONS': The observing conditions are to be described briefly; e.g. slight cloud; overcast.

Column headed 'AURORAL FORMS, ELEVATIONS, ETC': In the sub-column,

    × =decision about presence or absence of aurora impossible (e.g. because of poor observing conditions).

    0=observing conditions good; aurora clearly absent.

    ?=aurora suspected, but conditions not good enough for a firm decision.

    L=aurora observed. (L stands for Light.)

In the remaining part of the Column, Forms are represented by the symbols defined in **14.3**; and intensities are recorded by a numerical scale:

1. Weak: same as Milky Way.
2. Moderate: like cirrus cloud in moonlight.
3. Bright: like cumulus cloud in moonlight.
4. Very bright.

Colours are worth recording. The angular elevation, h, of the summit of the *base* of an arc should be indicated thus: e.g. $\nearrow 20°$. Elevation measurements may be done with a portable alidade.

Notes on colour, the development of a display, etc., will of course increase the value of the record, though the bare essentials recorded in the pro-forma are extremely valuable in themselves.

A more elaborate form of record includes the detailed description of the auroral forms observed and an account of their changes in the form of a log, with all times given to the nearest minute. An example of such a report is given below and is based on material supplied by the Director of the Auroral Section of the B.A.A.

REPORT SHEET LD	VISUAL AURORAL OBSERVATION								Completed report to be sent to BALFOUR STEWART AURORAL LABORATORY, Drummond Street, Edinburgh 8.
YEAR 1952?	MONTH ???EMBER				NIGHT 15–16			OBSERVER AND STATION N.A. Observer, CLEREVUE	SECTOR 80 · ZONE 58
DATE	TIME U.T.	AURORAL FORM adjective	symbol	BRIGHT-NESS	ELEVATION h	top	DIRECTION	Please leave blank	COLOUR, MOVEMENT, ETC., AND OBSERVING CONDITIONS
15	2020	observations begun							
	2020	quiet	G	2	–	20	NW–NE		little cloud; no Moon
	2035	diffuse	HA	2	05	10	at 350		yellow-green; continued for 15 minutes
	2038	one red	R	2	–	60	070		green; rising fairly steadily
	2045	HA →	RA	3	18	55	at 345		lasted about 20 seconds
	2048	some sharp	Rs	3	↑90		NE		broken and irregular; rising slowly
	2050	many	Rs	2–3	↑C				starting from RA; moderately active
	2054	large	S	2	see sketch				C formed only on N side
	2055	active	Rs	3	↑C				red
	2105	same	RA	3	27	85	at 350		C nearly always present from 2050 till 2120
	2108	sudden increase			to br. 4 of most Rs, lasted 20 seconds				
	2109	slow	F	2–3	through Rs, mainly E of N				
	2120	continued	F	2–3	—		observations ceased		
	2350	observations restarted							
	2350	quiet	G	3	–	40	NW–NE		cloud in E and S now moonlit
	2358	single narrow	R	2	–	45	335		green with red tinges
16	0003	diffuse	Rs	2	–	45	325		white, lasted 30 seconds, moving E → W
	0010	observations ceased							white, lasted for about a minute

Sketch: 2054 till 2057 — red 52, 25°, 10°, N 010 025

Full verbal reports of aurorae should if possible include the following data:

Date: the night should be specified by two dates, even if the observations are all made before or all after midnight.

Time (UT) of the appearance and disappearance of each form recorded; also times of any maxima, sudden flashes, conjunctions with stars, and fadings. The clock should be checked with TIM or the nearest radio time signal and any necessary corrections made to the record. Accurate timing is essential.

Whether or not the whole display was observed: whether it was already under way when observation began, or whether observation was suspended while it was still continuing. Also whether the observations were at any time interrupted by cloud, artificial lights, etc.

Auroral colours.

Intensities, given in brackets after the letter denoting the auroral form (e.g. HA(1)=homogeneous arc of intensity 1); if markedly nonuniform, specify the direction of maximum intensity.

Weather conditions.

Position and extent: The aim should be a complete description of the sky area covered by the display, though during a great display it is obviously impossible to realise this aim in detail; the general trends can, however, be kept track of. Azimuth should be recorded by compass points rather than bearings. Generally speaking, the azimuth of the E and W limits and the maximum and minimum central altitudes (H and h, respectively) should not be omitted, though to some extent this will depend on the form of the aurora. Relative positions of any conveniently placed stars should always be mentioned (binoculars are useful here, since the vicinity of the horizon is sparsely populated with stars). In the case of arcs—the most stable as well as one of the commonest forms—record (at stated times) the azimuth of the E and W ends and the central altitude of the upper and lower edges, and whether or not it reaches the horizon at each end. Moving forms call for a more general description.

Pictorial, rather than purely verbal, methods of recording auroral observations can also be employed. The use of star charts is not now encouraged by the Director of the Auroral Section of the B.A.A.; rather, observers willing to undertake accurately timed observations are encouraged to measure the elevations of auroral forms directly, using an alidade which is supplied to those who care to use it. (In practice, every keen observer uses an alidade.) The records can be used to give a general picture of the distribution (with colours noted) at a given time, to record the precise position of a particular auroral feature at a specified time, or to show the motion of a particular feature by recording its edge at regular intervals, the time being written against each. Drawings are particularly valuable as providing supplementary data for the photographic programme described in section 14.1: in this case the lower edge of the arc should be recorded at exact quarter-hours UT. The time must be given to the nearest 0^m5 for each feature drawn.

Observations should be sent in to the Section Director as soon as possible after the end of each calendar month, the records of individual displays being on separate (preferably quarto) sheets. They must include the observer's geographical position (longitude and latitude to the nearest 1′ if the record is verbal, or to the nearest 30″ if charts showing relative auroral and stellar positions are included) and height above MSL to the nearest 25 ft.

14.5 Photography

Auroral photography has, probably, greater entertainment than scientific value. The camera can, nevertheless, make useful records of the brighter displays (a commercial $f/3·5$, for example, recorded the brighter forms with exposures of 1^m to 2^m on ultra-rapid plates), while there is undoubted scope for wide-angle cameras of small focal ratio; for photographic determination of auroral parallaxes, see B. 203. Exposures are limited by the movements of the auroral forms themselves; a fixed mounting is of course all that is required.

If the camera field contains a distant and identifiable terrestrial object the bearing and altitude of the aurora can be determined from the plate (the plate-scale being known); given, further, the time of the exposure, the aurora's limits in RA and Dec can be derived. Star trails also help in fixing the positions of the auroral features.

The fastest available plates and a high-contrast developer should be used. Owing to falsification of contrast, the photograph seldom bears more than a superficial resemblance to the aurora as seen with the naked eye, but its utility for measurements is not thereby reduced.

14.6 Radio work on Aurorae

Radio studies of the aurorae may be carried out by observing the behaviour of radar pulses that are reflected from aurorae in a similar way to the radar 'pinging' of distant objects. Amateurs have also used the aurorae to bounce their transmissions over long distance paths.

Both the radar and amateur techniques are useful in studying aurorae.

In 1949 some Canadian observers heard radio noise from aurorae on a wavelength of 10 cms but similar attempts to detect radio emissions coming from auroral phenomena have not been successful. However, it is still possible that an aurora is a radio emitter, and highly directional arrays operated on a number of different wavelengths might confirm or deny the possibility.

Trans-auroral propagation characteristics have been the subject of a detailed examination by the amateurs of the Radio Society of Great Britain, observers in Scotland being more favoured with results than those in England. The Scottish observers were able to make contacts over a 400-mile path in the E–W direction and 600 miles in the N–S direction during periods of auroral activity.

The signals reflected from aurorae undergo a doppler shift due to the motion of the ionised region reflecting them, the amount of shift being a function of the velocity of the ionising region. The original continuous wave signal is thus noise-modulated when it arrives at the receiver. The R.S.G.B. amateurs have established that the higher the carrier frequency, the greater the doppler shift such that the listener hears a hiss.

Trans-auroral path propagation can be studied by observing the received signals from the American station WWV on 30, 20, 15 and 12 m.

SECTION 15

METEORS

15.1 Amateur work

Meteors offer an exceptionally fruitful field for amateur endeavour and initiative, though it is worth emphasising that the work is exacting and that desultory observations are unlikely to yield results of value. The observation of meteors is still to a large extent in the hands of amateurs, despite the pioneering work of the radar observers (notably those at Jodrell Bank) and Whipple's application of the super-Schmidt to meteor observation, which between them have revolutionised the subject in recent years. Furthermore, the visual observation of meteors requires no costly or complex equipment.

The observing programme operated by the Meteor Section of the B.A.A. falls into the following main categories:

1. Visual:
   - (a) Routine observations by a single observer—the determination of group radiants from individual meteor paths (see sections 15.2, 15.15).
   - (b) Routine observations within an observing group—real paths and absolute radiants (see sections 15.3, 15.16).
   - (c) Programme for meteor storms (see section 15.4).
   - (d) Routine meteor counts (see section 15.5).

2. Photographic:
   Individual photographs, two-station photographs and spectrograms (see sections 15.9.1, 15.9.2).

In addition, there is the wide field of telescopic meteors (see section 15.14) which is open to amateurs. Radar (section 15.10), though enormously fruitful, is a technique that is ruled out for the amateur by its prohibitive expense.

For the visual observation of meteors, the qualities most prized in the observer are accuracy, pertinacity, and a good knowledge of the

194

constellations. These qualities in combination will produce what is most needed: a body of observational data which is accurate enough and extensive enough to merit statistical discussion. As regards the third qualification, familiarity with the night sky, a knowledge of all stars to at least mag 4·0 or 4·5 is essential. The experienced observer will learn to go lower than this, and must develop his own technique for describing stars down to the naked-eye limit without reference to a map.

15.2 Individual paths: methods of observation

Although this work is not now accorded the same weight as during the period 1833–1930, it is likely that it will again become valuable when the correct principles for the determination of group radiants have been worked out (see section 15.15). Long watches are required, and generally a watch of from $3\frac{1}{2}$ to 4 hours may be considered a minimum for effective work on the minor streams, whilst watches of from 6 to 8 hours are preferable. The observer should pay careful attention to *all* the elements of the observation discussed in the subsections of 15.2 below, and not merely content himself with the determination of flight directions. It is probable that the accurate determination of magnitude, duration, and length of path will be found to be just as necessary in the determination of group radiants as the flight directions.

The isolated observer can also do valuable work in the determination of the distribution of magnitude within a major shower, discussed in section 15.5.

The normal path-plotting routine on a night when no major shower is in progress is to secure three primary data for each meteor observed:

Direction of flight.
Beginning and end points of its luminous path.
Duration of visibility.

When the hourly rate is higher than about 10, it will be found that it is impossible to obtain all these data fully.

15.2.1 Memorisation of the meteor's path (both orientation and extent), and its immediate transference to a map: This method is not recommended, for two reasons:

(*i*) Inaccuracy. It is difficult to determine the direction and end points of the path with the degree of precision obtainable by the method described in section 15.2.2 below.

(*ii*) Inconvenience. The path of a meteor being an arc of a **great** circle passing through its radiant, special maps in the gnomonic projection are required, such that the paths are represented by straight lines tangent to the celestial sphere at the radiant point.

If this method is used, each recorded path should be labelled with a serial number (referring to additional data in the Observing Book), and the flight direction indicated by an arrowhead.

15.2.2 Separate determination of the meteor's flight direction and of its beginning and end points: These data are recorded in descriptive, not graphical, form. The method—which was developed by Prentice, and has been proved by experience to be capable of great accuracy—is that employed by the Meteor Section of the B.A.A.

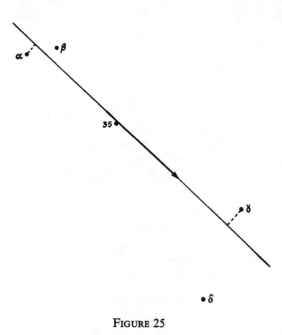

FIGURE 25

(*i*) *Orientation of the path, or flight direction:*

Immediately a meteor is seen, hold up a straight-edge or stretched string at arm's length against the sky overlying its path, and note whether this projection of the luminous path in both directions passes through or near any stars.

The flight direction should be defined by three points in order to eliminate (or at least reveal) casual errors of identification or recording. It can be done by either of two methods, which are often combined in the same observation:

(*a*) Fractional method (for which the reference stars should invariably be within 3° of the flight direction): e.g. (Figure 25)

$$\tfrac{1}{2}\alpha\beta \quad | \quad 35 \quad | \quad \tfrac{1}{4}\gamma\delta$$

indicates that the point midway between the stars α and β, the star 35, and the point one-quarter of the way from γ to δ all lie on the flight direction.

(*b*) Angular estimate method (for which the reference stars should be not more than 1° to 1½° from the flight direction): e.g. (Figure 25)

$$\tfrac{1}{2}° \, Np \, \alpha \quad | \quad 35 \quad | \quad 1° \, Sf \, \gamma$$

indicates that the flight direction passes through a point ½° North preceding the known reference star α, through the star 35, and through a point 1° South following γ.

(*ii*) *Determination of the luminous path:*

Two methods are used, (*a*) being appropriate for the longer paths, and (*b*) for path lengths of less than 5° or 6°:

(*a*) Separate determinations of the beginning and end points:

(*A*) Beginning and end points defined by perpendiculars dropped to the flight direction from individual stars.

(*B*) Beginning and end points defined by cross bearings between stars lying on opposite sides of the flight direction.

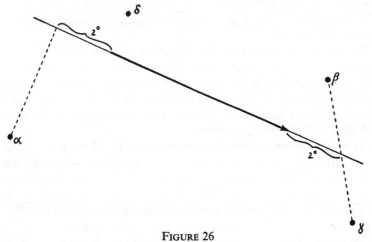

FIGURE 26

In recording these observations, use is made of the following conventions:

The direction of flight is counted positive; the reverse direction negative.

The point at which the perpendicular from star α cuts the flight direction is also denoted by α.

A cross-bearing between two stars is denoted by the prefix $\angle$.

e.g. (Figure 26)

$$\alpha + 2° \quad | \quad \angle \beta \gamma - 2°$$

indicates that the beginning point was estimated to lie 2° along the flight direction from the point at which it was intersected by the perpendicular from star α, measured in the direction of flight; and that the end point was estimated to lie 2° along the flight direction from the point at which it is intersected by the cross-bearing between stars β and γ, measured in the opposite direction to that of the meteor's flight.

(b) Determination of one point (beginning or end) and the length of the luminous path: e.g. (Figure 26)

	Beginning	End	Length of path
	$\alpha+2°$		$\beta\delta$
or			
		$\angle\beta\gamma-2°$	$\beta\delta$

indicating that the length of the luminous path was equal to the distance separating the stars β and δ. In practice, the end point is often preferable to the beginning point (assuming equally favourably placed reference stars), as tending to be the more accurately observed of the two. The description of the estimated length of the luminous path by comparison with the separation of a pair of stars is generally preferable to its quotation in degrees.

Three further examples of observations made and recorded in this way are to be found in the sample Observing Book layout in section 15.7. It is recommended that in order to become familiar with the method one should plot the flight directions and luminous paths on a celestial globe or gnomonic star chart (or even an ordinary star atlas) with the aid of the following notes:

(1) Flight direction defined by reference to the three stars η Leo, κ Gem, and ϵ Gem. The end of the luminous path was $\frac{1}{2}$° beyond (i.e. in the direction of the meteor's motion) κ Gem, which was the midpoint (M) of the three used to record the flight direction. The length of the luminous path was $\frac{3}{4}$° greater than the distance between α and β CMi.

(2) Flight direction defined by reference to the three stars ν UMa, μ UMa, and ι UMa. Luminous path defined by the point at which the line from ψ UMa to 37 LMi cuts the flight direction, and the point $\frac{1}{2}$° beyond the middle one of the three points defining the flight direction, namely μ UMa.

(3) Flight direction defined by reference to the stars ζ UMa and 30 LMi, and the point lying two-thirds of the way from χ UMa to 65 UMa. The luminous path began 4° short of the latter point and ended $\frac{3}{4}$° short of it.

15.2.3 Duration of visibility: There are two reasons why the duration estimates of a visual observer will be of little use in determining the linear velocities of meteors: (a) most estimates of this kind are distorted by large subjective errors; (b) for critical work an accuracy of better than 0·1 sec is necessary, and this is beyond the ability of a visual observer. The estimation of visible duration is nevertheless a valuable part of the total observation—partly for statistical reasons and partly for purposes of control in the determination of group radiants.

The normal meteor within the visual observer's range of perception has a duration of from 0·1 to 0·8 secs: it is clear, therefore, that nothing can be done whilst the meteor is actually in flight if its position, magnitude, etc, are also to be estimated with accuracy. For the average meteor the determination of duration must be an act of pure estimation. For the exceptional meteor (lasting from 1·5 to about 15 secs), it is true, a process of simultaneous counting is both possible and more accurate.

Three methods therefore suggest themselves, to cover the variety of cases actually encountered in observation:

(a) Pure estimation. The observer should endeavour to establish a subjective, uniform, and linear time scale. This can best be done by continuous practice against short time intervals of known duration; in its way the process is not dissimilar from the establishment of the 'step' in variable star work. When established, the scale error should be determined (a factor of ×2 need not be inconsistent with good observation, provided it is known and fixed), but the scale should not be adjusted to correct the error.

(b) A semi-automatic device such as a hand-operated chronograph has been used with successs. No attempt is made to operate this during the apparition of the meteor: after it has disappeared, the observer reproduces to the best of his ability a number of equivalent 'durations' on the chronograph, the weighted mean being taken. This method gives good results, but in practice is usually found to add too heavy a burden to an observer already overburdened with detail.

(c) Counting: the best way of dealing with meteors of long duration. The observer should learn to count at a uniform rate (8, 9 or 10 per 2·0 secs is usual).

Whether determining meteor durations by pure estimation or by counting, the observer will probably find that his time scale against the clock is different from his time scale in actual observation. The reason for this, certainly psychological, is obscure; but the scale error must nevertheless be determined. This can be done in either of two ways: (i) laboratory experiment, upon which few data have been published (but see B. 210); (ii) duplicate observations of those showers for which accurate velocities are known, such as

Leonids	72 km/sec
Perseids	61 „
Geminids	35 „
Taurids	28 „
Giacobinids	23 „

By taking the observed length of path and the known velocity of the shower, the scale error in the duration estimate may be evaluated within the limits of error of the observations.

15.2.4 The full procedure, and additional data: The complete procedure for logging the flight of a normal meteor may therefore be summarised as follows. Immediately it is seen, the observer forms an intense mental image of its flight direction, its position relative to the star field, and its stellar magnitude, and he simultaneously operates the subconscious timing process. With a controlled movement (and, in particular, without moving his head) he holds up the yardstick against the sky. The meteor, by this time, may have disappeared or it may still be in visible flight; but even in the former case the mental image will persist long enough to allow the observer to determine its position accurately. He notes and memorises, in order, the flight direction (three points) and the beginning and end of the luminous path. Only now can the yardstick be lowered. The observer then notes the time of observation (allowing for time lost) and extracts from his memory the stellar magnitude and the estimated duration of the meteor. All these quantities are then entered in the Observing Book.

Stellar magnitude should be determined and expressed by reference to stars at approximately the same altitude. Only for bright meteors—brighter, say, than mag 1—need recourse be had to the numerical magnitude scale, which should be avoided wherever possible.

Its accurate determination has the following important applications: (a) the magnitude distribution within a given shower; (b) it is a necessary element in the most recent method of determining group radiants; (c) it is valuable in correcting the observed hourly rate of a major shower for the effects of moonlight (see B. 255, 249).

The full observation, together with its recording in the Observation Book, will probably take at least a minute until practice in the technique has been gained; later, and assuming a detailed familiarity with the constellations, this can be cut down to about 30 secs. In addition to the basic data already mentioned, various other data are commonly obtained—as, for example, an estimate of the form of the meteor's light curve, whether a streak (or afterglow) was left, its colour, and a general description of its appearance if this is in any way unusual. Each

200

observer must decide for himself how many such data he can include without injuring his recollection of the basic and more vital data.

Except during specific showers, the early hours and nights of moonlight or mist or high cloud are better devoted to some branch of observation other than that of meteors. Ideally, for the observation of sporadic meteors, stars down to the 5th mag should be visible at the zenith; otherwise the number of observations that will be made will hardly justify the time spent in obtaining them.

15.3 Observational cooperation

The duplicated observation of a meteor (i.e. its simultaneous observation from two fairly widely separated stations) yields information about the meteor which is of an altogether different order from that yielded by a single-station observation. The latter gives the position of the meteor against the star field, its duration, and its brightness, but nothing more. A two-station observation, on the other hand, allows the meteor's actual path through the atmosphere to be derived (i.e. the geographical position of the points on the Earth's surface vertically below its beginning and end points, and its height at each of the latter points); the linear length of its path, combined with its duration, gives its linear velocity; the intersection of the flight directions as determined at the two stations gives its absolute radiant; and from these data its orbit round the Sun can be calculated.

A good duplicated observation is therefore of great value, and this type of work is at present (1953) yielding results of a far higher value than the work of isolated observers. In the Meteor Section of the B.A.A. regular combined watching has been continuously in operation (apart from the war years) since 1930.

Simultaneous observations are best made from stations about 45–100 miles apart. If they are nearer together, the parallax tends to be swamped by the observational errors. If further apart, various disadvantages follow—the loss of the fainter meteors under the inverse square law, unequal covering of the field, the increase of the linear equivalent of a given angular error, etc. If a third observation of the meteor is made, it is then possible to compute the probable error in the derived real path. Indeed, the effectiveness of the programme will be greatly increased if a network of four or more suitably placed stations can be staffed and operated. In such work the direction of the programme will naturally lie with the director of the group, and each member will do his utmost to carry out his own share of it.

The pooling of the observations of many observers, working individually and not in cooperation, is also essential: not only for the accidentally made duplicate observations that may be uncovered, but also because it provides the data required for statistical discussion. The Meteor Section Director is thus in a position to make much more fruitful use of the observations of each individual observer than that observer could himself.

See further, sections 15.16, 15.17.

15.4 Meteor storms

It is difficult for the observer to visualise beforehand how different will be the observational conditions during an exceptionally rich shower from those normally encountered. Unless the programme is carefully organised there will simply not be time to make any observations of value. Statistical work (determinations of HR, magnitude distribution, etc) must take priority over determinations of position, which are better left to the photographers or until the rate has dropped to a manageable level. For statistical work the following suggestions are made:

(*i*) Estimates are useless. All data should be based on careful counting.

(*ii*) Decide beforehand the exact limits of the sky area to be observed, and assess the geometrical factors involved in such choice. The area may be limited by star groups or by an artificial grid (see section 15.5).

(*iii*) Arrange means of defining smaller alternative areas for use in case the HR becomes unmanageable.

(*iv*) Arrange means whereby the observer can immediately ascertain minutes or smaller time intervals, and see that times are carefully recorded and checked. With a high HR, of the order of 2000 or more, time intervals should be short—say 1, 2, or 3 minutes.

(*v*) Keep a record of magnitudes as well as of numbers. If the rate is too high, either reduce the area or record the numbers above or below a preselected magnitude level.

(*vi*) Note the minimum stellar magnitude visible in the field of observation.

(*vii*) Supplement naked-eye work with telescopic if observing resources permit. The lower the magnitude limit, the more complete will be the final picture of the swarm. In all telescopic observing keep a careful record of the aperture, magnification, and field, especially if any of these are changed during the period of observation.

(*viii*) Be ready. Yours may be the only critical observations made, as occurred with the magnitude determinations of de Roy and the telescopic observations of Sandig and Richter at the unexpected Giacobinid storm of 1933 (B. 255).

15.5 Meteor counts and hourly rates

The procedure for determining statistically homogeneous meteor rates has been worked out by Öpik in his Double Count Method (B. 242, 243), and wherever possible it is desirable that a group of observers should employ this method. In practice, however, quite consistent results can be obtained by an isolated observer, and hourly rates are usually determined in this way.

The following investigations are suggested:

(*i*) The general level of meteoric activity should be determined once in every decade, and the routine statistical work of Gravier and of Schmidt in the nineteenth century and the more recent work of Hoffmeister should therefore be repeated.

(*ii*) The intensity of the annual meteor showers should be systematically investigated every year.

(*iii*) The distribution of meteor magnitudes within each of the annual showers should be similarly investigated.

(*iv*) Most of the statistical work on meteors has hitherto been done between geographical latitudes $+40°$ and $+55°$, and similar work in other latitudes would be of special importance.

In planning the programme of meteor counts the observer should follow, with the appropriate modifications, what has already been said in section 15.4, particularly paragraphs (*i*), (*ii*), (*v*), and (*vi*).

Three points are worth special mention in connexion with meteor counts:

(*i*) Both the linear area of sky that can be covered and the limiting zenithal magnitude observable will depend on the altitude of the observing field. Hence an observer watching near the horizon will see a different sample of the meteor population from an observer watching near the zenith. If it is assumed that the average height of appearance of meteors is a constant, then their distance from the observer depends on their ZD. At greater ZDs meteors will be intrinsically brighter (since more distant), and observable over a larger area for a given solid angle, than at smaller ZDs. The change in the observed frequency with changing ZD will be due to the balance of (*a*) decrease of absolute frequency with increasing luminosity, (*b*) increase of absolute area observed. This has been investigated by Öpik (B. 237). Taking the average height of appearance as 100 km, and an arbitrary unit of solid angle, the frequency of meteors observable by eye per unit angle at six ZDs from $0°$ to $82°$ is given below (Δm=difference between apparent and absolute magnitude):

		ZD					
		0°	45°	60°	75°	80°	82°
Δm { distance		0·0	0·8	1·5	2·7	3·4	3·7
absorption		0·0	0·1	0·3	0·6	1·0	1·2
Δm total		0·0	0·9	1·8	3·3	4·4	4·9
Limiting (zenithal) mag assuming 4·5=effective apparent mag limit		4·5	3·6	2·7	1·2	0·1	—0·4
Number		252	110	42	5·3	1·15	0·57
Area		1·00	2·81	7·34	41·0	93·5	138
Observable frequency		252	309	308	217	108	79

Thus it can be seen that the maximum observable frequency may be expected between ZDs of approximately 45° and 60°, and the figures in the final row may be used as correction factors dependent upon the altitude of the area of observation.

(*ii*) Counts of hourly numbers are by themselves of only secondary importance: the magnitude distribution is also required. The observer should therefore make a practice of recording the magnitudes of the meteors which he counts, and in order to enable these to be converted to zenithal magnitudes he should also record some nearby reference star from which the altitude may be derived.

(*iii*) Meteor counts can be combined very well with the routine recording of meteor paths up to an hourly rate of 40 at least, and probably 60 —i.e. for all normal returns of the annual major showers. If the standard B.A.A. practice of recording in complete darkness (entailing a guide to keep the written record on a single line, and some ingenuity in describing stars whose names are unknown) is adopted, no allowance need be made for the time spent in recording; if otherwise, this will be necessary.

The number of meteors visible per moonless hour varies to some extent from one observer to another, as also from one latitude to another. Figure 27 (*a*) gives some idea of the diurnal rates, averaged over the

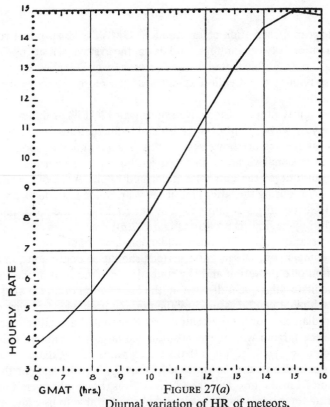

FIGURE 27(a)

Diurnal variation of HR of meteors,
averaged over the year (Olivier)

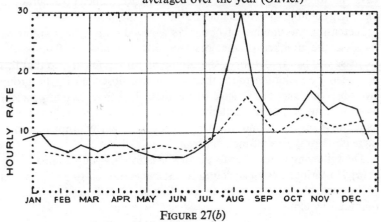

FIGURE 27(b)

Annual variation of HR of meteors :
———— fortnightly averages (Denning)
-------- monthly averages (Olivier)

whole year. Observation before about 8^h GMAT is less productive than observation between midnight and dawn, the average HR at 16^h GMAT being almost double that at 8^h. The evening (overtaking) meteors nevertheless require investigation as much as the more attractive morning ones.

The hourly number for a given hour (say 12^h–13^h) at different times of the year will be subject to considerable fluctuations due to the incidence of the major showers; and this is superimposed upon a well-marked seasonal variation in the mean hourly rate dependent on the mean altitude of the anti-solar point and of the Apex of the Earth's Way. Thus during the latter half of the year, in the latitude of England, the HR between given limits of time is about twice the corresponding rate during the first six months (Figure 27(b)).

Observations should be made under standard conditions, to facilitate their comparison. Observation periods should be continuous, and the direction of observation and sky state always mentioned in the record. To facilitate subsequent discussion, the observation of an equal area of sky each night can be assured by the use of a grid. This is a wire circle 3 ft in diameter, on whose central axis is mounted a smaller wire ring ('eyepiece'), from which eye position the large ring subtends the required angle. It will be found that a circular area of sky, diameter about 50°, is as much as can be watched effectively. The distance of the eye position from the grid will then be 3 ft 2 ins. Some observers find the wire ring 'eyepiece' inconvenient and uncomfortable to use, and in this case the direction of watch can be fixed with sufficient accuracy by choosing suitable stars to define the limits of the area.

Increasing the number of observers engaged on a meteor count will increase the number of meteors recorded, but not indefinitely. The increase will be rapid at first, smoothing off rather quickly, so that little is gained by including more than about five observers in the group: two observers may be expected to see about 1·75 times as many meteors as a single observer, but eight observers record less than 4 times as many as a single observer, and an increase beyond eight will not materially increase the number of meteors seen.*

The following notes refer to the organisation of group counts:

(a) No serious sky obstruction in the zone allotted to any observer.

(b) Each observer to keep to his allotted zone, even if temporarily obscured by cloud.

---

* Some workers claim that the numbers seen can be increased up to about 7·5 times before the curve of numbers seen against number of observers falls off appreciably (B. 268). The figures quoted in the text are probably nearer the mark.

(c) Each observer calls out his name every time he observes a meteor in his zone; many meteors will naturally pass through more than one zone.

(d) A non-observing member records the time each meteor is observed in a column headed with the observer's name. If the shower is too prolific for the recording of individual times, the recorder can mark each observation with a tick in the appropriate column, and draw a line across all columns at 5-minute intervals. A tape recorder can be used with great advantage, but it is necessary that frequent accurate time checks are recorded along with the observational material.

(e) The observers are best arranged back-to-back in a circle, looking upward at an altitude of 30° to 45°; deck-chairs are convenient. If more than four observers are available, one can profitably be allotted the zenith as his centre of observation.

References: B. 217, 218, 269.

15.6 Zenithal hourly rate, and zenithal magnitude

The ZHR is derived from the observational data by applying corrections for the altitude of the radiant and for moonlight, if any; generally, however, observations for statistical purposes are not made when there is strong moonlight.

If R is the observed hourly rate, then R_c (the HR corrected for radiant altitude a) is given by

$$R_c = R \operatorname{cosec}(a+6°)$$

The correction for moonlight depends upon the lunar phase and the incidence of diffusing matter in the atmosphere, and must be determined empirically by comparing the numbers per magnitude with similar figures relating to a previous, moonless, return of the swarm. (See also section 15.18.1.)

The zenithal magnitude is the stellar magnitude a meteor would have if it were at the observer's zenith and a standard height of 100 km. The correction, in units of the first decimal, to be applied to the observed magnitude in order to obtain the zenithal magnitude is given in the following Table (B. 246) for a range of values of the meteor's distance, r, and height, H (kms).

r \ H	60	80	100	120	140	160	180	200
60	+11							
80	4	+5						
100	−1	−1						
120	6	5	−4	−4				
140	10	9	8	7	−7			
160	14	12	11	11	10	−10		
180	17	16	15	14	14	13	−13	
200	−20	−18	−17	−16	−16	−16	−15	−15
220	23	21	20	19	18	18	17	17
240	25	23	22	21	21	20	20	19
260	28	26	24	23	23	22	22	21
280	30	28	26	25	24	24	23	23
300	−32	−30	−28	−27	−26	−26	−25	−25
320	34	32	30	29	28	27	27	26
340	37	34	32	31	30	29	29	28
360		35	34	32	31	31	30	30
380		37	35	34	33	32	31	31
400		−39	−36	−35	−34	−33	−33	−32

15.7 Observational records

The standard pro-forma used in the B.A.A. (with some specimen meteor records) is shown overleaf. It will be noticed that the individual observer is required to undertake no reduction of his own observations. The advantages of leaving all such work to the Director of the Section are, first, that the observer would be better employed in making more observations than in reducing those already made, and secondly, that subjective errors, clerical errors, and errors or merits of technique can still be deduced from the raw observational material, while they disappear from sight in the mass of figures which represents the reduced material.

The notes below refer to the respective columns of the Observation Book pro-forma:

(1): New series each night.

(2): To nearest $\frac{1}{2}$ min. In England GMAT is universally used in visual meteor work (radar observers use UT), owing to the convenience of not having to change date midway through a series of observations.

THE BRITISH ASTRONOMICAL ASSOCIATION: METEOR SECTION.

(Director: J. P. M. PRENTICE, Redcroft, Stowmarket, Suffolk.)

RECORD OF METEORS.

OBSERVER.
Name W. BROWN
Station BYFLEET

Year 1946 EPOCH.
Month Nov.

Serial Number	G.M.A.T. d. h. m.	Mag.	Dur.	Weight	ALIGNMENT (Direction of Flight) (1)	(2)	(3)	POSITION OF PATH Beginning	End	Length of Path	Notes on Appearance	Probable Radiant
1	7 10 42	1	0.7	AA	¾° Nβ. η Leo	¾°N κ Gem, 1° N ε Gem			M + ½	+β CMi +3/4		
2	10 50	βLMi	0.9	ABA	¼° Sp. ν UMa	½° Sp. μ UMa	ι· UMa LMi	L 4 UMa 57 LMi	M + ½			
3	11 01	2× ε UMa	0.6	CCC	1° Sβ. ξ UMa	⅓ χ 65 UMa 1° Sβ.	30 LMi	M–4	M – 3/4			

(3): Either as a direct magnitude estimate, or, preferably, compared with a named star.

(4): See section 15.2.3.

(5): The observer's degree of confidence in his observation. A scale of *A, B, C* is used for each of the separate elements—(*i*) flight direction, (*ii*) beginning point, (*iii*) end point. *A* denotes a normal sound observation; *B*, one obtained under some difficulty but considered satisfactory; *C*, one which is considered unreliable. Common causes of unreliability include interfering lights, such as moonlight or the approaching dawn; extreme tiredness; meteor observed near the edge of the field of vision; etc.

(6)–(11): See section 15.2.2.

(12): The observer is so busy securing the basic data of a meteor that there is usually little attention or time to spare for unusual features. However, any marked peculiarities of colour, varying brightness, train, etc, should if possible be mentioned.

15.8 Errors in meteor observation

The various sources of error in the observation of meteors have been rather fully investigated and are summarised below. Considering the shortness of the apparition of the average meteor (less than 1 sec) and the number of separate facts that have to be noted and memorised, before being recorded in the Observing Book, it is a matter for surprise that errors are not larger than, with experienced observers, they are. Forgetfulness, rather than carelessness or misobservation, is probably the most important single cause. The effects of fatigue appear to be less serious than might have been expected.

15.8.1 Hourly rates: It had for many years been assumed that fatigue causes an under-estimation of the HR towards the end of long spells of observation. A thorough investigation by Prentice (B. 250), however, suggests that the error from this cause is negligible.

15.8.2 Flight direction: The errors here depend very much on the experience of the observer, the technique employed, and the type of meteor. With inexperienced observers the errors are usually very large: thus Watson and Cook (B. 258), basing their conclusions upon the direct plotting of about 1500 Leonids (1933) on a gnomonic projection centred on the Leonid radiant, found that for inexperienced observers the probable error in an individual plot averaged $\pm 12°$ ($\pm 11°$ to $\pm 19°$), compared with only $\pm 4°$ for a bright meteor recorded by an experienced observer.

Similarly with technique. Öpik (B. 251, 238–241, 209) quotes $\pm 8°$ as the average probable error of all the members of the Arizona expedition; and the special technique used by this expedition was apparently unreliable where determinations of position were concerned. Porter, at any rate, from a discussion of 70 triple and multiple observations made by B.A.A. observers using the technique described in section 15.2.2, found a median error in flight direction of only $\pm 0°7$.

Experiments made at the Hague Planetarium in 1948 are not directly comparable with the figures quoted above, but are nevertheless of interest. It was found that when a string or yardstick was used to define the flight directions, these passed through a circle 4° in diameter, centred on the radiant; without a string or straight-edge, through a circle 5° in diameter.

15.8.3 Beginning and end points: Displacement of either end point along the flight direction by one or both observers has no effect upon the derived radiant, but introduces an error in the derived heights.

The Hague Planetarium tests gave $2°5$ as the mean error in the beginning and end points. As an example of the sort of accuracy obtainable by experienced observers, the mean deviations of the beginning and end points of one set of 309 meteors were 2·2 and 1·7 miles respectively. Porter's 'sliding errors' are in close agreement with the Hague figure (average errors $\pm 2°4$, $\pm 2°5$; median, $\pm 1°7$, $\pm 1°7$).

15.8.4 Time of flight: Boyd (B. 210), investigating the duration estimations of a group of 11 students (method employed is not mentioned, but was presumably counting or direct estimation), found that in 50% of the cases the scatter was random, while 50% showed a bias towards systematic under- or over-estimation. Observers should therefore test themselves with artificial 'meteors' to determine the nature of their personal error.

With durations between 0·38 and 1·80 secs, the errors ranged from 14% to 49%. Boyd found that although the error increased with increasing duration, it did so rather more slowly: hence the percentage errors decreased slightly as the duration to be estimated increased. Roughly speaking, an error of the order of 25% may be expected in the estimation of durations exceeding 0·5 secs; and a considerably larger percentage error for shorter durations.

15.8.5 Angular length of luminous path: There appears to be a pretty universal tendency among untrained observers to over-estimate the length of a meteor path, as of other angles and distances in the sky (cf. size of Sun or Moon when near the horizon). Thus members of the general public commonly over-estimate path lengths by as much as a factor of 5. Yet in the Hague Planetarium experiments the estimated paths were, surprisingly, 13% too short on the average.

The existence of a serious systematic error in angular length as a function of the angle of foreshortening has been known for some years, but at the time of writing no critical examination of this error has been published.

15.8.6 Magnitude: Trained observers—especially those used to the observation of variables—are surprisingly precise in their estimates of stellar magnitude. The magnitudes of 100 meteors, when reduced to zenithal magnitude (section 15.6), were found to be accurate to within 0·56 mag. Though this compares unfavourably with the accuracy obtained by variable star observers, the difference is hardly surprising considering the dissimilarity between the two types of observation.

15.8.7 Miscellaneous illusions and errors: Commonly encountered in the reports of fireballs made by inexperienced observers are: (a) 180°-error in the direction of flight; this strange error may be allied to the 'mirror failure' which makes it difficult for some people to distinguish quickly between b and d, 69 and 96, etc; (b) 'hearing a light', i.e. imagining that a synchronous 'swish' is audible, even though the meteor may be so distant that its noise, if any and if loud enough, could not reach the observer for many seconds; (c) inexperienced observers also tend to over-estimate the altitude of any celestial object; the majority of people, if asked to point to a spot at an altitude of 45°, will indicate an altitude in the neighbourhood of 30°.

See also B. 236, 258.

15.9 Photography

15.9.1 Direct: Photography is today a powerful technique for the study of meteors, owing primarily to the precision of its data—both as regards position and angular velocity at any point along the visible path: the former can only be estimated visually with an appreciable margin of error, even by a trained observer (see section 15.2.2), and the latter not at all. It is the most direct—or only—method for obtaining accurate data concerning stationary radiants, variations of brightness and speed during the meteor's visible flight, spectra, and the data necessary for the calculation of real paths and velocities.

It is, moreover, a field in which the sort of equipment found in amateur hands can be put to very good use and is an important complement to visual observations generally. It does, however, demand considerable patience from the observer, though perseverance and a rationally planned programme are all that are required to ensure eventual results.

The efficiency of a lens for meteor photography is determined by the intensity of its images and the size of the field over which they are tolerably defined. If a point image crosses a plate with an angular velocity of ω, the intensity of the photographic image is, per unit area, a function of $D^2/\omega F$, or, as in the case of a trailed asteroid (section 12.2),

$$b_p = k \cdot \frac{D^2}{F}$$

for a given value of ω. It is clear that, ω always being large, F must be made as small as possible for a given value of D. That is, considerations of image intensity alone indicate the use of small focal ratios.

On the other hand, the meteor-recording efficiency of a lens is directly proportional to the usable area of its field. Combining this factor with the above expression for the photographic brightness, and putting d=angular field diameter, the efficiency of the lens is given by

$$E = k \cdot \frac{(D \cdot d)^2}{F}$$

providing that, for an anastigmat, $F \geqslant 2\frac{1}{2}$ ins approximately, otherwise the image of an average meteor is in danger of being narrower than the grain of the emulsion. Hence the linear dimensions of the lens are irrelevant to E; furthermore, since d is inversely proportional to D/F, a lens of small focal ratio, though photographically fast, is not necessarily the most efficient for 'catching' meteors. In other words, a compromise must be struck between the conflicting demands of d and D/F. This, as a very rough guide, is represented by the lens of smallest focal ratio that is capable of giving a well-defined field of about 30° or 40° diameter; what its focal ratio will in fact be when this condition is satisfied will of course, depend on both the type and quality of the lens, though it will probably not be less than about $f/3$. The simplest way of testing the relative suitability of two lenses in practice is to expose trails of the same stellar field, for the same length of time and under identical atmospheric and other relevant conditions (such as altitude), with each lens in turn, and then to count the number of trails on the two plates.

Results obtained experimentally by Waters and Prentice with an artificial meteor show clearly that the essential factor is focal ratio, or a function of focal ratio, and that the linear values of D and F as such are irrelevant—though, of course, for a given value of the focal ratio the image intensity varies directly with D:

D	F	D/F	D²/F	Image intensity
1·3	6·0	0·22	0·28	1
2·3	10·5	0·22	0·50	3
2·0	6·0	0·33	0·67	6
4·25	8·5	0·50	2·17	9
2·75	6·0	0·46	1·26	10

The penultimate result appears to be 'wild', but the general drift is clear.

Instrumental requirements, then, are not elaborate. Portrait lenses are ideal, providing they are of good quality; if they are not, the field of good definition becomes unduly restricted—considerably more so than that of an equally fast, but very much more expensive, anastigmat. Focal ratios between about $f/2·5$ and $f/4·5$ and apertures from 2 to 6 ins can be put to good use. An anastigmat of 3 ins aperture or thereabouts, working at $f/3$ or $f/3·5$, is also a valuable adjunct to the meteor-photographer's equipment. Since the war it has been possible to buy various ex-R.A.F. camera lenses which—though rather comatic, reducing their usefulness for stellar work—are admirable for meteor work; the Kodak Aero-Ektar ($f/2·5$, 7 ins focus, giving a useful field of about 50° on a $8\frac{1}{2} \times 6\frac{1}{2}$-in plate), a $f/2·9$ Dallmeyer (of 8 ins focal length), and the $f/4$ Ross Xpres ($F=5$ ins, giving an abnormally wide field of about 65°), are good examples of this class of camera objective.

Speaking very generally, a $f/2$–$f/3$ objective will record most meteors of mag 1 and brighter, unless their angular velocities are abnormal, mag 2 meteors providing that they are fairly slow-moving and that other conditions are favourable, and meteors fainter than mag 2 only if they are abnormally slow-moving or if they possess a train. Lenses of focal ratios from about $f/3$ to $f/4·5$ will normally record only the brightest meteors or ones of abnormally low angular velocity.

There is great scope for the Schmidt camera—with its phenomenal reconciliation of the otherwise alternative characteristics of speed and width of field—in meteor work. They are being used in America, for example, by the Harvard meteor observers (see for instance, B. 259). Another way of escape from this particular dilemma is to mount a battery of three, four, or more fast but comparatively small-field cameras on a single equatorial mounting, their axes being arranged so that although there is a liberal overlap between their fields (to avoid the danger of meteors being lost in regions of inferior definition on the outer edges of the fields), they cover between them a large area of sky with good definition. A typical battery of this sort is described in B. 254, four portrait lenses covering an area of 50° × 60° with good definition.

It is essential that the camera, or battery of cameras, be used in a way calculated to increase the naturally rather poor chances of a meteor bright enough to be recorded crossing the field within a reasonable aggregate exposure time. Exposing at random for sporadic meteors is a waste of time. Be guided by the hourly rates quoted in sections 15.5, 15.18, concentrating particularly on the maxima of showers occurring when there is no Moon. Directing the camera at the radiant itself not only increases the probable number of meteors that may be expected to cross the field in a given time, but will also decrease their probable angular velocity, thus permitting fainter meteors to be recorded. Geminids, Perseids, Quadrantids, and Taurids, in particular, usually include a relatively high percentage of bright meteors. It is also worth bearing in mind that about 30% of all long-path meteors visible from a given station pass within 30° of that station's zenith (see also B. 229).

Some rough idea of the probable incidence of successful plates may be gauged from the table opposite, whose entries have been extracted at random from the literature. It must be borne in mind, however, that a great deal depends upon the lens speed, the plate speed, the effective field size, and the manner in which the camera is employed; also that improvements of lenses, and even more of emulsions, during the last 25 years have greatly increased the chances of success.

To end on a note of encouragement, there was the case of a single plate exposed during the Draconid storm of 1933 which on development was found to contain 25 trails!

A meteor camera may be either stationary or equatorially mounted and clock-driven. The latter is preferable, for the following reasons:

(a) With a camera recording star trails the only way of relating a meteor image to the positions of the stars is to terminate the exposure immediately a meteor is seen which crossed the field of the camera and which might have been bright enough to be recorded. Hence a visual watch must be kept throughout the photographic session (conveniently, with the aid of a wire grid which, from the observer's chair, outlines the limits of the camera field against the sky), the plate changed, and the time noted, each time a possibly recorded meteor appears.

(b) With a camera recording point stellar images, on the other hand, it is not necessary to know the time at which a meteor appeared in order that the plate may be used to determine the radiant. Hence a night-long visual watch is not necessary—for work of this type guiding is not essential, so long as there is no systematic gain or loss in the drive—

plate changing being dictated by fogging only, and being operated automatically at regular intervals. (See, for example, Collinson's ingenious and easily home-made automatic plate-changer, B. 213; also B. 214, 227.) If fogging does not necessitate changes of plate throughout the night, the final closing of the shutter before dawn, or when the radiant becomes unobservable, can easily be operated by means of an alarm clock.

(c) The importance of training the camera on shower radiants has already been stressed, and implies a clock-driven equatorial.

(d) Meteor trails are much more easily overlooked when examining a plate of star trails than one of point images. This becomes increasingly

Aggregate Exposure (hrs)	Number of Trails	Hours Exp. per Trail	Equipment	Camera Direction	Notes
724	4 } 2	121	$D=2$ ins, $f/3$ $D=2\frac{1}{2}$ ins, $f/2\cdot2$	Radiants	Rather slow plates used
2500	23	109	—	—	F. Whipple
738	12	61·5	$f/13$ (40° fd.)	—	Large f/ratio
411	20	20·5	$D=2$ ins, $f/3$ anastigmat	—	Exps. during peak period (Aug – Dec) 1928–1934
11·9	2	6	—	Perseid radiant	Aggregate of 2 yrs at Perseid max.
9	3	3	5 portrait lenses, $f/2 - f/4$ (50° × 60°)	Radiant at shower max.	
29·8	14	2	$f/2-f/4$	Leonid radiant	Aggregate of 3 yrs maxima
9	5	1·8	3 $f/4$ cameras ($D=4$–6 ins)	Perseid radiant	
12	16	0·75	10 portrait lenses ($D=$ 6–8 ins, F= 27–36 ins)	Leonid radiant	At 2 Harvard stns. 1898 Nov 13, 14

so in the case of faint meteor images and/or images which are approximately parallel to the star trails.

A rather strange device was constructed at Harvard many years ago which was in effect a half-way house between a stationary and a clock-driven meteor camera. The camera was mounted on a polar axis whose driving circle was a 144-toothed cog. This wheel was advanced mechanically one tooth every 10 minutes, the stars having been trailing during that period. The polar axis was slightly displaced from the NCP, with the result that each 10^m exposure left a separate trail of every star in the field. The time of appearance of every meteor had to be noted, so that its image could be related to the correct set of star trails.

Photography is particularly valuable in cooperative work by two or more observers designed to obtain parallactic observations of identical meteors from separated stations. From such accordances, true paths, heights, and mean geocentric velocities can be calculated. A baseline of from about 25 to 50 miles is suitable; if three observers are cooperating, their stations should lie as nearly as possible at the corners of an equilateral triangle. If the separation of the stations is too small, accuracy suffers through the measured parallax likewise being too small; if too great, there is a danger that a meteor included wholly in the field of one observer will be partially or even wholly outside the field of the other. The procedure is to synchronise exposures at the two stations, both cameras being set to the same RA and Dec and clock-driven.

An interesting account of the Harvard 2-station programme employing specially designed Schmidts fitted with rotating sectors (see below) is given in B. 259.

In connexion with the reduction of meteor photographs, reference may be made to B. 253.

If some recognisable modification of the meteor trail on the plate is made at equal known intervals of time, their linear separation will give the meteor's angular velocity at all points along its flight path. If an accordance has been obtained from another station, not only the angular velocity but also the linear geocentric velocity at all points, and hence the deceleration (the latter giving valuable information to meteorologists regarding atmospheric pressure at high altitudes) may be calculated.

Three main methods have been employed to introduce the modifications of the recorded trail:

(a) Vibrating the camera itself, a device suggested by the accidental discovery at Harvard many years ago that meteor trails taken with a certain camera were shown under microscopical examination to be regularly sinuous. The cause was traced to vibration imparted by the driving mechanism. The amplitude of the vibration in this particular case was less than 0·07 ins, but even so was accurately measurable with a microscope.

(*b*) Mounting an oscillating plane mirror in front of the camera objective in such a way that the reflected stellar point images are drawn out into circles; the image of a meteor then describes a symmetrical sinuous line.

(*c*) The most commonly employed device is a rotating shutter which passes between the objective and the sky at regular and known intervals. Experiments with a bicycle wheel fitted with 12 opaque sectors were made at Yale as long ago as 1894. Each revolution of the wheel, driven by a small electric motor, was recorded on a chronograph, so that its speed at all times was known. Speeds of from 30 to 50 r.p.m. (giving 6 to 10 interruptions of the trail per sec) were tried, but were found to be on the slow side. The optimum speed of rotation for a given meteor with a given equipment is determined by the meteor's angular velocity and the plate-scale (hence F) of the camera. No precise rule can be given, therefore, but interruptions of the order of 15–20 per sec will be found satisfactory in most cases. The two opposite dangers to be avoided are the difficulty of detecting the trail interruptions, even under high magnification, if the sectors are revolving too fast, and insufficient accuracy resulting from too few and two widely spaced interruptions if they are revolving too slowly. A 3-ply or aluminium disc with two or three open sectors cut in it is probably the most satisfactory arrangement, allowing lightness to be combined with strength. The disc should be as small as is compatible with cutting the whole field of the camera, or possibly battery of cameras; it should therefore be located close to the dewcaps. A synchronous motor or a mechanically governed non-synchronous electric motor would be suitable for the drive, and the speed of revolution must be accurately determined by a rev-counter, stroboscope, or similar device. A 2-vane home-made rotating sector of this type (Figure

FIGURE 28

28) is described in B. 254 (see also B. 261); in this instance a sector speed of 480 r.p.m. (giving 16 interruptions per sec) was found to be generally satisfactory with focal lengths of from 6 to $8\frac{1}{4}$ ins.

A method of synchronising the sectors at independent observing stations, as developed at the Brackett Observatory (B. 261), employs a radio signal initiated by a photoelectric cell upon which a flash of light falls once in every revolution of the sector.

Only the fastest plates can be used with any chance of success. This is necessitated by the invariably high angular velocity of meteors, and since there is no need for subsequent enlargement the graininess of the plate is not material. Speed must be combined with minimum production of sky fog during long exposures. Ilford Hypersensitive Panchromatic (HP3, 34° Scheiner) are good. Also recommended are the Ilford Press Ortho Series II plates, which are said to possess the necessary characteristic of great speed with short exposures combined with delayed fogging tendencies over long exposures. Development should aim at producing maximum density and contrast.

Plates (negatives) should be laid on a ground-glass screen, illuminated from below by a 150 watt lamp, and examined with a magnifying-glass for trails. As a matter of routine, an eye should always be kept open for comets and novae on non-trailed (stellar) plates.

Loss of meteor trails that should theoretically have been recorded is commonly due to: stars trailed (stationary camera); bad focusing; over-development of fog; dewing-up of lens during long exposures.

As regards the latter point, long dewcaps are essential, and it is also wise to install some form of heater—such as a coil of resistance-wire mounted on an insulating ring surrounding the lens cell.

15.9.2 Spectrograms: The photographic recording of meteor spectra offers great opportunities for the amateur, since it is a comparatively new field and very few good meteor spectrograms have been obtained. Its exploitation has been delayed by, as much as anything else, the lack of suitable plates, the necessary ultra-rapid panchromatic emulsions only having been developed during the early 1930s; before 1932 no more than a dozen meteor spectrograms had been secured. Despite the paucity of the material that is still available, the examination of meteor spectrograms has already led to the detection of free atmospheric hydrogen.

The whole field of correlating spectra with height, velocity, brightness, radiant, etc, is wide open for anyone having the requisite patience and imperturbability in the face of a mounting pile of fruitlessly exposed plates. For, inevitably, many hours' aggregate exposure must be anticipated as the price of each spectrogram bright enough to be of value. In the present state of the subject, however, each such success is of the first importance. It is on record that 73·6 hours' aggregate exposure of the Leonid radiant during two years yielded 8 spectra (1 per 9^h), and 84·9 hours of the Geminids in one year, 2 spectra (1 per 42^h), but these are insufficient data on which to base any general conclusions.

The only reasonable prospect of success is offered by an objective prism or grating; of these, the latter may be dismissed on the score of expense. The camera requirements are wide angle, large relative aper-

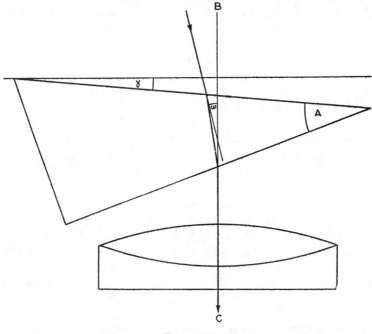

FIGURE 29

ture, and high quality, an anastigmat being preferable to a portrait lens since the best possible combination of field and relative aperture is required. An anastigmat of focal ratio $f/4·5$ or smaller, focal length about 6 ins, giving a well-defined field of about 30°, would be very useful for this type of work, and if the amateur's pocket can be made to stretch to a battery of three or four such lenses, so much the better. Fast panchromatic plates are essential, the ultra-rapid Ilford HP3 being probably as good as any. Development is tricky, a balance having to be struck between adequate contrast and a tolerable degree of graininess.

The objective prism must cover the objective completely. For stellar work with the plate exposed in the focal plane of a telescope, small-angle (3° to 5°) crown prisms are commonly used, otherwise the dispersion (at the relatively long F employed) would dilute the spectrum to an extent that would entail prohibitively long exposures. But for meteor spectrograms with short-focus cameras flint prisms of about 25° to 30° angle are more suitable; if less than this the dispersion is insufficient, and if much more, light loss by absorption becomes excessive.

The prism is mounted in front of the lens, rigidly fixed in the position of minimum deviation relative to the optical axis, BC (Figure 29). For an average flint prism of angle $A = 25°$, the angle of minimum deviation, ω, will be in the region of 15°, and γ, the angle between the forward face of the prism and the normal to the optical axis, about 5°.

Focusing should be carried out by exposing trial plates of star trails, using the absorption lines in the spectrum of a mag 1 star which is allowed to trail in the direction perpendicular to the direction of dispersion.

In operation, the camera is oriented so that the direction of dispersion is perpendicular to the line joining the field centre and the radiant (since the spectrum of a meteor travelling parallel to the direction of dispersion will not be recorded). If exposing for sporadic meteors (by comparison, a waste of time and plates) the camera and/or prism are best oriented so that the direction of dispersion is perpendicular to the hour circle through the centre of the field.

Three main types of meteor spectrum have so far been distinguished:

(a) those in which the H and K lines of ionised calcium are the predominant feature;

(b) those in which the calcium lines are weaker than magnesium emissions at 3830Å;

(c) those containing numerous iron lines and lacking the calcium emissions.

The calibration of the spectrograms and the identification of the emissions is a fairly technical job, involving the use of a comparator. B. 252, 225, 226 should be referred to.

15.10 Radar observation of meteors

This very powerful instrument of research cannot be passed over without some mention; at the same time, it lies outside the scope or means of the amateur and can therefore be referred to quite summarily.

The possibility of such a method of meteor observation was adumbrated by the work of Schafer and Goodall in America and Appleton in this country as long ago as the early 1930s. But the discovery of radio 'whistles' caused by meteors was only turned to good astronomical account with the development of radar in its civil applications, since the war. The detection of a meteor by the 'reflection' of an artificially projected beam by the ionised gases in its path is thus a comparatively recent development. Nevertheless its achievements have been phenomenal. By its means meteors have been observed continuously since 1950 in the non-stop survey at Jodrell Bank; meteors are observed which would have been missed by the visual or photographic observers on account of cloud; sporadic meteors and whole streams which could never have been discovered by the previous techniques (since they occur in daylight) have been detected—e.g. the unique May–August Piscids, discovered by Lovell and his colleagues at Jodrell Bank in 1947; visual systems have been studied, and their radiants determined, by an independent method; meteor velocities, a vitally important datum, have been determined; the distribution of mass within a given meteor stream has been effectively investigated.

A vast literature has already grown up; B. 228 provides an authoritative survey of the whole field of long-wavelength astronomical research.

15.11 Equipment

'The observer of meteors requires a clear sky, a thick coat, a notebook, a knowledge of the constellations, infinite patience, and a tendency to insomnia.'* From which it will be gathered that the equipment required by the meteor observer is not exclusively instrumental.

(a) Watch or clock (MT) correct to 0·5 mins, or with known error.

(b) A device, such as a chronograph, for registering time intervals (optional: see section 15.2.3).

(c) Light wooden straight-edge, about 3 ft long, or a 'string wand'. The standard B.A.A. practice is to use a stretched string just thick enough to be seen easily against the night sky.

(d) Star atlas showing designations down to at least mag 5·7, for confirming points used in defining flight directions and beginning and end points; Norton's, though not ideal for the purpose, is probably the best available. The experienced observer will, however, never need to refer to an atlas during the observing spell.

(e) Binoculars are useful, especially for the observation of trains.

* J. B. S. Haldane.

(*f*) Deck-chair, giving the degree of comfort essential during watches lasting several hours, while naturally tilting the head skywards.

(*g*) Observing Book, ready set out as a pro-forma; several pencils; drawing-board across knees.

(*h*) Dim, red-screened light clipped to back of chair and shining over the observer's shoulder, the switch being mounted in a convenient position such as the chair arm (optional).

(*i*) A thorough knowledge of the constellations, so as to eliminate time spent (and memory strained) poring over the atlas.

(*j*) Several thick rugs, since keeping warm is most important. An electric tubular heater for the hands is used by some observers.

(*k*) Vigilance, a good memory (at any rate over short periods), pertinacity, and some of the characteristics of a polar bear.

15.12 Meteor trains

Only a very small percentage of meteors leave trains visible to the naked eye, and of these the vastly greater number are ephemeral. On any occasion when an enduring train is seen, its observation should be given priority after the normal record of the meteor, and all other work temporarily suspended in order to record its appearance (colour, continuity, width, brightness, etc) and particularly its movements. It is absolutely essential that the latter should be recorded with accurate timing. The trail's linear velocity will probably be of the order of 100 to 300 km/hr, and therefore observations should be timed to the nearest 0·25 min, and the timepiece checked against a signal as soon afterwards as possible. The inadequacy of the time measurement is where nearly all previous observations have come to grief.

When nearing the limit of naked-eye vision, observation may be continued for a further period by binoculars or by a telescope using the lowest magnification available. Many bright meteors which appear to have no train will be found to have had one, if a telescope is immediately directed to the area; these, however, are usually too ephemeral to permit of more than the initial observation.

Numerous observations in the past have suggested that trains are tubular in structure; the physical and mechanical conditions of their formation are not completely understood. Duplicate observations of meteor trains give valuable information about the meteorology of the upper atmospheric levels.

Observations of an enduring train may be recorded in either of two ways: (*a*) drawing its position on a star chart at convenient intervals (one per minute should be possible); each position is labelled with the time, the clock error being known or subsequently corrected; (b) determining the orientation and end points of the train by the method already described for meteors in section 15.2.2; if the train becomes distorted it will be necessary to determine several points along it.

The aim should be to compile a record giving a detailed, accurate, and continuous picture of the train's shape, size, brightness, colour, position, and movements—a tall order, but not an impossible one.

15.13 Fireballs

Data which should be included in any report of a fireball or exceptionally bright meteor are:

(a) Date and time. If a casual timepiece is used, check it against a time signal as soon as possible. Summer Time, even if in force, must never be used in reporting fireballs (or, indeed, any other astronomical observation).

(b) Coordinates of beginning and end points:

Night: as for an ordinary meteor (section 15.2.2).
Day: note the horizon features immediately below the beginning and end points, the altitude of both points, and the exact position from which the observation was made. Later, measure the bearings (state whether true or magnetic are given) of these horizon marks by compass. The altitude will necessarily be less precisely determined than the azimuth, since a point in the featureless day sky cannot be memorised accurately enough to justify subsequent measurement. (See *A.A.H.*, section 36, for methods of making angular estimates.)

(c) Duration of visibility (see section 15.2.3).
(d) Details of appearance and behaviour:

Colour.
Brightness.
Explosions, if any. If possible, time the interval between seeing and hearing any explosion.
Curvature or other irregularities in the path.
Any variations of angular velocity along the path.

(e) Train, if any:

Night: see section 55.12.
Day: 1-min or $\frac{1}{2}$-min drawings, each including a distinctive feature on the horizon, and an estimate of the altitude of the train.

If too ephemeral for drawings to be made, estimate its duration in secs.

Subsequently the following data or amplifications should be added:

(*f*) Longitude and latitude of the observing station (from 1-in O.S.).

(*g*) Any sounds: detonations, thunder-like echoes, etc. If possible, relate these temporally to the visible phenomena.

(*h*) Whether one or more bodies were seen.

(*i*) Condition of sky at the time.

(*j*) Go back over the above items, indicating where necessary the estimated degree of accuracy of each.

It should not be, but is, necessary to stress the fact that unless a fireball report is accurate it is not worth making, and certainly not worth submitting.

15.14 Telescopic meteors

Telescopic meteors are exceedingly numerous: rather untrustworthy extrapolation (Watson, B. 256) suggests that even at mag 9 something like 10^9 enter the Earth's atmosphere daily, their numbers increasing by a factor of about 2·7 per magnitude. They have nevertheless been comparatively little observed, and the field offers scope for both individual and cooperative observation by anyone with the patience to tackle it.

The reason for the past neglect of the fainter meteors is, of course, that the naked eye, with its enormously wide field, is an incomparably more efficient instrument than the telescope for catching meteors. With telescopes of normal construction the fields are so restricted, even with the lowest permissible magnifications, that the crop of meteors is bound to be sparse compared with that of the naked-eye observer. Amateurs using low magnifications are quite familiar with the appearance of telescopic meteors,* while an observer with large instruments (18-in and 24-in) has been quoted as stating that he only saw one during a year's observing. Failing a specially constructed wide-field telescope,† binoculars probably offer the best chances of success; they should have an aperture of at least 6 cms or so, giving a magnitude threshold of 8 or 9. One set of observations with 6-cm and 8-cm binoculars (limiting mag 8·5, field about 8°) produced 14 meteors in 7½ hours. With this equipment, 47 meteors showed durations from

---

* Denning, for example, observed 635 during a total of 727 hours' comet-seeking with his 10-in reflector, though such a high rate would be impossible for sustained work.

† See *A.A.H.*, section 3.10, for an analysis of the difficulty and means of overcoming it.

0·05 to 1·0 sec (peak at 0·3 sec) and a magnitude range of 0–8·5 (peak at 6·0). See also B. 262, 209, 244.

The threshold of visibility of meteors is from 1·0 to 1·5 mags higher than that of stars, with given equipment; the faintest visible to the naked eye, for example, are of approximately mag 5·5.

The stellar magnitude of a meteor observed telescopically can be estimated in one of two ways. A telescope of aperture D increases the naked-eye brightness of a star* by

$$\Delta m' = 5 \log D - 5 \log \delta$$

The true apparent magnitude of a 'line' source, such as a meteor, whose apparent magnitude in a telescope is threshold (say, 5·0), is given by

$$m = 5 - 5 \log \delta + 5 \log D - 2 \cdot 5 \log M \qquad . \quad . \quad . \quad (1)$$

where M is the magnification. The telescope of aperture D increases the naked-eye brightness of the meteor by

$$\Delta m'' = 5 \log D - 5 \log \delta - 2 \cdot 5 \log M$$

Therefore,

$$\Delta m' - \Delta m'' = 2 \cdot 5 \log M$$

Hence:

(a) Estimate the true apparent magnitude (m_s) of a star in the field, such that it and the meteor are equally bright. Then the true apparent magnitude of the meteor is given by

$$m = m_s + 2 \cdot 5 \log M$$

Or:

(b) Estimate the brightness of the meteor by comparing it with that of a star observed with the naked eye, and use equation (1) above.

The anomalous fact that the majority of telescopic meteors cross the field with angular velocities comparable with those of naked-eye meteors suggests either that they are always observed near their radiants or that the atmosphere is very much more extensive than indicated by other lines of investigation. Neither suggestion is immediately acceptable. Observations have been published which would appear to indicate heights of from 400 to 1000 miles; some of Denning's meteors, assuming that their general characteristics were comparable with naked-eye meteors, indicated heights of the order of 2000 miles. Others, better authenticated, suggest more normal heights of the order of 100 km or so, and the cause of the anomalous angular velocities is almost certainly subjective, though unexplained.

* See, further, *A.A.H.*, section 1.1.

The observations of a single observer can be of value in improving our sparse knowledge of (a) the numbers of meteors of each telescopic magnitude in the major showers, and any variation in these data from year to year; (b) the determination of radiants by the group radiant method; this will be possible if the shower has a sharp radiant, but not if it is diffuse; (c) their appearance: colour, whether stellar or non-stellar, occurrence of streaks, etc; (d) statistics relating numbers seen with magnitudes and apertures.

What is really needed is a mass of two-station observations, allowing the real paths to be derived. The most hopeful way of overcoming the practical difficulty of the two observers obtaining observations of the same meteor within a reasonable number of observing hours would be to direct the telescope at the radiant of a major shower, using a low magnification and a large-scale map (e.g. Webb's, or the *BD* chart of the radiant area, enlarged several times by hand). Even so, the observers would probably have to be in continuous telephone contact to ensure the correct identification of the meteors. Any other way of organising a 2-station search for telescopic meteors would be virtually a waste of time.* Fatigue should be avoided, since it both reduces the accuracy of the observations and tends to promote the imagined observation of non-existent meteors; it is recommended that the observers should rest their eyes for a specified period at 5-min intervals (their watches being synchronised if they are not in telephone communication).

15.15 The determination of group radiants

In principle this is a simple matter. It is assumed that the meteors of a given shower enter the Earth's atmosphere in parallel paths, whence it follows that by an effect of perspective they appear to emanate from an infinitely distant point, known as the radiant. We therefore only have to observe the great-circle tracks of the meteors and plot them on a map of suitable projection in order to determine the radiant either by inspection or (if greater accuracy is justified) by a least square solution.

In the case of a dominant major shower with a sharp radiant this procedure can be carried out successfully. It can also be used to determine an approximate radiant centre for those more numerous major showers which have a diffuse radiant, such as the Quadrantids, Perseids, and Geminids. But the method does not give significant results where there are three, four, or more radiants in simultaneous activity, as

---

* Öpik, observing the Perseid radiant with an aperture of 5 ins, field diameter $2\frac{1}{2}°$, on 1921 August 10 and 12, mapped 15 telescopic meteors ranging from mag 5·5 to 9·5.

occurs in the diffuse major showers and (at a different intensity level) in all observations of minor streams. Here, if reliance is placed on the intersection of flight directions alone, a great number of spurious intersections are obtained, arising from real differences in the radiants; and among this tangle of intersections the correct radiants or radiant sub-centres cannot be found.

Some authorities have secured results from such data by arbitrarily rejecting those meteors which did not conform to their view of where the radiant should be. Such a process is obviously worthless. The only method of treatment which has given some successful results has been that of Hoffmeister, in which reliable radiants have in certain cases been derived by a process of successive elimination. The observations of many years were considered together, and group radiants were determined in the usual way. Then those which did not recur in n or more years were rejected, and their constituent meteors were combined to form other groups, the process being continued through five such stages of elimination. The method has numerous disadvantages. Even if the basic assumption is correct that a given radiant should be expected to recur two or more times in n years (and this may be doubted), the method is extremely laborious and at the same time wasteful of a large proportion of the observational material. It does, however, represent to date (1953) the only work on group radiants which can be considered to give even partially reliable results.

Certainly the simple process described earlier in this section—by which group radiants were determined during the period 1833 to about 1930—yielded results that were quite unreliable. Historically, the inherent weakness of the method was obscured by errors of technique whose correction took many years. A brief summary of these is given below as a guide to the observer in the avoidance of known pitfalls:

(*i*) It is erroneous to combine, for group radiants, sets of observations made on different nights, when the Sun's longitude differs by, say, more than 2° or 3°. This fundamental mistake has vitiated most of the work of the older observers, who frequently based group radiants on observations gathered over periods of up to 30 days. Such radiants are quite worthless, and it was to correct these that the American Meteor Society's rules for group radiants were formulated by Olivier in 1916. These are enumerated in paragraph (*iii*) below, and are a reliable guide for the combination of observations.

(*ii*) It is quite legitimate, on the other hand, to combine sets of observations made in different years, but when the Sun's longitude was the same.

(*iii*) The A.M.S. rules, so far as they concern the combination of observations, are as follows:

(*a*) A radiant shall be determined by not less than four meteors whose projected paths all intersect within a circle of 2° diameter and which are all observed within a period of at most four hours on one night by one observer.

(*b*) Or, by three meteors on one night and at least two on the next night, seen during the same approximate hours of GMT, and all five intersecting as described in (*a*).

(*c*) Or, by one stationary meteor.

(*d*) Under no circumstances shall a meteor be used to determine a radiant point whose projected path passes more than $3\frac{1}{2}°$ from the adopted point, and it is recommended that $2\frac{1}{2}°$ should be adopted as the usual limit.

(*e*) Three meteors which fulfil condition (*a*) shall be considered enough to give a radiant in confirmation of one determined on the same date of a previous year, i.e. where L, the meteoric apex, differs by less than 2°.

These rules are considered to be valuable as a guide to the combination of observations, though they are not themselves sufficient for the determination of group radiants.

(*iv*) The correction for zenithal attraction must often be applied. The correction is greatest where ϵ (the elongation from the apex) is large and h (the radiant altitude) is small; for most purposes the correction may be neglected when it amounts to less than $1°0$ to $1°3$. Where the Z.A. correction is applied to the individual meteors, that part of rule (*a*) of paragraph (*iii*) which limits the period of observation to at most four hours may be ignored. The correction for diurnal aberration is less important, and may be neglected for the purpose of classifying meteors for group radiants.

But although the observer may be careful to avoid the errors committed by his predecessors, he is still faced with the inherent weakness of the method of group radiants discussed at the beginning of this section. Evidently additional criteria must be found to enable us to distinguish between true radiants and chance points (or centres) of intersection. It is probable that these criteria will be found in the hypothetical lengths of paths of meteors of varying magnitudes and radiant altitudes, from which the approximate angle of foreshortening of the path may be deduced.

15.16 The determination of real paths

From a good double observation of a meteor its real path in the atmosphere (and hence its height at every point along this path, and its individual radiant) may be computed. The normal heights of meteors are now well recognised, but collections of data on these heights are still of considerable value.

Ideal separation of observing stations is about 50–100 miles (see also section 15.3). If less than 20 miles the observational errors are too great; if more than about 120 miles, not only is identification more difficult but the errors of observation become progressively more harmful.

The paths of the observed meteors may be described in either of two ways:

(a) With reference to the stars, as already described in section 15.2.2; this is the better method.

(b) With reference to an artificial coordinate system, stationary with respect to the Earth, which is duplicated at the two stations. This is provided by a wire grid at each station, identical in construction and orientation. Similar orientation of the two grids can be obtained either by compass and level or by reference to the stars at a predecided moment, the observers' watches being synchronised. A convenient design of grid consists of five concentric wire circles, of radii 8·75, 17·63, 26·79, 39·40, and 46·63 units. Six sets of cross-wires divide the circles into twelve 30° zones, and provide rigidity. The eye position is defined by a small wire ring located on the axis of the grid at a distance of 100 units from its centre; it should be just large enough for the outermost ring to be visible through it when the eye is placed as close to it as is comfortable. From this position the diameters of the rings will subtend angles of 10°, 20°, 30°, 40°, and 50° respectively. Beginning and end points of any meteor observed through the grid are described in terms of position angle and distance from the centre of the grid, estimated to the nearest 0·1 division; time is given to the nearest 0·5 min.

The advantages of this method, compared with (a), are more continuous observation of the sky (since less time spent making the records), and the more convenient form for reduction of the observations. Method (a), on the other hand, has been proved to be of far superior accuracy.

The most persistent source of error in such work is the lack of simultaneity between the first seeing of the meteor by the two observers, so that their estimated beginning points correspond to no single position of the meteor. This error, however, is taken care of in Davidson's method of reduction (see below).

Reductions can be made by a variety of methods:

(a) A 'beginner's method', employing only simple trigonometry, is described below:

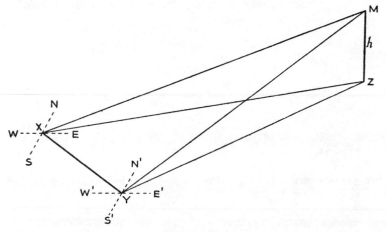

FIGURE 30

The observed RAs and Decs, or grid coordinates, from the two stations are first converted to altitude and azimuth.* If X, Y are the observing stations, and Z the point in the plane containing X and Y which is vertically below M, the beginning or end point of the path, then:

distance between the stations $= XY$
azimuth of X from Y $\quad = S'YX \quad$ or α
azimuth of Y from X $\quad =$ ext SXY or β
azimuth of meteor from Y $\quad =$ ext $S'YZ$ or γ
azimuth of meteor from X $\quad =$ ext SXZ or δ

all of which are known. Now

$$ZYX = \text{ext } S'YZ - S'YX = \gamma - \alpha$$
$$ZXY = \text{ext } SXY - \text{ext } SXZ = \beta - \delta$$
$$XZY = 180° - (ZYX + ZXY) = \epsilon$$

and

$$XZ = \frac{XY \sin (\gamma - \alpha)}{\sin \epsilon}$$

$$YZ = \frac{XY \sin (\beta - \delta)}{\sin \epsilon}$$

* Formulae for the commoner coordinate conversions will be found in *A.A.H.*, section 31.

Error in h due to neglecting the curvature of the Earth* can be brought within the range of ordinary and unavoidable observational error by adding to the observed altitudes MXZ and MYZ a quantity c whose values, dependent upon the values of XZ and YZ, are tabulated below:

XZ or YZ		c
150 miles		1·0
200	,,	1·5
250	,,	2·0
300	,,	2·0
350	,,	2·5
400	,,	3·0
450	,,	3·5
500	,,	3·5
550	,,	4·0
600	,,	4·5

Then the height of the meteor at point M can be independently derived from

$$h = XZ \tan (MXZ + c)$$
$$h = YZ \tan (MYZ + c)$$

and the mean taken.

M' and Z', respectively the other end point of the observed path and the ground point vertically beneath it, are derived in the same way, whence the length of the path is directly calculable. The weakness of this method is that it assumes the observations were simultaneous (i.e. both observers saw and described the same extent of the luminous path); nine times out of ten this condition is not satisfied, and the results are accordingly misleading.

(b) The neat method due to Davidson (B. 216) was designed to overcome this difficulty. The RA and Dec of the beginning and end points as observed from each of the two stations are first converted to azimuth and polar distance. These four positions are then referred to a system of rectangular coordinates (two horizontal, one vertical) set up on each station as origin. Since an observer often misses part of the luminous path immediately following the true beginning point, the larger of the two stations' z-coordinates (vertical) is taken as correct; since, on the other hand, an observer is unlikely to imagine he continues to see a meteor after its true end point, the smaller of the two z values is in this case taken.

Porter's simplification of this method, replacing the rectangular by equatorial coordinates, is described in B. 246 and is the method used by the B.A.A. computers. See also B. 247, 221, 260.

* Dip of 8 ins per mile, or 1 mile in 89.

(c) The best semi-graphical solution, employing a celestial globe and squared paper, is the so-called Newton-Denning or Tupman-King method; it is described in detail in B. 223 and 235. The essential stages are: first, the determination of the azimuth of the radiant (point of intersection on the star sphere of the two flight directions produced backward) and of the Earth point (i.e. the azimuth in which the altitude of the flight direction is zero) as seen from each station; these azimuths are then laid off from their respective stations plotted on squared paper, their point of intersection being the geographical position of the Earth point; secondly, the ground line of the meteor is laid off from the Earth point in the azimuth of the radiant; finally, the azimuths of the beginning and end points are drawn to intersect the ground line, and the two heights worked out by elementary trigonometry.

Summarised reductions of the B.A.A. Meteor Section's observations (heights of beginning and end points, length of real path, and velocity) are published periodically in *J.B.A.A.* and *Mem.B.A.A.* The reduction of meteor observations is a good introduction to astronomical computation generally, for those with a mathematical turn of mind.

15.17 The determination of meteor orbits

The requisite data are the apparent velocity and the radiant. Thence the geocentric velocity and radiant, and finally the heliocentric velocity and radiant, are calculated. From these the elements of the orbit are derived.

A graphical method described by Davidson (B. 220) involves the assumptions that the Earth's orbit is circular and that the meteor's velocity is parabolic; nevertheless, in most cases it is sufficiently accurate for the type of observation. All that is required is a 12-in celestial globe and a steel protractor at least 180° long, graduated in degrees.

See also B. 264–266 for a concise and useful account; also B. 236, 263, 219.

15.18 Meteor diary

15.18.1 Major streams: The data contained in the Table opposite refer to the major night-time meteor streams:

CLASSIFICATION OF STREAMS:

Meteor streams are classified under the following types (column 4 of Table opposite):

A. Streams giving regular annual meteor showers of good strength (ZHR 20–60) or intermediate strength (ZHR 10–20).

> *Examples:* Quadrantids, Lyrids, Perseids, Orionids, Geminids, and probably also the December Ursids.

B. Streams which have occasionally given exceptional meteor storms (ZHR 2000–30,000) but which are normally very weak.

> *Examples:* Leonids (period 33 years), Giacobinids (period 6·6 years).

C. Streams which have given occasional or periodic storms or rich returns in the past, but which are now extinct.

> *Examples:* Bielids, June Draconids (Pons-Winnecke meteors).

D. Major streams which owing to their latitude give very weak displays in this country.

> *Examples:* η Aquarids, δ Aquarids.

E. Streams only observable in daylight by radar techniques (see section 15.18.2).

F. Minor streams (see section 15.18.3).

Date UT	⊙	Stream		Radiant			ZHR *	LMT of Transit (UT)	Normal Limits
		Name	Type	α	δ	Type			
Jan. 4	282°9	Quadrantids	A	232	+50	Diffuse	40	8ʰ5	c. 24 hrs
Apr. 21	32	Lyrids	A	271	+33	Multiple centres	8 to 15	4·0	Apr. 20–22
May 6	45	η Aquarids	D	338	+ 1	Multiple centres?		7·6	May 4–13
June 29	97	June Draconids	C	231	+54	Diffuse		20·9	<24 hrs
July 28	125	δ Aquarids	D	342	−16	Diffuse		2·4	Jul. 25–Aug. 4
Aug. 12	139	Perseids	A	45	+58	Diffuse	50	5·6	Aug. 4–16
Oct. 10	196·3	Giacobinids	B	262	+54	Sharp?		16·2	<6 hrs
Oct. 21	208	Orionids	A	96	+15	Multiple centres?	10 to 20	4·4	Oct. 15–25
Nov. 14	232	Bielids	C	23	+43	Diffuse		22·0	?
Nov. 16	234	Leonids	B	152	+22	Sharp		6·5	Nov. 15–20 (?)
Dec. 13	261	Geminids	A	113	+32	Multiple centres	60	2·0	Dec. 9–13
Dec. 22	270	December Ursids	A?	207	+74	Sharp	18	7·7	c. 24 hrs

* The ZHR is given for type A showers only. For types B, C, and D refer to text below.

HOURLY RATES:

The hourly rate given in column 7 of the Table is the zenithal hourly rate at maximum. In order to forecast the HR at a given time it is necessary to know (*i*) the correction for radiant altitude, (*ii*) the rate of change of ZHR for the interval between the time of observation and the time of maximum, (*iii*) the annual variation in the intensity of the stream. Of these, (*ii*) and (*iii*) can only be stated with an approach to accuracy for the streams having sharp maxima, such as the Quadrantids and Giacobinids. In any case considerable statistical fluctuation in the tabulated values should be expected—particularly when the radiant is at a low altitude, and casual variations will have a correspondingly greater effect.

(*i*) Correction for radiant altitude:

The radiant altitude of the principal streams for an observer in latitude $+52°$ is given in the following Table at intervals of $t = \pm 0$, 1, 2, . . ., etc hours from the time of transit, and is based upon the radiant data in the Table on p. 245.

Altitude of Shower Radiants ($\phi = +52°$)

	Time from Transit in hours												
	0	1	2	3	4	5	6	7	8	9	10	11	12
Quadrantids	—	—	71	62	53	45	37	30	24	19	15	13	12
Lyrids	71	68	61	52	43	34	25	17	10	3	—	—	—
η Aquarids	—	—	—	—	—	10	1	—	—	—	—	—	—
δ Aquarids	22	21	17	12	4	—	—	—	—	—	—	—	—
Perseids	—	—	72	64	56	48	42	36	30	—	—	—	—
Giacobinids	—	—	72	63	55	47	39	33	27	22	19	17	16
Orionids	53	51	46	38	30	21	12	3	—	—	—	—	—
Leonids	60	58	52	44	35	26	17	8	1	—	—	—	—
Geminids	70	67	60	52	43	33	25	16	9	3	—	—	—
Dec. Ursids	—	67	65	61	57	53	49	45	42	39	37	36	35

The correction factor to be applied to the ZHR in order to correct for radiant altitude is given in the following critical Table, and is based on the expression

$$OHR = ZHR \sin (h + 6°)$$

Altitude	Factor	Altitude	Factor
	0·0		0·5
0·0		27·4	
	0·1		0·6
2·6		34·5	
	0·2		0·7
8·6		42·5	
	0·3		0·8
14·5		52·2	
	0·4		0·9
20·7		65·8	
	0·5		1·0
27·4		90·0	
	0·6		

In critical cases ascend*

This correction applies to visual work only—not to radar, where wholly different factors are involved.

(*ii*) *Correction for* $\Delta\odot$:

This correction is more uncertain. The correction curves for the Quadrantids and Giacobinids are quite well known, these being of short duration; the December Ursids are probably similar. They are less well established for the streams with long maxima, such as the Perseids and Geminids. The Table below gives the interval from the time of maximum in which the ZHR reaches a stated fraction of the ZHR at maximum:

	Units	$\Delta t-$		Max.	$\Delta t+$
		0·1	0·5	0·5	0·1
Quadrantids	hours	12	4	4	12
Lyrids	days	3?	1	1	3
Perseids	days	8	1	1	3
Giacobinids	hours	2·4	0·5	0·5	2·4
Orionids	days	8	5	5	8
Leonids	days	—	—	—	—
Geminids	days	3	1·0	0·8	1·2
Dec. Ursids	hours	12	4?	4?	12

* I.e. when the argument is one of the tabular values themselves, the functional value to take is the one immediately above, e.g. the factor for altitude 20°7 is 0·4, not 0·5.

(iii) Correction for annual variation:

(*a*) This does not apply to streams of types A and D, which are of fairly uniform annual richness. Occasional variations by a factor of ×2 or ×3 appear to be mainly of a random nature.

(*b*) The data for the recurrent streams are:

June Draconids: Associated with Pons-Winnecke's comet, period 6·1 years. The shower was discovered on 1916 June 28, ZHR *c*. 60. It made only one (perhaps three) known appearances, and is now extinct owing to the increase in *q* through perturbations.

October Draconids (Giacobinids): Associated with Giacobini's comet, period 6·6 years. The shower was discovered on 1926 October 9, ZHR *c*. 20. Rich returns (i.e. meteor storms) in 1933 and 1946; noteworthy return at sub-storm level (*c*. 200 per hour) in 1952.

Bielids: Associated with Biela's comet, period 6·6 years. Gave rich returns at major shower level frequently during the nineteenth century, with meteor storms on 1872 November 27 and 1885 November 27. Last known return in intermediate strength, 1899 November 24. Now extinct.

Leonids: Known from at least 1799. Associated with Tempel's comet, period 33·2 years. Major storms on 1833 November 13 and 1866 November 15. Owing to perturbations the 1899 return failed, but the shower returned at major shower intensity (ZHR *c*. 60) in 1932 and 1933, though far below storm intensity.

December Ursids: Possibly associated with comet Méchain-Tuttle. Discovered 1945 December 21 at major shower level (ZHR *c*. 100). In subsequent years has returned at 10–20 per hour.

15.18.2 Daylight streams: The following Table contains data concerning the principal daylight streams, i.e. those discovered and exclusively observable by radar techniques:

Maximum	⊙	Stream	α	δ	Transit HR	Normal limits
May 13	52°	υ Psc	17°	+26°	16	May 12–13
15	54	*o* Cet	26	− 3	25	May 14–23
June 8	77	ε Ari	46	+21	60	May 29–June 18
8	77	ζ Per	63	+21	40	June 1–16
27	95	β Tau	88	+17	25	June 24–July 5

The approximate date of maximum is given in column 1; usually it extends over many days. In column 5 is given the HR at transit for a receiver sensitivity adjusted to give approximately the HR of a visual observer under normal conditions.

15.18.3 Minor streams: The following Table includes the best of the minor streams found by duplicate observation mainly during the period 1946–1949; it is in no way a complete survey. These streams are all very weak, giving a ZHR at maximum of one meteor every one or two hours; the only exception is the Taurid system, which gives a ZHR of 5 or 6 over a long maximum.

Maximum	⊙	Stream	Radiant α δ	Normal limits
Apr. 9	19°	θ Vir	*196° −2°	Apr. 3–11
15	25	τ Her	*248 +46	Apr. 11–19
Jul. 26	123	θ Aql	*299 −3	Jul. 22–27
29	126	α Cap	307 −16	Jul. 23–31
Aug. 14	141	ζ Dra	261 +63	Aug. 14–16
14	141	θ Cyg	290 +54	Aug. 14–17
Sep. 8	165	δ Psc	8 +12	Sep. 5–11
30	187	ξ Psc	23 +2	Sep. 27–Oct. 3
30	187	ρ Cyg	325 +45	Sep. 27–Oct. 2
Oct. 11	198	ξ Ari	*36 +12	Oct. 2–16
21	207	ε Gem	*99 +26	Oct. 14–26
Nov. 4–9	225	Taurids	*55 +15	Oct. 26–Nov. 16

* These radiants exhibit the motion in longitude of approximately 1° per day that theory requires. The time interval in most cases is too short for the effect to be demonstrable.

SECTION 16

COMETS

16.1 Amateur work

Comets provide a fruitful field for amateur observers. The work includes:

(a) Observation of the appearance and structure of comets.
(b) Measurements of position, the fundamental data for the computers.
(c) Searching for new comets, and for returning periodic comets.
(d) Photometry.
(e) Spectroscopy (though with normal amateur equipment this is restricted to the brighter comets).
(f) Computation of orbits and ephemerides.

The observations may be made either visually or (see section 16.3) photographically.

The regular cometary observer will need to subscribe to the B.A.A. Circulars (50 p. per annum), which give early notification of cometary discoveries, reappearances, and other news.

Would-be members of the Comet Section of the B.A.A. are asked to supply the Director with the following information:

Details of equipment, including charts and catalogues available.
Types of work in which particularly interested.
Local observing conditions (horizon, artificial lights, etc).
Observational experience, and mathematical standard.
Approximate amount of time available.
Telephone number.

16.2 Visual observation

The continuous visual observation of comets is a necessary accompaniment of photography, since finer details and rapid changes cannot generally be so well recorded photographically. Observations of sudden developments should be reported immediately, and the wider the longitude distribution of observers the less likely it is that such developments will be missed.

As with the Moon and the planets, visual observation with a given aperture will show detail invisible in photographs taken with telescopes of many times larger aperture. Only with the smallest instruments is visual observation less useful than photographic, and even here this is far from being invariably the case.

Accurate timing of observations of position, and of sudden or rapid changes, is essential; an accuracy of one-tenth of a minute of time is usually sufficient. Other observations may be timed to the nearest minute and reported to one-tenth of a day.

For glimpsing the outermost regions of the tail very low magnifications, approaching M',* must be used. It is no uncommon experience to find that a comet (as also some very diffuse nebulae) can be clearly seen in the finder but is invisible in the main instrument. The general rule is to employ the smallest aperture that will show the comet clearly. Only when the nucleus and brighter central regions are being examined must the full aperture (and the highest magnification permitted by the atmospheric conditions) be used.

The visual observation of comets falls primarily into three categories:

(*a*) Structure (for which the head generally demands fairly high magnification—say about ×150—with progressively lower magnifications for the fainter outlying regions, so as to gain maximum contrast with the background):

Nucleus (not to be confused with the central condensation; the nucleus is typically either a small—few ″ arc—uniform disc with a sharp boundary, or a star-like point): single or multiple; if multiple, the relative positions of the components; disc or stellar; size of disc; sharp or diffuse.

Central condensation (if any): size and shape; if elliptical, p.a. of major axis.

Coma: size and shape (variations in these); hoods or haloes (if any): diameters, development, p.a. of major axes (if elliptical), whether separated by dark interspaces; jets (if any): length, p.a. (of tangent to the jet at the nucleus, if curved), p.a. and distance of several points on a curved jet (if possible).

Anomalous tails (i.e. directed towards the Sun): length p.a. or co-ordinates, curvature.

Tail: length and position (p.a. and distance, or coordinates, of points along its axis); any distortions or divisions; condensations: position

* Minimum useful magnification: see *A.A.H.*, section 3.3.

measures as often as possible; any fluctuations of light (points or areas) moving along the tail—probably physiological.

(b) Stellar magnitude of nucleus, and integrated magnitude of the whole comet (section 16.6); variations in these.

(c) Position (section 16.4): the point to measure is the nucleus, if present; failing that, the central condensation of the coma. If the comet is of sufficient angular size, its outline may be transferred at intervals to a tracing from a suitable star chart. This, however, is best done photographically.

16.3 Photographic observation

Comets should be photographed at every possible opportunity (plates being exposed in duplicate), so as to get as complete a record as possible both of position and of brightness variations. Structural detail is not likely to be shown effectively by amateur equipment except in the case of the largest comets, but given a reasonable plate-scale and adequate exposure, a comet's position, shape, and brightness can be deduced at leisure from a photographic plate with an accuracy at least comparable with that of visual observations. Measures of position* are still possible when a comet is too faint for effective visual observation, and can be made to within 2″ or 3″ if a machine is used, or to within 30″ or 1′ (according to plate-scale) with nothing more elaborate than a millimetre scale.

Prints from all plates should be submitted with the written records (or, at least, the date, time, exposure, and instrumental details of each), since any one of them may fill a gap in the series of other observers.

Newly announced discoveries may often be picked up photographically before they are even visible in the guide telescope. If the announcement includes information regarding the comet's motion, allow for this in the guiding; otherwise the image will be, at best, blurred, and at worst will not register at all. If d is the comet's diameter, and x mins the minimum exposure needed to record it, then no increase of exposure will show it if its motion is greater than d in x mins unless the camera follows it. Therefore displace the camera in the direction, and at the velocity, of its announced motion.

When searching for a returning comet with a battery of cameras, displace them in the direction, and by the amount, of its anticipated motion. Even partial elimination of its image's drift across the plate may make all the difference between visibility and invisibility. Inevitably,

* The possibilities of plate measurement by amateur observers are discussed in *A.A.H.*, section 20.3.

any image recorded thus will be so blurred as to be useless for any purpose other than the establishment of its mere existence; but this is all that is required in the case of rediscoveries. It is helpful to know the magnitude threshold of each camera of the battery for various exposures.

Fogging* is especially relevant to cometary photography, since comets are often near the Sun. The relation between exposure and visual magnitude varies considerably from comet to comet owing to different relative visible and actinic brightness; often comets are remarkably rich in actinic wavelengths. Long dewcaps help to reduce the speed of fogging to some extent. Experience with a given instrument, familiar plates, past successes and failures—these are the only reliable guide to estimating exposures in relation to fogging.

It is particularly important in the case of comets to record the times of beginning and end of each exposure.

As regards equipment, excellent work has been done with portrait lenses: 10 to 20 ins focal length is desirable; the smaller the f/ratio the better, $f/2$–$f/5$ being the suitable range. The recording of detail will usually necessitate use of the primary focus of the telescope. A shorter-F portrait lens is also useful for comets which develop long tails; projection lenses (e.g. F 5–6 ins, $f/4$–$f/5$ are quite cheap, and give a good wide field) are also recommended for long tails. Or two cameras can be used, their axes offset so as to cover the whole tail on overlapping plates. Where a single camera is used, it should be offset in the direction of the tail so that when the head is at the cross-webs of the guide telescope the maximum extent of tail lies across the plate area of best definition, i.e. the image is central in the camera field when the head is central in the guide field (Figure 31(a)).

Where a nucleus or small central condensation is visible it is best to

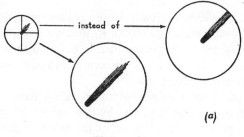

instead of

(a)

FIGURE 31

* The whole subject of sky fog, and magnitude and exposure limits, is discussed in greater detail in *A.A.H.*, section 20.5.

dispense with cross-webs—which are necessarily thick, and therefore hide the nucleus—and to guide by keeping the nucleus central on the tip of a tapered pointer, the so-called 'toffee-apple' method (Figure 31 (b)).

There is a variety of methods of guiding on a comet lacking a nucleus or central condensation (and a nucleus is usually absent just when most needed—with faint comets):

(a) Treat the coma like a star, and attempt to keep the intersection of the webs superimposed upon the same point in the image—the least satisfactory method.

(b)

FIGURE 31

(b) Compute the direction of motion and arrange the webs (which can afford to be rather thicker than usual) so that the coma is tangent to them and its direction of motion bisects the diametrically opposite quadrant (Figure 31 (c)).

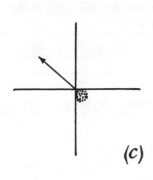
(c)

FIGURE 31

(c) The best method of all is to compute the comet's angular motion; set the cross-webs of a filar micrometer on a guide star; orient the micrometer to the p.a. of the comet's motion; at pre-calculated intervals (depending on the comet's angular velocity) displace the stellar image in the direction opposite to this motion, and bring it back to the intersection of the webs by means of the slow motions.

16.4 Measures of position

The accuracy required in order to justify the measuring of a comet's position depends to a large extent on how well it has already been observed. Where a good preliminary orbit has been established, it is a waste of time—that of the observer as well as of the computer, whose chief grouse is always at the large number of poor observations—to make and report rough eye-estimates of position. Where a preliminary orbit is not available, on the other hand, or where a check is required on an ephemeris, approximate measures of position can be valuable. Even an eye-estimate of the comet's position relative to known stars can be useful if it should happen to fall in a gap in the series of available micrometer measures, or before the first or after the last of these (e.g. when the comet is so near the Sun as to be barely visible). At all other times an accuracy of a few " arc must be achieved if the measures are to be of any value to the computer, and even so he will ignore such observations in favour of any likely to be more accurate. All observations claiming precision must be timed to the nearest 0·1 min.

Unless circle positions can be relied upon, good charts are essential to ensure the correct identification of the field stars. Given accurate circles, a diagram drawn at the telescope can be checked subsequently with the B.D. Catalogue (even without charts), and provides useful confirmation; or the comet's position can be indicated on a tracing from B. 409 or similar atlas.

(a) By eye:

Made by reference to field stars, the magnification being adjusted so that there are, if possible, not less than 5 or 6 such stars. Never fail to take advantage of the fact that the comet may lie on or close to the line joining two stars: the eye is capable of surprisingly accurate estimates of such a configuration and of the comet's distance along this line, expressed as a fraction of the total distance between the stars. If the comet is swift-moving in a region of the sky rich in stars, one or two such favourable configurations may be observable per night.

Otherwise recourse must be had to the less easily estimated distance of the comet from each of the field stars, expressed as a fraction of the separation of any two of them, chosen in each case according to convenience. In the case of the field illustrated below, for instance (comet at x), it may be judged that

$$xa = \tfrac{3}{4}ca$$
$$xc = 3bd$$
$$xb = \tfrac{1}{2}ab = \tfrac{3}{5}cb$$

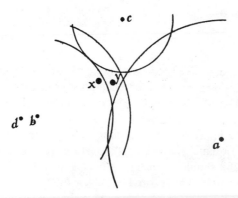

The field having been identified, the reference stars are plotted for any convenient (e.g. Catalogue) epoch,* the position of the comet plotted (y in Figure 32), its RA and Dec determined, and the precession correction applied to bring the position up to the mean equinox of the year of observation.

An accuracy of the order of 1′ can be achieved by this bow-and-arrow method; this may be superior to direct readings of the position circles unless these are finely divided and the mounting is very precisely adjusted.

As an alternative to the field sketch, $\Delta\delta$ between the comet and the comparison stars may be estimated in terms of the known field diameter, and $\Delta\alpha$ measured by the method of transits across a vertical (N–S) wire.

(b) By micrometer:

Any form of micrometer, even the simplest, can be used to advantage. Considering the ease with which a ring or cross-bar micrometer can be home-made, and the simplicity of the equipment with which it can be used,† no amateur intending to observe comets seriously need make use of the rather cumbersome and doubtfully accurate methods described above.

With a home-made cross-bar micrometer the position of a comet with a well-defined nucleus can be determined to within 2″ or 3″; if there is no nucleus, and especially if the coma is strongly elliptical, the inaccuracy may be as large as 10″, or one-sixth that to be expected from the eye method.

Owing to the dependence of the accuracy of the measures upon the nature of the nucleus (bright, faint, multiple, non-existent), this should always be specified in the observation record.

(c) By photography:

Methods of plate measurement adaptable to amateur needs are discussed in *A.A.H.*, section 20.3.

16.5 Comet seeking

Well suited to amateur effort by its instrumental requirements. Indeed, the most valuable items of equipment are not instrumental at all, but the ability to persevere for long periods without encouragement, and a retina of at least average sensitivity to faint illuminations.

---

* Durchmusterung positions, especially of the fainter stars, should be treated with some reserve, since they are not too reliable. Generally speaking, comparison stars brighter than mag 9 should be used wherever possible.

† See, e.g., *A.A.H.*, sections 18.4, 18.5.

Since 1600 some 600 comets have been discovered and observed well enough for their orbits to be determined. Between 1800 and 1940, 105 comets were visible to the naked eye—approximately 20% of the total. Comets are discovered at a current average rate of about 5 a year; 1947 (14 discovered, 9 of these being new) and 1948 (10 new discoveries) were exceptionally fruitful.

In recent years the ever-increasing use of photography has to some extent spoilt the pitch for the visual comet hunter, and it is no longer true to say that the vast majority of new comets are visible with a 3-in or 4-in at the time of their discovery. The picture has changed very considerably since the days of Caroline Herschel or Pons.* Even Denning† nowadays seems grossly over-optimistic when he estimated that comet seeking, if 'diligently pursued by a capable observer', might produce 2 discoveries per year, with the possibility of 300 fruitless hours at the telescope during the period. Nevertheless, such achievements as Peltier's, with a 6-in comet-seeker, or the successes of the Skalnaté Pleso observers (using 25×100 Somer binoculars), show that the field is by no means closed to the visual observer.

The effect in quite recent years of the large photographic reflectors, of the increasing number of Schmidts in operation, of survey cameras of all sorts exposing routine plates, and of such photographic programmes as those connected with minor planets, stellar proper motions, etc, can be seen by comparing Figures 33 and 34. The former is an arrangement by magnitudes of the cometary discoveries announced in the I.A.U. Circulars during the 23 years from October 1925 to December 1948. It will be seen that the majority of these comets were mag 8–13 at discovery, no allowance being made for the fact that the magnitudes were probably under-estimated (i.e. too faint) in many cases; they were thus within the range of quite small instruments.

Figure 34 shows the magnitude distribution at discovery of the 56 lettered comets of the 6 years 1946–1951.‡ The lower histogram, compared with Figure 33, shows how the camera has been instrumental in dredging up fainter and fainter comets, and the comparative infrequency of visual discoveries nowadays (10 visual discoveries, all brighter than

* The latter's record of 37 independent discoveries is still unbeaten, and likely to remain so.

† Over a period of years, Denning discovered 5 comets at a rate of 1 per 119 hours' systematic sweeping.

‡ Excluding mistaken identifications and the two 'freak' comets—1947*n*, which was already about mag −1 when first seen, and 1948*l*, discovered during total solar eclipse at a distance of less than 2° from the Sun's centre, when its magnitude also was better than 0.

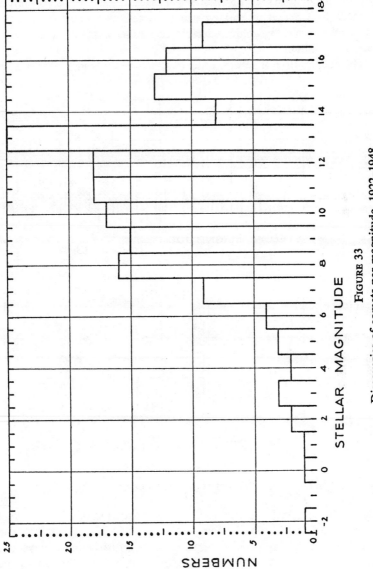

FIGURE 33

Discoveries of comets per magnitude, 1922–1948

mag 10·5, compared with 46 photographic discoveries ranging from mag 8 to 21). From the upper histogram it can be seen that over this period the majority of new comets were included in the magnitude range 9–14, whereas returning periodic comets were usually picked up by the large photographic reflectors and other cameras when about mag 16 or fainter.

The cooperation of several observers, between whom a large area of

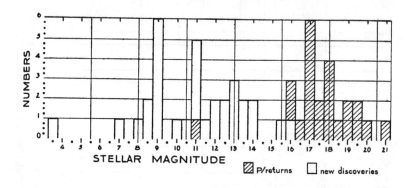

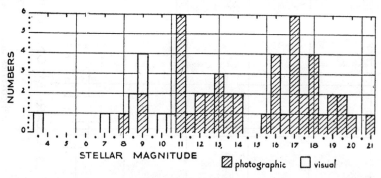

FIGURE 34

Discoveries of comets per magnitude, 1946–1951

sky can be parcelled out without wasteful duplication of effort, is likely to be fruitful in this—as in many another—field of observation. The B.A.A. had a good record for cometary discoveries in its early days, but more recently the cometary 'ashes' seem to have migrated across the Channel and the Atlantic.

Instrumentally, the most important factor is aperture. Not less than 4 ins is desirable, and an 8-in or 10-in reflector immensely increases the chances of success. Employing the corrected magnitude thresholds arrived at in *A.A.H.*, section 1.1 (columns (*e*) and (*f*) of the Table on p. 28), and assuming that the threshold for comets is 2 mags higher than for stars, it would appear from Figure 34 that 5 ins or 5½ ins aperture will show at the time of their discovery about 40% of all comets (including those discovered photographically), and about 2 out of every 3 new comets.

Focal length is not relevant to light grasp, although it is sometimes supposed that the large relative aperture of 'comet-seekers' contributes in some way analogous to camera 'speed' to increased brightness of extended images. On the contrary, F does not appear in the expression for the telescopic brightness of an extended image, but only in that for the photographic intensity.* Hence the brightness of an extended image is not increased by reducing F (the claims of some manufacturers of 'comet-seekers' notwithstanding), and the advantages of a small f/ratio for comet hunting are to be sought elsewhere: in the possibility of utilising the wide fields offered by LP oculars without increasing the diameter of the field lens to an unmanageable degree. Chromatic aberration, which would be intolerable with high powers when an ordinary Huyghenian is used with, say, a f/9 comet-seeker, is in fact not objectionable with the magnifications under about ×40 which are commonly used for sweeping. With a highly corrected ocular, even smaller f/ratios could of course be used.† Oculars providing flat fields, well defined to the edges, are most suitable for this work.

Large aperture (with low limiting magnitude) and short focal length (allowing wide fields) are therefore the instrumental characteristics to go for. A typical 3-in, f/9 comet-seeker, magnifying about ×20 (which is well over the safety margin, being about $2M'$), gives a field of nearly 3°. The magnitude threshold should be at least as low as 9, and sufficient magnification should be used to show a nebulous object 2′ in diameter. The following objects (all of which resemble telescopic comets with different apertures) should be clearly shown by any instrument intended for comet seeking: NGC 1068, 1501, 1514, 2022, 2392, 2440, 3242, 3379, 3587, 4472, 4736, 5024, 5272, 6093, 6341, 6402, 6779, 7089, 7099.‡

* See, respectively, *A.A.H.*, section 1.3, equation (*a*), and section 1.6.

† See *A.A.H.*, section 8.2.1.

‡ The following nebulae and clusters were originally described as 'cometic' by William Herschel (NGC numbers):

57	2592	3342	3872
524	3070	3423	4032
596	3078	3491	4578
1055	3166	3640	5248
1579	3169	3822/3825	

From *A.A.H.*, section 1.3, equation (*a*), it is apparent not only that a $f/3$ and a $f/15$ telescope will yield equally bright cometary images with a given magnification, providing that their apertures are the same, but also that two telescopes of unequal apertures D_1 and D_2 will yield equally bright images with magnifications M_1 and M_2 respectively, provided that $D_1 : M_1 :: D_2 : M_2$. The absolute magnification, rather than the magnification per inch of aperture, is therefore the important consideration. To reduce the magnification until it approaches M' is to run the risk of losing small comets through insufficient angular size to catch the eye; under about $\times 20$ there is also the wastage of time caused by mistaking small groups of faint stars for nebulous objects meriting HP examination. $\times 20$ may be taken as the absolute minimum with apertures up to about 4 ins, after which a magnification of from $1\frac{1}{2}M'$ to $2\frac{1}{2}M'$ should be used. The danger of over-magnification (quite apart from the reduction of the field) is the possibility of losing the comet owing to reduced contrast between it and the background.* Hence with any comet there is, depending upon its size and brightness, an optimum magnification.

Nevertheless, for general sweeping the following figures represent an effective compromise:

Aperture	Magnification
3–4 ins	$\times 20$
5	22–37
6	27–45
7	32–52
8	36–60

et cetera

In all cases the field diameter should not be less than about 1°5, and if it is nearer 3° so much the better, since four times the area of sky can be covered in the same time. The problem of arranging for wide-field eyepieces with all but the smallest instruments of normal f/ratio is referred to in *A.A.H.*, section 3.10.

Regular sweeping, carefully and systematically carried out, is the mode of working most likely to bring success. Even one hour's sweeping every clear night (atmospheric transparency is the *sine qua non*) of the moonless half of each month is better than spasmodic sessions of several hours' duration; a single constellation swept over with such care that the observer may be confident that it contains no comet within reach of his telescope is preferable to a much wider area skimpily covered. The beginning of each moonless period should not be missed,

* See also *A.A.H.*, section 1.3.

since any comet present may have brightened considerably since the area was last observed.

All comets must at some time pass near (angularly) to the Sun, and the majority of new comets are inside the orbit of Mars before they are spotted; furthermore they increase in brightness as they approach perihelion. Hence the western or NW sky should be swept as soon as it is quite dark, and the eastern or NE sky before sunrise (in the S hemisphere, W and SW, and E and SE, respectively); sweeping should be started in the evening, and finished in the morning, well outside the period of twilight. The low northern sky during the summer months is similarly a good region to sweep. Regions about 90° from the Sun should be given second priority, and both the plane and the poles of the Milky Way avoided; in such regions as Coma, Ursa Major, and Virgo the concentration of faint nebulae is so great that an undue proportion of the available observing time will be spent with one's nose in the catalogues. As sweeping moves further from the region of the Sun it should be carried out more and more carefully, since any comet encountered is likely to be faint and angularly small.

Despite such general indications, however, the truth remains that a new comet may appear in any part of the sky whatever.

Sweeps should be made slowly enough to permit the scrutiny of all parts of each successive field by indirect vision. Sweep, say, 20° in RA or azimuth; then alter the Dec or altitude setting of the telescope by not more than two-thirds of the diameter of the field, and sweep back again; this back and forth sweeping of overlapping strips is continued throughout the period of observation.

The sky contains innumerable objects (nebulae, clusters, and small star groups*) which under low magnification resemble telescopic comets; it is essential, in the interests of time-saving, to work out a quick method of checking these as they are swept up:

(a) An ocular adaptor, which allows the HP scrutiny of each suspicious object without incessant changing of oculars and re-focusing, is invaluable. Failing a rotating adaptor (e.g. B. 315), in which the alternative eyepieces are ready mounted, a great deal of time can be saved by scrapping the screw fitting of the oculars, mounting them instead in sections of brass tube which slip into the draw-tube; refocusing can be avoided by fixing flanges or stops on the eyepiece extensions in the required positions for a given setting of the drawtube adjustment.†

* Ghosts of bright stars are not likely to give any trouble, since the telescope is moving during sweeping, and the consequent motion of the ghost relative to the image of the star producing it is immediately noticeable.

† See also *A.A.H.*, section 22.9.

(*b*) If the instrument is fitted with circles, it is probably quickest to refer straight to a catalogue of nebulae and clusters; Dreyer's NGC (B. 543) is probably the most suitable.

(*c*) If the instrument is not fitted with circles, the identification of the field on a star chart, the determination of the approximate RA and Dec of the object, and finally reference to the catalogue, is a long process. Reference to a chart being quicker than to a catalogue, it is a good plan to keep a set of charts showing stars to mag 9 or thereabouts, and to insert in ink beforehand those NGC objects in the area of the night's sweeping which might be mistaken for a comet; any other object which is suspicious in the LP sweeping ocular is also inserted, in pencil, at the telescope. Before the next observing session the pencilled additions (it being assumed that their non-cometary nature has been established) are also inked in. Recommended charts for this purpose, B. 409, 414, 426, 435. As experience is gained, reference to charts and catalogues will become less and less frequent.

An occurrence with which the comet seeker soon becomes familiar is the passage across the moving field of a faint though perfectly visible nebulous object which vanishes as soon as the motion of the telescope is arrested for it to be more carefully inspected. This curious effect of a faint enough object being visible only while its image is moving relatively to the field has never been satisfactorily explained. It is quite independent of the indirect vision effect, since such an object is often perfectly visible to direct vision while in motion across the field. By the same token, it has nothing to do with motion of its image across the retina. A possible analogous example of apparently increased contrast between an object and its surroundings by the introduction of movement is the varying visibility of a page of print through a sheet of plain paper laid upon it: with a sheet of the right thickness it will be found that the print beneath is quite invisible when the sheet is lying motionless on it, and perfectly visible, even legible, when the sheet is moved about.

When an object not clearly non-cometary under HP is discovered, an accurate map of the field must be made; the field must be readily identifiable (RA and Dec if fitted with circles, or otherwise tied to some easily recognisable star) and the position of the object relative to the nearest three field stars put down with the greatest precision possible; a couple of micrometer measures of $\Delta\alpha$ and $\Delta\delta$ are better still. The field is then reobserved after the lapse of an hour or so; if no trace of motion on the part of the object is detectable with the HP ocular, it is almost certainly not a comet; in most cases $\frac{1}{4}$ hr is a long enough interval for change of position to become perceptible.* As a matter of routine, it is well to start each night's session with a check-up on any unidentified objects, apparently motionless, that were found during the previous night. An object showing no change of position relative to the stars after 24 hrs, in a HP ocular, is certainly not a comet.

Once proper motion has been confirmed, the discovery should be reported with the minimum of delay, so that other observers may be notified and observations in all terrestrial longitudes be initiated as early as possible (also in the interests of establishing priority). The announcement should be made by telegram or phone to the nearest observatory (in the British Isles, to the Royal Greenwich Observatory, Hurstmonceaux, Sussex, or to the Director of the Comet Section of the B.A.A.). See also section 16.7.

16.6 Photometric observations

The laws governing the variations in the brightness of comets are still imperfectly understood, a fact not unconnected with the practical difficulties involved in obtaining accurate observational data.

Presumably the apparent brightness of a comet varies inversely as the square of its distance both from the observer and from the Sun, in so far as it shines by reflected light. That is to say, its brightness at any moment will be proportional to

$$\frac{1}{r^2 \Delta^2}$$

where r is its heliocentric distance and Δ its geocentric. If it is further assumed that the proportion of its total radiation which consists of emission is produced through the agency of solar radiation acting upon the material in the nucleus, we might expect its brightness due to this factor to vary with $1/r^2$. Hence the preliminary expression for the brightness of a comet is

$$b = \frac{b_0}{r^4 \Delta^2} \quad \ldots \quad \ldots \quad \ldots \quad (1)$$

where b is its observed brightness, and b_0 a constant.

However, no comet behaves accurately in accordance with this expression, which has to be made more general:

$$b = \frac{b_0}{r^n \Delta^2} \quad \ldots \quad \ldots \quad \ldots \quad (2)$$

* A daily motion of only $1°$ is equivalent to a displacement of $2''\!.6$ per minute. This would be clearly perceptible in 12 minutes ($0''\!.5$) providing there are reasonably nearby stars for comparison.

where the value of the exponent n is different for different comets, and even for a given comet may vary (e.g. before and after perihelion); and the fractions of the total brightness due to reflected light and to solar action are respectively proportional to

$$\frac{1}{r^2 \Delta^2} \quad \text{and} \quad \frac{1}{r^{n-2}}$$

Expression (2), converted to terms of stellar magnitudes and adopting the more convenient logarithmic form, becomes

$$m = m_0 + 2 \cdot 5n \log r + 5 \log \Delta$$

where $m =$ observed magnitude,

$m_0 =$ magnitude when $r = \Delta = 1$, or $b = b_0$.

Values of m for different values of r and Δ are given by observation, and m_0 and n are derived by the method of least squares.

The brightness of the majority of comets is at any rate roughly represented by the so-called 'r^4 law' or 'r^6 law'; i.e. by putting $n = 4$ or $n = 6$ in equation (2) above, we obtain, respectively,

$$m = m_0 + 10 \log r + 5 \log \Delta$$
$$m = m_0 + 15 \log r + 5 \log \Delta$$

Generally the former is likely to be more correct for new comets (parabolic), and the latter for short-period comets.

The different values of m_0 for different comets presumably reflect differences in their physical and chemical composition, but other factors must be looked for to explain, *inter alia*:

(a) Fluctuations unrelated to Δ occurring in comets whose eccentricity is so small that r is also insufficiently variable to account for them. For example, Comet Schwassmann-Wachmann, 1925*ii*, $e = 0 \cdot 142$, r varying by only 1·8 A.U., whose average magnitude of 18 is liable to sudden decreases of several mags—in one case a brightening of 5 mags within 4 days. 1925*ii* is visible at aphelion, and has been continuously observed since its discovery.

(b) Fluctuations occurring when r is so large that the temperature is too low for the expulsion of gaseous material from the nucleus, as a result of solar heating, to be feasible. For example, at mean solar distance Comet Whipple-Fedtke, 1942*g*, has a temperature in the neighbourhood of $-160°C$; yet the presence of gaseous material in comets is proved spectroscopically.

(c) Sudden decreases in brightness, not susceptible of explanation by the hypothesis that seeks to account for some fluctuations in terms of collision with meteor swarms, or of that which suggests that ultraviolet radiation or streams of ionised particles from the Sun produce an excitation effect in the gaseous material of the coma and tail. As regards the latter hypothesis, a possible correlation was established between the sudden brightening of Comet Whipple by 3 mags with solar activity in February 1943, at a time when both r and Δ were increasing.

(d) The fading of many comets before they reach perihelion.

(e) The rough periodicity in the light variation of many comets, investigated by Bobrovnikoff (B. 276). Comet Whipple-Fedtke, for example, brightened during the 1943 return five times, these exhibiting a periodicity of roughly 30 days (B. 279).

The photometric behaviour of a comet is most conveniently studied in terms of the difference of its observed brightness from that predicted, that is, of $O-C$, where C is the computed value of its magnitude at suitable intervals, and O is the corresponding observed value. A plot of the values of $O-C$ will show clearly the nature and extent of any anomalous variations of brightness. The calculated values are derived as follows. Suppose that on a given date

$$\left.\begin{array}{l} \Delta_1 = 1\cdot126 \\ r_1 = 1\cdot626 \end{array}\right\} \text{ from the ephemeris}$$

$$m_1 = 6\cdot7 \qquad \text{from observation}$$

It is required to find m_2, the comet's magnitude on some subsequent date. From the ephemeris, for this latter date,

$$\Delta_2 = 2\cdot542$$
$$r_2 = 2\cdot321$$

Then[*] $\qquad \log r_2^4 \Delta_2^2 - \log r_1^4 \Delta_1^2 = 0\cdot4\,(m_2 - m_1)$

hence $\qquad 2\cdot2730 - 0\cdot9474 = 0\cdot4\,(m_2 - 6\cdot7)$

$$m_2 = 10\cdot01$$

The r^6 law would in this case yield $m_2 = 10\cdot76$.

The 'Light' of a comet is given in ephemerides that have been telegraphed. Since the telegraphic code has to cover minor planet discoveries the 'Light' is derived from the proportion

$$\frac{r^2\Delta^2 \text{ at discovery}}{r^2\Delta^2 \text{ at ephemeris date}}$$

Although not really satisfactory for comets, this quantity does indicate if the brightness is likely to be increasing or decreasing.

[*] From equation (1), p. 248, and *A.A.H.*, section 1.7, equation (e).

When a nucleus is present, its magnitude can be estimated by any of the visual methods employed by variable star observers. Except when the comet is faint, and showing little coma, the photographic method tends to be unreliable, since the photographic image of the nucleus is probably several times larger than the true image and therefore includes light from the surrounding central condensation.

The brightness of a comet is, however, normally taken to mean the integrated magnitude of the coma, and such estimates are very much more difficult to make. Comparisons of the comet with nebulae or clusters of known magnitude (B. 548, 552) can at times yield good estimates of the integrated magnitude, but this method is necessarily limited in its scope. The usual, and most satisfactory, method of making visual estimations of the integrated magnitude of a comet is to compare it with extrafocal stellar images, expanded till their angular size is similar to that of the comet's focused image. Two applications of this method are available:

(*a*) (*i*) Observe the comet, memorising its brightness and angular size.
(*ii*) Rack out the drawtube till the images of the field stars are of the same size as the focused image of the comet.
(*iii*) Attempt to find one or more nearby stars, as nearly as possible at the same altitude as the comet, the brightness of whose expanded images matches that of the comet. If their altitude is much different from that of the comet, a correction for atmospheric absorption must be made.
(*iv*) Take the position of each comparison star (circles or chart) and identify it later. If brighter than mag 9 it is most likely to be in the Henry Draper Catalogue (B. 498, 499), but with faint comets the difficulty of obtaining the magnitudes of the comparison stars is a perennial source of trouble, and method (*b*) will probably have to be used.
(*b*) (*i*) and (*ii*) as before.
(*iii*) Still carrying the memory of the comet's brightness in mind, swing the telescope on to the NPS (B. 479, 483, 485, 486, 488, 493) and match it with a star of known magnitude. Allowance must in this case be made for the difference in altitude.

Several independent estimations should be made during the course of each night's work.

Factors affecting accuracy include:

(*a*) Nearness of suitable comparison stars, permitting the comparisons to be made quickly.

(*b*) Brightness of the comet: the brighter it is, the further one will probably have to look for comparison stars; on the other hand, if it is fainter than about mag 9 the mags of the comparison stars may have to be established by comparison with the NPS.

(*c*) Number and brightness of the comparison stars: ideally not less than three should be used—one slightly brighter than the comet, one slightly fainter, and one matching.

(*d*) Altitude of the comparison stars must be approximately the same as the comet's—or the necessary correction made.

(*e*) Comparison stars should be of roughly the same colour as the comet, i.e. in most cases of types B, A, or F.

(*f*) The derived magnitude will depend heavily on the angular expanse of comet visible, and this in turn depends upon the instrument used. The diameter of Comet Schaumasse (1951), for example, was given as 8' in ordinary telescopes and eyepieces, and at the same time was seen as 20' diameter in a finder, while a photoelectric photometer recorded it over a diameter of 160'. Under such circumstances, more or less true of all comets, the term 'integrated magnitude' loses its meaning.

It was in an endeavour to avoid this last source of error that Merton recently proposed a method based on a standard angular area of comet, suggested as $1'/\Delta$ (Δ=geocentric distance), which would roughly correspond with a fixed volume of comet at different times. 1' arc was chosen since it gives an area which most observers can observe in most comets, and therefore eliminates the uncertain and often large peripheral area which may or may not be seen and recorded. The technique is to expand the image of a nearby star, not until it is the same *size* as the image of the comet, but until its surface *brightness* matches that of the comet's central condensation. The diameter of the expanded image is measured, and the light for the standard $1'/\Delta$ area computed and translated into magnitudes.*

The consistency of the results is as important as their absolute accuracy, and with experience a consistency of about one-third of a magnitude may be hoped for. The absolute values of the derived mags will be much wider of the mark—by as much, in difficult cases, as 2 or even 3 mags—since differences of brightness in extended images are much harder to perceive and estimate accurately than those between point images. Factors affecting the consistency of the results include:

(*a*) Nature of the background against which the comet, with its extended image and indefinite boundary, is observed. A bright ground

* *Trans. I.A.U.*, **8**, 1952; see Commission 15.

will appear to dim a comet out of proportion to the dimming of star images, though this effect is reduced by placing the latter out of focus. Moonlight, haze, high cloud, and the nature of the stellar background all introduce variable factors into a set of measures made at different times, and must therefore be specified in the observational record.

(b) Magnification, for the same reason, affects the results, since increased magnification dilutes the extended image more than the point images; it likewise must always be recorded. It is usually wise to use the lowest magnification that permits easy observation of the comet.

(c) Aperture and type of instrument must be specified. If more than one instrument is used during the observations of the same comet (e.g. naked eye and binoculars, binoculars and telescope, or telescope with reduced and full aperture) a series of overlap estimates should be made to determine the systematic difference, if any, between them. Speaking very generally (since the angular size of the coma is also relevant), the limiting magnitude for comets, with a given aperture, is about 2 mags higher than for stars. The normal tendency is to under-estimate the brightness of a comet, partly, no doubt, owing to neglect of this higher threshold in the case of extended objects; announcements of discoveries not infrequently under-quote the brightness by as much as 2 mags.

(d) The observational record should contain sufficient indication of the photometric method used, and the identity of the comparison stars.

Though the use of extrafocal images for comparison represents an improvement upon that of focused images, a telescopic comet (or the head of a brighter one) is nevertheless very unlike the comparison objects, both as regards the intensity gradient across its diameter and the definiteness of its boundary. A system of instrumental photometry, giving more consistent results than the stellar comparison method, might be based upon the injection into the field of a comparison image more closely resembling the comet.

The whole subject of cometary brightness is still in a rudimentary state, and more observational data are urgently required for discussion. There is great scope here for amateur work, both in the accumulation of reliable data and in the investigation of possible correlations between cometary fluctuations and, for example, spectrohelioscopic solar events.

16.7 Communication of observations

If, for the announcement of a cometary discovery, a telegraphic code is not used, the telegram should include the following data:

(a) Nature of object.

(*b*) Position: For a preliminary announcement an accuracy of 2′ or 3′ is good enough to allow the object to be identified. This order of accuracy can be obtained for α by timing the interval between the transits of the object and of a known star at a vertical (N–S) web in the eyepiece, and for δ by eye estimation of $\varDelta\delta$ from a known star based upon the known field diameter. If the telegram is followed up with a chart of the comet's position, ensure that (*i*) the field is made readily identifiable by linking it to some nearby bright star or stars, (*ii*) the relative positions of comet and field stars are put down as accurately as possible, (*iii*) the scale and orientation of the chart are given.

(*c*) Direction (p.a.) and estimated daily rate of motion.

(*d*) Estimated integrated magnitude.

(*e*) Whether there is a nucleus; if so, estimated stellar magnitude.

(*f*) Whether there is a tail; if so, direction (p.a.) and length.

(*g*) Name and address of discoverer.

(*e*) and (*f*) may be omitted, but the remainder are essential.

It is recommended, however, that the standardised telegraphic code adopted by the I.A.U. (which has replaced Holden's code) be used. This consists of 13 groups, three of which may be omitted according to the nature of the observation reported; five of the groups consist of a single word, and the remainder of figures (5 in each group). The significance of the groups, and the order in which they occur, are as follows:

1. Name of discoverer. Or, in the case of a recovered periodic comet, the generally used name of the object (in which case the discoverer counts as 'observer'—see below, 3).

2. Nature of object (comet, nova, object, etc).

3. Name of observer.

4. 5-figure group:

      2 figures: day of month,

      2 figures: stellar magnitude,

      1 figure: description of object according to Table below:

	No report on tail	*Tail* $<1°$	*Tail* $>1°$
Appearance stellar	0	–	–
No report on appearance	1	2	3
Diffuse; no nucleus	4	5	6
Diffuse; with nucleus	7	8	9

5. Name of month.

6. 5-figure group: Time (UT) of observation:
   - 2 figures: hours,
   - 2 figures: minutes,
   - 1 figure: tenths of a minute.

7. 5-figure group: Right Ascension:
   - 2 figures: hours,
   - 2 figures: minutes,
   - 1 figure: tenths of a minute (for approximate position), tens of seconds (for accurate position).

8. 5-figure group: Declination:
   - 1 figure: *1* for S Dec, *2* for N Dec,
   - 2 figures: degrees,
   - 2 figures: minutes of arc.

9. (Omitted unless an accurate position is communicated.) 5-figure group:
   - 1 figure: the figure *8*,
   - 2 figures: units and tenths of the seconds (time) of RA,
   - 2 figures: seconds (arc) of Dec.

10. (Omitted unless daily motion is communicated.) 5-figure group: Daily motion in RA:
   - 1 figure: *1* if motion is−, *2* if motion is +,
   - 2 figures: minutes (time),
   - 2 figures: seconds (time).

11. (Omitted unless daily motion is communicated.) 5-figure group: Daily motion in Dec:
   - 1 figure: *1* if motion is −, *2* if motion is +,
   - 2 figures: degrees,
   - 2 figures: minutes (arc).

12. 5-figure group: Check number consisting of the sum of the preceding 5-figure groups; if this total exceeds 99999, the first (i.e. left-hand) figure is omitted.

13. Name of communicator.

The letter y is used (rather than — or 0) for any figure which is unknown or uncertain. y's are counted as zero when computing the check number.

For example:

> 'BROWN COMET BROWN 07*yy*8 FEBRUARY 21300 08469 21557
> 11020 20150 89504 BROWN.'

announcing the discovery of a comet, the position being given approximately, would read as follows:

'Brown / has discovered a comet / observed by Brown / on the 7th; magnitude not stated; diffuse, with nucleus, tail < 1° long / the month of discovery is February / the observation was made at 21^h 30^{m}0 UT / RA 8^h 46^{m}9 / Dec +15° 57' / [Since this next group does not begin with 8, it cannot be the 8th group devoted to the accurate position; therefore:] daily motion in RA −10^m 20^s / daily motion in Dec +1° 50' / check number / discovery communicated by Brown.'

Announcements of discoveries should be sent to the nearest large observatory (see section 16.5).

When communicating routine observations to the B.A.A. Comet Section, the following data are required, a separate sheet being devoted to the observations of each comet:

(*a*) Date and time (UT), or date and first decimal.

(*b*) Place of observation.

(*c*) Approximate RA and Dec.

(*d*) Estimated magnitude.

(*e*) Diameter of coma (' arc) and other descriptive data, including degree of condensation of coma:

    0 no condensation,

    9 sharply condensed at centre.

(*f*) Aperture and magnification.

(*g*) Observational conditions: sky, Moon, etc. Scale adopted for describing atmospheric transparency:

    0 hopeless (mist, fog, etc),

    5 average,

    6 Milky Way pretty clear,

    9 perfect: clear down to horizon.

(*h*) If field sketch is added: location, orientation, scale.

All observations of sudden changes or developments should be reported immediately.

Below is printed a facsimile of the observing card now used in the Section for all observation reports, exemplifying a convenient form of layout:

OBSERVATION OF COMET......................................

Date (and decimal U.T.)   Place

Approx. R.A.   Dec.

Obs. conditions

Magnitude estimates (and comp. stars)

Description (Coma diam.; degree of condensation; nucleus; tails, length and p.a.) and remarks

Instrument (and ×)   Observer

                            (Continue over, e.g. field sketch)

16.8 Orbits

From a series of observations of the position of a comet, its orbit may be computed. The more widely spaced in time and the more numerous the observations, the more precisely may the orbit be derived. Crommelin's 3-observation method (B. 291) is a good introduction to the subject, but yields less reliable elements than the more complicated methods involving long series of observations (see, e.g., B. 332, 272, 287, 327, 333).

Methods of orbit computation fall into three main groups:

(*a*) *Gauss's method* (see B. 332), of which Merton's is a modern version (B. 317, 318; B. 309 gives a detailed account of the method, with applications). The observational data are converted into the comet's heliocentric coordinates at two different times, the elements then being derived from these two completely defined positions.

(*b*) *Laplace's method.* In its formulation by Leuschner this method has been much used in America (e.g. B. 287, 312), but generally elsewhere the Gaussian method has been preferred. From the observational data are derived the three heliocentric coordinates of the comet at a single time, and the three components of its velocity at the same time. The elements are then deduced from this complete description of its position and velocity at a single moment. B. 330 describes Väisälä's Laplacian modification, which is interesting and practical for the general orbit.

(*c*) *Graphical.* The main advantage offered by graphical methods is that they allow the worker who is new to the subject to apprehend more clearly what is involved and the direction that successive steps are taking, and to form a clearer mental picture of the whole problem than the analytical methods provide. It is, however, prohibitively inaccurate unless the observations are very widely spaced; when the comet's angular motion is large an observational period of several weeks may provide data from which an orbit can be derived with an accuracy comparable with that given by computation, but in most cases several months are required. See B. 280; B. 323, of which B. 305 is a detailed account, with applications; and B. 283.

The following are recommended to the newcomer to this type of work: B. 296–298, 301–303, 308.

An elliptical orbit, and the position of the comet in it at a given time, can be completely defined by the six elements T, Ω, ω, i, a, and e; a parabolic orbit by the five elements T, Ω, ω, i, and q (see Figure 35). i and Ω determine the plane, passing through the Sun's centre, in which the orbit lies; q or a and e describe the size and shape of the conic section; ω defines the conic's orientation in the plane of the orbit. Additional data are usually included in ephemerides.

In detail, the elements and associated quantities are:

T: *time of perihelion passage* (i.e. comet at *P*); thus, with ω, defining the comet's position at a single instant.

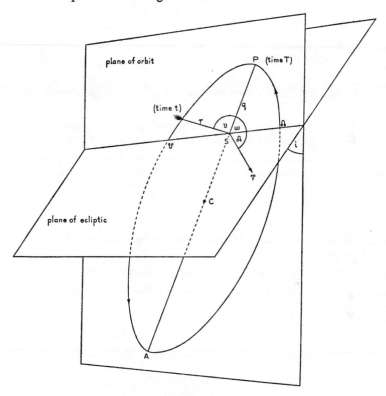

FIGURE 35

Comet direct : therefore *i* = smaller angle between the two planes
Comet past perihelion: therefore *t* is positive, (*t* − *T*), and *v* is positive
Perihelion reached before ☊ : therefore ω < 180°
Orbit elliptical: therefore *e* = *CS*/*CP* < 1

☊: *longitude of the ascending node* (i.e. angle ☊*S*♈, measured in the plane of the ecliptic); thus defining the line of nodes.
ω: *argument of perihelion* (i.e. angle ☊*SP* measured from ☊ to *P* in the plane of the orbit and in the direction of the comet's motion); thus defining the orientation of the major axis.

If $\omega < 180°$: perihelion is reached after Ω,
$\omega > 180°$: perihelion is reached before Ω.

π: (obsolete: $\tilde{\omega}$) *longitude of perihelion*, sometimes quoted instead of ω.
$\pi = \Omega + \omega$, i.e. the angle $\Upsilon S\Omega$ measured in the plane of the ecliptic,
plus the angle ΩSP measured along the orbit in the direction of the
comet's motion.

If $\Omega + \omega > 360°$, then $\pi = (\Omega + \omega) - 360°$.

i: *inclination of orbit* (i.e. the angle between the planes containing the
orbit and the ecliptic); thus defining the plane of the orbit. If the
motion is direct,* i lies between $0°$ and $90°$; if retrograde, between
$90°$ and $180°$. In a now obsolete terminology, the smaller angle
between the two planes was always given, irrespective of the direction of motion. To convert to the current usage, the following
corrections must be applied:

Direct: none,
Retrograde: $i = 180° -$ given i,
$\pi = 2\Omega -$ given π.

q: *perihelion distance* (i.e. *PS*, expressed in A.U.s). In the case of an
elliptical orbit, $q = a\,(1-e)$; aphelion distance (i.e. *AS*):
$Q = a\,(1+e)$.

a: *semimajor axis* (i.e. *AP*/2); thus defining the size of the ellipse. In the
case of elliptical orbits, a is usually given instead of q, which can be
derived from it by means of $q = a\,(1-e)$.

e: *eccentricity* (i.e. *CS/CP* in the case of an elliptical orbit, C being the
midpoint of *AP*); thus defining the shape of the conic.

If $e < 1$: ellipse,
$e = 1$: parabola,
$e > 1$: hyperbola.

ϕ (or φ): may be used instead of e, ϕ being the angle such that

$$\sin \phi = e = \sqrt{\frac{a^2 - b^2}{a}}$$

ϕ is related to the semimajor axis by $b = a \cos \phi$.

P: *period* in years, a function of a. In the case of a comet (mass assumed
zero) moving in an elliptical orbit:

* Anticlockwise as seen from the North Pole of the ecliptic.

264

$$P = a^{3/2} \text{ years (sidereal)},$$
$$= 365 \cdot 256898 a^{3/2} \text{ mean solar days},$$
$$= 360/n° \text{ mean solar days},$$

or, $\log a = \frac{2}{3} \log P$ (from Kepler III).

Epoch: an arbitrarily chosen zero point in time (elliptical orbits only).

n (obsolescent : μ): *mean daily motion*. Previously expressed in " arc, now usually in decimals of a degree:

$$n° = \frac{0 \cdot 9856077}{a^{3/2}}$$

M_O: *mean anomaly at the Epoch*. The value of the mean anomaly, M, varies at a uniform rate of n from 0° at time T.

t: time interval between T and the present position:

after perihelion: t is $+$,
before perihelion: t is $-$.

v: *true anomaly* (i.e. angle at S from P to position at time t, measured in the plane of the orbit):

after perihelion: v is $+$,
before perihelion: v is $-$.

r: *radius vector* measured in A.U.s from the Sun's centre at time t.

$\varDelta$ (or ρ): distance from the centre of the Earth, measured in A.U.s at time t.

16.9 Ephemerides

The full procedure for obtaining a search ephemeris for a periodic comet is to apply to the best available orbit from the comet's last return the perturbations of Jupiter and Saturn (normally the others may be neglected in the construction of a search ephemeris), and to compute the ephemeris from this corrected orbit. If the perturbations to which the comet has been subjected during its last revolution are neglected, the resulting ephemeris will naturally be less accurate, though in many cases still good enough for search purposes.

The first stage in the computation of an ephemeris for a comet moving in either a parabolic or an elliptical orbit is to derive the six Gaussian constants A, B, C, a, b, c, and the additional constants A', B', C'. These are functions of Ω, i and ϵ (obliquity of the ecliptic), and are independent of t.

Put
$$\left. \begin{array}{l} a \sin A = \cos \Omega \\ a \cos A = -\cos i \sin \Omega, \quad \text{and} \quad A' = A + \omega \end{array} \right\} \quad \cdot \quad \cdot \quad \cdot \quad (3)$$

where a is taken as positive, so that the signs of $\sin A$ and $\cos A$ are clear and the quadrant of A determined. Tan A is given by dividing the first expression by the second, and hence A. Knowing A, and thus $\sin A$ or $\cos A$, we can also obtain a.

Similarly B, b, C, c are obtained from

$$\left. \begin{aligned} &b \sin B = \sin \Omega \cos \epsilon \\ &b \cos B = \cos i \cos \Omega \cos \epsilon - \sin i \sin \epsilon, \quad \text{and } B' = B + \omega \end{aligned} \right\} \quad \cdot \quad \cdot \quad (4)$$

and

$$\left. \begin{aligned} &c \sin C = \sin \Omega \sin \epsilon \\ &c \cos C = \cos i \cos \Omega \sin \epsilon + \sin i \cos \epsilon, \quad \text{and } C' = C + \omega \end{aligned} \right\} \quad \cdot \quad \cdot \quad (5)$$

Great care is needed to check that the correct trigonometrical functions are taken from the tables. It is easy to take a sine for a cosine and vice versa, and to get the signs wrong, and the numerical checks given below will not detect such errors.

The heliocentric rectangular coordinates of a comet in parabolic motion, x, y, z, and the radius vector r, are then obtained from

$$\left. \begin{aligned} x &= qP_x\left(1 - \tan^2 \frac{v}{2}\right) + 2qQ_x \tan \frac{v}{2} \\ y &= qP_y\left(1 - \tan^2 \frac{v}{2}\right) + 2qQ_y \tan \frac{v}{2} \\ z &= qP_z\left(1 - \tan^2 \frac{v}{2}\right) + 2qQ_z \tan \frac{v}{2} \\ r &= q\left(1 + \tan^2 \frac{v}{2}\right) \end{aligned} \right\} \quad \cdot \quad \cdot \quad \cdot \quad (6)$$

where

$$\left. \begin{aligned} P_x &= a \sin A' \quad & P_y &= b \sin B' \quad & P_z &= c \sin C' \\ Q_x &= a \cos A' \quad & Q_y &= b \cos B' \quad & Q_z &= c \cos C' \end{aligned} \right\} \quad \cdot \quad \cdot \quad (7)$$

and $\tan^2 v/2$, $\tan v/2$ may be obtained from B. 328.

A convenient arrangement for obtaining P_x, Q_x, etc direct from the elements ω, Ω, and i by machine is given by Merton in B. 318:

$\sin \omega \sin \Omega = (8)$	$\cos \omega \sin \Omega = (11)$	$(12) - (8) \cos i = (14)$
$\sin \omega \cos \Omega = (9)$	$\cos \omega \cos \Omega = (12)$	$(12) \cos i - (8) = (15)$
$\sin \omega \sin i = (10)$	$\cos \omega \sin i = (13)$	$-(9) - (11) \cos i = (16)$
		$(9) \cos i + (11) = (17)$

Then

$$\left. \begin{aligned} P_x &= (14) & Q_x &= (16) \\ P_y &= (17) \cos \epsilon - (10) \sin \epsilon \quad & Q_y &= (15) \cos \epsilon - (13) \sin \epsilon \\ P_z &= (10) \cos \epsilon + (17) \sin \epsilon & Q_z &= (13) \cos \epsilon + (15) \sin \epsilon \end{aligned} \right\} \quad \cdot \quad (18)$$

266

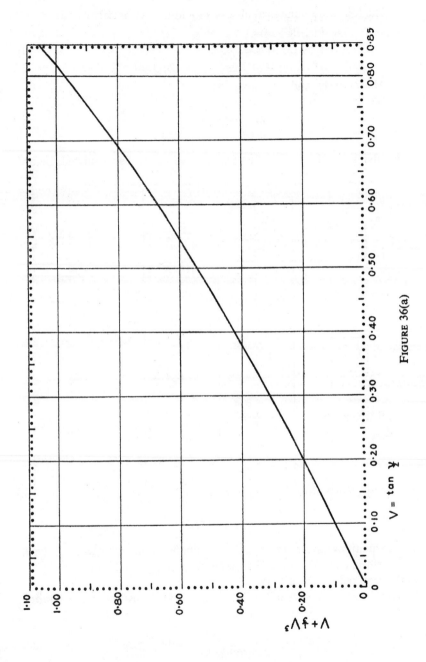

FIGURE 36(a)

The following numerical checks should always be calculated:

$$\left.\begin{array}{l} P_x^2+P_y^2+P_z^2=1 \\ Q_x^2+Q_y^2+Q_z^2=1 \\ qP_x.2qQ_x+qP_y.2qQ_y+qP_z.2qQ_z=0 \end{array}\right\} \quad . \quad . \quad . \quad (19)$$

Alternatively, and more tediously,

$$\left.\begin{array}{l} x=ar\sin(A'+v) \\ y=br\sin(B'+v) \\ z=cr\sin(C'+v) \end{array}\right\} \quad . \quad . \quad . \quad . \quad (20)$$

involving r and v as variables which have still to be calculated. Before

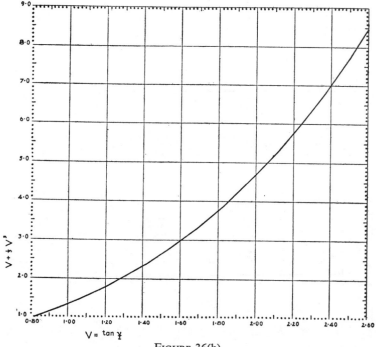

FIGURE 36(b)

the equations for the heliocentric coordinates of the comet can be solved, therefore, equations must first be set up giving the values of r and v for the required values of t.

In the case of a parabolic orbit v is derived by substituting the required value of t (days) in the equation

$$\tan\frac{v}{2}+\tfrac{1}{3}\tan^3\frac{v}{2}=\frac{3\cdot14159t\sqrt{2}}{365\cdot257q^{3/2}}=0\cdot0121637\frac{t}{q^{3/2}} \quad . \quad . \quad (21)$$

and solving the cubic for v by means of the tables of $V+\frac{1}{3}V^3 \sim v$ (where $V=\tan v/2$) which are to be found in, e.g. B. 322; or a first approximation may be obtained by means of Figures 36 (a) and (b).

The value of r corresponding to this value of v is derived from

$$\left.\begin{aligned} r &= q \sec^2 \frac{v}{2} \\ &= q\left(1+\tan^2 \frac{v}{2}\right) \end{aligned}\right\} \quad \cdots \cdots \cdots \quad (22)$$

Insertion of these values of r and v in the three Gaussian equations (20) gives x, y, z, defining the heliocentric position of the comet at time t measured in days from the perihelion date.

It remains to convert these to rectangular geocentric coordinates (ξ, η, ζ), and thence to the equatorial coordinates α and δ.

Using the values of the Sun's equatorial rectangular coordinates X, Y, Z, given in the A.E., ξ, η, and ζ are given by

$$\left.\begin{aligned} \xi &= x+X = \varDelta \cos \delta \cos \alpha \\ \eta &= y+Y = \varDelta \cos \delta \sin \alpha \\ \zeta &= z+Z = \varDelta \sin \delta \end{aligned}\right\} \quad \cdots \cdots \quad (23)$$

The RA and Dec of the comet at time t are thus derived from

$$\left.\begin{aligned} \tan \alpha &= \frac{\eta}{\xi} \quad \text{(observing the sign rule of Figure 37 and} \\ &\qquad\qquad \text{converting from arc to time)} \\[2mm] \varDelta \cos \delta &= \xi \sec \alpha \quad \text{(if } \cos \alpha > \sin \alpha \text{ numerically)} \\ &= \eta \operatorname{cosec} \alpha \quad \text{(if } \sin \alpha > \cos \alpha \text{ numerically)} \\[2mm] \tan \delta &= \frac{\zeta}{\varDelta \cos \delta} \\[2mm] \varDelta &= (\varDelta \cos \delta) \sec \delta \end{aligned}\right\} \quad . \quad (24)$$

In the case of an elliptical orbit the derivation of the Gaussian constants, their employment to derive the comet's heliocentric coordinates, and the conversion of these to RA and Dec are the same as before, but it is convenient to eliminate r and v and to employ E, the eccentric anomaly, instead.

E is a function of t, $e=\sin \phi$, and n (mean motion), and must be found from Kepler's equation:

$$E-e° \sin E = nt = M \quad \cdots \cdots \quad (25)$$

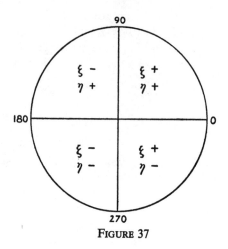

FIGURE 37

where $e°=180e/\pi=57\cdot295780e$, and all are in degrees. This equation has to be solved by trial, which may be done quickly with a slide rule, and an approximate value E_0 found, which may then be corrected by calculating the equivalent M_0:

$$M_0=E_0-e° \sin E_0$$

and the error

$$\Delta M=M-M_0$$

Then the correction to E_0, usually with sufficient accuracy, is

$$\Delta E=\frac{\Delta M}{1-e \cos E_0} \quad \text{(using } e, \text{ not } e°)$$

The coordinates are then derived from

$$\left.\begin{array}{l} x=aP_x(\cos E-e)+bQ_x \sin E \\ y=aP_y(\cos E-e)+bQ_y \sin E \\ z=aP_z(\cos E-e)+bQ_z \sin E \end{array}\right\} \quad . \quad . \quad . \quad (26)$$

a and b are here not Gaussian constants but, respectively, the semi-major axis and the semiminor axis, $a \cos \phi$.

The third numerical check, on the equatorial constants in this case, is:

$$aP_x.bQ_x+aP_y.bQ_y+aP_z.bQ_z=0 \quad . \quad . \quad (27)$$

For a fuller treatment, see B. 292, one of a series of papers by Crommelin which forms a useful introduction to ephemeris computation generally: B. 290, 292, 293. B. 271 (see also B. 285, 300) describes a simple and recommended method, while B. 329 is also a clear and straightforward account. For a graphical method, see B. 306. B. 313, 314, 325 should also be referred to.

Wood's method of extending an ephemeris (B. 334) often proves useful, especially to overseas observers, who are liable to find that the published ephemeris has run out by the time it reaches them; see also Merton's table to facilitate the working of this method (B. 319).

It is sometimes necessary, when continuing an ephemeris from one year to the next, to change the constants by the amount of one year's precession in order to obtain them for the mean equinox of the next year. This is conveniently done by

$$\left.\begin{aligned} \text{new } aP_x &= aP_x - 0 \cdot 0002235aP_y - 0 \cdot 0000972aP_z \\ \text{new } aP_y &= aP_y + 0 \cdot 0002235aP_x \\ \text{new } aP_z &= aP_z + 0 \cdot 0000972aP_x \end{aligned}\right\} \quad . \quad . \quad (28)$$

and similarly for bQ_x, bQ_y, bQ_z. The constants qP_x, $2qQ_x$, etc, in the parabolic orbit can, of course, be treated similarly. For correcting for longer periods than one year, see B. 13, Table V.

16.10 B.A.A.H. data

Elements and ephemerides of periodic comets whose returns are expected during the year. Ephemerides contain the following data:

Date.

RA } for the mean equinox of the beginning of the year, or for a
Dec } standard equinox, e.g. 1950·0.

r (solar distance, in A.U.s).

Δ (distance from Earth, in A.U.s).

Magnitude.

In addition, search ephemerides usually give:

$\left.\begin{aligned} \Delta\alpha \\ \Delta\delta \end{aligned}\right\}$ for $\Delta T = +1^d$.

$\Delta\alpha$ and $\Delta\delta$ give the corrections that must be applied to the RA and Dec for an increase of 1^d in the time of perihelion passage.

16.11 A.E. data

X, Y, Z: the Sun's equatorial rectangular coordinates at midnight throughout the year (required in computing ephemerides).

VARIABLES

17.1 Amateur work

The majority of the several thousand variables that have been studied at all have still been very inadequately observed. There are, in addition, the thousands of stars whose suspected variability has never been confirmed, and the equally numerous cases where variation has been established but which have never been classified owing to insufficient observation.

Variable stars provide one of the most noteworthy examples of a field in which the amateur can render valuable assistance to the professional astronomer. The technique of observation is within the accomplishment of anyone, and even the most modest types of amateur equipment can be turned to valuable work.

Instrumental photometry, as distinguished from visual methods, is demanded by a small minority of variables whose insignificant amplitudes render them unobservable visually or photographically, and for the detection of secondary variations in stars whose general characteristics are already well known. An obvious field for photoelectric investigation is the red giant stars, the vastly greater number of which are slightly variable, the amplitude in most cases being below the limit of effective eye-estimation.

Photography (e.g. section 17.11) in amateur hands is of limited though real usefulness in the observation of variables.

Observations—however accurate and however badly needed—are wasted if they never get further than the pages of the Observing Book. The value of pooling observations of certain types of variable*—since it allows smoothed interpolation curves to be constructed from a very much greater number of observations (and with corresponding weight) than any single observer could make—indicates the desirability of joining an observing group, such as that provided in this country by the

---

* E.g. LPVs, and some rapidly varying stars like R CrB and U Gem. In the case of variables of small amplitude, the work of each observer must be discussed separately.

Variable Star Section (V.S.S.) of the B.A.A., or in America by the American Association of Variable Star Observers (A.A.V.S.O.). The V.S.S. keeps about 70 variables of different types under observation; the majority are LPVs with an amplitude of several mags and period of about 1 year. Anyone wishing to strike out on his own may refer to Campbell's list of 100 miscellaneous variables which are in particular need of further study (B. 352); 12 of Campbell's stars are at the time of writing on the V.S.S. observing list.

The V.S.S. Director issues general instructions, lists of comparison stars, and the necessary charts. The Section Director also performs such tasks as the construction of the standard light curves, the determination of periods, and the determination of maxima and minima.* Observations should be submitted annually; they are published and discussed in the annual Interim Reports in *J.B.A.A.* and in the 5-yearly Memoirs (*Mem. B.A.A*).

The frequency with which variables should be observed depends upon their period. The following instructions are intended as no more than rough guides:

Class I:† Nightly, or (e.g. I.1 and I.4(*a*)) at the beginning and end of each night's work. During periods of rapid change, observations can profitably be made at almost hourly intervals.

Class II: Twice a week, or even less frequently, is adequate in most cases.

Class III: Hourly, nightly, or still less frequently, according to the lapse of time required for the brightness of the star to change appreciably.

It is important to reduce, as much as possible, each variable's annual season of invisibility when it is near to the Sun. Observations in twilight (both evening and morning), though made under difficult circumstances, and therefore of reduced accuracy, are nevertheless particularly valuable. An approach to continuity of observation is especially desirable in the case of Class I variables.

17.2 Visual estimation of stellar magnitudes

The methods which permit the magnitude of a star to be accurately derived by direct eye-estimations fall into two fundamentally dissimilar

---

* For the methods employed in the discussion of observations, see B. 353, Chapter 3, and B. 355, Chapters 9, 10 and 11.

† See section 17.13.

categories: Step methods and Fractional methods. These are described in detail in the subsequent sections, but some preliminary remarks of a general and ground-clearing nature may be helpful.

All branches of observation are to some extent an art as well as a science—in so far as proficiency involves mental processes of which the observer is largely unconscious—and this is truer of the visual estimation of stellar magnitudes than of most. Although there are a favoured few who appear to be able to divine the brightness of a star to one-tenth of a magnitude by some aptitude akin to clairvoyance, such feats are not really inspired shots in the dark, but rather the result of unconsciously applied experience accumulated through years of observation according to the 'rules'. There are no short cuts in astronomical observation: proficiency can only come from experience in the use of those techniques which trial has proved to be the most reliable. Such techniques in the case of variable-star observation have been worked out in some detail: but it is worth emphasising that although the 'rules' may be more numerous than in some other branches of observation, they have not been formulated for the fun of it, but simply because they represent the most efficient and reliable means of attaining the desired goal—accurate results.

It is precisely because the visual estimation of stellar magnitudes is so beset with pitfalls that special techniques have been evolved; and if he is to avoid these pitfalls, the newcomer to variable-star observation cannot afford to disregard the 'rules'. In comparing by eye the brightness of a variable and a comparison star the observer is performing an exercise in point photometry. He must allow the image of each star in turn to fall upon the same spot on his retina, and by means of the techniques described in the following sections make an estimate of the stars' relative brightness. The purpose of these techniques, as was said above, is simply and solely to enable the observer to make the estimate with reasonable accuracy: hit-or-miss methods just will not produce accurate results, and the apparent complexity of the recognised methods of observation is the inescapable result of the necessity for circumventing the various errors (mostly physiological) that afflict visual point photometry.

It is also essential to be quite clear in one's mind regarding the precise nature of the Step and Fractional methods, and the manner in which they differ from one another. In making an observation by a Step method, the elements involved are 2 stars and the light interval (or brightness difference) between them; the variable may afterwards be compared with other comparison stars, but each such comparison is an entirely independent operation, each involves the same three elements —2 stars and 1 interval—and each consists, first, in forming a correct impression of the brightness of the two stars, and then in assessing the light interval between them in terms of a scale of 'steps'.

With the Fractional method the unit observation involves a greater number of elements—3 stars and the 2 light intervals between them (the variable, and a brighter and a fainter comparison star)—and the assessment consists in weighing these two intervals against one another, not against a known scale of 'steps'.

The making of an estimate by the Fractional method is to this extent a longer and more complicated process than making a Step estimate. For this reason the latter is generally to be preferred when comparison stars at small enough light intervals are available. Both the Fractional and the Pogson Step methods are employed by the V.S.S.

For a fuller discussion of these methods, and their relative advantages and weaknesses, see B. 363.

17.2.1 The Herschel-Argelander Step method: Commonly called, simply, the Argelander method. Independent comparisons are made of the variable with as many comparison stars in turn as are available. The selected comparison star is brought to the centre of the field, steadily regarded for not longer than several seconds, and an impression taken of its brightness; the same operation is then carried out with the variable; on the basis of these two impressions, two judgments are made—first, a qualitative one as to which star is the brighter, and then a quantitative one as to the size of interval between them, expressed in terms of the scale of steps described below.

The smaller the mag difference between each comparison star and the variable, and the more evenly their brightnesses are distributed on either side of the variable, the better will be the derived magnitude. Unlike the Fractional method, the Argelander and other Step methods thus permit the estimation of the brightness of a variable by comparison with a single field star, though it is desirable that more than one should be used if available.

The mags of the comparison stars do not have to be known at the time of observation—in fact it is psychologically most undesirable that they should be. The relative brightness of the variable and each usable comparison star in turn is estimated as so many 'steps'. The step is, strictly speaking, incapable of general definition, since it is a subjective unit. But broadly speaking it may be described as the smallest difference of brightness between two stars observed in fairly quick succession that is clearly distinguishable. Subjectively, the steps may be described as follows. Suppose that at a single casual glance two stars, *a* and *b*, appear to be equally bright. Suppose, further, that *a* is now observed intently for several seconds, its brightness memorised, star *b* similarly observed, a judgment made as to which is the brighter (assuming that, as will often be the case, they no longer appear to be *exactly* equal), and the whole procedure then repeated several times. Then if *a* was judged to be brighter than *b* as often as *b* was judged to be brighter than *a*, they may be taken to be as nearly equal as the eye is capable of distinguishing, and their step difference will be 0. If one star is only occasionally judged to be brighter than the other, then their difference is 1 step; if one is never brighter than the other, but occasionally equal to it, the difference is 2 steps; if one is always brighter than the other, but at times only just so, their difference is 3 steps; and if one is continuously and clearly brighter than the other, 4 steps or more. Thus the final opinion regarding the step-difference between two stars is made up by the accumulation of individual estimates. It can be seen that the Herschel-Argelander method is precisely that one which attempts to utilise the observer's eye to its most critical limit.

For the average observer with a trained eye, the value of the step is not far from 0·1 mag; and although its value varies slightly from one observer to another, it appears to remain tolerably constant for a given observer over long periods. With practice, differences of up to 3 or 4 steps can be estimated quite accurately and consistently, but if the magnitude difference exceeds about 0·4 or 0·5 it is better to use the Fractional method.

When recording observations, the brighter of the two stars is given first and the fainter last, with the step-difference in brackets between them. Thus *b*(1)*V* means that the star designated *b* is 1 step brighter than the variable, *V*(2)*a* that the variable is 2 steps brighter than star *a*, etc.

The symbols $>$ and $<$ should not be used for 'brighter than' and 'fainter than', the correct symbols being respectively] and [.* Thus [37 would mean that the variable was fainter than the comparison star 37, the faintest visible on that occasion (i.e. the variable was below the threshold of the telescope); this might be recorded more specifically as [37 N.S. (variable fainter than star 37, and not seen); or amplified to [37 gl. (variable fainter than star 37, but glimpsed).

On every occasion when a variable is invisible (no matter what

---

* Round brackets,) and (, are used in typewritten work, and sometimes in printed work also.

method is being used), the faintest visible comparison star should be specified in this way.

17.2.2 Pogson's Step method: Like the Herschel-Argelander method, this is a true Step method: it can be used with a single comparison star, and in ignorance of any actual magnitudes. The only difference is that whereas the former is based upon a scale of subjective units, Pogson's step is a consciously memorised difference of 0·1 mag. (That the Herschel-Argelander physiological step also happens in most cases to be *about* 0·1 mag is purely fortuitous.)

The Pogson method thus involves a preliminary training of the eye to recognise intervals of 0·1 mag, 0·2 mag, 0·3 mag, etc, when it sees them. Comparison stars are the most convenient objects to use when memorising the appearance of the Pogson steps, since they are easily found and cover a wide range of accurately determined magnitudes.

To avoid confusion with observations made by other methods, Pogson step observations are recorded as follows: the comparison star is named first, and is followed by + and the number of steps that the variable is brighter than it, or − and the number of steps that the variable is fainter than it. Thus $a-2$ means that the variable is 2 steps (i.e. 0·2 mag)* fainter than star a, $b+4$ that it is 4 steps brighter than star b, etc.

The derivation of the variable's magnitude from the observational data (columns 6 and 7 of the Permanent Record: see section 17.6.2) is performed as follows. At the end of each observational session the mags of the comparison stars used are inserted against the observations in the 'Light Estimate' column. A typical entry in this column, with the corresponding entry in the 'Deduced Magnitude' column, might then read:

Light Estimate	Deduced Magnitude
$e-2$ (7·0)	7·2
$a-1$ (6·9)	7·0 }7·10
$b+4$ (7·5)	7·1

It is important to realise that—this being a Step and not a Fractional method—these three observations are absolutely independent of one another. Although the second and third observations quoted above do

* Note that in the Argelander method, $a(2)V$ would also mean that the variable is 2 steps fainter than a, but in this case we could not go on to say that the difference was 0·2 mag.

in fact place the variable between a and b at a point one-fifth of the total a-to-b interval fainter than a, and four-fifths of the interval brighter than b, these two observations were made quite independently of one another in two separate operations, each of which involved 2 stars and 1 interval—and not, as with the Fractional method (section 17.2.4), in a single operation involving 3 stars and 2 intervals.

Also it should be clearly realised that the observations are, at the time they are made, absolutely independent of any known magnitudes. It is, indeed, a thoroughly undesirable practice to go to the telescope armed with the magnitude values of the comparison stars that one intends using.

It is possible to determine the mean value of the observational error in a series of observations, for if no such error (due to mis-estimation of the number of steps, and/or to the use of a step differing in value from 0·1 mag) occurs, then

$$(b-a) - \frac{(a'+b')}{10} = 0$$

$$(b-e) - \frac{(e'+b')}{10} = 0$$

where e, a, b are the magnitudes of the comparison stars so designated, and e', a', b' are the estimated step-differences between them and the variable.

It will be found, however, that in many cases this equality does not hold. If we write, in the case of either equation, m for the known mag difference of the comparison stars, and s and s' for the corresponding step values divided by 10, we shall have instead

$$m - (s+s') = x$$

where x is a small number representing (in mags) the error of the observation. If the variable is observed a number of times we shall have, for each pair of comparison stars, a set of equations of the general form

$$m - (s_1 + s_1') = x_1$$
$$m - (s_2 + s_2') = x_2$$
$$\cdot \quad \cdot \quad \cdot \quad \cdot \quad \cdot \quad \cdot$$
$$m - (s_n + s_n') = x_n$$

And the mean error of the series will be given in the ordinary way by

$$E = \frac{x_1 + x_2 + \ldots x_n}{n}$$

17.2.3 Pogson's Mixed method: Pogson himself proposed a development of his true Step method, which is a sort of half-way house between the Step and the Fractional methods. It remains a Step method, since the estimation is made in terms of steps, while resembling the Fractional method in that each single observation involves 3 stars and 2 intervals.

In the Mixed method the observer goes to the telescope knowing the mag interval between the comparison star immediately brighter than the variable and that immediately fainter than it. Suppose, for the sake of illustration, that the mags of the two comparison stars, a and b, are respectively 10·0 and 10·5. The observer then knows that the number of steps in his observation comparing the variable with a, and the number of steps in his observation comparing the variable with b, must sum to 5. He goes ahead and makes his two independent step estimations, each concerning 2 stars and the 1 interval that separates them, and if these estimates should be $a-1$, $b+4$ or $a-2$, $b+3$ or $a-3$, $b+2$ or $a-4$, $b+1$, all is well. But if his observation is, let us say, $a-2$, $b+4$ he cannot let it rest at that (as he could with Pogson's pure Step method, when he is ignorant of what the sum of the steps in the two intervals really is) since $4+2\neq5$, and his observation must be in error. He therefore has to recompare a and V, and b and V, and decide whether he wants to change his observation to $a-2$, $b+3$ or to $a-1$, $b+4$. But he does this by a reconsideration of the number of $0^{m}1$ steps in the two intervals, and not (as in the Fractional method) by thinking in terms of the proportion of 1 : 4 or 2 : 3.*

It is the standardised procedure in the V.S.S. to record the observations themselves, and to deduce the magnitude of the variable from them later (see section 17.6.2). In the A.A.V.S.O., on the other hand, the result is written straight down in mags, and the 'Light Estimate' column goes out of commission.

17.2.4 The Fractional method: Two comparison stars are chosen, one slightly brighter and one slightly fainter than the variable, thus immediately fixing the magnitude of the latter between definite limits. In constructing the B.A.A. sequences of comparison stars the aim has been to avoid jumps of more than 0·4 mag. Where this has not been practicable, however, the Fractional method is preferable to one of the Step methods, since the assessment of intervals up to 1 mag is a feasible undertaking by its means.

The brightness difference between stars a and b is divided mentally into any convenient number of parts, depending on the size of the

---

* If the observation were made fractionally, it would be recorded in the form $a,1,V,4,b$ or $a,2,V,3,b$ (see section 17.2.4).

interval (3, 4, 5, or 6 for normal intervals; only exceptionally more than 7), and the position of the variable within this interval is estimated in terms of the fraction of the total interval separating it from each star. For example, if the brightness of the variable is reckoned to be one-quarter of the way from a to b, and $\frac{3}{4}$(a-to-b) brighter than b, the observation would be recorded in the form $a,1,V,3,b$*; if the variable is estimated to be midway from a to b, the observation would be recorded as $a,1,V,1,b$; if the difference between the comparison stars is great enough for one-fifth of it to be perceptible, and the variable is judged to be three-fifths of the way from a to b, the observational record would read $a,3,V,2,b$.

Interval assessments of from 1 : 1 up to about 1 : 5 (e.g. $a,1,V,1,b$ to $a,1,V,5,b$) can be made with sufficient accuracy to justify placing reasonable confidence in them. But mentally to divide a light interval into 7 parts (as is involved in the observation $a,1,V,6,b$), or more, and to place the variable correctly within this range, is too difficult for much weight to be attached to such an observation.

Pickering's decimal notation, in which the numerators of the two fractions into which the variable divides the whole interval between a and b always sum to 10 (e.g. $a,6,V,4,b$, $a,2,V,8,b$, etc), is open to the double objection that it either encourages the observer to claim a precision which in fact he cannot attain, or is capable of simplification. Thus 5 : 5 is the same as 1 : 1; 6 : 4 simplifies to 3 : 2; 7 : 3 is in practice indistinguishable from 2 : 1; 8 : 2 simplifies to 4 : 1; and a 9 : 1 observation means in practice that the difference between V and b is only *just* distinguishable, and is therefore given the minimum value of 1, the other 9 being in no sense an accurate estimate of the size of the a-to-V interval relative to V-to-b, but merely being dictated by the fact that the sum must be 10.

It can be seen that it is unnecessary to know the mags of the comparison stars at the time the observation is made. The observation is reduced subsequently as follows:

Observation: $a,3,V,2,b$.

Mags of comparison stars: a 5·27,

b 6·05.

Then mag difference $(b-a)=0\cdot78$,

$\therefore \frac{1}{5}(b-a)=0\cdot156$.

Hence,

Mag of variable$=6\cdot05-(2\times0\cdot156)=5\cdot738$ $\left.\right\}=5\cdot74.$

or$=5\cdot27+(3\times0\cdot156)=5\cdot738$

* The brighter star is always written first.

Observations should be reduced to the nearest 0·01 mag, the combined observations of independent observers subsequently being given (e.g. by the V.S.S. Director) to the nearest 0·1 mag.

It is impossible to say anything about the relative accuracy of the Fractional and Step methods without specifying the conditions under which they are being used: thus a step comparison when the available comparison stars are spaced at not more than about 0·5 mags is likely to be as accurate as a fractional assessment when the interval is larger than this. It is the present practice of the V.S.S., in systematising the observations of its members, to give double the weight to a fractional observation as compared with a single step observation. The reason for this is that in the former case 2 comparison stars were employed, and in the latter only 1, i.e. unit weight is given to each comparison star. Though this may appear reasonable enough at first glance, it is by no means certain that the practice is always and necessarily valid, for it does not follow that an observation like $a,1,V,4,b$ must be twice as valuable as $a-1$: an experienced observer's estimate of 1 step is so precise that the accuracy of $a-1$ is unlikely to be doubled merely by tying V to a second comparison star b and making a fractional assessment of 1 : 4.

A small point that might be noticed in passing is that in the Fractional method it is the arithmetical ratio of the brightnesses of the stars that is estimated, whereas the magnitude scale is geometric. The discrepancy involved is, however, too small to be taken into account when small intervals are concerned, and with large intervals is likely to be swamped by the considerable observational error that must be anticipated anyhow. Thus if the brightness of V is exactly midway between that of a and that of b (as estimated by the Fractional method), and the mags of a and b are respectively 3·5 and 5·0, then the mag of the variable is not 4·25 (the arithmetical mean of the mags) but 4·01. At the same time, the assessment of such large light intervals may be expected to involve an error of more than 0·24 mag anyway, so that a correction for the divergence between the brightness and magnitude scales is not worth introducing.

When taking up this type of work, the eye should be subjected to a thorough course of training in the estimation of relative brightnesses. This is most conveniently undertaken by making long series of observations among the comparison stars on the V.S.S. charts, their magnitudes being referred to later and the accuracy of the observations checked.

17.3 Making the comparisons

In point photometry the most important condition for securing consistency of results is that the images being compared should be received by the same spot on the observer's retina. In practice this must mean the fovea, whence each star must be brought in turn to the centre of the telescopic field, and there regarded (for not more than 2 or 3 seconds) by direct vision. The fact that a *simultaneous* comparison is not possible —the impression of the brightness of one star having to be carried in the memory while the next star is being brought to the field centre and observed—does not in practice appear to be a source of material error.

Simultaneous observation of two stars by averted vision, the eye being fixed on a point midway between them, results in large and unsystematic errors due to the enormous range of sensitivity of different regions of the retina: for whereas when the two stars are looked at directly (though necessarily in succession) the image of each is known to fall on the same retinal spot—the fovea—in the case of indirect vision there is no such guarantee. The indirect method is also subject to position-angle error* and to error arising from the fact that a star tends to appear slightly brighter at the edge of the field than at the centre. The physiological sources of error are, however, much more important, and are the reason why foveal vision has been universally adopted by variable-star observers. The danger to be constantly on one's guard against when using this method is the unconscious use of averted vision—by allowing the fixation point to wander from the star whose brightness is being impressed upon the visual memory, or by allowing the extrafoveal image of the first star, as the telescope is being shifted to bring the second to the field centre, to influence the original impression of its brightness gained whilst it itself was at the centre of the field.

The only occasion where the use of averted vision is justified is when no observation at all would be possible without it—i.e. when either the variable or the comparison star is so near the magnitude threshold of the instrument that even with magnification pushed to the limit (to increase the star's visibility by darkening the sky background) it is still inaccessible to foveal vision. Every effort must then be made to fix the eye on the same point in the field when each star is at the field centre. Even so, the observation must be recognised as a *faute de mieux* makeshift, and of doubtful accuracy.

17.4 Comparison stars

Charts are specially constructed for variable-star observers, and issued

---

* *A.A.H.*, section 24.9.

by such bodies as the A.A.V.S.O., and the V.S.S. of the British Astronomical Association. Each chart shows the area of sky containing the variable in question; those field stars suitable for use as comparison stars are indicated by letters, numbers (referring to a separate table of magnitudes), or according to Pickering's system whereby they are denoted on the chart by their magnitudes (to tenths), decimal points being omitted (e.g. 12=mag 1·2, 101=mag 10·1, etc).

The magnitudes of the standard comparison stars have been very carefully determined; but errors do occur, many having been corrected in the past, and among the thousands of comparison stars in use there are still wrongly ascribed magnitudes. The detection of these errors lies with the variable-star observers themselves, and any anomalous observations, suggestive of wrongly ascribed comparison-star magnitudes, should be reported to the V.S.S. Director.

V.S.S. magnitudes are based on the scale of the Harvard photometries and B. 360, though in most cases 'adopted magnitudes'—derived from both photometric measures and step estimates—are used. With certain reservations, these are the mags of the A.A.V.S.O. charts.

Each variable should ideally have a set of comparison stars whose mags are accurately known and which are distributed in not more than half-magnitude steps over the whole of the variable's amplitude plus 0·5 mag at each end. Thus at any time two comparison stars could be found whose mags are within 0·5 above and below that of the variable. They should be included in the same telescopic field which shows the variable clearly, but should be neither too close to one another nor to any much brighter star; double stars are unsuitable. Finally, they should be of the same colour as the variable.

Needless to say, all these conditions cannot in most cases be fulfilled.

17.5 The observation of coloured variables*

The kernel of the difficulty has been put succinctly by P. M. Ryves: 'In comparing a red star with a white star we are trying to equate things which are essentially different; rather like trying to decide whether one cup of tea is as strong as another is hot.'

There are several physiological bases, among them:

1. The effect of colour upon the perceived brightness of two equally bright stars.

2. The eye's non-instantaneous adaptation to red light. Thus, as a red star is stared at, it appears to grow brighter over a period of a few

* This section should be read in conjunction with *A.A.H.*, section 24.4.

seconds. This is less troublesome than 1, and can be avoided by substituting quick glances for a steady scrutiny.

3. The Purkinje effect. If R and W are the intensities of a red and a white star respectively, and it is estimated that $R = W$, then $2R$ will appear to be greater than $2W$. Examples: if $R = W$ when the stars are viewed with the naked eye, R will appear up to 0·5 mag brighter than W when seen with a telescope of moderate aperture, owing to the increased intensities of the telescopic images; again, U Cyg at maximum appears, with moderate apertures, virtually equal to a bright nearby comparison star, but if the aperture is reduced till the variable is almost invisible it appears about 0·5 mag fainter than the comparison star; again, T Cas observed with a 10-in is estimated to be about 0·5 mags brighter than with a 3-in.

The varying effects of colour can be clearly seen when combining the observational data of different observers: whereas in the case of red stars the greatest scatter is found around maxima, in the case of blue stars it increases with decreasing brightness.

The error can be circumvented in various ways, of unequal practicality:

(a) Only compare a red variable with a red comparison star. This is the radical and ideal solution, but infrequently possible.

(b) Use a red filter to reduce the difference between the tints of the two stars. The disadvantages here are (i) the mags of all the standard comparison stars would have to be redetermined, (ii) identical filters would have to be used by all observers whose observations are to be combined for discussion, (iii) the visible range of each variable would be reduced, (iv) a discontinuity with previous estimates would be introduced.

(c) Reduce the aperture by an amount (depending on the brightness of the variable at the time) that brings its intensity down to its minimum as seen with full aperture, or to a faint but clearly perceptible intensity, whichever is the greater. The justification for this procedure is that whereas the eye's sensitivity to colour decreases with decreasing intensity, it becomes more sensitive to intensity-differences at a low intensity level (providing this is not too near the threshold). In this way the Purkinje effect is harnessed to reduce the perceived colour difference between the variable and the comparison star. It should be noted (i) that the presence of haze or high cloud will affect the estimated brightness of a red star, (ii) that owing to the darker field of a HP ocular, a red star (compared with a white one) will appear brighter with a high magnification than with a low.

(d) Use indirect vision, the periphery of the retina being less sensitive to colour than the macula. A single series of observations must not include both direct-vision and indirect-vision items. This is a less effective method than (c); and see also section 17.3.

(e) Determine the personal colour equation by estimating the subsequently verifiable magnitudes of a large number of red stars of different intensities, by comparison with white stars. In this way a curve may be constructed showing the error plotted against magnitude, which with a change of sign becomes the correction to be systematically applied to all observations of red variables.

Two scales are in common use for the description of star colours, Hagen's (sometimes called Osthoff's) and Franks':

Hagen		Franks
0^c	white	W
1^c	yellowish white	YW
2^c	pale yellow	WY
3^c	pure yellow	Y
4^c	deep yellow	OY
5^c	pale orange	YO
6^c	orange	O
7^c	deep orange	RO
8^c	reddish orange	OR
9^c	red, with tinge of orange	R
10^c	spectrum red (never encountered)	SR

See further: B. 342, 344.

17.6 Observational records

As usual, it is necessary to keep two separate records: an Observing Book for the direct recording of observations as they are made, and a Permanent Record made up from the Observing Book.

17.6.1 Observing Book: A convenient form of layout is as follows:

Date...................................

(1)	(2)	(3)		(4)	(5)	(6)	(7)
Star	Time GMAT (0^h=noon)	Sky State		Instrument	Observations	Class	Notes
		General	Local				

Date: Day of week, GMAT date, and Julian date (see section 17.14), e.g. Sunday, 1950 Nov 12, JD 2433598.

Col. (1): The generally used name; in most cases this will be Argelander's designation (see section 17.12).

Col. (2): GMAT. Either to the nearest minute in all cases, or in the case of SPVs and Irregular Variables only; or to the nearest 5 mins, according to the variable's period. Even with LPVs it is useful to record the approximate time, since this gives an indication of the star's altitude in doubtful cases.

Col. (3): Clarity, rather than freedom from turbulence, is the important factor. The General State refers to the whole sky, and need be entered only at the beginning and end of each observing session. Local State refers to the immediate vicinity of the variable, and should be entered against each observation. A scale recognised by the B.A.A. is:

    1: good,
    2: fair, to fairly good,
    3: poor.

Other useful abbreviations are:

    C: clouds,
    H: haze, mist, or uniform high cloud,
    W: windy.

If the General State is apparently uniform, the mag of the faintest visible star near the zenith may be quoted. The following stars of UMi are also useful in this connexion:

α . . . . mag 2·2
γ . . . .   3·2
δ . . . .   4·3
θ . . . .   5·3
λ . . . .   6·5

Col. (4): Abbreviations recognised by the B.A.A. include:

    NE: naked eye,
    B: binoculars,
    T: telescope, followed by the magnification, e.g. T 30. If two telescopes are regularly employed, T is used for the larger and t for the smaller.

This scheme can be elaborated. For instance:

    F: finder
    RR: refractor ⎱ plus aperture and magnification, e.g. RL 6/40 indicates
    RL: reflector ⎰ a 6-in reflector, ×40.

Col. (5): See sections 17.2.1–17.2.4.

Col. (6): The degree of reliability of the observation, as judged by the observer at the time he makes it:

    1: reliable, complete confidence,
    2: fair,
    3: unreliable.

It is important that this should be entered at the time of the observation, taking account of all relevant factors, and that it should under no circumstances be altered later.

Col. (7): Any notes on conditions in relation to which the observations should be considered, e.g. trouble from artificial lights or aurorae, observation hurried or otherwise suspect, etc. Suggested abbreviations:

    M: Moon above horizon. If it is near the variable, the fact should be mentioned.
    T: Twilight.
    Z 70: Zenith Distance of variable 70°; the ZD should be recorded if greater than 65°.
    L: Star low. (Used as an alternative to ZD, sometimes.)

OBSERVATIONS of..............................

By..............................

Date (0ʰ=noon)	Time G.M.A.T.	Sky	Instr.	Class	Light Estimate	Ded. Mag.	Remarks
	ᵐ						

17.6.2 Permanent Record: Made up daily from the Observing Book. Cards are more convenient than a book, unless loose-leaf. Separate card or page for each variable. It is assumed that the Permanent Record is kept in duplicate, one copy being sent annually to a central pool for the correlation and discussion of different observers' work. This copy will include a covering note giving the observer's locality, longitude and latitude, and any other general information that he may think relevant. It is most important, however, that *each individual sheet* sent to the B.A.A. or elsewhere should contain the observer's name, a statement of the apertures of T and t (see notes on column (4) of the Observing Book, above), and whether they are refractors or reflectors.

The form recommended by the V.S.S., and in use by all its members, is shown on the opposite page.

Observers working on their own (i.e. not as members of a group, such as the V.S.S., with its own recognised methods and procedures) should, when publishing or submitting their results, always quote the observations *as made* and recorded in the Observing Book, and should indicate clearly the method used—Argelander Step (e.g. $a(1)V$, $V(2)b$), Pogson Step ($a-1$, $b+2$), Fractional ($a,1,V,2,b$), etc.

17.7 Observational errors

Two equally experienced observers, observing the same star under identical conditions, may differ systematically in their estimates by as much as a fifth of a magnitude, even though each series is homogeneous. The discrepancy may grow to a whole magnitude, or even more, when the star is very bright (e.g. nova at maximum). It might therefore be useful (though extremely laborious) for each observer to investigate the value and sign of his own personal equation by means of long series of test observations of comparison stars. It is essential, however, that no personal correction arrived at in this way should be applied by the observer himself, though he should report it in the covering note accompanying his observations to the V.S.S. Such an investigation is primarily of interest to the observer himself, for a curve drawn through the plots of half a dozen individually homogeneous though uncorrected sets of observations may be expected to be accurate to within 0·2 mags or thereabouts.

van der Bilt (B. 350) found that accidental errors tend to cancel one another out in a large mass of observational material; in particular, no systematic correlations of error with type of instrument or aperture were possible. Readers interested in the problem of discussing a large quantity of heterogeneous material are recommended to refer to this paper.

The sources of accidental error are manifold, and include:

(a) Wrong identification of the variable, or of one or more of the comparison stars. Because of this danger, and also because the locating of his variables often wastes a great deal of time with the newcomer to variable-star work, a separate section (17.8) is devoted to this subject. The importance of correctly identifying the variable, and the comparison stars used, need hardly be stressed.

(b) Erroneous mags of the comparison stars. If not working from B.A.A. or A.A.V.S.O. charts (see section 17.4), B. 360, 366, 367, 368, 369 should wherever possible be used.

(c) The use of different comparison stars by different observers.

(d) Variations in atmospheric transparency, background brightness, etc.

(e) Different colour sensitivity of different instruments, leading to different estimates of the star's colour, and thence to divergent estimates of its brightness.

(f) The employment of different instruments or photometric methods in a single series of observations.

(g) Unsystematic use of direct and averted vision. Owing to the uncertainties of indirect vision, direct vision is clearly indicated as a general rule, and averted vision should only be resorted to if the star is otherwise invisible (see section 17.3). Any variable whose observation requires, around minimum, the use of averted vision should be observed in this manner at all times, an effort being made to systematise the distance and p.a. of the fixation point relative to the observed point. If, however, the variable should be perceptible by direct vision, estimates should be made by both direct and averted vision, in order to secure a check 'overlap'.

(h) Unsystematic dark adaptation. Always wait until adaptation is complete, or virtually so, before starting the night's work (not less than 15 mins). Any light at the observing site should be heavily red-screened; screen out any external light shining on to the observing site (street lamps, etc).

(i) Decreased accuracy when the variable is very bright.

(j) Decreasing accuracy as the variable fades through about 2 mags above the instrument's threshold.

(k) Giving the observation an emotional bias by looking up, or thinking about, the star's expected magnitude beforehand; the telescope should be approached with a mind empty of preconceptions.*

* Comment of the Director of the V.S.S. [then W. M. Lindley—ed.], when he read this in manuscript: 'I would like you to print note (k) in block letters!'

(*l*) Position-angle error.* That the apparent brightness of a star depends upon its position in the field, and that the perceived relative brightness of two stars depends upon the inclination of the line joining them to that joining the observer's eyes, is well established. But in detail the evidence of different observers is conflicting. Most commonly it appears that when the line-of-stars and the line-of-eyes are parallel, equally bright stars appear equally bright; when the two lines are perpendicular,† maximum inequality in the apparent brightness of the two stars occurs. The rotation of the field through 90° may cause discrepancies of the order of 0·5 to more than 1·0 mag, the lower of the two stars usually, though not invariably, appearing the brighter. The quantity of the error appears to be independent of the brightness of the stars.

One's own p.a. equation can be investigated by observing a pair of stars over a wide range of hour angles, the estimate being made first with the usual inverted field, *a*, and then with an erect field, *b*, at each hour angle. The p.a. error at each hour angle is then $(a-b)/2$.

Even though the variable-star observer is, in principle, making successive observations of two stars, each at the centre of the field, the line-of-stars does not for that reason effectively cease to exist, nor the rule 'keep the line-of-eyes parallel to the line-of-stars' lose its validity. For star *b* does not instantaneously and miraculously replace star *a* at the centre of the field: in fact the telescope has to be moved so that a path can be traced out from *a* to *b* with the help of the known star patterns of the field, *b* being the point of aim but the observer also being unconsciously aware of *a* as the point of departure. One cannot in practice expunge from memory and awareness everything that happens between the moment that *a* ceases to be observed at the field centre and the moment when *b* occupies that position.

(*m*) Purkinje effect and colour-brightness equation.‡ The former begins to obtrude when the intensity has fallen to a level at which rod-vision is being used more than cone-vision. Probably because of different thresholds at which this change-over occurs, two observers of a red variable over an amplitude of 8 mags found a relative personal equation which varied with magnitude, being 0·0 at both ends of the range but 0·7 in the middle.

(*n*) Scale error.§

* See also section 17.3, and *A.A.H.*, section 24.9.
† In one case, maximum divergence from equality occurred systematically when the line-of-stars was inclined at 30° to the vertical, the line-of-eyes being horizontal.
‡ See also section 17.5, and *A.A.H.*, section 24.
§ *A.A.H.*, section 24.3.14.

17.8 Locating variables

A great deal of time can be wasted locating a variable that has just been added to one's observing list unless a rational procedure is adopted. After it has been observed a number of times, of course, the observer's familiarity with the field and immediate surroundings, as well as with the particular course that has been adopted for locating the field, will reduce the time spent on finding to a matter of seconds in most cases, and at worst to two or three minutes.

Once this familiarity with the stars on the observing list has been gained, it is as quick to pick them up by the visual method described below as by using circles; and it has the additional advantage of gradually increasing one's familiarity with the whole face of the night sky.

Whether using circles or the visual method, what the observer is trying to locate is not the variable but the field. Hence the finding operation is not affected by the possible faintness or even the invisibility of the variable itself. For the same reason it is helpful to study the field chart beforehand and memorise the configuration of its brighter stars, so that it will be immediately recognised when it enters the field of the telescope or finder.

The visual method consists in effect of nothing more than the intelligent use of a star atlas, starting with the whole visible hemisphere of sky and narrowing down the position of the variable to within smaller and smaller areas. Suppose the variable sought is X Peg. Its position, $21^h 18^m6$, $+14° 14'$, is plotted on Norton. Then starting from the nearest well-known star group, which in this case may be the Great Square of Pegasus, work nearer to the variable: the southern side of the Square will lead to the rapid identification of ϵ Peg, which is only 8° Sf the variable. Using ϵ Peg as a springboard for further operations, note from the map that the variable lies midway between it and γ Del, and about 3° Nf the centre of the line joining them. At this stage it should be possible to direct the finder at the field with sufficient accuracy for it to be picked up with little or no sweeping; a preliminary examination of the vicinity with binoculars will prove a great help. The field having been located, identify all the visible comparison stars from the X Peg chart (the variable itself may or may not be visible), making yourself so familiar with the pattern of stars that the field's identification will be even quicker next time. The rule to remember when locating V.S. fields by this method is never to go on to the next stage before being quite sure of the last—it is a waste of time, for example, trying to narrow down the position of the X Peg field to within less than 8° if the star you are working from, in the belief that it is ϵ Peg, is in fact β Aqu.

17.9 Equipment

(a) Type of telescope:

Refractors and reflectors are equally suitable, the secondary spectrum of the former merely resulting in a systematic over-estimation of the brightness of red stars, when compared with white, amounting to about 0·1 mags or less. In the case of Newtonians it is essential that the flat should be uniformly silvered, and also large enough to intercept the cone from the whole of the field.

(b) Aperture:

Telescopes of from 3 ins upward can do useful work in the field of variable stars; optical quality much inferior to that demanded by, for example, planetary observation will be tolerated. Moderately large apertures are required to reach many variables at minimum, and the owners of such instruments should concentrate on these, since they are in many cases beyond the reach of smaller apertures. The disadvantages of large apertures are (*i*) excessive brightness of the images; this can be overcome by stopping; (*ii*) small fields; (*iii*) weight and difficulty of handling make readjustments of position between the variable and the comparison star rather slow, with consequent deterioration of the accuracy of the estimates.

(c) Mounting:

An equatorial fitted with circles is a convenience, since it saves some time in the location of unfamiliar or difficult fields, but it is in no sense a necessity.

(d) Oculars:

Wide, flat fields with good definition to the edge are the ideal, since they offer the greatest choice of comparison stars with minimum movement of the telescope. For the same reason, magnifications as low as possible are used. A bar in the field of the HP ocular used for variable-star work is useful for eliminating bright field stars which would otherwise render the comparisons difficult and the results unreliable.

(e) Accessory instruments:

Brightness estimations being most accurate when made in the range of roughly 2 to 4 mags above the instrument's threshold, it follows that a diversity of available aperture is required. The brighter variables can be wholly observed with the naked eye; those lying within the approximate magnitude range 4 to 7, wholly with binoculars; and those fainter than mag 7 at maximum, telescopically. In general, estimates made with binoculars tend to be more accurate than those made with the naked eye, and telescopic estimates than either. Variables of large amplitude cannot always be wholly observed with the same equipment, being too faint at minimum for accurate observation with binoculars or the naked eye, whilst at maximum the telescopic field is too restricted for any suitably bright comparison stars to be anywhere near it. The undesirable switch from monocular to binocular vision can be eliminated over a certain range by means of a predictor telescope or a small hand telescope of the coastguard type.* Nevertheless, any attempt to combine observations made with different apertures inevitably introduces errors into a series of observations, since they can only be made consonant by reducing them to the values that would have been derived by the use of a standard aperture; and the nature of the necessary corrections is not known with any accuracy.

(*f*) *Photometers:*
See *A.A.H.*, section 21; especially 21.3.7, Danjon's photometer.

17.10 Novae
17.10.1 Scope for work:
(*a*) Discovery (see section 17.10.2).

(*b*) Keeping past novae under survey, especially the recurrent novae which may brighten without warning at any time. This work requires considerable aperture, however.

(*c*) Photometric and spectroscopic observations, especially valuable being those made in the stages immediately following the discovery announcement. The early stages in the development of novae are still badly under-observed, since they are so often past before the nova is even discovered. (See also section 17.10.3.)

17.10.2 Searching: Naked-eye discoveries of novae (of which, during the past half-century, there have been two per year on the average) fall surprisingly often to regular meteor observers, giving a clue to one at least of the desiderata for success in this direction: an intimate knowledge of the constellations, so that the appearance of even a 4-mag star in an unusual position catches the eye. Figure 38 shows the magnitude distribution of 21 novae discovered between 1922 and 1948, 38% of which were above the naked-eye threshold at discovery.

Given sufficient familiarity with the galactic region, it is worth while making a quick survey with binoculars at the commencement of each night's observing period. Even a naked-eye nightly survey of the zones

* See *A.A.H.*, section 22.2, for further details.

bounding the Milky Way is likely to bring ultimate success, and is undertaken in a matter of minutes once the stars down to mag 4 or 5 are known.

There is a strong case to be made for cooperative searching: each observer is then responsible for a smaller section of the sky than when on his own, can learn it more thoroughly, and can get through his routine nightly survey more quickly. He should gradually learn the

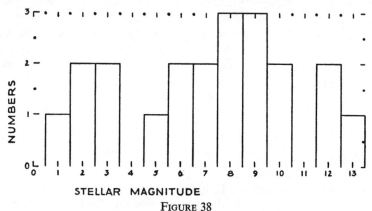

FIGURE 38

Discoveries of novae per magnitude, 1922–1948

positions of all the stars in his zone, making mag 4 his first objective and the naked-eye limit his ultimate one. Allotted zones should be based on the galactic equator as median line. The subjoined Table of galactic distributions refers to the 84 novae known in about 1935:

Number of novae	Galactic Latitude	Galactic Longitude	Number of novae
50	0°– 10°	0°– 90°	21
19	10 – 20	90 – 180	13
9	20 – 40	180 – 270	10
6	40	270 – 360	40

As regards galactic longitude, it should be noted that the preponderance of novae occurs in the quadrant containing the galactic centre (330°).

Searches for novae, their early spectra being so distinctive, could be carried out with an objective prism. Whipple's Nova Monocerotis 1939, and Anderson's novae of 1891 and 1900, for example, were spotted by their spectra.

For photographic searching, see section 17.11.

17.10.3 Spectroscopy: The complex spectroscopic changes concurrent with the brightness variations of novae are described in the text-books. Early observations, in particular, are likely to be of value even when made with modest equipment. An ordinary slitless star spectroscope, used with a LP ocular and an aperture of 3 or 4 ins, is capable of showing bright enough spectra down to about mag 4. No possible spectroscopic observations of novae, at any stage, should be neglected, however.

17.10.4 Supernovae: Occur primarily in the extragalactic nebulae, where instrumental means outside the usual amateur range is needed. So far as is known, three supernovae have appeared in the Galaxy: (*a*) what is now the Crab nebula, (*b*) N. Cassiopeiae 1572, which has not been certainly identified with any object now visible, (*c*) Kepler's nova of 1604, recently identified as a small fan-shaped nebulosity with an emission spectrum similar to that of the Crab nebula.

17.11 Photography

Except in the case of novae there is no scope for the amateur use of photography as a means of discovery (the only means nowadays employed). Although there are countless undiscovered LPVs fainter than mag 10 or 11, and variables of other types brighter than this, it is lack of time for the examination and comparison of plates, rather than lack of the plates themselves, that is the important factor: the Harvard collection alone, containing over 200,000 plates, is so enormous that the amateur working in this field is reasonably certain to be duplicating existing data. Furthermore, 'mass-production' methods*—such as the use of the blink microscope and, in the case of LPVs with their easily recognised emissions, the objective prism—will beat the lone amateur every time. On the other hand, there is nothing to prevent the amateur using these methods† himself, providing he has sufficient instrumental strength to warrant them.

As a photometer, the camera is particularly applicable to: (*a*) the following of faint variables through that section of their curve that might be unobservable visually; (*b*) the determination of photovisual magnitudes of red variables with a yellow filter (e.g. Wratten 12 or 15) and panchromatic plates; an exposure factor of 3 or 4 must be reckoned with, however.

Only for the discovery of novae is the camera well adapted to the conditions of amateur work. Patrol plates should be exposed regularly,

---

* Harvard College Observatory alone had discovered 10,000 by 1939, the majority of these never having been observed since their discovery.

† See section 15.9.2 (objective prism); *A.A.H.*, section 22.8 (blink microscope).

as part of a planned programme of work; variations of stellar brightness, or the appearance of an image on one plate only, are quickly spotted (in the absence of a blink microscope) by superimposing the negative of one photo over the positive print of another.

Instrumental requirements are large D (to provide low magnitude thresholds without excessive exposures) and reasonably small F (for small plate-scale, and therefore wide sky-coverage); excessively short focal lengths, however, will yield impossibly crowded plates. Apertures should not be less than about 2 ins, and if nearer 6 ins, so much the better. Anastigmats, or batteries of portrait lenses, of large linear aperture are therefore indicated.

The chief weakness of portrait and aircraft camera lenses for patrol work—as for wide 'views' of the constellations, photographs of the Milky Way, etc—is the marked aberrational distortion of the outlying images. The chief disadvantage of anastigmats—for the average amateur —is of course their cost.

Barnard's fine Milky Way photographs were taken with a 6-in lens of 31 ins focus, but surprisingly good results have been obtained with apertures of 2 ins and 3 ins at focal ratios of from $f/2$ to $f/5$. More realistic photographs of large sections of the Milky Way are, however, obtainable with a relatively slow wide-angle lens (at, say, $f/11$) using long exposures, since the faster lenses ($f/2$ to $f/6$) produce too rapid a falling off of light towards the edges of the plate.

Patrol plates must be stored and catalogued,* since they may provide valuable negative evidence concerning the pre-outburst condition and history of later novae.

Most novae, however, have been detected visually at the time of their occurrence, photography having been chiefly of value in the 'posthumous' discovery of faint novae.

The spectroscopic study of novae being one of the most powerful lines of attack upon the many still unsolved problems associated with these objects, spectrograms of novae are of great value. The object being a point source and its radiation being parallel, no slit or collimator is needed. The spectrum, which is usually widened by means of a cylindrical lens in visual observation, is most conveniently widened photographically by rotating the spectroscopic unit to make the direction of dispersion coincide with the hour circle through the field, and then to expose the plate with the driving clock running slightly fast or slow. The straightness and definition of the spectral lines then depends, given good seeing, upon the accuracy of the guiding in Dec.

* See *A.A.H.*, section 32.

The factors governing the performance of an objective prism are the familiar ones of D, F, F/D, and fog-rate. A compromise has to be made between, on the one hand, large D (for light grasp) and small F (to reduce the effects of atmospheric turbulence), indicating a small focal ratio and high photographic speed, and, on the other, large F to reduce the fogging rate by increasing the focal ratio. $f/5$ for a 2^h exposure, and *pro rata*, will be found to be about right. Given the dispersion (determined by the prism or grating), the width of spectrum (determined by the clock rate), and the maximum exposure time (determined by the focal ratio and fogging), then the magnitude threshold attainable is a function of D. Given F, D, and the minimum useful spectrum width, the limiting magnitude is a function of the dispersion, and the resolution a function of the atmospheric condition and the resolution of the photographic emulsion.

If an objective prism is used with the telescope itself, it can afford to be of fairly small angle, but if with a camera of relatively short F, the prism angle needs to be 25° or 30° at least, in order to provide sufficient dispersion. Examples of amateur equipment that have produced useful stellar spectrograms: objective prisms of from 45° to 60°, with a 2-in objective working at from $f/5$ to $f/10$; 35° prism covering a 2 in × 2¼ in area of a 3-in telescope objective (the remainder being masked); 60° prism in conjunction with a portrait lens of 5½ ins focus; 20° prism with a 6-in lens at $f/4$.

17.12 Nomenclature

(*a*) Standard system, originated by Argelander, adopted by the Astronomische Gesellschaft, and now universally employed:

(*i*) If the variable had a previous name, this is retained.

(*ii*) In each constellation, 334 variables are designated by a capital Roman letter, or combination of two letters, followed by the constellation abbreviation,* and thereafter by the letter V and a number, this series of numbers opening at 335:

R, S, T . . . . . . Z   9 stars ⎫
RR, RS, RT . . . . RZ   9 stars ⎪
SS, ST, SU . . . . SZ ⎫   ⎪
                     ZZ ⎭ 36 stars   ⎬ 334
AA, AB, AC . . . . AZ (omitting J) 25 stars ⎪ stars
BB, BC, BD . . . . BZ ⎫ (omitting J) 255 stars ⎪
                     QZ ⎭   ⎭

V 335, V 336 . . . . . (see paragraph (*d*) below).

* If given in full, the genitive of the constellation name is used.

(b) Harvard College Observatory positional designations:
6 figures, the 1st two being the hrs of the star's RA (1900),

       ,, 2nd   ,,   mins   ,,   RA,

       ,, last   ,,   degrees ,,   Dec.

N and S Dec are distinguished by italicising or underlining the last two figures, or by preceding them with a minus sign, if the variable is in S Dec.

(c) Chandler's number: A 4-figure group, representing the star's RA (1900), expressed in secs and divided by 10. These are not used nowadays, but are to be found in some of the older catalogues and papers, as well as in Hagen's charts.

(d) Chambers-André-Nijland nomenclature: Variables in each constellation numbered according to order of discovery, the number being prefixed by V; it is this system which is now used from V 335 onward, in each constellation.

(e) Various provisional and 'private' nomenclatures, notably the series of numbers, each prefixed by the letters HV, allotted by the Harvard College Observatory to its own discoveries.*

17.13 Classification

No classification of the more than 10,000 well-known variables based solely upon a single feature of the light-curve (such as period), or solely upon physical causation, is convenient for the practical observer. The following is based upon the classifications of Pickering, Ludendorff, and Campbell and Jacchia, but reference should be made to the more recent classification in the second edition of B. 509; and to B. 349a.

I. IRREGULAR

1. Novae:	(a)	Supernovae:	S And,
	(b)	Normal:	N. Aql 1945,
	(c)	Recurring:	T CrB.
2. Nova-like:	(a)	Steady, with sudden rises: U Gem- and SS Cyg-type,	
	(b)	Z Cam-type,	
	(c)	Miscellaneous: variables with nova-like spectroscopic or other features: Z And etc.	
3. Red giants:	(a)	Irregular:	TU Aur,
	(b)	Semi-regular:	V Hya.
4. Miscellaneous:	(a)	Rapid: RW Aur,	
	(b)	Nebular: T Ori,	
	(c)	Steady, with sudden falls: R CrB,	
	(d)	Be-type stars: γ Cas,	
	(e)	Flare stars: UV Cet.	

* Similarly HN for nebulae discovered at Harvard.

VARIABLES

II. LONG-PERIOD

(a)	Me-type stars:	o Cet,
(b)	Se-type stars:	R Cam,
(c)	Ne-type stars:	R Lep,
(d)	Re-type stars:	RU Vir.

III. SHORT-PERIOD

1. Eclipsing:
   - (a) Algol-type: λ Tau,
   - (b) β Lyr-type: u Her,
   - (c) W UMa-type: RR Cen.
2. Pulsating:
   - (a) Long-period Cepheids: δ Cep,
   - (b) Short-period Cepheids ('Cluster Variables'): RR Lyr,
   - (c) Semi-regular: RV Tau,
   - (d) β CMa-type: β UMa.
3. Ellipsoidal: ζ And.

The characteristics of each type are summarised below:

I.1(a): Average absolute mag at maximum, −15; remain at maximum longer, and fade more slowly and steadily, than normal novae.

I.1(b): Average amplitude about 13 mags; great variety among the individual curves; average absolute mag at maximum, about −6; galactic concentration.

I.1(c): Amplitude less than that of normal novae (average, 7–8 mags); extraordinarily rapid rise to maximum; 30–40 years between outbursts seems to be the favoured interval.

I.2(a): About 80 known; binary nature discovered 1944; steady minima with sudden rises; all faint, blue-white stars, showing no galactic concentration; variation of spectra with magnitude rather reminiscent of novae; amplitudes typically 3–5 mags; periods from about 15^d to 350^d.

I.2(b): About a dozen known; amplitude about 3 mags; shorter minima than I.2(a), separated by steady periods (weeks, or even a year) and periods of erratic behaviour.

I.3: Hydrogen emissions weak or absent, and no period/spectral type correlation (cf. II); complex curves often due to superposition of two simpler curves, the median magnitude having a long-period variation; amplitudes small; several hundred known. No sharp demarcation between (a) and (b). Periods, 40–530^d, concentration around 180^d; periods of (b) may vary by 100%.

I.4(a): Large amplitudes; rapid and erratic brightness variation; less than a dozen known.

I.4(b): Small amplitudes; all associated with nebulosity; normally of types B, A, and F.

I.4(c): Large amplitudes (5–9 mags); long maxima (which may continue for years) with sudden fadings and slower recoveries at completely irregular intervals.

I.4(d): B-type stars with hydrogen emissions and variable spectra; variations slow, including long steady periods.

I.4(e): Dwarfs, with emission lines in spectra (type dMe); flares, supposedly analogous to solar flares, at times produce startling increases of brightness, e.g. UV Cet on one occasion increased 6 mags in less than 1 minute; only 5 members known (1952), one being Proxima Centauri.

II: Numerous. Periods from 120^d to 1400^d, majority between 200^d and 400^d, with concentration about 275^d. Great variety of curves, but secondary minima rare. Spectra of the vast majority contain emissions, primarily hydrogen. Giants, red or reddish; pulsating; no galactic concentration.

299

II(*a*): About 2600 known diversity of curves; amplitudes 4–10 mags, average about 6 mags; minor irregularities usual in amplitude, period, and form of curve. Spectra characterised by titanium oxide bands, and strong hydrogen emissions at maxima.

II(*b*): About 25 members; periods from 200^d to 600^d; zirconium oxide bands; otherwise generally similar to (*a*).

II(*c*): About 25 members; average amplitude about 4 mags; periods from 254^d to 580^d, average about 420^d; broad maxima and narrow minima; carbon, cyanogen, and hydrocarbon bands; very red stars.

II(*d*): Very few known; similar to (*c*).

III.1: About 2000 known.

III.1(*a*): About 1200 members; largest amplitudes in III.1; periods from $0^d.197$ to 9883^d, majority 2–3^d, caused by the mutual eclipses of undistorted stars; brightness therefore constant (or very nearly so) between eclipses.

III.1(*b*): About 200 members; amplitudes normally less than 15 mags; periods from *c.* $0^d.48$ to 199^d, average $0^d.8$; caused by the mutual eclipses of distorted, unequally bright stars; brightness variation therefore continuous, with secondary minima.

III.1(*c*): About 200 members; average amplitude 0·65 mags; average period $0^d.48$, limits $0^d.219$–$1^d.327$; caused by the mutual eclipses of distorted, equally bright stars; variation therefore continuous, with equal minima.

III.2: The observed relation between the radial velocity and magnitude of these stars cannot be explained on the supposition of a *comes*.

III.2(*a*): Over 450 known in the Galaxy, about 2500 in the extragalactic nebulae; periods, 1–45^d, majority about 5^d; stars of great luminosity; spectra of the shorter-period Cepheids vary from F at maximum to G at minimum, of those with longer periods from G at maximum to K at minimum; variation characteristically regular, with rise steeper than fall; galactic concentration.

III.2(*b*): About 600 known in the globular clusters, 900 outside them; periods from 1·5 to 24^h, the majority between 9^h and 17^h, with a concentration about 13^h; spectra, A at maximum to F at minimum; form of curves similar to III. 2(*a*); no galactic concentration.

III.2(*c*): About 65 known; high luminosities; same spectrum/period relation as the Cepheids; characteristically have two equal maxima and two unequal minima.

III.2(*d*): About 20 members; extremely small amplitudes—normally a few hundredths of a mag, never more than 0·25 mags; short periods—majority between 2^h and 8·5; characteristic spectral type, B; variation of radial velocity more striking than that of brightness.

III.3: Revolving distorted stars which do not eclipse one another; amplitudes very small, average about 0·2 mags.

17.14 The Julian Date

In computations and records covering wide time-intervals it is inconvenient to have to deal in miscellaneous units, such as years, months, and days.

The Julian Calendar consists of a continuous series of numbered days, originating at a sufficiently distant past date to ensure that no date prior to JD 1 will be required. The date of the origin of the series is 4713 B.C., whence 1950=Julian Year 6663.

In the following table are tabulated the last 4 figures of the Julian dates of the zero day of each month from 1970 to 1995. The figures must be added to 2,440,000 to derive the full Julian date. Thus the JD of

$$
\begin{array}{rr}
1970 \text{ Feb 10 is} & 2,440,000 \\
& 0,618 \\
& 10 \\
\hline
& 2,440,628 \\
\\
1984 \text{ Apr 1 is} & 2,440,000 \\
& 5,791 \\
& 1 \\
\hline
& 2,445,792
\end{array}
$$

	Jan.	Feb.	Mar.	Apr.	May	Jun.	Jul.	Aug.	Sep.	Oct.	Nov.	Dec.
1970	0587	0618	0646	0677	0707	0738	0768	0799	0830	0860	0891	0921
71	0952	0983	1011	1042	1072	1103	1133	1164	1195	1225	1256	1286
72	1317	1348	1377	1408	1438	1469	1499	1530	1561	1591	1622	1652
73	1683	1714	1742	1773	1803	1834	1864	1895	1926	1956	1987	2017
74	2048	2079	2107	2138	2168	2199	2229	2260	2291	2321	2352	2382
1975	2413	2444	2472	2503	2533	2564	2594	2625	2656	2686	2717	2747
76	2778	2809	2838	2869	2899	2930	2960	2991	3022	3052	3083	3113
77	3144	3175	3203	3234	3264	3295	3325	3356	3387	3417	3448	3478
78	3509	3540	3568	3599	3629	3660	3690	3721	3752	3782	3813	3843
79	3874	3905	3933	3964	3994	4025	4055	4086	4117	4147	4178	4208
1980	4239	4270	4299	4330	4360	4391	4421	4452	4483	4513	4544	4574
81	4605	4636	4664	4695	4725	4756	4786	4817	4848	4878	4909	4939
82	4970	5001	5029	5060	5090	5121	5151	5182	5213	5243	5274	5304
83	5335	5366	5394	5425	5455	5486	5516	5547	5578	5608	5639	5669
84	5700	5731	5760	5791	5821	5852	5882	5913	5944	5974	6005	6035
1985	6066	6097	6125	6156	6186	6217	6247	6278	6309	6339	6370	6400
86	6431	6462	6490	6521	6551	6582	6612	6643	6674	6704	6735	6765
87	6796	6827	6855	6886	6916	6947	6977	7008	7039	7069	7100	7130
88	7161	7192	7221	7252	7282	7313	7343	7374	7405	7435	7466	7496
89	7527	7558	7586	7617	7647	7678	7708	7739	7770	7800	7831	7861
1990	7892	7923	7951	7982	8012	8043	8073	8104	8135	8165	8196	8226
91	8257	8288	8316	8347	8377	8408	8438	8469	8500	8530	8561	8591
92	8622	8653	8682	8713	8743	8774	8804	8835	8866	8896	8927	8957
93	8988	9019	9047	9078	9108	9139	9169	9200	9231	9261	9292	9322
94	9353	9384	9412	9443	9473	9504	9534	9565	9596	9626	9657	9687
1995	9718	9749	9777	9808	9838	9869	9899	9930	9961	9991	10022	10052

17.15 Conversion of hours and minutes to decimals of a day

Observers are asked to report their observations to the B.A.A. timed in ʰ ᵐ GMAT (see section 17.6.2), as in their Observational Record, and to leave the conversion to decimals of a GMAT day or Julian day (in those cases where it is necessary to specify the time of an observation more precisely than by date alone) to the Section Director.

It is the usual practice, however, to quote times of variable-star observations by decimals of a day rather than in hours and minutes, and it is often convenient to have a conversion table handy. The following table gives results correct to the nearest $0\overset{d}{\cdot}005$, or $\pm 7\overset{m}{\cdot}2$.

To convert Hours and Minutes to Decimals of a Day:

h	m		h	m		h	m		h	m	
0	00										
		·00									
	07		4	12		8	16		12	21	
		·01			·18			·35			·52
	21			26			31			36	
		·02			·19			·36			·53
	36			40		8	45		12	50	
		·03			·20			·37			·54
0	50		4	55		9	00		13	04	
		·04			·21			·38			·55
1	04		5	09			14			19	
		·05			·22			·39			·56
	19			24			28			33	
		·06			·23			·40			·57
	33			38			43		13	48	
		·07			·24			·41			·58
1	48		5	52		9	57		14	02	
		·08			·25			·42			·59
2	02		6	07		10	12			16	
		·09			·26			·43			·60
	16			21			26			31	
		·10			·27			·44			·61
	31			36			40		14	45	
		·11			·28			·45			·62
2	45		6	50		10	55		15	00	
		·12			·29			·46			·63
3	00		7	04		11	09			14	
		·13			·30			·47			·64
	14			19			24			28	
		·14			·31			·48			·65
	28			33			38			43	
		·15			·32			·49			·66
	43		7	48		11	52		15	57	
		·16			·33			·50			·67
3	57		8	02		12	07		16	12	
		·17			·34			·51			·68
4	12			16			21			26	

VARIABLES

h	m		h	m		h	m		h	m	
16	26		18	21		20	16		22	12	
		·69			·77			·85			·93
	40			36			31			26	
		·70			·78			·86			·94
16	55		18	50		20	45			40	
		·71			·79			·87			·95
17	09		19	04		21	00		22	55	
		·72			·80			·88			·96
	24			19			14		23	09	
		·73			·81			·89			·97
	38			33			28			24	
		·74			·82			·90			·98
17	52		19	48			43			38	
		·75			·83			·91			·99
18	07		20	02		21	57			52	
		·76			·84			·92			1·00
	21			16		22	12		23	59	

In critical cases ascend.

SECTION 18

BINARIES

18.1 Work

Professional observatories hold all the trumps in this field, though double stars provide a field for gaining experience in the technique of micrometer measures and orbit computation, and there is a limited scope for amateur photography (see section 18.4). Primarily, however, binaries are of interest to the amateur as tests of instrumental performance.

As regards the discovery of new faint binaries, Jonckhere has recently denied the truth of Aitken's dictum that the need today is not for more discoveries, but for more numerous and more accurate measures of already known doubles.

18.2 Measures of position

With 6-ins aperture or more, work of value can be done with micrometer or camera; but it should be remembered that unpublished measures are valueless. With apertures smaller than 6 ins it is a waste of time to concentrate on binaries. Dawes, the eagle-eyed, worked with instruments ranging from 3·8 to 8·5 ins, mostly 7 to 8·5 ins, all refractors.

With an ordinary filar micrometer a clock-driven 12-in can make reliable measures of doubles with separations down to about $0.''5$, but by the method of matching ellipses this threshold has been considerably lowered, with still reasonable accuracy (θ to within $15°$ and r to $\pm 0.''025$ on the average):

D	R (theoretical threshold)	Measurable threshold of r
3 ins	$1.''82$	$0.''75–1.''10$
5	$1·09$	$0·45–0·65$
8	$0·68$	$0·3–0·4$
11	$0·49$	$0·2–0·3$

The method is to match as nearly as possible the observed elongated star image (unresolved) with one of a series of white ellipses photographed on a dark ground. A set of five such ellipses is employed, one axis being 1·0 cms in each case, the other progressing from 0·96 to 1·16 cms in 0·04 cm steps. The reliability of the measures falls off sharply outside the range of eccentricities 1·04–1·12; also if the magnitude difference exceeds 2. For this work a high magnification is recommended (75D), and good seeing is absolutely essential.

The choice of stars for observation is important:

(*a*) For reliable measures, the pair should be well above the instrument's theoretical resolution threshold; Aitken's opinion was that to secure the greatest accuracy possible with a given equipment, the separation should not be less than twice the instrument's theoretical threshold, given good seeing.

(*b*) Rapidly moving pairs are, generally, those most needing observation: those with separations of less than 0″5, say (implying an aperture of not less than 10 ins), for which one set of measures every 1 to 5 years is sufficient. For those with separations of 1″–5″, measures every 20 years or so are adequate.

(*c*) Stars which are shown by the catalogues to have been poorly observed in the past or to be at a critical point in their orbit.

Separation is measured in ″ arc; position angle from 0° (N), through 90° (*f*), 180° (S), and 270° (*p*), where the hour circle of the primary passes through the N and S points of the field (see *A.A.H.*, Figure 192).

For the measurement of θ and r by the filar micrometer, see *A.A.H.*, section 18.6.

For the use of objective and exit-pupil diaphragms in the observation of binaries, see *A.A.H.*, section 27.1.

The observer should be aware of the following precautions and sources of error in double-star measurements:

(*a*) Seeing is the all-important factor in the measurement of difficult pairs, and measures should not be attempted when the seeing is poor; inferior results are inevitable, and these are worse than merely useless. For this reason it is well to have prepared working lists, supplemented where necessary by charts, so that full use can be made of periods of good seeing when they occur.

(*b*) Each final measure should be the mean of about 3 nights' observations (more if the measures are discordant, or the pair is very difficult), each night's observations consisting of at least three measures of θ and three of the double distance. In this way errors due to seeing and the physiological condition of the observer may be to some extent reduced.

(*c*) Systematic errors are more difficult to eliminate. They are mainly dependent on the personal idiosyncrasy of the observer, the relative brightness of the two stars, their separation, and the inclination of the radius vector to the horizontal. Some mitigation of these can be achieved by taking the mean of measures made on either side of the meridian, and with and without a totally reflecting prism, placed between the eye and the ocular, which inverts the field. According to Voûte, more trouble is encountered when the radius vector is vertical than when horizontal.

(*d*) Tilt the head so that the line through the eyes is systematically either parallel or perpendicular (preferably the former) to the line through the components.

(*e*) See that the observing position (especially of the head and neck) is comfortable.

(*f*) With unequally bright pairs there is a tendency when measuring θ to set the web tangential to the discs instead of bisecting them or setting it parallel to their centres. Therefore bring the stars nearly into contact with the web, first from one side and then from the other, taking an equal number of readings on either side of the web.

(*g*) Between successive measures of θ, throw the web off in opposite directions. Also remove the eye from the telescope between measures and attempt to come to the next measure with no recollection of the last one.

(*h*) Separations, when small, tend to be over-estimated, owing to the dilation of the star image when the web is placed across it. Small instruments hence have a systematic tendency to over-estimate r, since they cannot use sufficient magnification to separate out the images (it being assumed, of course, that the instrument's resolving power is adequate in the first place). This factor becomes increasingly important as the value of r is reduced from about twice the theoretical resolution threshold. There are two alleviants: (*i*) a Barlow lens placed forward of the primary focus increases the separation of the images in the field without increasing the apparent thickness of the webs; (*ii*) before the measures are made, the appearance of each star when accurately bisected by the web should be carefully noted and memorised; when making the measures, a conscious attempt is made to reproduce these appearances accurately.

(*i*) Webs and stars must be simultaneously in accurate focus.*

(*j*) The accuracy with which θ is measurable depends, *inter alia*, upon the accuracy of the setting of the polar axis. The gravity of the errors from this cause increases with increasing Dec, and for

* See, further, *A.A.H.*, section 18.2.

satisfactory results to be obtained in the vicinity of the Pole itself extreme precision in the orientation and elevation of the polar axis is demanded. For Innes's modification of the Struve method of dealing with errors of this nature, see B. 373.

18.3 Magnification

The general subject of magnification limits is discussed in *A.A.H.*, section 3; it is of relevance here since the measurement of double stars normally entails magnifications near the upper limit. The atmosphere is therefore frequently the limiting factor in this work; when turbulence forbids the use of adequate magnification it is advisable to restrict observation to pairs of sufficient separation to be observable with low magnifications. Aitken, for example, never attempted to observe the closer pairs with the Lick 36-in refractor unless a magnification of $\times 1500$ ($42D$) was feasible. Burnham's invariable rule was to use the lowest magnification yielding sufficient separation for a good measure to be made, thus exposing himself as little as possible to the effects of inferior seeing.

Taking $70D$ as an average permissible magnification on good nights, at any rate over the small and moderate aperture range, and following Aitken's usual practice with the 36-in of using

    $\times 520$ on pairs wider than 2″,
    $\times 1000$ on pairs between 2″ and 1″,
    $\times 1000 - \times 3000$ on pairs closer than 0″.5,

we have, as a very rough guide, that

    an 8-in will tackle pairs wider than 2″,
    a 14-in will tackle pairs wider than 1″,
    a 20-in will tackle pairs wider than 0″.5.

This agrees more or less with W. H. Pickering's dictum that for work of value, atmosphere and instrument must be capable of supporting a magnification of at least $\times 800$. Most of Burnham's measures with the 36-in were made with $\times 1000 - \times 1500$ ($28D$–$42D$), $\times 2600$ ($72D$) being reserved for the very closest pairs; Barnard employed the same magnifications, finding that $\times 2600$ could be used very rarely indeed.

Lewis (B. 377) carried out a valuable investigation into the magnifications actually employed by 36 double-star observers in all parts of the world, using instruments from 3·8 to 36 ins aperture. His results are summarised below. The actual magnifications most used with the different apertures in col. (1) are tabulated in col. (2), the equivalent

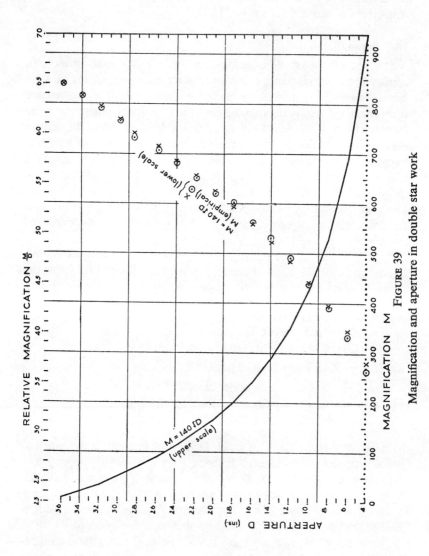

FIGURE 39

Magnification and aperture in double star work

magnification per inch of aperture in col. (3). Lewis found that these empirical figures could be nearly represented by the formula

$$M = 140\sqrt{D}$$

as can be seen from cols. (4) and (5) and Figure 39.

(1) D	(2) M	(3) Equivalent M per in	(4) $M=140\sqrt{D}$	(5) Equivalent M per in
4	264	66·0	280	70·0
6	333	55·5	344	57·3
8	392	49·0	396	49·5
10	440	44·0	443	44·3
12	492	41·0	485	40·4
14	532	38·0	524	37·4
16	563	35·2	560	35·0
18	604	33·6	594	33·0
20	620	31·0	626	31·0
22	651	29·6	657	29·9
24	682	28·4	686	28·6
26	707	27·2	714	27·5
28	731	26·1	741	26·5
30	765	25·5	767	25·6
32	790	24·7	792	24·7
34	816	24·0	816	24·0
36	840	23·3	840	23·3

It will be seen that the maximum practicable magnification, when expressed in terms of aperture, is not constant over the range of apertures employed, but falls continuously with increasing aperture.*

From these empirical figures it might appear that 70*D* is in fact seldom realised, even with small instruments, and that the conclusions reached on the preceding page need fairly drastic amendment. It must be pointed out, however, that the figures derived by Lewis represent the most commonly employed magnification with each aperture, and were obtained by weighting each in proportion to the number of times it was employed over a period of time. Considerably higher magnifications can be used, all along the range of apertures, when the seeing is better than average; 70*D* is not infrequently practicable at least into the moderate-aperture range, though by the time *D* reaches 36 ins the

* See also, in this connexion, *A.A.H.*, section 3.

experience of Burnham and Barnard indicates that it can be very rarely used.

18.4 Photography

The measurement of wide pairs can be undertaken more accurately from photographic plates than by direct observation with a micrometer. Given a moderate aperture the measurement of pairs wider than about 3″ may be undertaken, but the necessity for a plate-measuring machine and the fact that this field is covered by the professional observatories make the work somewhat ill-adapted to amateur requirements and qualifications.

18.5 Apparent orbits

The true orbit of the *comes* about the primary (it is assumed for simplicity that only the *comes* is in motion, the primary being used as the reference point for this motion) is observed as projected upon a plane perpendicular to the line of sight. Its projection in this plane is known as the apparent orbit. The determination of the apparent orbit can be made either from the observed position angles and separations at different times, or from the elements of the true orbit.

Two simple graphical methods of establishing the apparent orbit of a binary are described below. The first, modified from J. Herschel, is both the more elegant and the more accurate. It is instructive occasionally to use both methods on the same set of observational material and to compare the results obtained. For the construction of the apparent orbit from the elements of the true orbit, see B. 370.

First method:

Given: θ (position angle) and r (angular separation) at a variety of dates, t.

The advantage of this method is that it employs θ only, which is in general a more accurately observable quantity than r, in establishing the form of the orbit.

1. Construct a pro-forma for the following Table:

(1)	(2)	(3)	(4)	(5)	(6)	(7)	(8)
θ	t	Δt	$\Delta\Delta t$	$\dfrac{1}{v}$	$\sqrt{\dfrac{\Delta t}{\Delta \theta}}$	r	r'

2. Plot the given values of θ against t. Through these points draw the best possible freehand curve; this is known as the interpolating curve.

3. In col. (1) set down a series of equally spaced position angles (say every 5° or 10° throughout the given series of values of θ), read off the corresponding values of t from the interpolating curve, and tabulate these in the left-hand side of col. (2). It will probably be necessary to smooth this curve.

4. In the left-hand side of col. (3) tabulate the difference between each pair of values of t; in the left-hand side of col. (4) tabulate the difference between each pair of values of Δt. The first differences in col. (3) should increase or decrease steadily; the existence of any sudden jumps is more easily seen in the column of second differences, which, however, can be omitted when some experience has been gained.

Any such sudden increase or decrease must be eliminated by adjusting the date in col. (2) which is responsible for it. A second interpolating curve is then constructed from the values in col. (1) and the adjusted values which have been entered in the right-hand side of col. (2). This in turn is tested for smoothness and when satisfactory is known as the smoothed interpolating curve.

5. Take the mean of the values of Δt on either side of each value in col. (2), divide it by the constant difference between the values in col. (1), and enter in col. (5).

6. The square roots of the values in col. (5) are taken and entered in col. (6); these values are now, by Kepler II, proportional to the radii vectores at each position angle in col. (1).

7. From a central point on a sheet of graph paper lay off the radii vectores in col. (1). Using the largest scale that the sheet allows, cut off on each radius vector a length proportional to the corresponding value in col. (6).

8. Through these points draw the best possible ellipse (ellipsograph or pins and cotton loop).

9. If any points lie far from any possible curve, work back to the smoothed interpolating curve, make the necessary correction, and draw a new ellipse.

To find the scale of this apparent orbit:

10. Plot the observed values of r against the times, t, at which the observations were made.

11. Draw the interpolating curve through these points.

12. Tabulate in col. (7) the values of r, read off this curve, corresponding to the values of t in col. (2).

13. In col. (8) tabulate the scale values of the radii vectores of the apparent orbit corresponding to the values of θ in col. (1).

14. The value in " arc of one scale division is then given by dividing the sum of the values in col. (7) by the sum of those in col. (8).

Second method:

Given: a set of values of θ and r at different times, as before.

1. Construct a pro-forma for the following Table:

(1)	(2)	(3)	(4)	(5)	(6)	(7)	(8)
t	θ	r	Δt	$\Delta\theta$	$\dfrac{\Delta t}{\Delta\theta}$	$\sqrt{\dfrac{\Delta t}{\Delta\theta}}$	$\sqrt{\dfrac{\Delta t}{\Delta}} \times$

2. Enter the observational data in cols. (1)–(3).

3. In col. (4) tabulate the intervals separating the dates tabulated in col. (1).

4. In col. (5) tabulate the differences between the values of θ in col. (2).

5. The angular velocity at each time in col. (1) is obtained by dividing each corresponding value of Δt by that of $\Delta\theta$. These are entered in col. (6).

6. Take the square roots of these values and enter them in col. (7).

7. From a central point, representing the primary, lay off the position angles tabulated in col. (2); mark each with the corresponding date from col. (1); lay off on each, using the largest scale that the paper will allow, a distance proportional to the corresponding value in col. (3). The points so plotted will probably show a considerable scatter, but draw through them the best ellipse that is possible.

8. From this first rough orbit estimate as nearly as possible the period (p), and measure the major and minor axes (a, b), converting them (the scale being known) to " arc.

9. The radius of the circle whose area is equal to that of the orbit is given by $\frac{1}{2}\sqrt{ab}$. Calculate the value of $\frac{1}{2}\sqrt{ab} \cdot \sqrt{\dfrac{360}{p}}$; call this k.

10. Insert this value at the head of col. (8), thus: $\sqrt{\dfrac{\Delta t}{\Delta \theta}} \times [k]$, and tabulate the values.

11. Each of these values, in $''$ arc, represents the radius of a circle whose segment bounded by the corresponding radii vectores is equal in area to the segment of the orbital ellipse bounded by the same radii vectores. On the diagram of the approximate orbit draw the arcs of these circles, using in turn the radii tabulated in col. (8). By their means the necessary corrections can be applied to the rough orbit. A surprising degree of accuracy can be obtained, though this stage of the process requires practice.

18.6 True orbits

If one of the foci of the apparent orbit coincides with the primary, it is also the true orbit. If, however, the plane of the true orbit is not perpendicular to the line of sight, this coincidence will not occur.

The true orbit is defined by the following elements:

P: Period (mean solar years),
T: Time of periastron passage,
e: Eccentricity,
a: Semimajor axis ($''$ arc),
Ω (or ω):   Position angle of the node which lies between $0°$ and $180°$,
i (or γ):   Inclination of the orbital plane to the plane of projection,
λ (or ω):   Angle between the line of nodes and the major axis, measured in the plane of the true orbit.

There are numerous methods of computing the elements of the true orbit, among them:

(a) The Thiele-Innes method (B. 370).
(b) Kowalsky's analytical method: derivation of the elements from the constants of the general equation of the apparent orbit (B. 370, 382).
(c) Zwiers' graphical method: involves the prior construction of an accurate apparent orbit (B. 370).
(d) Russell's method (B. 378).

18.7 Spectroscopic binaries

The orbit of a spectroscopic binary may be determined by a variety of methods:

(a) The Lehmann-Filhés method (B. 370).

(*b*) Schwarzschild's method (B. 370).

(*c*) Zurhellen's methods (B. 370).

(*d*) King's method (B. 370, 375).

(*e*) Russell's short method (B. 370, 379).

18.8 Eclipsing binaries

See section 17.

For methods of computing the orbits of eclipsing binaries, see B. 370, 381; also B. 380.

SECTION 19

NEBULAE AND CLUSTERS

The scope for original and valuable work in this field lies with the large instruments of the professional observatories. Nebulae and clusters are nevertheless among the more exciting discoveries of the telescopic beginner who is making his first survey of the heavens.

They also represent a fruitful field for the photographer using even quite modest equipment. Nebulae being extended objects of, for the most part, small angular dimensions, the instrumental requirement for their successful photography is the difficult one of large linear F and small focal ratio—i.e. the linear values of both F and D are large. Clusters, though consisting of stellar points, still ideally require large linear dimensions of the objective, their angular smallness demanding large F and their faintness a wide aperture.

Generally speaking, clusters and small nebulae are best photographed at the telescopic focus with amplification, and probably with some subsequent enlargement as well. More extended nebulosity may be photographed with portrait lenses of fairly long F (20 ins, say), with some subsequent enlargement. At $F=20$ ins, for example, fine photographs can be obtained of the Orion nebula, although M32 remains stellar in appearance with all but the giant instruments.

Telephoto lenses have also been used with success in this field. A $2\frac{1}{2}$-in of 20 ins F, for example, provided much resolution of the Perseus double cluster in as little as 30^m, and of the Orion nebula in 8^m. A $f/4.5$ anastigmat of $3\frac{1}{2}$ ins aperture showed the spiral form of M31 in $1\frac{1}{2}^h$, as well as producing recognisable photographs of the Horsehead nebula, the Cygnus filamentous nebula, and others. As results of what can be achieved at the telescopic focus of a 12-in reflector, the following may be mentioned: the spiral structure of M101 in 2^h, considerable detail and extent of the Orion nebula in 30^m (the Trapezium already lost in over-exposure), and the open clusters M46 and M35 in 30^m.

BIBLIOGRAPHY

[See pages 347–349 for a Supplemental Bibliography listing books published since the original bibliography was compiled.]

Abbreviations used in this Bibliography are listed below; wherever possible the style of the *Astronomischer Jahresbericht* or the *World List of Scientific Periodicals* has been followed. Bibliographical data are enclosed in round brackets ( ); my own comments, if any, in square brackets[ ]. Each division of the Bibliography is arranged alphabetically by authors unless some other arrangement (e.g. chronological) is specified.

A.J. Astronomical Journal.

A.N. Astronomische Nachrichten.

Ann. Cape Obs. Annals of the Cape Observatory.

Ann. d'Astrophys. Annales d'Astrophysique.

Ann. Lowell Obs. Lowell Observatory Annals.

Ann. Obs. Strasbourg. Annales de l'Observatoire de Strasbourg.

Ap. J. Astrophysical Journal [previously 'Sidereal Messenger', 1883–92; 'Astronomy and Astro-Physics', 1892–95].

Astr. Mitt. Göttingen. Astronomische Mittheilungen der Königlichen Sternwarte zu Göttingen.

Astr. Pap., Wash. Astronomical Papers of the American Ephemeris & Nautical Almanac.

B.A.A.H. Handbook of the British Astronomical Association.

Brit. J. Physiol. Optics. British Journal of Physiological Optics.

B.S.A.F. Bulletin de la Société Astronomique de France ['L'Astronomie'].

Connais. Temps. Connaissance des Temps.

Contr. Dunsink Obs. Dunsink Observatory Contributions.

Contr. Lick Obs. Contributions from the Lick Observatory.

Contr. Perkins Obs. Perkins Observatory Contributions.

Contr. Princeton Obs. Princeton University Observatory Contributions.

C.R. Comptes Rendus des Séances de l'Académie des Sciences.

Engl. Mech. English Mechanics [formerly 'The English Mechanic'].

Harv. Ann. Annals of Harvard College Observatory.

Harv. Bull. Harvard Bulletins.

Harv. Circ. Harvard College Observatory Circulars.

Harv. Monogr. Harvard Observatory Monographs.

Harv. Repr. Harvard Reprints.

H.d.A. Handbuch der Astrophysik (Julius Springer, Berlin).

H.M.S.O. Her Majesty's Stationery Office.

I.A.U. International Astronomical Union.

Internat. Ass. Acad. International Association of Academies.

Irish Astr. J. Irish Astronomical Journal.
J. Appl. Phys. Journal of Applied Physics.
J.B.A.A. Journal of the British Astronomical Association.
J. Can. R.A.S. Journal of the Royal Astronomical Society of Canada.
J. Opt. Soc. Amer. Journal of the Optical Society of America.
J. Sci. Instr. Journal of Scientific Instruments.
L.O.B. Lick Observatory Bulletins.
Lund. Medd. Meddelande från Lunds Astronomiska Observatorium.
Mem. Amer. Acad. Arts Sci. Memoirs of the American Academy of Arts and
Sciences.
Mem. B.A.A. Memoirs of the British Astronomical Association.
Mem. R.A.S. Memoirs of the Royal Astronomical Society and Memoirs of
the Astronomical Society of London [consecutive volume numbering].
M.N. Monthly Notices of the Royal Astronomical Society.
M.W.C. Mount Wilson Contributions.
N.A. The Nautical Almanac and Astronomical Ephemeris (H.M.S.O.,
annually).
Nat. Nature.
Obs. The Observatory.
Perkins Obs. Repr. Perkins Observatory Reprints.
Phil. Trans. Philosophical Transactions of the Royal Society.
Photogr. J. Photographic Journal.
Phys. Rev. Physical Review [U.S.A.].
Pop. Astr. Popular Astronomy.
Proc. Amer. Acad. Arts Sci. Proceedings of the American Academy of Arts
and Sciences.
Proc. Amer. Phil. Soc. Proceedings of the American Philosophical Society.
Proc. Phys. Soc. Lond. Proceedings of the Physical Society.
Proc. R. Irish Acad. Proceedings of the Royal Irish Academy.
Proc. Roy. Soc. Proceedings of the Royal Society.
Publ. A.A.S. Publications of the American Astronomical Society.
Publ. A.S.P. Publications of the Astronomical Society of the Pacific.
Publ. Tartu. Publications de l'Observatoire Astronomique de l'Université de
Tartu (Dorpat).
Publ. Astrophys. Obs. Potsdam. Publikationen des Astrophysikalischen Ob-
servatoriums zu Potsdam.
Publ. Carneg. Instn. Carnegie Institution Publications, Washington.
Publ. Cincinn. Obs. Cincinnati Observatory Publications.
Publ. Dom. Astrophys. Obs. Dominion Astrophysical Observatory Publica-
tions.
Publ. Lick Obs. Lick Observatory Publications.
Publ. L. McC. Obs. Publications of the Leander McCormick Observatory of
the University of Virginia.
Publ. Michigan Obs. Michigan Observatory Publications.
Publ. Univ. Pa. Pennsylvania University Publications (Astronomical Series).
Publ. Yale Obs. Yale University Observatory Publications.
Result. Obs. Nac. Argent. Resultados del Observatorio Nacional Argentino.
Rev. d'Opt. Revue d'Optique Théorique et Instrumentale.
Rev. Mod. Phys. Review of Modern Physics.

Rev. Sci. Instr. Review of Scientific Instruments.
Sci. Amer. Scientific American.
Sci. Progr. Science Progress.
Sky & Telesc. Sky and Telescope [amalgamation of 'Sky' and 'Telescope'].
Smithson. Contr. Smithsonian Contributions to Knowledge.
Trans. I.A.U. Transactions of the International Astronomical Union.
Veröff. Univ. Berlin-Babelsberg. Veröffentlichungen der Universitätsstern-warte zu Berlin-Babelsberg.
Veröff. König. Astron. Rechen-Instit. Veröffentlichungen des Königlichen Astronomischen Rechen-Instituts zu Berlin.
Wash. Nat. Ac. Proc. Proceedings of the National Academy of Science of the United States of America.

Solar System—Miscellaneous

1. s. CHAPMAN & J. BARTELS, *Geomagnetism* (Oxford, 1940).
2. J. A. FLEMING (ed.), *Terrestrial Magnetism* (McGraw-Hill, 1939).
3. F. J. HARGREAVES, [Report of Presidential Address to the B.A.A., 1944] (*J.B.A.A.*, **55**, No. 1, 1).
4. [JARRY-DESLOGES], *Observations des Surfaces Planétaires* [made at the Jarry-Desloges Observatory] (Gauthier–Villars, Paris (vols. 1–3), Paillart, Abbeville (vols. 4–10), 1908–1946).
5. H. JEFFREYS, *The Earth: its Origin, History, and Physical Constitution* (Cambridge, 2nd edn., 1929).
6. H. JEFFREYS, *The Future of the Earth* (Kegan Paul, 1929).
7. H. SPENCER JONES, *Life on Other Worlds* (English Universities Press, Lond., 1952).
8. H. N. RUSSELL, *The Solar System and its Origin* (Macmillan, 1935).
9. V. M. SLIPHER, Spectrographic Studies of the Planets (*M.N.*, **93**, No. 9, 657). [George Darwin Lecture, 1933.]
9a. A. G. SMITH & T. D. CARR, Radio Frequency Observations of the Planets in 1957–1958 (*Ap.J.*, **130**, 641).
10. H. T. STETSON, *Earth, Radio and Stars* (McGraw-Hill, N.Y., 1934).
11. F. L. WHIPPLE, *Earth, Moon and Planets* (Blakiston, Philadelphia, 1941).
12. —*Planetary Co-ordinates for the Years 1800–1940* (H.M.S.O., 1933).
13. —*Planetary Co-ordinates for the Years 1940–1960* (H.M.S.O., 1939).
13a.—*Planetary Co-ordinates for the Years 1960–1980* (H.M.S.O., 1958).

Sun

14. G. ABETTI (trans. J. B. SIDGWICK), *The Sun* (Faber, 1955).
15. G. ABETTI, Solar Physics (*H.d.A.*, **4**, 57).
16. C. G. ABBOT, *The Sun* (Appleton, Lond., and N.Y., 2nd edn., 1929).
17. A. F. ALEXANDER, Longitudinal Distribution of Sunspot Areas, 1925–36 (Rotations 964–1113): Relative Positions of the Most and Least Spotted Regions (*J.B.A.A.*, **54**, No. 2, 31).
18. A. F. O'D. ALEXANDER, Area, Distribution and the Sunspot Cycle (*J.B.A.A.*, **55**, No. 2, 43).
19. A. J. ÅNGSTRÖM, *Spectre Normal du Soleil* (Upsala, 1868).
19a. R. G. ATHAY, A Model of the Chromosphere from Radio and Optical Data, p. 98 (*Radio Astronomy*, ed.: R. N. Bracewell, Stanford Univ. Press).

20. H. D. BABCOCK & C. E. MOORE, *The Solar Spectrum, λ6600 to λ13495* (*Publ. Carneg. Instn.*, 579, 1947).

21. B. F. BAWTREE, Solar Eclipses (*Mem. B.A.A.*, **30**, No. 3, 94).

22. B. F. BAWTREE, Tables for the Calculation of Astronomical Quantities (*Mem. B.A.A.*, **34**, No. 4, 1).

22a. E. J. BLUM & A. BOISCHOT, Occultation of the Crab Nebula by the Solar Corona (*Obs.*, **77**, 206, 1957).

23. G. BRUHAT (rev. L. D'AZAMBUJA) *Le Soleil* (Presses Universitaires de France, 1951).

23a. W. N. CHRISTIANSEN & J. A. WARBURTON, The Distribution of Radio Brightness over the Solar Disc at a Frequency of 21 cms. (*Aust. J. Sci. Res.* **6**, 262, 1953).

23b. W. N. CHRISTIANSEN & D. S. MATHEWSON, The Origin of the Slowly Varying Component (*Radio Astronomy*, ed.: R. N. Bracewell, Stanford Univ. Press, 1959).

24. A. L. CORTIE, The Stonyhurst discs for Measuring the Positions of Sunspots (*J.B.A.A.*, **18**, No. 1, 26).

25. A. L. CORTIE, On the Types of Sun-Spot Disturbances (*Ap. J.*, **13**, No. 4, 260).

26. M. DAVIDSON, The Computation of Total Solar Eclipses (*J.B.A.A.*, **49**, No. 8, 299).

27. F. DYSON & R. v. d. R. WOOLLEY, *Eclipses of the Sun and Moon* (Oxford, 1937).

28. B. EDLÉN, The Identification of the Coronal Lines (*M.N.*, **105**, No. 6, 323). [George Darwin Lecture, 1945.]

29. M. A. ELLISON, Problems of the Motions of Solar Prominences (*Nat.*, **147**, 662).

29a. M. A. ELLISON, *The Sun and Its Influence*, Routledge & Kegan Paul.

29b. M. A. ELLISON, The Recording of Sudden Enhancements of Atmospherics, (S.E.A's) for Purposes of Flare Patrol (*J.B.A.A.*, **69**, No. 3, 1959).

29c. F. F. GARDNER, The Effect of S.I.D's on 2·28 mcs Pulse Reflections from the Lower Ionosphere (*Aust. J. Phys.*, **12**, 42, 1959).

29d. R. G. GIOVANELLI & J. A. ROBERTS, Optical Observations of the Solar Disturbances causing Type II Radio Bursts (*Aust. J. Phys.*, **11**, 353, 1958).

30. G. E. HALE, The Spectrohelioscope and its Work, I (*Ap. J.*, **70**, No. 5, 265=*M.W.C.*, 388).

31. F. J. HARGREAVES, Camera Work in the Eclipse (*J.B.A.A.*, **37**, No. 6, 212).

31a. A. HEWISH, Radio Observations of the Solar Corona at Sunspot Minimum, I.A.U. Symposium No. 4 (*Radio Astronomy* p. 298. Cambridge, 1957).

31b. A. HEWISH, The Occultation of the Crab Nebula by the Solar Corona (*Obs.*, **77**, 152, 1957).

31c. A. HEWISH, The Scattering of Radio Waves in the Solar Corona (*Mon. Notices of R.A.S.*, **118**, No. 6 (1958), p. 534).

31d. J. S. HEY & V. A. HUGHES, Centimetre Wave Observations of the Solar Eclipse of June 30 1954 (*Obs.*, **76**, 226, 1956).

BIBLIOGRAPHY

32. A. HUNTER, Recent Advances in Astronomy (*Sci. Progr.*, **34**, No. 136, 751).

32a. C. DE JAGER, The Structure of the Chromosphere and the Low Corona (*Radio Astronomy*, ed.: R. N. Bracewell, Stanford Univ. Press, 1959).

32b. M. KOMESAROFF, Polarization Measurements of the Three Spectral Types of Solar Radio Burst (*Aust. J. Phys.*, **11**, 201, 1958).

33. J. C. MABY, A Programme for the Observation and Photography of Sunspots (*J.B.A.A.*, **41**, No. 4, 190).

34. J. C. MABY, Sunspot Photography with a small Visual Refractor (*J.B.A.A.*, **47**, 321).

35. E. W. MAUNDER, Eclipse Suggestions (*J.B.A.A.*, **15**, No. 8, 317).

36. E. W. MAUNDER, Carrington's Method of Determining the Positions of Sun-spots (*J.B.A.A.*, **21**, No. 2, 94).

37. E. W. MAUNDER, Carrington's Method of Observing Sun-spots (*Mem. B.A.A.*, **23**, No. 2, 65).

37a. D. J. MCCLEAN, Solar Radio Emission of Spectral Type 4 and its Association with Geomagnetic Storms (*Aust. J. Phys.*, **12**, 404, 1959).

38. D. H. MENZEL, *Our Sun* (Harvard University Press, 1949).

39. M. MINNAERT, G. F. W. MULDERS & J. HOUTGAST, *Photometric Atlas of the Solar Spectrum from λ6312 to λ8771, with an Appendix from λ3332 to λ3637* (Amsterdam, 1940). [The Utrecht Atlas.]

40. S. A. MITCHELL, *Eclipses of the Sun* (*H.d.A.*, **4**, 231; Columbia University Press, 4th edn., 1935).

40a. S. K. MITRA, *The Upper Atmosphere* (Royal Asiatic Society of Calcutta, Second edn: 1952).

41. H. W. NEWTON, Early Visual Observations of Bright Chromospheric Eruptions on the Sun's Disk (*J.B.A.A.*, **50**, No. 8, 273).

42. H. W. NEWTON, A Famous Sunspot and its Epilogue (*J.B.A.A.*, **54**, No. 9, 244).

43. H. W. NEWTON, Sunspots, Bright Eruptions and Magnetic Storms (*Obs.* **62**, No. 787, 318).

43a. A. A. NEYLAN, An Association between Solar Radio Bursts at Metre and Centimetre Wavelengths (*Aust. J. Phys.*, **12**, 399, 1959).

44. T. VON OPPOLZER, *Canon der Finsternisse* (Vienna, 1887). [Data of 8000 solar and 5000 lunar eclipses from B.C. 1205 to A.D. 2152.]

45. E. PETTIT, The Properties of Solar Prominences as Related to Type (*Ap. J.*, **98**, 6).

46. H. PINNOCK, Photographing the Sun (*J.B.A.A.*, **55**, 124).

47. J. G. PORTER, The Heliographic Co-ordinates of Sunspots (*J.B.A.A.*, **53**, No. 2, 63).

47a. K. RAWER, *The Ionosphere* (Crosby-Lockwood, 1958).

47b. J. A. ROBERTS, Evidence of Echoes in the Solar Corona from a New Type of Radio Burst (*Aust. J. Phys.*, **11**, 215, 1958).

48. H. A. ROWLAND, *Preliminary Table of Solar Spectrum Wave-lengths* (Chicago University Press, 1896).

49. F. J. SELLERS, Estimation of Sunspot Areas (*J.B.A.A.*, **49**, No. 7, 256).

50. F. J. SELLERS, Co-operative Sunspot Observation (*J.B.A.A.*, **49**, No. 2, 75).

51. F. J. SELLERS, Motions of Solar Prominences (*J.B.A.A.*, **51**, No. 6, 221).

51a. C. A. SHAIN & C. S. HIGGINS, Location of the Sources of 19 mc/s Solar Bursts (*Aust. J. Phys.*, **12**, 357, 1959).

51b. O. B. SLEE, The Occultation of a Radio Star by the Solar Corona (*Obs.*, **76**, 228, 1956).

52. H. T. STETSON, *Sunspots in Action* (N.Y., 1947).

53. H. T. STETSON, *Sunspots and Their Effects* (McGraw-Hill, N.Y., 1937).

54. C. E. ST. JOHN *et al.*, *Revision of Rowland's Preliminary Table of Solar Spectrum Wave-lengths, with an extension to the present limit of the infra-red* (*Publ. Carneg. Instn.*, 396, 1928).

55. F. J. M. STRATTON, *Modern Eclipse Problems* (Oxford, 1927). [Halley Lecture, 1927.]

55a. G. SWARUP & R. PARTHASARATHY, Solar Brightness Distribution at a Wavelength of 60 cms. (*Aust. J. Phys.*, **11**, 338, 1958).

55b. J. P. WILD, K. V. SHERIDAN, & A. A. NEYLAN, An Investigation of the Speed of the Solar Disturbances responsible for Type III Radio Bursts (*Aust. J. Phys.*, **12**, 369, 1959).

56. W. REES WRIGHT, Solar Observations with Unsilvered Mirrors (*J.B.A.A.*, **54**, No. 4/5, 103).

57. *Publ. Astrophys. Obs.*, *Potsdam*, **2**, Tables 33, 34; 1881.

58. *Publ. Astrophys. Obs.*, *Potsdam*, **1**, 1879.

59. *Quarterly Bulletin on Solar Activity* (I.A.U., Zurich, 1939–). [Formerly *Bulletin for Character Figures of Solar Phenomena* (Zurich, 1917–1938).]

60. Solar Flares in White Light (*Obs.*, **67**, No. 839, 156).

MOON

[*a*. Maps and descriptive works; arranged chronologically.]

61. W. BEER & J. H. MÄDLER, *Der Mond nach seinen kosmischen und individuellen Verhältnissen oder Allgemeine vergleichende Selenographie* (Berlin, 1837). [Marks the birth of modern selenography.]

62. W. BEER & J. H. MÄDLER, *Mappa Selenographica* (Berlin, 1837). [Accompanying B. 61.]

63. J. F. J. SCHMIDT, *Der Mond* (Leipzig, 1856).

64. E. NEISON, *The Moon, and the Condition and Configurations of its Surface* (Longmans, Green, 1876). [Comprehensive but rather out of date. Map (diameter 24 ins) included in sections in text.]

65. J. F. J. SCHMIDT, *Charte der Gebirge des Mondes* (Reimer, Berlin, 1878). [Schmidt's great contribution to selenography.]

66. W. G. LOHRMANN: *Mondcharte* (Leipzig, 1878). [25 charts, with descriptions.]

67. R. A. PROCTOR, *The Moon—Her Motions, Aspect, Scenery, and Physical Condition* (Longmans, Green, 1878). [Includes a 12-in map based on B. 62. One of the standard works in English, though now rather badly dated.]

68. T. G. ELGER, *The Moon—A Full Description and Map of its Principal Physical Features* (Philip, Lond., 1895). [Map, diameter 18 ins, in 4 quadrants, with index of formations; new edition of Map, edited by H. P. Wilkins (Philip, 1950).]

69. M. M. LOEWY & M. P. PUISEUX, *Atlas Photographique de la Lune* (Paris Observatory, 1896–1900). [Issued in 12 parts.]
70. N. S. SHALER, A Comparison of the Features of Earth and the Moon (*Smithson. Contr.*, 1903).
71. J. NASMYTH & J. CARPENTER, *The Moon considered as a Planet, a World, and a Satellite* (Murray, 4th edn., 1903; 1st edn., 1874). [Rather badly out of date.]
72. W. H. PICKERING, *The Moon—A Summary of Existing Knowledge of Our Satellite, with a Complete Photographic Atlas* (Doubleday, Page, N.Y., 1903). [Moon divided into 16 areas, each photographed 5 times (sunrise, morning, noon, evening, sunset), plus key photographs and charts of the 4 quadrants.]
73. P. FAUTH, *The Moon in Modern Astronomy* (Owen, Lond., 1907).
74. P. PUISEUX, *La Terre et la Lune—Forme Extérieure et Structure Interne* (Gauthier-Villars, Paris, 1908).
75. W. GOODACRE, *Lunar Map* (1910). [One of the most accurate; based on 1433 surveyed points. Original 77 ins diameter; published in 25 sections reduced to 60 ins diameter. Reproduced in B. 80.]
76. J. N. KRIEGER, *Mond-Atlas* (Vienna, 1912) [Vol. 1, text; vol. 2, atlas.]
77. M. A. BLAGG, Collated List of Lunar Formations Named or Lettered in the Maps of Neison, Schmidt and Mädler. (*Internat. Ass. Acad.*, Edinburgh, 1913).
78. H. P. WILKINS, *A New Map of the Moon* (Lond., 1924) [24 sections plus index map; diameter about 60 ins.]
79. K. ANDĚL, *Mappa Selenographica* (Prague, 1926) [Single sheet, diameter about 24 ins, with key map of same size.]
80. W. GOODACRE, *The Moon, with a Description of its Surface Formations* (Bournemouth, 1931) [One of the finest modern works on the Moon. The lunar map, B. 75 is reproduced here on reduced scale.]
81. M. A. BLAGG & K. MÜLLER, *Named Lunar Formations* (Lund, Humphreys, 1935).
82. W. H. WESLEY & M. A. BLAGG, *I.A.U. Map of the Moon* (Lund, Humphreys, 1935). [Being vol. 2 of B. 81. 14 charts; lunar diameter about 35 ins.]
83. P. FAUTH, *Unser Mond* (Breslau, 1936).
84. P. FAUTH, *Übersichtskarte des Mondes* (Breslau, 1936). [6 charts measuring about 12 × 17 ins.]
85. F. C. LAMÈCH, *Carte Générale de la Lune* (Gizard, Barrère et Thomas, Paris, 1946). [Single sheet, diameter about 24 ins.]
86. H. P. WILKINS, *Map of the Moon* (Lond., 3rd edn. 1951). [The great 300-in diameter map; in 22 sections and 3 special Libratory Maps.]
87. R. B. BALDWIN, *The Face of the Moon* (University of Chicago Press, 1949).
88. D. W. G. ARTHUR, *The Diameters of Lunar Craters* (pub. by the author, 1951). [Part 1 (including 1000 craters) of a catalogue of crater diameters.]

[*b*. Papers and miscellaneous works referred to in the text, alphabetically arranged.]

89. R. BARKER, Physical Change on the Moon (*J.B.A.A.*, **48**, No. 9, 347).
90. L. F. BALL, The Lunar Mare Marginalis (*J.B.A.A.*, **47**, No. 7, 260).

BIBLIOGRAPHY

91. L. J. COMRIE, *A Short Semi-Graphical Method of Predicting Occultations* (H.M.S.O., 1926). [Copies obtainable from Scientific and Computing Service, 23 Bedford Square, London, W.C.1.]

92. M. DAVIDSON, The Reduction of Occultations for Stars Fainter than Magnitude 7·5 (*J.B.A.A.*, **48**, No. 3, 120). [See also B. 105, 93.]

93. M. DAVIDSON, Note on Mr F. Robbins' Paper (*J.B.A.A.*, **48**, No. 4, 175). [Refers to B. 105.]

94. J. T. FOXELL, Lunar Occultation Maps (*Mem. B.A.A.*, **30**, No. 3, 107).

95. W. H. HAAS, Colour Changes on the Moon (*Pop. Astr.*, **45**, No. 6, 337).

96. W. H. HAAS, Does Anything Ever Happen on the Moon? (*J. Can. R.A.S.*, **36**, No. 6, 237; No. 7, 317; No. 8, 361; No. 9, 397).

97. C. H. HAMILTON, Lunar Changes (Eratosthenes region) (*Pop. Astr.*, **32**, 237).

98. J. J. HILL, Some Notes on Lunar Photography with a 4¼-inch Refractor (*J.B.A.A.*, **55**, No. 3, 77).

99. R. T. A. INNES, Reduction of Occultations of Stars by the Moon (*A.J.*, **35**, No. 835, 155).

99a. B. LYOT, Recherches sur la polarisation de la lumière des planètes. . . . (*Ann. d'Obs. de Paris, sect. de Meudon*, **8**, part 1, 38).

99b. N. A. KOSYREV, Luminescence of the Lunar Surface and the Intensity of Corpuscular Radiation from the Sun (*Publ. Crimean Astrophys. Obs.*, **16**, 148).

99c. N. A. KOSYREV, Observation of a Volcanic Process on the Moon (*Sky and Tel.*, **18**, 184).

99d. P. Moore, Report on Transient Phenomena (*J.B.A.A.*, **77**, No. 1, 47).

99e. P. Moore, Transient Lunar Phenomena: A Review, 1967 (*J.B.A.A.*, **78**, No. 2, 138).

100. T. L. MACDONALD, The Altitudes of Lunar Craters (*J.B.A.A.*, **39**, No. 8, 314).

    T. L. MACDONALD, Studies in Lunar Statistics (*J.B.A.A.*, **41**, 172, 228, 288, 367; **42**, 291).

101. E. PETTIT & S. B. NICHOLSON, Lunar Radiation and Temperatures (*Ap. J.*, **71**, No. 2, 102=*M.W.C.*, 392).

102. E. PETTIT, Radiation Measurements on the Eclipsed Moon (*Ap.J.*, **91**, No. 4, 408=*M.W.C.*, 627).

103. W. H. PICKERING, Eratosthenes, I: A Study for the Amateur (*Pop. Astr.*, 27, 579); No. 2 (*ibid.*, **29**, 404); No. 3 (*ibid.*, **30**, 257); No. 4 (*ibid.*, **32**, 69); No. 5 (*ibid.*, **32**, 302); No. 6 (*ibid.*, **32**, 393).

103a. T. RACKHAM, *Astronomical Photography at the Telescope* (Faber, London, 1959).

104. W. F. RIGGE, *The Graphic Construction of Eclipses and Occultations* (Loyola University Press, Chicago, 1924).

105. F. ROBBINS, Remarks on Dr Davidson's Paper, (*J.B.A.A.*, **48**, No. 4, 171). [See also B. 92, 93.]

106. D. H. SADLER & M. W. P. RICHARDS, The Prediction and Reduction of Occultations (H.M.S.O., Supplement to *N.A.*, 1938).

107. S. A. SAUNDER, The Determination of Selenographic Positions and the Measurement of Lunar Photographs (*M.N.*, **60**, No. 3, 174).

108. S. A. SAUNDER, The Determination of Selenographic Positions . . .

Determination of a first group of Standard Points by Measures made at the Telescope and on Photographs (*M.N.*, **62**, No. 1, 41).

109. S. A. SAUNDER, The Determination of Selenographic Positions . . . Results of the Measurement of Four Paris Negatives (*Mem. R.A.S.*, **57**, 1).

110. V. VAND, A Theory of the Evolution of the Surface Features of the Moon (*J.B.A.A.*, **55**, 47).

111. C. T. WHITMELL, Stellar Occultation (*J.B.A.A.*, **23**, No. 4, 182).

112. H. P. WILKINS, The Lunar Mare 'X' (*J.B.A.A.*, **48**, No. 2, 80).

113. H. P. WILKINS, The Lunar Mare Australe (*J.B.A.A.*, **50**, No. 9, 304).

114. H. P. WILKINS, Total Lunar Eclipse, 1942 March 2 (*J.B.A.A.*, **52**, No. 3, 108).

115. H. P. WILKINS, The Total Eclipse of the Moon, 1942 Aug 26 (*J.B.A.A.*, **52**, No. 9, 297).

116. H. P. WILKINS, Lunar Thermal Researches (*J.B.A.A.*, **53**, No. 2, 86).

117. H. P. WILKINS, A Thermal Eyepiece (*J.B.A.A.*, **54**, No. 2, 38).

118. J. YOUNG, A Statistical Investigation of the Diameters and Distribution of Lunar Craters (*J.B.A.A.*, **50**, No. 9, 309).

119. —Lunar Occultations (*N.A.*, 1950, pp. 592–597).

120. —Lunar Memoirs of the B.A.A. (*Mem. B.A.A.*, 1, 2, 3, 7, 10, 13, 20, 23, 32, 34, 36).

121. —Report of the General Ordinary Meeting (*J.B.A.A.*, **54**, No. 8/9, 150).

MERCURY

122. E. M. ANTONIADI, *La Planète Mercure et la Rotation des Satellites* (Gauthier-Villars, 1934).

123. P. LOWELL, New Observations of Mercury (*Mem. Amer. Acad. Arts Sci.*, **12**, 1897).

124. H. MCEWEN, Mercury, Part III (*J.B.A.A.*, **39**, No. 8, Plates VII, VIII).

125. H. MCEWEN, The Markings of Mercury (*J.B.A.A.*, **46**, No. 10, 382).

126. H. MCEWEN, *Mercury and Venus Section Observing Notes* (B.A.A. Sectional Notes, No. 3).

127. G. V. SCHIAPARELLI, Sulla rotazione di Mercurio (*A.N.*, **123**, No. 2944, 242).

128. —Planispheres of Mercury (*J.B.A.A.*, **46**, No. 10, 357, Plate I).

VENUS

129. E. M. ANTONIADI, The Markings and Rotation of the Planet Venus (*J.B.A.A.*, **44**, No. 9, 341).

130. C. FLAMMARION, *La Planète Vénus—discussion général des observations* (Paris, 1897).

130a. P. MOORE, *The Planet Venus* (Faber, London, 1959).

130b. P. MOORE, The Future of the Mercury and Venus Section (*J.B.A.A.*, **70**, No. 4, pp. 167–173, 1960).

MARS

131. E. M. ANTONIADI *et al.*, Reports of the Mars Section of the B.A.A. (*Mem. B.A.A.*, 2, 1892; 4 & 7, 1896; 27, 1919–20; 37, 1941).

132. E. M. ANTONIADI, *La Planète Mars, 1659–1929* (Hermann, Paris, 1930).

133. E. M. ANTONIADI, La Planète Mars en 1935 (*B.S.A.F.*, **49**, 401).

134. W. W. COBLENZ, Climatic Conditions on Mars (*Pop. Astr.*, **33**, No. 5, 310; No. 6, 363).

135. W. W. COBLENZ & C. O. LAMPLAND, Radiometric Measurements on Mars in 1924 (*Pop. Astr.*, **32**, No. 9, 570).

136. C. FLAMMARION, *La Planète Mars* (Gauthier-Villars, Paris, vol. 1 1892, vol. 2 1909).

137. N. E. GREEN, Observations of Mars at Madeira, August and September 1877 (*M.N.*, **38**, No. 1, 38).

138. N. E. GREEN, Observations of Mars at Madeira, in August and September 1877 (*Mem. R.A.S.*, **44**, No. 3, 123).

139. P. LOWELL, *Mars* (Longmans, Green, 1896).

140. P. LOWELL, *Mars and its Canals* (N.Y., 1906).

141. P. LOWELL, *Mars as the Abode of Life* (Macmillan, N.Y., 1909).

142. E. PETTIT & S. B. NICHOLSON, Measurements of the Radiation from the Planet Mars (*Pop. Astr.*, **32**, No. 10, 601).

143. W. H. PICKERING, Mars Reports: Nos. 1–7 (*Pop. Astr.*, **22**, 1914); Nos. 8–12 (*ibid.*, **23**, 1915); Nos. 13–17 (*ibid.*, **24**, 1916); No. 18 (*ibid.*, **25**, 1917); Nos. 19–20 (*ibid.*, **26**, 1918); No. 21 (*ibid.*, **27**, 1919); No. 22 (*ibid.*, **28**, 1920); No. 23 (*ibid.*, **29**, 1921); No. 24 (*ibid.*, **30**, 1922); Nos. 25–26 (*ibid.*, **31**, 1923); Nos. 27–28 (*ibid.*, **32**, 1924); Nos. 29–31, (*ibid.*, **33**, 1925); Nos. 32–37 (*ibid.*, **34**, 1926); Nos. 38–40 (*ibid.*, **35**, 1927); Nos. 41–42 (*ibid.*, **36**, 1928); No. 43 (*ibid.*, **37**, 1929); No. 44 (*ibid.*, **38**, 1930).

144. G. DE VAUCOULEURS (trans., P. A. MOORE), *The Planet Mars* (Faber, 1950).

145. —*Ann. Lowell Obs.*, **3**, Supplement, 24, 1905.

JUPITER

145a. L. E. ALSOP et al., in *Radio Astronomy*, p. 69 (ed: R. N. Bracewell, Stanford Univ. Press, 1959).

145b. C. H. BARROW, Thesis, London Univ. (1958).

145c. C. H. BARROW, The Latitudes of Radio Sources on Jupiter (*J.B.A.A.*, **69**, 211, 1959).

145d. C. H. BARROW & T. D. CARR, A Radio Investigation of Planetary Radiation (*J.B.A.A.*, **67**, 200, 1957).

146. D. P. BAYLEY, Colour of Jupiter's Polar Regions (*J.B.A.A.*, **55**, No. 5, 116).

147. M. DAVIDSON (ed.), *Astronomy for Everyman* (Dent, 1953).

148. F. J. HARGREAVES, How to Observe Jupiter, and Why (*J.B.A.A.*, **60**, No. 7, 187).

149. A. E. LEVIN, [Presidential Address to the B.A.A., 1931] (*J.B.A.A.*, **42**, No. 1).

150. A. E. LEVIN, Mutual Eclipses and Occultations of Jupiter's Satellites (*Mem. B.A.A.*, **30**, No. 3, 149).

151. B. LYOT, Observations Planétaires au Pic du Midi en 1941 (*B.S.A.F.*, April 1943).

151a. E. F. MCCLAIN & R. M. SLOANAKER, *Radio Astronomy*, p. 61 (ed.: R. N. Bracewell, Stanford Univ. Press, 1959).

152. R. A. MCINTOSH, Colour Variation in Jupiter's Equatorial Zone (*J.B.A.A.*, **46**, No. 8, 285).

153. R. A. MCINTOSH, Disturbance on Jupiter's South Equatorial Region (*J.B.A.A.*, **60**, No. 8, 247).

154. D. W. MILLAR, Variations of Surface Features on Jupiter (*J.B.A.A.*, **54**, No. 8/9, 162).

155. B. M. PEEK, A Hint to Observers of Jupiter (*J.B.A.A.*, **47**, No. 4, 154).

156. B. M. PEEK, [Presidential Address to the B.A.A., 1939] (*J.B.A.A.*, **50**, No. 1).

157. B. M. PEEK, [Presidential Address to the B.A.A., 1940] (*J.B.A.A.*, **51**, No. 1).

157a. B. M. PEEK, *The Planet Jupiter* (Faber, London, 1958).

157b. B. M. PEEK, The Determination of the Longitudes of Sources of Emission of Radio Noise on Jupiter (*J.B.A.A.*, **69**, 70, 1959).

158. W. DE SITTER, Jupiter's Galilean Satellites (*M.N.*, **91**, No. 7, 706). [George Darwin Lecture, 1931.]

159. C. F. O. SMITH, The Colour of Jupiter's Polar Regions (*J.B.A.A.*, **55**, No. 1, 23).

160. C. F. O. SMITH, Jupiter in Retrospect (*J.B.A.A.*, **57**, No. 1, 37).

160a. F. G. SMITH, A Search for Radiation from Jupiter at 38 mc/s and at 85 mc/s. (*Obs.*, **75**, 252, 1955).

161. A. STANLEY WILLIAMS, *Zenographical Fragments—The Motions and Changes of the Markings of Jupiter in the Apparition 1886–87* (Mitchell & Hughes, Lond., 1889).

162. A. STANLEY WILLIAMS, *Zenographical Fragments II—The Motions and Changes of the Markings on Jupiter in 1888* (Taylor & Francis, Lond., 1909).

163. A. STANLEY WILLIAMS, On the Observed Changes in the Colour of Jupiter's Equatorial Zone (*M.N.*, **80**, No. 5, 467).

164. A. STANLEY WILLIAMS, Periodic Variation in the Colours of the Two Equatorial Belts of Jupiter (*M.N.*, **90**, No. 7, 696).

165. A. STANLEY WILLIAMS, The Colour Variations of Jupiter's Equatorial Zones (*J.B.A.A.*, **47**, No. 2, 68).

166. A. STANLEY WILLIAMS, The Colour Variations of Jupiter's Equatorial Belts (*Obs.*, **60**, No. 754, 74).

167. W. H. WRIGHT, On Photographs of the Brighter Planets by Light of Different Colours (*M.N.*, **88**, No. 9, 709). [George Darwin Lecture, 1928.]

168. —33 Reports of the Jupiter Section of the B.A.A., 1891—(*Mem. B.A.A.*, 1–35), especially Reports No. 27, 29, 32, 33.

169. —*J.B.A.A.*, **44**, 219; **43**, 86, 404; **42**, 205, 362; **37**, 62; *Mem. B.A.A.*, **34**, No. 2.

SATURN

170. M. A. AINSLIE, Photographs of Saturn by the Lick Observatory (*J.B.A.A.*, **55**, No. 5, 125).

171. A. F. O'D. ALEXANDER, The Future of the Saturn Section [of the B.A.A.] (*J.B.A.A.*, **57**, No. 1, 45).

172. A. F. O'D. ALEXANDER, Intensities of Belts, Zones and Rings, 1946–48 (*J.B.A.A.*, **59**, No. 7, 207).

173. E. M. ANTONIADI, Observations of Saturn in 1936–1937, when his Ring was seen more or less edgewise (*J.B.A.A.*, **47**, No. 7, 252).

174. R. BARKER, Saturn in 1932 (*J.B.A.A.*, **43**, No. 2, 56).

175. R. BARKER, Notes on Saturn in 1933 (*J.B.A.A.*, **44**, No. 2, 74).

176. R. BARKER, Notes on Saturn in 1934 (*J.B.A.A.*, **45**, No. 1, 41).

177. R. BARKER, Saturn's Satellites in 1936 (*J.B.A.A.*, **47**, No. 4, 152).

178. L. J. COMRIE, Phenomena of Saturn's Satellites (*Mem. B.A.A.*, **30**, No. 3, 97).

179. F. O'B. ELLISON, Some Observations on Saturn near the Time of the Ring Plane passing through the Sun and the Earth, 1936–1937 (*J.B.A.A.*, **50**, No. 6, 213). [See also *J.B.A.A.*, **50**, No. 7, 230.]

180. [W. HAY], Interim Report of the Saturn Section [dealing with observations of Will Hay's prominent white spot on Saturn] (*J.B.A.A.*, **44**, No. 6, 220).

181. M. B. B. HEATH, Latitude of Saturn's South Equatorial Belt (*J.B.A.A.*, **62**, No. 6, 202).

182. P. H. HEPBURN, The Diameters and Densities of the Six Inner Satellites of Saturn (*J.B.A.A.*, **33**, No. 6, 244).

183. P. H. HEPBURN, Note and Correction to [the above paper] (*J.B.A.A.*, **33**, No. 7, 284).

184. H. M. JOHNSON, The White Spot on Saturn's Rings (*J.B.A.A.*, **51**, No. 9, 309).

185. T. E. R. PHILLIPS, Micrometer Measures of the Rings and Ball of Saturn (*J.B.A.A.*, **34**, No. 5, 185).

186. T. E. R. PHILLIPS, The Rotation of Saturn (*J.B.A.A.*, **44**, No. 1, 29).

187. T. E. R. PHILLIPS, Report of Saturn Section [of the B.A.A.] (*J.B.A.A.*, **46**, No. 10, 361).

188. R. A. PROCTOR, *Saturn and its System* (Longmans, Green, Lond., 1865).

189. E. D. SHERLOCK, Colour of Saturn's Polar Regions (*J.B.A.A.*, **56**, No. 1, 16).

ASTEROIDS

190. N. T. BOBROVNIKOFF, The Spectra of Minor Planets (*L.O.B.*, **14**, No. 407).

191. A. O. LEUSCHNER, Research Surveys of the Orbits of Minor Planets 1–1091, from 1801.0 to 1929.5 (*Publ. Lick Obs.*, **19**, 1935).

ZODIACAL LIGHT, ETC

191a. D. E. BLACKWELL, The Zodiacal Light and its Interpretation (*Endeavour*, **19**, 14).

192. R. B. BOUSFIELD, The Zodiacal Band (*M.N.*, **94**, No. 9, 824).

193. A. COLEMAN, The Photography of the Zodiacal Light (*J.B.A.A.*, **44**, No. 7, 262).

194. A. E. DOUGLASS, Zodiacal Light and Counterglow and the Photography of Large Areas and Faint Contrasts (*Photogr. J.*, New Series, **40**, No. 2, 44).

195. C. T. ELVEY, Photometry of the Gegenschein (*Ap. J.*, **77**, No. 1, 56).

196. C. HOFFMEISTER, Beitrag zur Photometrie der Südlichen Milchstrasse und des Zodiakallichts (*Veröff. Univ. Berlin-Babelsberg*, **8**, No. 2, 1930).

197. W. B. HOUSMAN, *Aurora and Zodiacal Light Section Observing Notes* (B.A.A. Sectional Notes, No. 4).

197a. R. O. REDMAN, Dust and Gas Between the Earth and the Sun (*Obs.*, **79**, No. 912, 172).

198. A. THOM, The Zodiacal Light (*J.B.A.A.*, **49**, No. 3, 103).

199. —Reports of the Aurora and Zodiacal Light Section of the B.A.A. (*Mem. B.A.A.*, **19**, 1914—35, 1944).

AURORAE

200. B. BURRELL, Photographs of the Great Aurora, 17th April 1947 (*J.B.A.A.* **57**, No. 5, 205).

201. J. R. CAPRON, *Aurorae—Their Characters and Spectra* (Lond., 1879).

202. L. HARANG, *The Aurorae* (Chapman & Hall, 1951).

203. J. PATON, Proposed Survey of the Frequency of Aurorae over the British Isles (*J.B.A.A.*, **62**, No. 7, 226).

204. J. PATON, Aurora Borealis: Photographic measurements of height (*Weather*, **1**, No. 6, 8, 1946).

205. J. PATON, Aurora Borealis (*Science News*, **11**, No. 9, 15, 1949).

206 —*Photographic Atlas of Auroral Forms and Scheme for Visual Observations of Aurorae* (International Geodetic & Geophysical Union, Oslo, 1930).

206a. G. M. C. STONE, *Bull. R.S.G.B.*, **34**, pp. 13 and 15 (I.G.Y. V.H.F. Programme and Progress Report, 1958).

206b. G. M. C. STONE, *Bull. R.S.G.B.*, **35**, p. 395 (Amateur Radio Participation in I.G.Y., 1950).

METEORS

207. I. S. ASTAPOWITSCH, On the Cosmic Nature of Telescopic Meteors (*Obs.*, **60**, No. 762, 285).

208. A. BEER, Meteors (*Obs.*, **63**, No. 786, 229).

209. S. L. BOOTHROYD, Results of the Arizona Expedition: IV. Telescopic Observations of Meteor Velocities. (*Harv. Circ.*, 390). [See also B. 251, 238-241.]

210. B. BOYD, The Accuracy of Estimated Meteor Durations (*Pop. Astr.*, **44**, No. 1, 39).

211. H. CHRÉTIEN, Les Perséids en 1904 (*B.S.A.F.*, **18**, 482).

212. E. H. COLLINSON & J. P. M. PRENTICE, The Photography of Meteors (*J.B.A.A.*, **37**, No. 7, 266).

213. E. H. COLLINSON, An Automatic Meteor Camera (*J.B.A.A.*, **39**, No. 5, 150).

214. E. H. COLLINSON, An Improved Automatic Meteor Camera (*J.B.A.A.*, **44**, No. 4, 157).

215. E. H. COLLINSON, Meteor Photography, 1928-31 (*J.B.A.A.*, **46**, No. 3, 116).

216. M. DAVIDSON, The Computation of the Real Paths of Meteors (*J.B.A.A.*, **46**, 292).

217. M. DAVIDSON, Variation in the Number of Meteors Observed for Different Hours and Different Times of the Year (*J.B.A.A.*, **24**, 352, 411).

218. M. DAVIDSON, Variation in the Number of Meteors observed for different Periods of the Year (*J.B.A.A.*, **24**, 477).

219. M. DAVIDSON, Computation of the Orbit of a Meteor Stream (*J.B.A.A.*, **44**, 116, 146).

220. M. DAVIDSON, A Simple Method of determining the Orbit of a Meteor by means of a Celestial Globe (*J.B.A.A.*, **24**, 307).

221. M. DAVIDSON, Note on Mr Porter's Paper (*J.B.A.A.*, **47**, 120). [see B. 247.]

222. W. F. DENNING, General Catalogue of the Radiant Points of Meteoric Showers and of Fireballs and Shooting Stars observed at more than one Station (*Mem. R.A.S.*, **53**, 203). [A classic work, but now obsolete and not always reliable.]

223. W. J. FISHER, The Newton-Denning Method for Computing Meteor Paths with a Celestial Globe (*Proc. Nat. Acad. Sci.*, **19**, No. 2, 209= *Harv. Repr.*, 85).

224. C. HOFFMEISTER, *Die Meteore* (Leipzig, 1937).

225. J. S. HOPKINS, A Tentative Identification of Lines in a Meteor Spectrum (*Pop. Astr.*, **45**, No. 4, 214).

226. A. S. KING, A Spectroscopic Examination of Meteorites (*Ap. J.*, **84**, No. 5, 507).

227. F. A. LINDEMANN & G. M. B. DOBSON, Note on the Photography of Meteors (*M.N.*, **83**, No. 3, 163).

228. B. LOVELL & J. A. CLEGG, *Radio Astronomy* (Chapman & Hall, 1952).

229. P. M. MILLMAN, The Theoretical Frequency Distribution of Photographic Meteors (*Selected Papers from Wash. Nat. Ac. Proc.*, **19**, 34, 1933).

230. P. M. MILLMAN, Amateur Meteor Photography (*Pop. Astr.*, **41**, No. 6, 298).

231. P. M. MILLMAN, An Analysis of Meteor Spectra (*Harv. Ann.*, **82**, No. 6, 113).

232 P. M. MILLMAN & D. HOFFLEIT, A Study of Meteor Photographs Taken through a Rotating Shutter (*Harv. Ann.*, **105**, No. 31, 601).

233. P. M. MILLMAN & D. W. R. MCKINLEY, Three-Station Radar and Visual Triangulation of Meteors (*Sky & Telesc.*, **8**, No. 5, 114).

234. C. P. OLIVIER, Calculation of the Heights of Meteors observed by H. L. Alden and C. P. Olivier (*Pop. Astr.*, **32**, No. 10, 591).

235. C. P. OLIVIER, Methods for Computing the Heights and Paths of Fireballs and Meteors (*Supplt. to the Pilot Chart of the North Atlantic Ocean for 1931*, Washington, 1931).

236. C. P. OLIVIER, *Meteors* (Williams & Wilkins, Baltimore, 1925).

237. E. ÖPIK, On the Visual and Photographic Study of Meteors (*Harv. Bull.*, 879, 5).

238. E. ÖPIK, Results of the Arizona Expedition: II. Statistical Analysis of Group Radiants (*Harv. Circ.*, 388). [See also B. 209, 239–241, 251.]

239. E. ÖPIK, Results of the Arizona Expedition: III. Velocities of Meteors observed visually (*Harv. Circ.*, 389). [See also B. 251, 238, 209, 240, 241.]

240. E. ÖPIK, Results of the Arizona Expedition: V. On the Distribution of Heliocentric Velocities of Meteors (*Harv. Circ.*, 391). [See also B. 251, 238–9, 209, 241.]

241. E. ÖPIK, Results of the Arizona Expedition: VI. Analysis of Meteor Heights (*Harv. Ann.* **105**, No. 30, 1937). [See also B. 251, 238-9, 209, 240.]

242. E. ÖPIK, A Statistical Method of Counting Shooting Stars and its Application to the Perseid Shower of 1920 (*Publ. Tartu*, **25**, No. 1, 1922).

243. E. ÖPIK, Results of Double-Count Observations of the Perseids in 1921 (*Publ. Tartu*, **25**, No. 4, 1923).

244. E. ÖPIK, Telescopic Observations of Meteors at the Tartu Observatory (*Publ. Tartu*, **27**, No. 2, 1930).

245. F. A. PANETH, *The Origin of Meteorites* (Oxford, 1940). [Halley Lecture, 1940.]

246. J. G. PORTER, The Reduction of Meteor Observations (*Mem. B.A.A.*, **34**, No. 4, 37).

247. J. G. PORTER, The Reduction of Meteor Observations (*J.B.A.A.*, **47**, 118). [See B. 221.]

248. J. G. PORTER, An Analysis of British Meteor Data (*M.N.*, **103**, No. 3, 134).

249. J. P. M. PRENTICE, The Giacobinids, 1946 (*J.B.A.A.*, **57**, No. 2, 86).

250. J. P. M. PRENTICE, Fatigue and the Hourly Rate of Meteors (*J.B.A.A.*, **52**, No. 3, 98).

251. H. SHAPLEY, E. J. ÖPIK & S. L. BOOTHROYD, The Arizona Expedition for the Study of Meteors (*Wash. Nat. Ac. Proc.*, **18**, No. 1, 16=*Harv. Repr.*, 74). [See also B. 238-241, 209.]

252. J. SKYORA, La Photographie des Étoiles Filantes (*B.S.A.F.*, **38**, 64).

253. H. H. TURNER, On the Measurement of a Meteor Trail on a Photographic Plate (*M.N.*, **67**, No. 9, 562).

254. H. H. WATERS, The Photography of Meteors (*J.B.A.A.*, **46**, No. 4, 152).

255. F. WATSON, The Luminosity Function of the Giacobinids (*Harv. Bull.*, 895, 9).

256. F. WATSON, A Study of Telescopic Meteors (*Proc. Amer. Phil. Soc.*, **81**, No. 4, 493).

257. F. G. WATSON, *Between the Planets* (Cambridge, Mass., 1941).

258. F. WATSON & E. M. COOK, The Accuracy of Observations by Inexperienced Meteor Observers (*Pop. Astr.*, **44**, No. 5, 258).

259. F. L. WHIPPLE, The Harvard Photographic Meteor Programme (*Sky & Telesc.*, **8**, No. 4, 90=*Harv. Repr.*, 319).

260. B. S. WHITNEY, New Methods for Computing Meteor Heights (*M.N.*, **96**, 544).

261. W. T. WHITNEY, The Determination of Meteor Velocities (*Pop. Astr.*, **45**, No. 3, 162).

262. J. D. WILLIAMS, Binocular Observations of 718 Meteors (*Proc. Amer. Phil. Soc.*, **81**, No. 4, 505).

263. E. WILLIS, *Tables for the Computation of Meteor Orbits* (privately printed, 1939).

264. C. C. WYLIE, The Calculation of Meteor Orbits (Formulas) (*Pop. Astr.*, **47**, No. 8, 425).

265. C. C. WYLIE, The Calculation of Meteor Orbits (Tables) (*Pop. Astr.*, **47**, No. 9, 478)

266. C. C. WYLIE, The Calculation of Meteor Orbits (Examples) (*Pop. Astr.*, **47**, No. 10, 549).

267. C. C. WYLIE, Psychological Errors in Meteor Work (*Pop. Astr.*, **47**, No. 4, 206).

268. C. C. WYLIE, The Relation of Group to Solo Counts in Meteor Work (*Pop. Astr.*, **42**, No. 3, 157).

269. —*American Meteor Society Bulletins* (Flower Observatory, University of Pennsylvania).

270. —Reports of the Meteor Section of the B.A.A., 1893–1937 (*Mem. B.A.A.*, **1–32**).

See also B. 311, 325.

COMETS

271. C. E. ADAMS, Calculation of a Comet's Coordinates (*J.B.A.A.*, **32**, No. 6, 231). [See B. 285, 300.]

272. J. BAUSCHINGER, *Die Bahnbestimmung der Himmelskörper* (Engelmann, Leipzig, 1928).

273. N. T. BOBROVNIKOFF, Physical Theory of Comets in the Light of Spectroscopic Data (*Rev. Mod. Phys.*, **14**, No. 2–3=*Perkins Obs. Repr.*, 31).

274. N. T. BOBROVNIKOFF, On the Systematic Errors in the Photometry of Comets (*Contr. Perkins Obs.*, 19).

275. N. T. BOBROVNIKOFF, On the Organisation of Physical Observations of Comets (*Pop. Astr.*, **42**, No. 1, 2).

276. N. T. BOBROVNIKOFF, Investigations of the Brightness of Comets (Part I, *Contr. Perkins Obs.*, 15, 1941; Part II, *ibid.*, 16, 1942).

277. N. T. BOBROVNIKOFF, Observation of the Brightness of Comets (*Pop. Astr.*, **49**, No. 9, 467=*Perkins Obs. Repr.*, 28).

278. N. T. BOBROVNIKOFF, On the Brightness of Comets (*Pop. Astr.*, **50**, No. 9, 473=*Perkins Obs. Repr.*, 29).

279. N. T. BOBROVNIKOFF, The Brightness of Comet 1942g (Whipple) (*Pop. Astr.*, **51**, No. 9, 481=*Perkins Obs. Repr.*, 32).

280. G. F. CHAMBERS, *A Handbook of Descriptive and Practical Astronomy* (Oxford, 1890, 3 vols).

281. G. F. CHAMBERS, *The Story of the Comets* (Oxford, 1909).

282. S. C. CHANDLER, Note on a Practical Problem for Beginners in Cometary Computation (*Pop. Astr.*, **6**, 459).

283. T. CLOSE, To Find the Parabolic Orbit of a Comet by a Graphical Method (*J.B.A.A.*, **49**, No. 6, 216).

284. L. J. COMRIE, Telegraphic and Published Positions of Comets and Asteroids (*Pop. Astr.*, **33**, No. 6, 382).

285. L. J. COMRIE, Note on Dr Adams's Paper and the Computation of Ephemerides (*J.B.A.A.*, **32**, No. 6, 234). [See B. 271, 300.]

286. L. J. COMRIE, On Transferring Solar Co-ordinates etc from One Annual Equinox to Another (*J.B.A.A.*, **43**, No. 4, 158). [See B. 299.]

287. R. T. CRAWFORD, *Determination of Orbits of Comets and Asteroids* (McGraw-Hill, N.Y., 1930).

288. A. C. D. CROMMELIN, Comet Catalogue—Sequel to Galle's 'Cometenbahnen' (*Mem. B.A.A.*, **26**, No. 2).

289. A. C. D. CROMMELIN, Continuation of Comet Catalogue (*Mem. B.A.A.*, **30**, No. 1).

290. A. C. D. CROMMELIN, On the Computation of a Comet's Ephemeris (*J.B.A.A.*, **6**, No. 3, 105).

291. A. C. D. CROMMELIN, On the Determination of the Orbit of a Comet or Planet by three Observations made at Intervals of a few days (*J.B.A.A.*, **7**, No. 3, 121; No. 5, 260; No. 6, 327).

292. A. C. D. CROMMELIN, The Computation of an Ephemeris of a Body moving in an Ellipse (*J.B.A.A.*, **26**, No. 4, 150).

293. A. C. D. CROMMELIN, Simplification of the Computation of an Ephemeris of a Comet moving in a Parabola (*J.B.A.A.*, **32**, No. 8, 305).

294. A. C. D. CROMMELIN & M. PROCTOR, *Comets* (Technical Press, Lond., 1937).

295. M. DAVIDSON, Variation in the Brightness of Comets (*J.B.A.A.*, **53**, No. 6, 175).

296. M. DAVIDSON, The Determination of the Parabolic Orbit of a Comet (*Mem. B.A.A.*, **30**, No. 1). [See also B. 297.]

297. M. DAVIDSON, The Determination of the Parabolic Orbit of a Comet (*J.B.A.A.*, **43**, No. 2, 84). [See also B. 298, 308.]

298. M. DAVIDSON, Remarks on the Relative Advantages of the Equator and the Ecliptic as Planes of Reference in Computing Cometary Orbits (*J.B.A.A.*, **43**, No. 3, 114).

299. M. DAVIDSON, Comet Whipple, 1933*f* (*J.B.A.A.*, **44**, No. 7, 267). [See also B. 286.]

300. M. DAVIDSON, The Computation of Ephemerides (*J.B.A.A.*, **44**, No. 5, 185). [See also B. 271, 285.]

301. M. DAVIDSON, A Method for Computing Approximate Elements in the Case of a General Orbit (*Mem. B.A.A.*, **30**, No. 1).

302. M. DAVIDSON, The Range of Solution in the Orbits of Comets (*J.B.A.A.*, **44**, No. 2, 68).

303. M. DAVIDSON, Note on Comet 1935*a* (Johnson) (*J.B.A.A.*, **45**, No. 5, 183). [See also B. 302.]

304. M. DAVIDSON, Remarks on Mr Kellaway's Paper (*J.B.A.A.*, **53**, No. 4/5, 160). [Refers to B. 310.]

305. E. DOOLITTLE, A Simple Method devised by F. C. Penrose for Finding the Orbit of a Heavenly Body by a Graphical Process (*Pop. Astr.*, **17**, 65, 138, 200, 292, 365). [See B. 323.]

306. J. GRIGG, A Graphic Method of Computing a Search Ephemeris for a Periodic Comet (*J.B.A.A.*, **9**, No. 8, 382).

307. W. P. HENDERSON, The Computation of the Perturbations of a Periodic Comet by Jupiter and Saturn (*Mem. B.A.A.*, **34**, No. 4, 21).

308. R. T. A. INNES, Comments on Dr Davidson's Paper (*J.B.A.A.*, **43**, No. 3, 115). [Refers to B. 297.]

309. R. T. A. INNES, Comet 1927*f* (Gale) (*Mem. B.A.A.*, **30**, No. 1). [See B. 317, 305.]

310. G. F. KELLAWAY, A Note on the Orbit of Comet Whipple-Fedtke (1942*g*) (*J.B.A.A.*, **53**, No. 4/5, 159). [See B. 304.]

311. A. KOPFF, Kometen und Meteore (*H.d.A.*, **4**, 426).

312. A. O. LEUSCHNER *et al.*, A Short Method of Determining Orbits from

BIBLIOGRAPHY

Three Observations [and other papers] (*Publ. Lick Obs.*, **7**, Nos. 1–3, 7–10).

313. A. E. LEVIN, Cometary Ephemerides: Correction Coefficients for change in date of perihelion (*J.B.A.A.*, **43**, No. 10, 429). [See also B. 314.]

314. A. E. LEVIN, Cometary Ephemerides (*J.B.A.A.*, **44**, No. 1, 41). [See also B. 313.]

315. A. F. LINDEMANN, A Revolving Eyepiece, electrically warmed (*M.N.*, **58**, 362).

316. G. MERTON, Comets and their Origin (*J.B.A.A.*, **62**, No. 1, 1951). [Also contains useful bibliography.]

317. G. MERTON, A Modification of Gauss's Method for the Determination of Orbits (*M.N.*, **85**, No. 8, 693). [See B. 318.]

318. G. MERTON, A Modification of Gauss's Method for the Determination of Orbits (*M.N.*, **89**, No. 5, 451). [See B. 317, 309.]

319. G. MERTON, Note on the above Paper of Mr Wood (*J.B.A.A.*, **36**, No. 5, 151). [Refers to B. 334.]

320. C. P. OLIVIER, *Comets* (Baillière, Tindall & Cox, 1930).

321. J. H. OORT, The Origin and Development of Comets (*Obs.*, **71**, 129). [1951 Halley Lecture.]

322. T. VON OPPOLZER, *Lehrbuch zur Bahnbestimmung der Kometen und Planeten* (Engelmann, Leipzig, 1882; trans. PACQUIER, Paris, 1886).

323. F. C. PENROSE, On a Method for Finding the Elements of the Orbit of a Comet by a Graphical Process (*M.N.*, **42**, No. 2, 68). [See also B. 305.]

324. G. B. PETTER, The Determination of a Cometary Orbit (*Mem. B.A.A.*, **21**, No. 2).

325. J. G. PORTER. *Comets and Meteor Streams* (Chapman & Hall, 1952). [Excellent modern treatment, with valuable bibliographies.]

326. W. C. RAND, A Nomogram for Comet Data (*J.B.A.A.*, **52**, No. 3, 104).

327. G. STRACKE, *Bahnbestimmung der Planeten und Kometen* (Julius Springer, Berlin, 1929).

328. B. STRÖMGREN, Tables giving $\tan \frac{v}{2}$ and $\tan^2 \frac{v}{2}$ in Parabolic Motion, with Argument $M=(t-T)q^{-3/2}$, to facilitate the Computation of Ephemerides from Parabolic Elements (*Mem. B.A.A.*, **27**, No. 2).

329. M. C. TRAYLOR, The Computation of an Ephemeris of a Planet or a Comet (*Pop. Astr.*, **9**, 311).

330. Y. VÄISÄLÄ & L. OTERMA, Formulae and Directions for Computing the Orbits of Minor Planets and Comets (*Publ. Astron. Obs.*, Turku, 1951).

331. J. VINTER-HANSEN, The Orbits of Comets (*Pop. Astr.*, **52**, 370).

332. J. C. WATSON, *Theoretical Astronomy* (Lippincott, Philadelphia, 1900).

333. K. P. WILLIAMS, *The Calculation of the Orbits of Asteroids and Comets* (Principia Press, Indiana, 1934; Williams & Norgate, Lond., 1934).

334. H. E. WOOD, A Rapid Method of extending an Ephemeris (*J.B.A.A.*, **36**, No. 5, 149). [See also B. 319.]

See also B. 257.

Stars and Astrophysics: General

334a. R. HANBURY BROWN & A. C. B. LOVELL, *The Exploration of Space by Radio* (Chapman & Hall, London, 1957).

335. W. W. CAMPBELL, *Stellar Motions* (Yale University Press, 1913).

336. R. H. CURTISS, Classification and Description of Stellar Spectra (*H.d.A.*, 5/1, 1).

336a. R. D. DAVIES & H. P. PALMER, *Radio Studies of the Universe* (D. van Nostrand & Co., Inc., Princeton, 1959).

337. P. DOIG, *An Outline of Stellar Astronomy* (Hutchinson, 1947).

338. A. S. EDDINGTON, *The Internal Constitution of the Stars* (Cambridge, 1926).

339. A. S. EDDINGTON, *Stars and Atoms* (Oxford, 1927).

340. G. GAMOW, *The Birth and Death of the Sun* (N.Y., 1940).

341. L. GOLDBERG & L. H. ALLER, *Atoms, Stars and Nebulae* (Churchill, Lond., 1947).

342. J. G. HAGEN, Various Scales for Colour Estimates (*Ap. J.*, 34, No. 4, 261).

343. G. E. HALE, *Signals from the Stars* (Scribners, Lond., 1932).

343a. A. C. B. LOVELL & J. A. CLEGG, *Radio Astronomy* (Chapman & Hall, 1952).

344. K. LUNDMARK, Luminosities, Colours, Diameters, Densities, Masses of the Stars (*H.d.A.*, 5/1, 210; 5/2, 575).

345. D. H. MENZEL & H. SEN, *Stellar Constitution* (Chapman & Hall, forthcoming).

345a. J. L. PAWSEY & R. N. BRACEWELL, *Radio Astronomy* (Oxford, 1955).

346. C. H. PAYNE, *Stellar Atmospheres* (*Harv. Monogr.*, 1).

347. S. ROSSELAND, *Theoretical Astrophysics* (Oxford, 1936).

348. F. J. M. STRATTON, *Astronomical Physics* (Methuen, 1925).

349. O. STRUVE, *Stellar Evolution* (Princeton University Press, 1950).

Variables

349a. R. G. ANDREWS, The Classification of Variable Stars (*J.B.A.A.*, 70, No. 5, 214.)

350. J. VAN DER BILT, The Light Curve of U Cygni (*Mem. B.A.A.*, 33, 1937).

351. A. N. BROWN & F. DE ROY, The Observation of Variable Stars (*J.B.A.A.*, 33, No. 4, 143).

352. L. CAMPBELL, One Hundred Important Variable Stars (*Trans. I.A.U.* 6, 237; Cambridge University Press, 1939).

353. L. CAMPBELL & L. JACCHIA, *The Story of Variable Stars* (Harvard University Press, 1941).

354. R. S. DUGAN, A Finding List for Observers of Eclipsing Variables (*Contr. Princeton Obs.*, 15). [Data on 269 eclipsing variables.]

355. C. E. FURNESS, *An Introduction to the Study of Variable Stars* (Houghton Mifflin, 1915).

356. M. E. J. GHEURY, Notes pratiques sur l'Observation visuelle des Étoiles variables (*Ciel et Terre*, 1913, pp. 287, 319, 351; 1914–1919, pp. 1, 35, 78, 153, 180, 246; 1920, p. 36; Brussels).

356a. F. M. HOLBORN, The Methods of the Variable Star Section (*J.B.A.A.*, 68, No. 8, 1958).

357. Z. KOPAL, *The Computation of Elements of Eclipsing Binary Systems* (*Harv. Monogr.*, 8, 1950).

358. Z. KOPAL, *An Introduction to the Study of Eclipsing Variables* (*Harv. Monogr.*, 6, 1946).

359. S. A. MITCHELL, Observations of 204 Long Period Variables (*Publ. L. McC. Obs.*, **60**, No. 1, 1935).

360. S. A. MITCHELL, Magnitudes and Coordinates of Comparison Stars (*Publ. L. McC. Obs.*, **60**, No. 2, 1935).

361. C. P. OLIVIER *et al.* (*Publ. Univ. Pa.*, **5**, No. 3). [Comparison stars for 52 variables.]

362. C. PAYNE-GAPOSCHKIN & S. GAPOSCHKIN, *Variable Stars* (*Harv. Monogr.*, 5, 1938).

363. F. DE ROY, Tenth Report of the Variable Star Section of the B.A.A., 1920–1924 (*Mem. B.A.A.*, **28**, 1929).

364. F. J. M. STRATTON, Novae (*H.d.A.*, **6**, 251).

365. A. D. THACKERAY, The Long-period Variables (*Obs.*, **58**, No. 737, 285).

366. —Observations of Circumpolar Variable Stars during the Years 1889–1899 (*Harv. Ann.*, **37**, No. 1, 1, 1900).

367. —Observations of 58 Variable Stars of Long Period during the Years 1890–1901 (*Harv. Ann.*, **37**, No. 2, 149, 1902).

368. —Observations of 75 Variable Stars of Long Period during the Years 1902–1905 (*Harv. Ann.*, **57**, No. 1, 1, 1907).

369. —Comparison Stars for 252 Variables of Long Period (*Harv. Ann.*, **57**, No. 2, 215, 1908).

BINARIES

370. R. G. AITKEN, *The Binary Stars* (McGraw-Hill, 1935).

371. R. G. AITKEN, What we know about Double Stars (*M.N.*, **92**, No.7, 596).

372. E. CROSSLEY, J. GLEDHILL & J. W. WILSON, *A Handbook of Double Stars, with a Catalogue of 1200 Double Stars and Extensive Lists of Measures* (Macmillan, Lond., revised edn., 1880).

373. M. A. ELLISON, A Note upon the Measurement of Double-Star Position-Angles near the Pole (*J.B.A.A.*, **54**, No. 8/9, 169).

374. F. C. HENROTEAU, Double and Multiple Stars (*H.d.A.*, **6**, 299).

375. W. F. KING, Determination of the Orbits of Spectroscopic Binaries (*Ap. J.*, **27**, 125).

376. T. LEWIS, *Double Star Astronomy* (Taylor & Francis, Lond., 1908). [Reprint of *Obs.*, **31**, 88, 125, 162, 205, 242, 279, 307, 339, 379.]

377. T. LEWIS, Double Star Astronomy (*Obs.*, **36**, 426).

378. H. N. RUSSELL, A Rapid Method for Determining Visual Binary Orbits (*M.N.*, **93**, 599).

379. H. N. RUSSELL, A Short Method of Determining the Orbit of a Spectroscopic Binary (*Ap. J.*, **40**, 282).

380. H. N. RUSSELL, On the Determination of the Orbital Elements of Eclipsing Variable Stars (*Ap. J.*, **35**, 315; **36**, 54).

381. B. W. SITTERLEY, A Graphical Method for Obtaining the Elements of Eclipsing Variables (*Pop. Astr.*, **32**, 231).

382. W. M. SMART, On the Derivation of the Elements of a Visual Binary Orbit by Kowalsky's Method (*M.N.*, **90**, 534).

383. O. STRUVE, Spectroscopic Binaries (*M.N.*, **109**, No. 5, 487). [George Darwin Lecture, 1949.]

NEBULAE AND CLUSTERS; COSMOLOGY

384. B. J. & P. F. BOK, *The Milky Way* (Blakiston, Philadelphia, 1941).

385. P. COUDERC (trans. J. B. SIDGWICK), *The Expansion of the Universe* (Faber, 1952).

386. H. D. CURTIS, The Nebulae (*H.d.A.*, **5/2**, 774).

387. A. S. EDDINGTON, *The Expanding Universe* (Cambridge, 1933).

388. A. S. EDDINGTON, *The Rotation of the Galaxy* (Oxford, 1930). [Halley Lecture, 1930.]

389. G. E. HALE, *The Depths of the Universe* (Scribners, Lond., 1924).

390. G. E. HALE, *Beyond the Milky Way* (Scribners, Lond., 1926).

391. F. J. HARGREAVES, *The Size of the Universe* (Pelican Books, 1948).

392. E. HUBBLE, *The Realm of the Nebulae* (Oxford, 1936).

393. E. HUBBLE, *The Observational Approach to Cosmology* (Oxford, 1937).

394. E. HUBBLE, *Red Shifts in the Spectra of Nebulae* (Oxford, 1934). [Halley Lecture, 1934.]

395. J. H. JEANS, *Astronomy and Cosmogony* (Cambridge, 1928).

396. J. S. PLASKETT, *The Dimensions and the Structure of the Galaxy* (Oxford, 1935). [Halley Lecture, 1935.]

397. J. H. REYNOLDS, The Galactic Nebulae (*M.N.*, **96**, No. 4, 393).

398. I. ROBERTS, *A Selection of Photographs of Stars, Star-Clusters and Nebulae* (Lond., 1893).

399. I. ROBERTS, *Photographs of Stars, Star-Clusters and Nebulae* (Lond., 1899).

400. H. SHAPLEY, *Galaxies* (Blakiston, Philadelphia, 1943).

401. H. SHAPLEY, *Galactic and Extragalactic Studies—First Collection* (Harvard Observatory, 1940).

402. H. SHAPLEY, On Some Structural Features of the Metagalaxy (*M.N.*, **94**, No. 9, 791). [George Darwin Lecture, 1934.]

403. H. SHAPLEY, Stellar Clusters (*H.d.A.*, **5/2**, 698).

404. H. SHAPLEY, *Star Clusters* (*Harv. Monogr.* 2, McGraw-Hill, 1930).

STAR ATLASES AND CHARTS

[See also various entries under 'Star Catalogues'.]

405. F. W. A. ARGELANDER,* *Atlas des Nördlichen Gestirnten Himmels 1855.0* (Bonn, 1863; ed. KÜSTNER, Bonn, 1899). [40 charts covering the sky N of Dec—2° to mag 9 on scale of 2 cms/degree.]

406. E. E. BARNARD (ed. E. B. FROST & M. R. CALVERT), *A Photographic Atlas of Selected Regions of the Milky Way* (Publ. Carneg. Instn., 247, 1927). [Part I, photographs and descriptions; Part II, charts and tables.]

407. A. BEČVÁŘ, *Atlas Coeli Skalnaté Pleso 1950.0* (Praha, 1948; Sky Publishing Corporation, Harvard, 1949). [16 maps covering the whole

*Best known as *Bonner Durchmusterung*.

sky to mag 7·75 on scale of 7·5 mm/degree, including doubles, variables, nebulae, etc.]

408. A. BEČVÁŘ, *Atlas Coeli Skalnaté Pleso II* (Praha, 1951). [Catalogue of interesting objects, and Tables.]

409. M. BEYER & K. GRAFF, *Stern-Atlas* (Hamburg, 1925, repr. 1952). [27 charts covering the whole sky N of Dec−23° to mag 9 (plus brighter nebulae and clusters) on scale of 1 cm/degree, epoch 1855. *B.A.A.H.*, 1926 contains a Table of Precession Corrections, 1855 to 1926, for application to the positions of the Beyer-Graff Atlas.]

410. G. BISHOP, *Ecliptic Chart* (Lond., 1848, etc). [24 charts, to mag 10, extending 3° on each side of the ecliptic, epoch 1825.]

411. K. F. BOTTLINGER, *Galaktischer Atlas* (Julius Springer, Berlin, 1937). [8 charts showing stars and nebulae to about mag 5·5 in galactic coordinates based on Pole at $12^h 40^m$, $+28°$.]

412. E. DELPORTE, *Atlas Céleste* (I.A.U., Cambridge, 1930). [26 maps covering whole sky to mag 6; I.A.U. constellation boundaries; lists of mags. spectroscopic types, and positions at 1875 and 1925 of all stars to mag 4·5, and principal doubles, variables, nebulae, etc.]

413. E. DELPORTE, *Délimitation Scientifique des Constellations* (*Tables et Cartes*) (I.A.U., Cambridge, 1930). [Virtually a quotation from B. 412.]

414. J. FRANKLIN-ADAMS, *Photographic Chart of the Sky* (R.A.S., 1914). [206 sheets, each 16° square, covering the whole sky to mag 15·5 on scale of about 1 in/1°36. Charts 1–67, Dec −90° to −30°; charts 68–139, −15° to +15°; charts 140–206, +30° to +90°. See also *M.N.*, **64**, 608, 1904; *ibid.*, **97**, 89, 1936.]

415. E. HEIS, *Atlas Coelestis Eclipticus: Octo Continens Tabulas ad Delineandum Lumen Zodiacale* (1878). [8 charts of the zodiacal region, especially made for the Zodiacal Light observer.]

416. *Mappa Coelestis Nova* (Sky Publishing Corpn., Harvard, 1949). [Single chart, about 33 × 30 ins, covering sky N of Dec −42° to mag 5; stars of spectral types B–M printed in different colours; also novae, radiants, nebulae, clusters.]

417. *New Popular Star Atlas, Epoch 1950* (Gall & Inglis, *N.D.*). [Virtually a cheaper and simplified B. 418, and without the latter's 'Handbook' section; stars to mag 5·5.]

418. A. P. NORTON, *A Star Atlas and Reference Handbook, Epoch 1950* (Gall & Inglis, 5th edn., 1964). [The stand-by of every amateur; some 7000 stars to mag 6·5, plus nebulae, clusters, etc, and a mass of general information and reference material of use to the amateur.]

419. J. PALISA & M. WOLF, *Palisa-Wolf Charts* (Vienna, 1908–31). [210 photographic charts in 11 Series; epoch 1875; scale 36 mm/degree.]

420. *Palomar Sky Atlas.* [Two-colour photographic survey of the whole sky visible from Mt Palomar, made with the 48-in Schmidt; about 2000 plates anticipated, each 14 ins square; to mag 20; sponsored by the National Geographical Society of America; in progress.]

421. W. PECK, *The Observer's Atlas of the Heavens* (Gall & Inglis, 1898). [Same general type as B. 418, but superseded by the latter. 30 charts, plus positions and mags of over 1400 doubles, variables, nebulae, etc.]

422. F. E. ROSS & M. R. CALVERT, *Atlas of the Northern Milky Way* (University of Chicago Press, 1934). [39 plates, each about 13¼ ins square, exposed in a $D=5$, $F=35$-in camera at Mt Wilson and Flagstaff.]

423. E. SCHÖNFELD,* *Atlas der Himmelszone zwischen 1° und 23° südlicher Declination, 1855* (*Bonner Sternkarten, Zweite Serie*) (Bonn, 1887). [24 charts continuing B. 405 to Dec −23°.]

424. P. STUKER, *Sternatlas für Freunde der Astronomie* (Stuttgart, 1925). [Photographic; to mag 7·5; epoch 1900.]

425. O. THOMAS, *Atlas der Sternbilder* (Salzburg, 1945). [32 main charts; also useful section on objects of interest.]

426. H. B. WEBB, *Atlas of the Stars* (privately printed, N.Y., 2nd edn., 1945). [110 charts covering the sky N of Dec −23° to about mag 9·5 on scale 1 cm/degree; epoch 1920.0, with coordinate intersections for 2000.0. Very useful supplement to B. 418.]

STAR CATALOGUES—POSITIONAL

427. A. KOPF, Star Catalogues, especially those of Fundamental Character (*M.N.*, **96**, No. 8, 714). [George Darwin Lecture, 1936; an extremely useful summary of 19th- and 20th-century work.]

[The following selection of the catalogues of the last 120 years, devoted primarily to star positions, is arranged chronologically.]

428. F. BAILY, *A Catalogue of Those Stars in the Histoire Céleste Française of J. Lalande* [etc] (British Association, Lond., 1837). [47,390 stars reduced to epoch 1800.0 from Lalande's observations.]

429. S. GROOMBRIDGE (ed. G. B. AIRY), *A Catalogue of Circumpolar Stars* (Murray, Lond., 1838). [4243 stars, epoch 1810.0; see also B. 446.]

430. F. BAILY, *British Association Catalogue* (Lond., 1845). [8377 stars, epoch 1850.]

431. M. WEISSE, *Positiones mediae stellarum fixarum* [etc] (Petropoli, 1846). [Weisse's reductions of 31,085 stars within 15° of the equator to epoch 1825.0, using Bessel's observations; see also B. 432. Abbrev: *WB*.]

432. M. WEISSE, *Positiones mediae stellarum fixarum* [etc] (Petropoli, 1863). [Continuation of B. 431; 31,445 stars between Dec +15° and +45°. Abbrev: *WB2*.]

433. W. OELTZEN, *Argelanders Zonen-Beobachtungen vom 45° bis 80° nördlicher Declination in mittleren Positionen für 1842·0* (Wien, 1851–52). [Oeltzen's reductions of 26,425 stars from Argelander's observations. Abbrev: *OA(N)*.]

434. W. OELTZEN, *Argelanders Zonen-Beobachtungen vom 15° bis 31° südlicher Declination in mittleren Positionen für 1853·0* (Wien, 1857–58). [Continuation of B. 433. Abbrev: *OA(S)*.]

435. F. W. A. ARGELANDER,* *Bonner Durchmusterung des nördlichen Himmels* (Bonn, 1859–62; reprint 1903; 3 vols). [Approximate positions and visual mags to nearest 0·1 mag, to about mag 9·5. Arranged in successive 1°-wide Dec zones from +90° to −2°. Charts, scale 2 cms/degree, have been issued in photostat. Abbrev: *BD*. See B 438, 441.]

*Best known as *Bonner Durchmusterung*.

436. HEIS, *Atlas [and] Catalogus Coelestis Novus* (Cologne, 1872). [Abbrev: *H'*.]

437. J. BIRMINGHAM, The Red Stars: Observations and Catalogue (*Trans. Roy. Irish Acad.*, **26**, 1877; ed. T. E. ESPIN, Dublin, 1890). [Abbrevs: *B* and *E-B* respectively.]

438. E. SCHÖNFELD,*Durchmusterung* (1886). [Continuation of B. 435 to Dec −23°. Abbrev: *BD*.]

439. B. A. GOULD, The Argentine General Catalogue (*Result. Obs. Nac. Argent.*, **14**, Cordoba, 1886). [32,448 southern stars plus additional stars in clusters. Abbrevs: *CGA, AGC*.]

440. *Astronomische Gesellschaft Katalog* (Leipzig, 1890 etc). [The most complete catalogue of precision; epoch 1875. Abbrevs: *AG, AGC, CAG.* See B. 464.]

441.†J. M. THOME, Cordoba Durchmusterung (*Result. Obs. Nac. Argent.*, **16**, 1892 etc). [Continuation of B. 438 to Dec −52° in 10° vols. To mag 10 approximately; with visual mags and charts. Abbrev: *CD*.]

442. *The Astrographic Catalogue*. [Initiated at the Paris Congress, 1887; work shared by observatories over the world, began 1892, still in progress. Positions taken from photographic charts, scale 6 cms/degree. Abbrev: *AC*.]

443. D. GILL & J. C. KAPTEYN, The Cape Photographic Durchmusterung, 1875.0 (*Ann. Cape Obs.*, **3**, 1896– **5**, 1900). [Mags and approximate positions from Dec −19° to −90°, to mag 9. Abbrev: *CPD*.]

444. J SCHEINER, Photographische Himmelskarte (*Publ. Astrophys. Obs. Potsdam*, 1899–1903). [Mags and positions, epoch 1900.0.]

445. S. NEWCOMB, Catalogue of Fundamental Stars for the Epochs 1875 and 1900 (*Astr. Pap., Wash.*, **8**, No. 2, 77, 1905).

446. F. W. DYSON & W. G. THACKERAY, *New Reduction of Groombridge's Circumpolar Catalogue, Epoch 1810.0* (H.M.S.O., 1905). [See B. 429.]

447. H. B. HEDRICK, Catalogue of Zodiacal Stars, for the Epochs 1900 and 1920 (*Astr. Pap., Wash.*, **8**, No. 3, 405, 1905). [1607 stars to mag 7·5. Abbrev: *WZC.* See also B. 463.]

448. J. BOSSERT, *Catalogue d'Étoiles Brillantes, 1900.0* (Gauthier-Villars, Paris, 1906). [3799 stars in 1° NPD zones.]

449. J. &. R AMBRONN, *Sternverzeichnis enthaltend alle Sterne bis zur 6.5 Grösse* (Julius Springer, Berlin, 1907). [Positions of 7796 stars to mag 6·5 for epoch 1900, and proper motions of 2226 stars.]

450. A. AUWERS, Neue Fundamentalkatalog des Berliner Astronomischen Jahrbuchs (*Veröff. König. Astron. Rechen-Instit.*, **33**, 1910). [925 stars; one of the best fundamental catalogues; abbrev: *NFK*. See also B. 459.]

451. L. BOSS, *Preliminary General Catalogue of 6188 Stars for the Epoch 1900* (Publ. Carneg. Instn., 115, 1910). [Accurate positions and proper motions of all naked-eye stars; abbrev: *PGC*.]

452. T. W. BACKHOUSE, *Catalogue of 9842 Stars, or all Stars Very Conspicuous to the Naked Eye* (Sunderland, 1911). [Epoch 1900; useful for Amateurs.]

453. *Geschichte des Fixstern-Himmels* (Karlsruhe, 1922–23). [Collection of pre-1900 observations reduced to 1875.0.]

*Best known as *Bonner Durchmusterung*.

†441A. C. D. PERINNE, Cordoba Durchmusterung. [Continuation of B.441 to the South Pole, to 10ᵐ0, 1910, Cordoba Obs.]

454. E. C. PICKERING & J. C. KAPTEYN, Durchmusterung of Selected Areas between δ=0 and δ=+90° (*Harv. Ann.*, **101**, 1918).

455. E. C. PICKERING, J. C. KAPTEYN & P. J. VAN RHIJN, Durchmusterung of Selected Areas between δ=−15° and δ=−30° (*Harv. Ann.*, **102**, 1923).

456. E. C. PICKERING, J. C. KAPTEYN & P. J. VAN RHIJN, Durchmusterung of Selected Areas between δ=−45° and δ=−90° (*Harv. Ann.*, **103**, 1924).

457. L. BOSS & B. BOSS, *San Louis Catalogue of 15,333 Stars for the Epoch 1920.0* (Publ. Carneg. Instn., 386, 1928). [To mag 7; mostly southern.]

458. R. SCHORR & W. KRUSE, *Index der Sternörter 1900–25* (Bergedorf, 1928). [Monumental analysis of over 400 catalogues. Vol. 1, northern stars, vol. 2, southern.]

459. *Dritter Fundamentalkatalog des Berliner Astronomischen Jahrbuchs* (Berlin, 1934). [Abbrev: *FK3*. See B. 450.]

460. F. SCHLESLINGER, Catalogue of Bright Stars containing all important data known in June 1930 (*Publ. Yale Obs.*, 1930). [9110 stars to visual mag 6·5, and some fainter. Abbrev: *BS*.]

461. B. BOSS, *Albany Catalogue of 20,811 Stars for the Epoch 1910* (Carnegie Institution of Washington, 1931).

462. B. BOSS, *General Catalogue of 33,342 Stars for the Epoch 1950* (Carnegie Institution of Washington, 1937, 5 vols).

463. J. ROBERTSON, Catalogue of 3539 Zodiacal Stars for the Equinox 1950.0 (*Astr. Pap., Wash.*, **10**, No. 2, 175, 1940.) [Revision and enlargement of B. 447; abbrev: *NZC*.]

464. R. SCHORR & A. KOHLSCHÜTTER, *Zweiter Katalog der Astronomische Gesellschaft, Äquinoktium 1950* (Hamburg-Bergedorf, 1951). [Vols 1–8, Dec + 90° to −2°. See B. 440 Abbrev: *AGK2*.]

465. *Apparent Places of Fundamental Stars* (H.M.S.O., annually since 1941). [Mean and Apparent places of the 1535 stars of the *FK3* (B. 459) and its Supplement.]

STAR CATALOGUES—MOTIONS AND PARALLAXES

466. W. S. ADAMS & A. H. JOY, The Radial Velocities of 1013 Stars (*Ap. J.*, **57**, No. 3, 149=*M.W.C.*, 258).

467. J. BOSSERT, *Catalogue des mouvements propres des 5671 étoiles* (Paris, 1919).

468. W. W. CAMPBELL & J. H. MOORE, Radial Velocities of Stars brighter than Visual Magnitude 5·51 (*Publ. Lick. Obs.*, **16**, 1928).

469. W. S. EICHELBERGER, Positions and Proper Motions of 1504 Standard Stars, 1925.0 (*Astr. Pap., Wash.*, **10**, Part 1, 1925).

470. H. KNOX-SHAW & H. G. SCOTT BARRETT, *The Radcliffe Catalogue of Proper Motions in Selected Areas 1 to 115* (Oxford University Press, 1934). [To mag 14 in the Selected Areas on and N of the equator.]

471. J. H. MOORE, General Catalogue of Radial Velocities of Stars, Nebulae and Clusters (*Publ. Lick. Obs.*, **18**, 1932).

472. J. S. PLASKETT & J. A. PEARCE, A Catalogue of the Radial Velocities of O and B Type Stars (*Publ. Dom. Astrophys. Obs.*, **5**, No. 2, 99).

473. J. G. PORTER, E. I. YOWELL & E. S. SMITH, A Catalog of 1474 Stars with proper motion exceeding four-tenths of a second per year (*Publ. Cincinn. Obs.*, **20**).

474. F. SCHLESINGER, *General Catalogue of Stellar Parallaxes* (Yale, 1924). [Includes all determinations available in 1924 Jan.]

475. F. SCHLESINGER & L. F. JENKINS, General Catalogue of Stellar Parallaxes (*Publ. Yale Obs.*, 1935). [B. 474 revised to 1935.]

476. R. SCHORR, *Eigenbewegungs-Lexikon* (Hamburg Observatory, Bergedorf, 1 vol, 1923; 2 vols, 1936). [2nd edn. includes all proper motions available at the end of 1935; 94,741 stars, with mags and spectral types. Vol 1, N stars; vol 2, S stars. Abbrev: *EBL*.]

STAR CATALOGUES—PHOTOMETRIC

477. S. I. BAILEY, A Catalogue of 7922 Stars observed with the Meridian Photometer, 1889–91 (*Harv. Ann.*, **34**). [The 'Southern Meridian Photometry', abbrev: *SMP*. Continuation of B. 489 to the S Pole.]

478. A. BRUNN, *Atlas photométrique des Constellations de* $+90°$ *à* $-30°$ (privately printed, France, 1949). [55 sheets showing all *BD* stars to mag 7·5, scale 1 cm/degree, epoch 1900. Against each star is printed its visual mag, to 0·01 mag for stars of mag 6·50 and brighter, to 0·1 mag for those fainter than 6·50. Other data include photometric mags of all extragalactic nebulae brighter than mag 12·0 photographic.]

479. S. CHAPMAN & P. J. MELOTTE, Photographic Magnitudes of 262 Stars within 25' of the North Pole (*M.N.*, **74**, No. 1, 40).

480. B. G. FESSENKOFF, *Photometrical Catalogue of 1155 Stars* (Kharkow, 1926).

481. W. FLEMING, Spectra and Photographic Magnitudes of Stars in Standard Regions (*Harv. Ann.*, **71**, No. 2, 27).

482. B. A. GOULD, *Uranometria Argentina* (Buenos Aires, 1879). [Visually determined mags, and positions, of stars to mag 7 South of Dec $+10°$. Abbrevs: *UA, G.*]

483. [Harvard], Stars near the North Pole (*Harv. Ann.*, **48**, No. 1, 1).

484. Harvard Standard Regions (*Harv. Ann.*, **71**, No. 4, 233).

485. H. S. LEAVITT, The North Polar Sequence (*Harv. Ann.*, **71**, No. 3, 47).

486. Magnitudes of Stars of the North Polar Sequence (*B.A.A.H.*, 1926, 32).

487. G. MÜLLER & P. KEMPF, Photometrische Durchmusterung des nördlichen Himmels (*Publ. Astrophys. Obs. Potsdam*, Nos. 31, 43, 44, 51, 52, 1894–1907).

488. E. C. PICKERING, Adopted Photographic Magnitudes of 96 Polar Stars (*Harv. Circ.*, 170).

489. E. C. PICKERING, Observations with the Meridian Photometer, 1879–82 (*Harv. Ann.*, **14**, 1884). [The Harvard Photometry (*HP*): magnitudes of 4260 stars, including all brighter than mag 6 N of Dec $-30°$.]

490. E. C. PICKERING, Revised Harvard Photometry (*Harv. Ann.*, **50**). [Positions, visual mags, and spectral types of 9110 stars, mostly mag 6·5 and brighter. Abbrevs: *HR, RHP.*]

491. E. C. PICKERING, A Catalogue of 36,682 Stars Fainter than Magnitude

6·50 . . . forming a Supplement to the Revised Harvard Photometry (*Harv. Ann.*, **54**).

492. C. PRITCHARD, *Uranometria Nova Oxoniensis* (Oxford, 1885). [Wedge-photometer redeterminations of Argelander's *Uranometria Nova* magnitudes; 2784 entries. Abbrev: *UO*.]

493. F. H. SEARES, Magnitudes of the North Polar Sequence. (Report of the Commission de photométrie stellaire) (*Trans. I.A.U.*, **1**, 69).

494. F. H. SEARES, J. C. KAPTEYN & P. J. VAN RHIJN, *Mt Wilson Catalogue of Photographic Magnitudes in Selected Areas 1–139* (Carnegie Institution, Washington, 1930).

495. F. H. SEARES, F. E. ROSS & M. C. JOYNER, *Magnitudes and Colours of Stars North of +80°* (Publ. Carneg. Instn., 532, 1941).

STAR CATALOGUES—SPECTROSCOPIC

[Many of the catalogues mentioned elsewhere in this Bibliography quote spectroscopic types. Specially demanding mention, however, are the following.]

496. E. C. PICKERING, The Draper Catalogue of Stellar Spectra (*Harv. Ann.*, **27**, 1890).

497. A. C. MAURY, Spectra of Bright Stars (*Harv. Ann.*, **28**, 1897). [Together with B. 496 constitutes the 'old' Draper Catalogue of over 10,000 stars.]

498. A. J. CANNON & E. C. PICKERING, The Henry Draper Catalogue of Stellar Spectra (*Harv. Ann.*, **91–99**, 1918–24).

499. A. J. CANNON, The Henry Draper Extension (*Harv. Ann.*, **100**). [Together with B. 498 constitutes the 'new' Draper Catalogue (*HD*): mags, spectral types and positions of 225,000 stars to mag 10 approximately.]

500. A. SCHWASSMANN & P. J. VAN RHIJN, *Bergedorfer Spektral-Durch-musterung* (Bergedorf, 1935, 1938). [To mag 13 (photographic) in the northern Kapteyn areas.]

STAR CATALOGUES—VARIABLE STARS

501. A. J. CANNON,* Second Catalogue of Variable Stars (*Harv. Ann.*, **55**, 1907). ['Second' with reference to B. 512; 1957 variables.]

502. S. C. CHANDLER,* Catalogue of Variable Stars (*A.J.*, **8**, No. 11/12, 82, 1888). [225 variables.]

503. S. C. CHANDLER,* Second Catalogue of Variable Stars (*A.J.*, **13**, No. 12, 89, 1893). [260 variables.]

504. S. C. CHANDLER,* Third Catalogue of Variable Stars (*A.J.*, **16**, No. 9, 145, 1896). [393 variables.]

505. S. C. CHANDLER,* Revision of Elements of the Third Catalogue of Variable Stars (*A.J.*, **24**, No. 1, 1, 1904).

506. J. G. GHAEN, *Atlas [et Catalogus] Stellarum Variabilium* (9 Series, 1899–1941). [Charts and lists of about 24,000 comparison stars for 488 variables. The 5th Series (Berlin, 1906) is particularly useful, including

* Primarily of historical value, B. 507–8 and B. 509 now being the standard works.

all variables wholly observable with the naked eye or binoculars (minima brighter than mag 7). See also B. 513.]

507. *Katalog und Ephemeriden Veränderlicher Sterne* (Vierteljahrsschrift der Astronomischen Gesellschaft, annually 1870–1926).

508. *Katalog und Ephemeriden Veränderlicher Sterne* (Berlin-Babelsberg, annually to 1941).

509. B. V. KUKARKIN & P. P. PARENAGO, *General Catalogue of Variable Stars* (Academy of Sciences of the U.S.S.R., 1948; annual Supplements 1949–52 second edn.: 1958). [In Russian, but with English translations of the Introductions. The I.A.U.-recognised standard work.]

510. R. PRAGER, *Geschichte und Literatur des Lichtwechsels der Veränderlichen Sterne* (Ferd. Dümmlers Verlagsbuchhandlung, Berlin; vol. 1, 1934; vol. 2, 1936). [See also B. 511.]

511. R. PRAGER, History and Bibliography of the Light Variations of Variable Stars (*Harv. Ann.*, **111**, 1941). [Vol. 3 of B. 510.]

512. Provisional Catalogue of Variable Stars* (*Harv. Ann.*, **48**, No. 3, 91, 1903). [1227 variables.]

512a. H. SCHNELLER, *Geschichte und Literatur des Lichtwechsels der Veränderlichen Sterne* (Berlin, 1957).

513. J. STEIN & J. JUNKERS, [Index to the 9 Series of B. 506.] (*Ricerche Astronomiche*, **4**; Specola Vaticana, 1941).

STAR CATALOGUES—BINARY STARS

514. R. G. AITKEN, *New General Catalogue of Double Stars within 120° of the North Pole* (Publ. Carneg. Instn., 417, 2 vols, 1932). [Includes all measures of 17,181 doubles prior to 1927; epochs 1900.0 and 1950.0. Abbrev: *ADS*.]

515. S. W. BURNHAM, *A New General Catalogue of Double Stars within 121° of the North Pole* (Publ. Carneg. Instn., 5, 2 vols, 1906). [Measures etc of 13,665 doubles; epochs 1880.0 and 1900.0. Part I, The Catalogue: Part II, Notes to the Catalogue. Abbrev: *BGC*.]

516. W. W. CAMPBELL & H. D. CURTIS, First Catalogue of Spectroscopic Binaries (*L.O.B.*, 3, No. 79, 136). [Complete to 1905; 140 stars.]

517. W. W. CAMPBELL, Second Catalogue of Spectroscopic Binary Stars (*L.O.B.*, 6, No. 181, 17). [To 1910; 306 stars. See also B. 516, 532–4.]

518. F. W. DYSON, *Catalogue of Double Stars from observations made at The Royal Observatory Greenwich with the 28-inch Refractor, 1893–1919* (H.M.S.O., 1921).

519. J. F. W. HERSCHEL, Descriptions and approximate Places of 321 new Double and Triple Stars (*Mem. R.A.S.*, 2, No. 29, 459).

520. J. F. W. HERSCHEL, Approximate Places and Descriptions of 295 new Double and Triple Stars (*Mem. R.A.S.*, 3, No. 3, 47).

521. J. F. W. HERSCHEL, Third Series of Observations . . . Catalogue of 384 new Double and Multiple Stars; completing a first 1000 of Those Objects (*Mem. R.A.S.*, 3, No. 13, 177).

---

* Primarily of historical value, B. 507–8 and B. 509 now being the standard works.

522. J. F. W. HERSCHEL, Fourth Series of Observations . . . containing the Mean Places . . . of 1236 Double Stars [etc] (*Mem. R.A.S.*, **4**, No. 17, 331).

523. J. F. W. HERSCHEL, Fifth Catalogue of Double Stars . . . Places, Descriptions, and measured Angles of Position of 2007 of those objects [etc] (*Mem. R.A.S.*, **6**, No. 1, 1).

524. J. F. W. HERSCHEL, Sixth Catalogue of Double Stars . . . 286 of those objects (*Mem. R.A.S.*, **9**, No. 7, 193).

525. J. F. W. HERSCHEL, Seventh Catalogue of Double Stars (*Mem. R.A.S.*, **38**, 1870).

526. J. F. W. HERSCHEL (ed. R. MAIN & C. PRITCHARD), Catalogue of 10,300 Multiple and Double Stars (*Mem. R.A.S.*, **40**, 1874).

527. W. HERSCHEL, Catalogue of Double Stars (*Phil. Trans.*, **72**, 112, 1782).

528. W. HERSCHEL, Catalogue of Double Stars (*Phil. Trans.*, **75**, 40, 1785).

529. W. HERSCHEL, On the places of 145 new Double Stars (*Mem. R.A.S.*, **1**, 166, 1821).

530. R. JONCKHEERE, Catalogue and Measures of Double Stars discovered visually from 1905–1916 within 105° of the North Pole and under 5″ Separation (*Mem. R.A.S.*, **17**, 1917). [Virtually a Supplement to B. 515.]

531. T. LEWIS, Measures of the Double Stars contained in the Mensurae Micrometricae of F. G. W. Struve (*Mem. R.A.S.*, **56**). [See B. 537.]

532. J. H. MOORE, Third Catalogue of Spectroscopic Binary Stars (*L.O.B.*, **11**, No. 355, 141). [To 1924; 1054 stars. See also B. 516–5, 533–4.]

533. J. H. MOORE, Fourth Catalogue of Spectroscopic Binary Stars (*L.O.B.*, **18**, No. 483, 1). [375 stars.]

534. J. H. MOORE & F. J. NEUBAUER, Fifth Catalogue of the Orbital Elements of Spectroscopic Binary Stars (*L.O.B.*, No. 521).

535. J. SOUTH & J. F. W. HERSCHEL, *Observations of the Apparent Distances and Positions of 380 Double and Triple Stars, made in the Years 1821, 1822 and 1823* (Lond., 1825).

536. F. G. W. STRUVE, *Catalogus Novus Stellarum Duplicium et Multiplicium* (Dorpat, 1827). [The Dorpat Catalogue (*Σ*).]

537. F. G. W. STRUVE, *Stellarum Duplicium et Multiplicium Mensurae Micrometricae* (Petropoli, 1837). [See B. 531.]

538. F. G. W. STRUVE, *Stellarum Fixarum imprimis Duplicium et Multiplicium Positiones Mediae pro Epocha 1830.0* (Petropoli, 1852).

539. O. STRUVE, *Revised Pulkova Catalogue* (Pulkova, 1850). [Abbrev: *OΣ*; Part II denoted by *OΣΣ*.]

NEBULAE AND CLUSTERS—CATALOGUES

[See also under 'Star Atlases and Charts'.]

540. S. I. BAILEY, Globular Clusters—A Provisional Catalogue (*Harv. Ann.*, **76**, No. 4, 43). [113 clusters.]

541. E. E. BARNARD, On the Dark Markings of the Sky, with a Catalogue of 182 Such Objects (*Ap. J.*, **49**, No. 1, 1). [See *Ap. J.*, **49**, No. 5, 360 for list of errata.]

542. H. D. CURTIS, Descriptions of 762 Nebulae and Clusters Photographed with the Crossley Reflector (*Publ. Lick Obs.*, **13**, No. 1, 9).

543. J. L. E. DREYER, New General Catalogue of Nebulae and Clusters of Stars (*Mem. R.A.S.*, **49**, 1888). [NGC. Based on B. 544.]
—Index Catalogue (*Mem. R.A.S.*, **51**, 1895). [IC. Extension of NGC.]
—Second Index Catalogue (*Mem. R.A.S.*, **59**, 1908). [Extension of NGC.]*

544. J. F. W. HERSCHEL, *General Catalogue of Nebulae and Clusters of Stars of the Epoch 1860* (Lond., 1864).

545. W. HERSCHEL, Catalogue of 1000 new Nebulae and Clusters of Stars (*Phil. Trans.*, **76**, 457, 1786).

546. W. HERSCHEL, Catalogue of a second 1000 of New Nebulae and Clusters of Stars (*Phil. Trans.*, **79**, 212, 1789).

547. W. HERSCHEL, Catalogue of 500 new Nebulae, Nebulous Stars, Planetary Nebulae, and Clusters of Stars (*Phil. Trans.*, 1802, 477).

548. J. HOLETSCHEK, Catalogue of Nebular Magnitudes (*Ann. K.K. Univ.-Stern.*, **20**, 114, Vienna, 1907).

549. P. J. MELOTTE, A Catalogue of Star Clusters shown on Franklin-Adams Chart Plates (*Mem. R.A.S.*, **60**, No. 5, 175). [245 objects.]

550. C. MESSIER, *Catalogue of 103 Nebulae and Clusters* (1771–84). [Abbrev: *M*. See also B. 551.]

551. H. SHAPLEY & H. DAVIES, Messier's 'Catalogue of Nebulae and Clusters' (*Obs.* **41**, No. 529, 318). [Reprint of B. 550, with corresponding NGC (B. 543) numbers.]

552. C. WIRTZ, Flächenhelligkeiten von 566 Nebelflecken und Sternhaufen (*Lund. Medd.*, **2**, No. 29, 1923).

AMATEUR OBSERVATIONAL ASTRONOMY

[With the exception of B. 556 the following are rather elementary or dated, or both, and are chiefly of value for the lists of telescopically interesting objects which they contain. A number of Star Atlases (*q.v.*) contain similar lists.]

553. C. E. BARNES, *1001 Celestial Wonders as observed with Home-built Instruments* (California, 1929).

554. W. F. DENNING, *Telescopic Work for Starlight Evenings* (Taylor & Francis, Lond., 1891).

555. F. M. GIBSON, *The Amateur Telescopist's Handbook* (Longmans, Green, 1894).

556. R. HENSELING (ed.), *Astronomisches Handbuch* (Stuttgart, 1924).

557. W. NOBLE, *Hours with a Three-inch Telescope* (Longmans, Green, 1886).

558. W. T. OLCOTT, *In Starland with a Three-inch Telescope* (Putnam, 1909).

559. T. E. R. PHILLIPS & W. H. STEAVENSON (eds), *Splendour of the Heavens* (Hutchinson, 1923).

* A one-volume edition of *New General Catalogue of Nebulae and Clusters of Stars, the Index Catalogue and the Second Index Catalogue* was issued by the R.A.S. in 1953.

560. R. A. PROCTOR (rev. W. H. STEAVENSON), *Half-Hours with the Telescope* (Longmans, Green, 1926).

561. G. P. SERVISS, *Astronomy with an Opera Glass* (Lond., 1902).

562. G. P. SERVISS, *Pleasures of the Telescope* (Hirschfield, Lond., 1902).

563. J. B. SIDGWICK, *Introducing Astronomy* (Faber, 1951).

564. W. H. SMYTH, *A Cycle of Celestial Objects* (1st edn., 1844, 2 vols [vol 2 being the *Bedford Catalogue*]; 2nd edn., edited G. F. CHAMBERS, Oxford, 1881).

565. T. W. WEBB (rev. ESPIN), *Celestial Objects for Common Telescopes* (Longmans, Green, 1917, 2 vols.; rev. and enl. repub. of 6th edn., (MAYALL & MAYALL), Dover, 1962).

OBSERVATIONAL AIDS

566. *Nautical Almanac and Astronomical Ephemeris* (H.M.S.O., annually).

567. *Connaissance des Temps, ou des Mouvements Celéstes . . . publiée par le Bureau des Longitudes* (Gauthier-Villars, Paris, annually).

568. *American Ephemeris and Nautical Almanac* (Washington, annually).

569. *Berliner Astronomisches Jahrbuch* (Akademie Verlag, Berlin).

570. *Handbook of the British Astronomical Association* (B.A.A. Computing Section, annually).

571. *Journal of the British Astronomical Association* (B.A.A., approximately monthly).

572. *British Astronomical Association Circulars* (B.A.A., at irregular intervals).

573. *The British Astronomical Association: Its Nature, Aims and Methods* (London, 1948).

SECTION 21

SUPPLEMENTARY BIBLIOGRAPHY

Arranged alphabetically unless otherwise stated.

SUN

S1. SVESTKA, *Solar Flares* (Reidel, 1976).
S2. TANSBERG-HANSEN, *Solar Activity* (Blaisdell, 1967).
S3. M. WALDMEIER, *Ergebnisse und Probleme der Sonnenforschung* (Leipzig, 1955).
S4. H. ZIRIN, *The Solar Atmosphere* (Blaisdell, 1966).

MOON

[*a*. Maps and descriptive works; arranged chronologically.]

S5. H. P. WILKINS & P. MOORE, *The Moon* (Faber & Faber, 1969).
S6. NASA (ed.), *Lunar Orbiter Photographic Atlas of the Moon* (1971).
S7. P. MOORE, *New Guide to the Moon* (Norton, 1976).
S8. H. R. POVENMIRE, *Graze Observer's Handbook*, privately printed, 2nd edn., 1979.

MERCURY

S9. C. A. CROSS & P. MOORE, *The Atlas of Mercury* (Crown, 1977).

MARS

S10. P. MOORE, *Guide to Mars* (Norton, 1978).
S11. P. MOORE & C. A. CROSS, *Mars* (Crown, 1973). [An atlas.]
S12. NASA (ed.), *The Martian Landscape* (1978).

JUPITER

S13. T. GEHRELS (ed.), *Jupiter* (University of Arizona Press, 1976).
S14. NASA (ed.), *Pioneer Odyssey* (1977).

SATURN

S15. A. F. O'D. ALEXANDER, *The Planet Saturn* (Faber and Faber, 1962; Dover reprint, 1980).
S16. I. ASIMOV, *Saturn and Beyond* (Lothrop, Lee, 1979).
S17. NASA (ed.), *The Rings of Saturn* (1977).

347

BIBLIOGRAPHY

URANUS

S18. A. F. O'D. ALEXANDER, *The Planet Uranus* (Faber & Faber, 1972).

PLANETARY SATELLITES

S19. J. A. BURNS (ed.), *Planetary Satellites* (University of Arizona Press, 1977).

METEORS

S20. D. W. R. MCKINLEY, *Meteor Science and Engineering* (McGraw-Hill, 1961).
S21. NASA (ed.), *Meteor Orbits and Dust* (1965).

COMETS

S22. B. G. MARSDEN (ed.), *1979 Catalogue of Cometary Orbits* (Smithsonian, 1979).
S23. P. MOORE, *Comets* (Scribner's, 1976).
S24. NASA (ed.), *Comet Kohoutek* (1975).
S25. NASA (ed.), *The Study of Comets* (1977).

STARS AND ASTROPHYSICS: GENERAL

S26. A. UNSÖLD, *The New Cosmos* (Springer, 2nd edn., 1977).

VARIABLE STARS

S27. J. S. GLASBY, *Variable Stars* (Constable, 1969).
S28. B. V. KUKARKIN *et al.*, *General Catalogue of Variable Stars* (USSR Academy of Sciences, Moscow, 1969, 1975, 3 vols., 2 supplements).

BINARIES

S29. W. D. HEINTZ, *Double Stars* (D. Reidel [cloth]; Kluwer [paper], 1978).

NEBULAE AND CLUSTERS: COSMOLOGY

S30. J. H. MALLAS & E. KREIMER, *The Messier Album* (Sky Publishing, 1978).

STAR ATLASES AND CHARTS

S31. S. MITTON (ed.), *Star Atlas* (Crown, 1979). [8 maps, over 4000 stars to 6^m0 with some introduction, similar to B. 417.]
S32. C. PAPADOPOULOS, *True Visual Magnitude Photographic Star Atlas* (Pergamon, 1978, 1980).
S33. *Smithsonian Astrophysical Observatory Star Atlas* (M.I.T. Press, 1966). [152 maps, 258,997 stars of the entire sky to 9^m0.]
S34. H. VEHRENBERG, *Atlas of Deep Sky Splendors* (Treugesell Verlag, 3rd. edn., 1978).
S35. H. VEHRENBERG, *Atlas of Selected Areas* (Treugesell Verlag, 1976). [206 maps of the famous Kapteyn's areas down to 15^m9.]
S36. H. VEHRENBERG, *Atlas Stellarum* (Treugesell Verlag, 1974). [486 maps of the whole sky down to 14^m0.]

BIBLIOGRAPHY

S37. H. VEHRENBERG, *Photographic Star Atlas* (Treugesell Verlag, 1972). [464 maps covering the whole sky to 13^m.]

S37a. *AAVSO Star Atlas* (Sky Publishing, 1980). [Similar to the *Smithsonian*.]

STAR CATALOGUES—POSITIONAL

S38. *Dritter Katalog der Astronomischen Gesellschaft* (Hamburg-Bergedorf, 1970, 8 vols.). [See B. 464: abbrev *AGK3*.]

S39. D. HOFFLEIT, *Bright Star Catalogue of the Yale University Observatory* (Yale University Observatory, 3rd rev. edn., 1964). [See B. 460.]

S40. *Smithsonian Astrophysical Observatory Star Catalog* (U.S. Government Printing Office, 1966, 4 vols.). [The catalogue to above S33.]

S41. *Vierter Fundamental Katalog* (Karlsruhe, 1963). [Abbrev: *FK4*.]

STAR CATALOGUES—VARIABLE STARS

S42. B. V. KUKARKIN *et al.*, *General Catalogue of Variable Stars* (USSR Academy of Sciences, Moscow, 1969, 1975, 3 vols., 2 supplements).

STAR CATALOGUES—BINARY STARS

S43. H. M. JEFFERS, W. H. V. D. BOS & F. M. GREEBY, *Index Catalogue of Visual Double Stars*, 1961.0 (Publication of the Lick Observatory, Vol. 21, 1963, 2 vols.).

NEBULAE AND CLUSTERS—CATALOGUES

S44. J. W. SULENTIC & W. G. TIFFT, *The Revised New General Catalogue of Nonstellar Astronomical Objects* (University of Arizona Press, 1976). [See also B. 543.]

AMATEUR OBSERVATIONAL ASTRONOMY

S45. R. BURNHAM, JR., *Burnham's Celestial Handbook—An Observer's Guide to the Universe Beyond the Solar System* (Dover, 1978, 3 vols.). [The best of such handbooks.]

S46. G. D. ROTH (ed.), *Astronomy—A Handbook for Amateur Astronomers* (Springer, 1967).

S47. H. VEHRENBERG & D. BLANK, *Handbook of the Constellations* (Treugesell Verlag, 3rd edn., 1977).

INDEX

351

A CATALOGUE OF
SELECTED DOVER BOOKS
IN ALL FIELDS OF INTEREST

A CATALOGUE OF SELECTED DOVER
BOOKS IN ALL FIELDS OF INTEREST

RACKHAM'S COLOR ILLUSTRATIONS FOR WAGNER'S RING. Rackham's finest mature work—all 64 full-color watercolors in a faithful and lush interpretation of the *Ring*. Full-sized plates on coated stock of the paintings used by opera companies for authentic staging of Wagner. Captions aid in following complete Ring cycle. Introduction. 64 illustrations plus vignettes. 72pp. 8⅝ x 11¼.   23779-6 Pa. $6.00

CONTEMPORARY POLISH POSTERS IN FULL COLOR, edited by Joseph Czestochowski. 46 full-color examples of brilliant school of Polish graphic design, selected from world's first museum (near Warsaw) dedicated to poster art. Posters on circuses, films, plays, concerts all show cosmopolitan influences, free imagination. Introduction. 48pp. 9⅜ x 12¼.
                                                23780-X Pa. $6.00

GRAPHIC WORKS OF EDVARD MUNCH, Edvard Munch. 90 haunting, evocative prints by first major Expressionist artist and one of the greatest graphic artists of his time: *The Scream, Anxiety, Death Chamber, The Kiss, Madonna*, etc. Introduction by Alfred Werner. 90pp. 9 x 12.
                                                23765-6 Pa. $5.00

THE GOLDEN AGE OF THE POSTER, Hayward and Blanche Cirker. 70 extraordinary posters in full colors, from Maitres de l'Affiche, Mucha, Lautrec, Bradley, Cheret, Beardsley, many others. Total of 78pp. 9⅜ x 12¼.   22753-7 Pa. $5.95

THE NOTEBOOKS OF LEONARDO DA VINCI, edited by J. P. Richter. Extracts from manuscripts reveal great genius; on painting, sculpture, anatomy, sciences, geography, etc. Both Italian and English. 186 ms. pages reproduced, plus 500 additional drawings, including studies for *Last Supper*, Sforza monument, etc. 860pp. 7⅞ x 10¾. (Available in U.S. only)
                           22572-0, 22573-9 Pa., Two-vol. set $15.90

THE CODEX NUTTALL, as first edited by Zelia Nuttall. Only inexpensive edition, in full color, of a pre-Columbian Mexican (Mixtec) book. 88 color plates show kings, gods, heroes, temples, sacrifices. New explanatory, historical introduction by Arthur G. Miller. 96pp. 11⅜ x 8½. (Available in U.S. only)   23168-2 Pa. $7.95

UNE SEMAINE DE BONTÉ, A SURREALISTIC NOVEL IN COLLAGE, Max Ernst. Masterpiece created out of 19th-century periodical illustrations, explores worlds of terror and surprise. Some consider this Ernst's greatest work. 208pp. 8⅛ x 11.   23252-2 Pa. $5.00

DRAWINGS OF WILLIAM BLAKE, William Blake. 92 plates from Book of Job, *Divine Comedy, Paradise Lost,* visionary heads, mythological figures, Laocoon, etc. Selection, introduction, commentary by Sir Geoffrey Keynes. 178pp. 8⅛ x 11. 22303-5 Pa. $4.00

ENGRAVINGS OF HOGARTH, William Hogarth. 101 of Hogarth's greatest works: *Rake's Progress, Harlot's Progress, Illustrations for Hudibras, Before and After, Beer Street and Gin Lane,* many more. Full commentary. 256pp. 11 x 13¾. 22479-1 Pa. $12.95

DAUMIER: 120 GREAT LITHOGRAPHS, Honore Daumier. Wide-ranging collection of lithographs by the greatest caricaturist of the 19th century. Concentrates on eternally popular series on lawyers, on married life, on liberated women, etc. Selection, introduction, and notes on plates by Charles F. Ramus. Total of 158pp. 9⅜ x 12¼. 23512-2 Pa. $5.50

DRAWINGS OF MUCHA, Alphonse Maria Mucha. Work reveals draftsman of highest caliber: studies for famous posters and paintings, renderings for book illustrations and ads, etc. 70 works, 9 in color; including 6 items not drawings. Introduction. List of illustrations. 72pp. 9⅜ x 12¼. (Available in U.S. only) 23672-2 Pa. $4.00

GIOVANNI BATTISTA PIRANESI: DRAWINGS IN THE PIERPONT MORGAN LIBRARY, Giovanni Battista Piranesi. For first time ever all of Morgan Library's collection, world's largest. 167 illustrations of rare Piranesi drawings—archeological, architectural, decorative and visionary. Essay, detailed list of drawings, chronology, captions. Edited by Felice Stampfle. 144pp. 9⅜ x 12¼. 23714-1 Pa. $7.50

NEW YORK ETCHINGS (1905-1949), John Sloan. All of important American artist's N.Y. life etchings. 67 works include some of his best art; also lively historical record—Greenwich Village, tenement scenes. Edited by Sloan's widow. Introduction and captions. 79pp. 8⅜ x 11¼. 23651-X Pa. $4.00

CHINESE PAINTING AND CALLIGRAPHY: A PICTORIAL SURVEY, Wan-go Weng. 69 fine examples from John M. Crawford's matchless private collection: landscapes, birds, flowers, human figures, etc., plus calligraphy. Every basic form included: hanging scrolls, handscrolls, album leaves, fans, etc. 109 illustrations. Introduction. Captions. 192pp. 8⅞ x 11¾. 23707-9 Pa. $7.95

DRAWINGS OF REMBRANDT, edited by Seymour Slive. Updated Lippmann, Hofstede de Groot edition, with definitive scholarly apparatus. All portraits, biblical sketches, landscapes, nudes, Oriental figures, classical studies, together with selection of work by followers. 550 illustrations. Total of 630pp. 9⅛ x 12¼. 21485-0, 21486-9 Pa., Two-vol. set $15.00

THE DISASTERS OF WAR, Francisco Goya. 83 etchings record horrors of Napoleonic wars in Spain and war in general. Reprint of 1st edition, plus 3 additional plates. Introduction by Philip Hofer. 97pp. 9⅜ x 8¼. 21872-4 Pa. $3.75

THE EARLY WORK OF AUBREY BEARDSLEY, Aubrey Beardsley. 157 plates, 2 in color: *Manon Lescaut, Madame Bovary, Morte Darthur, Salome,* other. Introduction by H. Marillier. 182pp. 8⅛ x 11. 21816-3 Pa. $4.50

THE LATER WORK OF AUBREY BEARDSLEY, Aubrey Beardsley. Exotic masterpieces of full maturity: *Venus and Tannhauser, Lysistrata, Rape of the Lock, Volpone,* Savoy material, etc. 174 plates, 2 in color. 186pp. 8⅛ x 11. 21817-1 Pa. $4.50

THOMAS NAST'S CHRISTMAS DRAWINGS, Thomas Nast. Almost all Christmas drawings by creator of image of Santa Claus as we know it, and one of America's foremost illustrators and political cartoonists. 66 illustrations. 3 illustrations in color on covers. 96pp. 8⅜ x 11¼. 23660-9 Pa. $3.50

THE DORÉ ILLUSTRATIONS FOR DANTE'S DIVINE COMEDY, Gustave Doré. All 135 plates from Inferno, Purgatory, Paradise; fantastic tortures, infernal landscapes, celestial wonders. Each plate with appropriate (translated) verses. 141pp. 9 x 12. 23231-X Pa. $4.50

DORÉ'S ILLUSTRATIONS FOR RABELAIS, Gustave Doré. 252 striking illustrations of *Gargantua and Pantagruel* books by foremost 19th-century illustrator. Including 60 plates, 192 delightful smaller illustrations. 153pp. 9 x 12. 23656-0 Pa. $5.00

LONDON: A PILGRIMAGE, Gustave Doré, Blanchard Jerrold. Squalor, riches, misery, beauty of mid-Victorian metropolis; 55 wonderful plates, 125 other illustrations, full social, cultural text by Jerrold. 191pp. of text. 9⅜ x 12¼. 22306-X Pa. $7.00

THE RIME OF THE ANCIENT MARINER, Gustave Doré, S. T. Coleridge. Dore's finest work, 34 plates capture moods, subtleties of poem. Full text. Introduction by Millicent Rose. 77pp. 9¼ x 12. 22305-1 Pa. $3.50

THE DORE BIBLE ILLUSTRATIONS, Gustave Doré. All wonderful, detailed plates: Adam and Eve, Flood, Babylon, Life of Jesus, etc. Brief King James text with each plate. Introduction by Millicent Rose. 241 plates. 241pp. 9 x 12. 23004-X Pa. $6.00

THE COMPLETE ENGRAVINGS, ETCHINGS AND DRYPOINTS OF ALBRECHT DURER. "Knight, Death and Devil"; "Melencolia," and more—all Dürer's known works in all three media, including 6 works formerly attributed to him. 120 plates. 235pp. 8⅜ x 11¼. 22851-7 Pa. $6.50

MAXIMILIAN'S TRIUMPHAL ARCH, Albrecht Dürer and others. Incredible monument of woodcut art: 8 foot high elaborate arch—heraldic figures, humans, battle scenes, fantastic elements—that you can assemble yourself. Printed on one side, layout for assembly. 143pp. 11 x 16. 21451-6 Pa. $5.00

THE COMPLETE WOODCUTS OF ALBRECHT DURER, edited by Dr. W. Kurth. 346 in all: "Old Testament," "St. Jerome," "Passion," "Life of Virgin," "Apocalypse," many others. Introduction by Campbell Dodgson. 285pp. 8½ x 12¼. 21097-9 Pa. $7.50

DRAWINGS OF ALBRECHT DURER, edited by Heinrich Wolfflin. 81 plates show development from youth to full style. Many favorites; many new. Introduction by Alfred Werner. 96pp. 8⅛ x 11. 22352-3 Pa. $5.00

THE HUMAN FIGURE, Albrecht Dürer. Experiments in various techniques—stereometric, progressive proportional, and others. Also life studies that rank among finest ever done. Complete reprinting of *Dresden Sketchbook*. 170 plates. 355pp. 8⅜ x 11¼. 21042-1 Pa. $7.95

OF THE JUST SHAPING OF LETTERS, Albrecht Dürer. Renaissance artist explains design of Roman majuscules by geometry, also Gothic lower and capitals. Grolier Club edition. 43pp. 7⅞ x 10¾ 21306-4 Pa. $3.00

TEN BOOKS ON ARCHITECTURE, Vitruvius. The most important book ever written on architecture. Early Roman aesthetics, technology, classical orders, site selection, all other aspects. Stands behind everything since. Morgan translation. 331pp. 5⅜ x 8½. 20645-9 Pa. $4.50

THE FOUR BOOKS OF ARCHITECTURE, Andrea Palladio. 16th-century classic responsible for Palladian movement and style. Covers classical architectural remains, Renaissance revivals, classical orders, etc. 1738 Ware English edition. Introduction by A. Placzek. 216 plates. 110pp. of text. 9½ x 12¾. 21308-0 Pa. $10.00

HORIZONS, Norman Bel Geddes. Great industrialist stage designer, "father of streamlining," on application of aesthetics to transportation, amusement, architecture, etc. 1932 prophetic account; function, theory, specific projects. 222 illustrations. 312pp. 7⅞ x 10¾. 23514-9 Pa. $6.95

FRANK LLOYD WRIGHT'S FALLINGWATER, Donald Hoffmann. Full, illustrated story of conception and building of Wright's masterwork at Bear Run, Pa. 100 photographs of site, construction, and details of completed structure. 112pp. 9¼ x 10. 23671-4 Pa. $5.50

THE ELEMENTS OF DRAWING, John Ruskin. Timeless classic by great Viltorian; starts with basic ideas, works through more difficult. Many practical exercises. 48 illustrations. Introduction by Lawrence Campbell. 228pp. 5⅜ x 8½. 22730-8 Pa. $3.75

GIST OF ART, John Sloan. Greatest modern American teacher, Art Students League, offers innumerable hints, instructions, guided comments to help you in painting. Not a formal course. 46 illustrations. Introduction by Helen Sloan. 200pp. 5⅜ x 8½. 23435-5 Pa. $4.00

THE ANATOMY OF THE HORSE, George Stubbs. Often considered the great masterpiece of animal anatomy. Full reproduction of 1766 edition, plus prospectus; original text and modernized text. 36 plates. Introduction by Eleanor Garvey. 121pp. 11 x 14¾.   23402-9 Pa. $6.00

BRIDGMAN'S LIFE DRAWING, George B. Bridgman. More than 500 illustrative drawings and text teach you to abstract the body into its major masses, use light and shade, proportion; as well as specific areas of anatomy, of which Bridgman is master. 192pp. 6½ x 9¼. (Available in U.S. only)
22710-3 Pa. $3.50

ART NOUVEAU DESIGNS IN COLOR, Alphonse Mucha, Maurice Verneuil, Georges Auriol. Full-color reproduction of *Combinaisons ornementales* (c. 1900) by Art Nouveau masters. Floral, animal, geometric, interlacings, swashes—borders, frames, spots—all incredibly beautiful. 60 plates, hundreds of designs. 9⅜ x 8-1/16.   22885-1 Pa. $4.00

FULL-COLOR FLORAL DESIGNS IN THE ART NOUVEAU STYLE, E. A. Seguy. 166 motifs, on 40 plates, from *Les fleurs et leurs applications decoratives* (1902): borders, circular designs, repeats, allovers, "spots." All in authentic Art Nouveau colors. 48pp. 9⅜ x 12¼.
23439-8 Pa. $5.00

A DIDEROT PICTORIAL ENCYCLOPEDIA OF TRADES AND IN-DUSTRY, edited by Charles C. Gillispie. 485 most interesting plates from the great French Encyclopedia of the 18th century show hundreds of working figures, artifacts, process, land and cityscapes; glassmaking, paper-making, metal extraction, construction, weaving, making furniture, clothing, wigs, dozens of other activities. Plates fully explained. 920pp. 9 x 12.
22284-5, 22285-3 Clothbd., Two-vol. set $40.00

HANDBOOK OF EARLY ADVERTISING ART, Clarence P. Hornung. Largest collection of copyright-free early and antique advertising art ever compiled. Over 6,000 illustrations, from Franklin's time to the 1890's for special effects, novelty. Valuable source, almost inexhaustible.
Pictorial Volume. Agriculture, the zodiac, animals, autos, birds, Christmas, fire engines, flowers, trees, musical instruments, ships, games and sports, much more. Arranged by subject matter and use. 237 plates. 288pp. 9 x 12.
20122-8 Clothbd. $14.50

Typographical Volume. Roman and Gothic faces ranging from 10 point to 300 point, "Barnum," German and Old English faces, script, logotypes, scrolls and flourishes, 1115 ornamental initials, 67 complete alphabets, more. 310 plates. 320pp. 9 x 12.   20123-6 Clothbd. $15.00

CALLIGRAPHY (CALLIGRAPHIA LATINA), J. G. Schwandner. High point of 18th-century ornamental calligraphy. Very ornate initials, scrolls, borders, cherubs, birds, lettered examples. 172pp. 9 x 13.
20475-8 Pa. $7.00

ART FORMS IN NATURE, Ernst Haeckel. Multitude of strangely beautiful natural forms: Radiolaria, Foraminifera, jellyfishes, fungi, turtles, bats, etc. All 100 plates of the 19th-century evolutionist's *Kunstformen der Natur* (1904). 100pp. 9⅜ x 12¼. 22987-4 Pa. $5.00

CHILDREN: A PICTORIAL ARCHIVE FROM NINETEENTH-CENTURY SOURCES, edited by Carol Belanger Grafton. 242 rare, copyright-free wood engravings for artists and designers. Widest such selection available. All illustrations in line. 119pp. 8⅜ x 11¼.
23694-3 Pa. $3.50

WOMEN: A PICTORIAL ARCHIVE FROM NINETEENTH-CENTURY SOURCES, edited by Jim Harter. 391 copyright-free wood engravings for artists and designers selected from rare periodicals. Most extensive such collection available. All illustrations in line. 128pp. 9 x 12.
23703-6 Pa. $4.50

ARABIC ART IN COLOR, Prisse d'Avennes. From the greatest ornamentalists of all time—50 plates in color, rarely seen outside the Near East, rich in suggestion and stimulus. Includes 4 plates on covers. 46pp. 9⅜ x 12¼. 23658-7 Pa. $6.00

AUTHENTIC ALGERIAN CARPET DESIGNS AND MOTIFS, edited by June Beveridge. Algerian carpets are world famous. Dozens of geometrical motifs are charted on grids, color-coded, for weavers, needleworkers, craftsmen, designers. 53 illustrations plus 4 in color. 48pp. 8¼ x 11. (Available in U.S. only) 23650-1 Pa. $1.75

DICTIONARY OF AMERICAN PORTRAITS, edited by Hayward and Blanche Cirker. 4000 important Americans, earliest times to 1905, mostly in clear line. Politicians, writers, soldiers, scientists, inventors, industrialists, Indians, Blacks, women, outlaws, etc. Identificatory information. 756pp. 9¼ x 12¾. 21823-6 Clothbd. $40.00

HOW THE OTHER HALF LIVES, Jacob A. Riis. Journalistic record of filth, degradation, upward drive in New York immigrant slums, shops, around 1900. New edition includes 100 original Riis photos, monuments of early photography. 233pp. 10 x 7⅞. 22012-5 Pa. $7.00

NEW YORK IN THE THIRTIES, Berenice Abbott. Noted photographer's fascinating study of city shows new buildings that have become famous and old sights that have disappeared forever. Insightful commentary. 97 photographs. 97pp. 11⅜ x 10. 22967-X Pa. $5.00

MEN AT WORK, Lewis W. Hine. Famous photographic studies of construction workers, railroad men, factory workers and coal miners. New supplement of 18 photos on Empire State building construction. New introduction by Jonathan L. Doherty. Total of 69 photos. 63pp. 8 x 10¾.
23475-4 Pa. $3.00

THE DEPRESSION YEARS AS PHOTOGRAPHED BY ARTHUR ROTH-STEIN, Arthur Rothstein. First collection devoted entirely to the work of outstanding 1930s photographer: famous dust storm photo, ragged children, unemployed, etc. 120 photographs. Captions. 119pp. 9¼ x 10¾.
23590-4 Pa. $5.00

CAMERA WORK: A PICTORIAL GUIDE, Alfred Stieglitz. All 559 illustrations and plates from the most important periodical in the history of art photography, Camera Work (1903-17). Presented four to a page, reduced in size but still clear, in strict chronological order, with complete captions. Three indexes. Glossary. Bibliography. 176pp. 8⅜ x 11¼.
23591-2 Pa. $6.95

ALVIN LANGDON COBURN, PHOTOGRAPHER, Alvin L. Coburn. Revealing autobiography by one of greatest photographers of 20th century gives insider's version of Photo-Secession, plus comments on his own work. 77 photographs by Coburn. Edited by Helmut and Alison Gernsheim. 160pp. 8⅛ x 11.
23685-4 Pa. $6.00

NEW YORK IN THE FORTIES, Andreas Feininger. 162 brilliant photographs by the well-known photographer, formerly with Life magazine, show commuters, shoppers, Times Square at night, Harlem nightclub, Lower East Side, etc. Introduction and full captions by John von Hartz. 181pp. 9¼ x 10¾.
23585-8 Pa. $6.00

GREAT NEWS PHOTOS AND THE STORIES BEHIND THEM, John Faber. Dramatic volume of 140 great news photos, 1855 through 1976, and revealing stories behind them, with both historical and technical information. Hindenburg disaster, shooting of Oswald, nomination of Jimmy Carter, etc. 160pp. 8¼ x 11.
23667-6 Pa. $5.00

THE ART OF THE CINEMATOGRAPHER, Leonard Maltin. Survey of American cinematography history and anecdotal interviews with 5 masters—Arthur Miller, Hal Mohr, Hal Rosson, Lucien Ballard, and Conrad Hall. Very large selection of behind-the-scenes production photos. 105 photographs. Filmographies. Index. Originally Behind the Camera. 144pp. 8¼ x 11.
23686-2 Pa. $5.00

DESIGNS FOR THE THREE-CORNERED HAT (LE TRICORNE), Pablo Picasso. 32 fabulously rare drawings—including 31 color illustrations of costumes and accessories—for 1919 production of famous ballet. Edited by Parmenia Migel, who has written new introduction. 48pp. 9⅜ x 12¼. (Available in U.S. only)
23709-5 Pa. $5.00

NOTES OF A FILM DIRECTOR, Sergei Eisenstein. Greatest Russian filmmaker explains montage, making of Alexander Nevsky, aesthetics; comments on self, associates, great rivals (Chaplin), similar material. 78 illustrations. 240pp. 5⅜ x 8½.
22392-2 Pa. $4.50

HOLLYWOOD GLAMOUR PORTRAITS, edited by John Kobal. 145 photos capture the stars from 1926-49, the high point in portrait photography. Gable, Harlow, Bogart, Bacall, Hedy Lamarr, Marlene Dietrich, Robert Montgomery, Marlon Brando, Veronica Lake; 94 stars in all. Full background on photographers, technical aspects, much more. Total of 160pp. 8⅜ x 11¼. 23352-9 Pa. **$6.00**

THE NEW YORK STAGE: FAMOUS PRODUCTIONS IN PHOTO-GRAPHS, edited by Stanley Appelbaum. 148 photographs from Museum of City of New York show 142 plays, 1883-1939. *Peter Pan, The Front Page, Dead End, Our Town,* O'Neill, hundreds of actors and actresses, etc. Full indexes. 154pp. 9½ x 10. 23241-7 Pa. **$6.00**

DIALOGUES CONCERNING TWO NEW SCIENCES, Galileo Galilei. Encompassing 30 years of experiment and thought, these dialogues deal with geometric demonstrations of fracture of solid bodies, cohesion, leverage, speed of light and sound, pendulums, falling bodies, accelerated motion, etc. 300pp. 5⅜ x 8½. 60099-8 Pa. $4.00

THE GREAT OPERA STARS IN HISTORIC PHOTOGRAPHS, edited by James Camner. 343 portraits from the 1850s to the 1940s: Tamburini, Mario, Caliapin, Jeritza, Melchior, Melba, Patti, Pinza, Schipa, Caruso, Farrar, Steber, Gobbi, and many more—270 performers in all. Index. 199pp. 8⅜ x 11¼. 23575-0 Pa. $6.50

J. S. BACH, Albert Schweitzer. Great full-length study of Bach, life, background to music, music, by foremost modern scholar. Ernest Newman translation. 650 musical examples. Total of 928pp. 5⅜ x 8½. (Available in U.S. only) 21631-4, 21632-2 Pa., Two-vol. set $11.00

COMPLETE PIANO SONATAS, Ludwig van Beethoven. All sonatas in the fine Schenker edition, with fingering, analytical material. One of best modern editions. Total of 615pp. 9 x 12. (Available in U.S. only) 23134-8, 23135-6 Pa., Two-vol. set $15.00

KEYBOARD MUSIC, J. S. Bach. Bach-Gesellschaft edition. For harpsichord, piano, other keyboard instruments. English Suites, French Suites, Six Partitas, Goldberg Variations, Two-Part Inventions, Three-Part Sinfonias. 312pp. 8⅛ x 11. (Available in U.S. only) 22360-4 Pa. **$6.95**

FOUR SYMPHONIES IN FULL SCORE, Franz Schubert. Schubert's four most popular symphonies: No. 4 in C Minor ("Tragic"); No. 5 in B-flat Major; No. 8 in B Minor ("Unfinished"); No. 9 in C Major ("Great"). Breitkopf & Hartel edition. Study score. 261pp. 9⅜ x 12¼.
23681-1 Pa. $6.50

THE AUTHENTIC GILBERT & SULLIVAN SONGBOOK, W. S. Gilbert, A. S. Sullivan. Largest selection available; 92 songs, uncut, original keys, in piano rendering approved by Sullivan. Favorites and lesser-known fine numbers. Edited with plot synopses by James Spero. 3 illustrations. 399pp. 9 x 12. 23482-7 Pa. **$9.95**

PRINCIPLES OF ORCHESTRATION, Nikolay Rimsky-Korsakov. Great classical orchestrator provides fundamentals of tonal resonance, progression of parts, voice and orchestra, tutti effects, much else in major document. 330pp. of musical excerpts. 489pp. 6½ x 9¼.   21266-1 Pa. **$7.50**

TRISTAN UND ISOLDE, Richard Wagner. Full orchestral score with complete instrumentation. Do not confuse with piano reduction. Commentary by Felix Mottl, great Wagnerian conductor and scholar. Study score. 655pp. 8⅛ x 11.   22915-7 Pa. **$13.95**

REQUIEM IN FULL SCORE, Giuseppe Verdi. Immensely popular with choral groups and music lovers. Republication of edition published by C. F. Peters, Leipzig, n. d. German frontmaker in English translation. Glossary. Text in Latin. Study score. 204pp. 9⅜ x 12¼.
23682-X Pa. **$6.00**

COMPLETE CHAMBER MUSIC FOR STRINGS, Felix Mendelssohn. All of Mendelssohn's chamber music: Octet, 2 Quintets, 6 Quartets, and Four Pieces for String Quartet. (Nothing with piano is included). Complete works edition (1874-7). Study score. 283 pp. 9⅜ x 12¼.
23679-X Pa. **$7.50**

POPULAR SONGS OF NINETEENTH-CENTURY AMERICA, edited by Richard Jackson. 64 most important songs: "Old Oaken Bucket," "Arkansas Traveler," "Yellow Rose of Texas," etc. Authentic original sheet music, full introduction and commentaries. 290pp. 9 x 12.   23270-0 Pa. **$7.95**

COLLECTED PIANO WORKS, Scott Joplin. Edited by Vera Brodsky Lawrence. Practically all of Joplin's piano works—rags, two-steps, marches, waltzes, etc., 51 works in all. Extensive introduction by Rudi Blesh. Total of 345pp. 9 x 12.   23106-2 Pa. **$14.95**

BASIC PRINCIPLES OF CLASSICAL BALLET, Agrippina Vaganova. Great Russian theoretician, teacher explains methods for teaching classical ballet; incorporates best from French, Italian, Russian schools. 118 illustrations. 175pp. 5⅜ x 8½.   22036-2 Pa. **$2.50**

CHINESE CHARACTERS, L. Wieger. Rich analysis of 2300 characters according to traditional systems into primitives. Historical-semantic analysis to phonetics (Classical Mandarin) and radicals. 820pp. 6⅛ x 9¼.
21321-8 Pa. **$10.00**

EGYPTIAN LANGUAGE: EASY LESSONS IN EGYPTIAN HIERO-GLYPHICS, E. A. Wallis Budge. Foremost Egyptologist offers Egyptian grammar, explanation of hieroglyphics, many reading texts, dictionary of symbols. 246pp. 5 x 7½. (Available in U.S. only)
21394-3 Clothbd. **$7.50**

AN ETYMOLOGICAL DICTIONARY OF MODERN ENGLISH, Ernest Weekley. Richest, fullest work, by foremost British lexicographer. Detailed word histories. Inexhaustible. Do not confuse this with *Concise Etymological Dictionary*, which is abridged. Total of 856pp. 6½ x 9¼.
21873-2, 21874-0 Pa., Two-vol. set **$12.00**

A MAYA GRAMMAR, Alfred M. Tozzer. Practical, useful English-language grammar by the Harvard anthropologist who was one of the three greatest American scholars in the area of Maya culture. Phonetics, grammatical processes, syntax, more. 301pp. 5⅜ x 8½. 23465-7 Pa. $4.00

THE JOURNAL OF HENRY D. THOREAU, edited by Bradford Torrey, F. H. Allen. Complete reprinting of 14 volumes, 1837-61, over two million words; the sourcebooks for *Walden*, etc. Definitive. All original sketches, plus 75 photographs. Introduction by Walter Harding. Total of 1804pp. 8½ x 12¼. 20312-3, 20313-1 Clothbd., Two-vol. set $50.00

CLASSIC GHOST STORIES, Charles Dickens and others. 18 wonderful stories you've wanted to reread: "The Monkey's Paw," "The House and the Brain," "The Upper Berth," "The Signalman," "Dracula's Guest," "The Tapestried Chamber," etc. Dickens, Scott, Mary Shelley, Stoker, etc. 330pp. 5⅜ x 8½. 20735-8 Pa. $4.50

SEVEN SCIENCE FICTION NOVELS, H. G. Wells. Full novels. *First Men in the Moon, Island of Dr. Moreau, War of the Worlds, Food of the Gods, Invisible Man, Time Machine, In the Days of the Comet*. A basic science-fiction library. 1015pp. 5⅜ x 8½. (Available in U.S. only) 20264-X Clothbd. $8.95

ARMADALE, Wilkie Collins. Third great mystery novel by the author of *The Woman in White* and *The Moonstone*. Ingeniously plotted narrative shows an exceptional command of character, incident and mood. Original magazine version with 40 illustrations. 597pp. 5⅜ x 8½. 23429-0 Pa. $6.00

MASTERS OF MYSTERY, H. Douglas Thomson. The first book in English (1931) devoted to history and aesthetics of detective story. Poe, Doyle, LeFanu, Dickens, many others, up to 1930. New introduction and notes by E. F. Bleiler. 288pp. 5⅜ x 8½. (Available in U.S. only) 23606-4 Pa. $4.00

FLATLAND, E. A. Abbott. Science-fiction classic explores life of 2-D being in 3-D world. Read also as introduction to thought about hyperspace. Introduction by Banesh Hoffmann. 16 illustrations. 103pp. 5⅜ x 8½. 20001-9 Pa. $2.00

THREE SUPERNATURAL NOVELS OF THE VICTORIAN PERIOD, edited, with an introduction, by E. F. Bleiler. Reprinted complete and unabridged, three great classics of the supernatural: *The Haunted Hotel* by Wilkie Collins, *The Haunted House at Latchford* by Mrs. J. H. Riddell, and *The Lost Stradivarious* by J. Meade Falkner. 325pp. 5⅜ x 8½. 22571-2 Pa. $4.00

AYESHA: THE RETURN OF "SHE," H. Rider Haggard. Virtuoso sequel featuring the great mythic creation, Ayesha, in an adventure that is fully as good as the first book, *She*. Original magazine version, with 47 original illustrations by Maurice Greiffenhagen. 189pp. 6½ x 9¼. 23649-8 Pa. $3.50

UNCLE SILAS, J. Sheridan LeFanu. Victorian Gothic mystery novel, considered by many best of period, even better than Collins or Dickens. Wonderful psychological terror. Introduction by Frederick Shroyer. 436pp. 5⅜ x 8½.   21715-9 Pa. $6.00

JURGEN, James Branch Cabell. The great erotic fantasy of the 1920's that delighted thousands, shocked thousands more. Full final text, Lane edition with 13 plates by Frank Pape. 346pp. 5⅜ x 8½.
                                                          23507-6 Pa. $4.50

THE CLAVERINGS, Anthony Trollope. Major novel, chronicling aspects of British Victorian society, personalities. Reprint of Cornhill serialization, 16 plates by M. Edwards; first reprint of full text. Introduction by Norman Donaldson. 412pp. 5⅜ x 8½.   23464-9 Pa. $5.00

KEPT IN THE DARK, Anthony Trollope. Unusual short novel about Victorian morality and abnormal psychology by the great English author. Probably the first American publication. Frontispiece by Sir John Millais. 92pp. 6½ x 9¼.   23609-9 Pa. $2.50

RALPH THE HEIR, Anthony Trollope. Forgotten tale of illegitimacy, inheritance. Master novel of Trollope's later years. Victorian country estates, clubs, Parliament, fox hunting, world of fully realized characters. Reprint of 1871 edition. 12 illustrations by F. A. Faser. 434pp. of text. 5⅜ x 8½.   23642-0 Pa. $5.00

YEKL and THE IMPORTED BRIDEGROOM AND OTHER STORIES OF THE NEW YORK GHETTO, Abraham Cahan. Film *Hester Street* based on *Yekl* (1896). Novel, other stories among first about Jewish immigrants of N.Y.'s East Side. Highly praised by W. D. Howells—Cahan "a new star of realism." New introduction by Bernard G. Richards. 240pp. 5⅜ x 8½.   22427-9 Pa. $3.50

THE HIGH PLACE, James Branch Cabell. Great fantasy writer's enchanting comedy of disenchantment set in 18th-century France. Considered by some critics to be even better than his famous *Jurgen*. 10 illustrations and numerous vignettes by noted fantasy artist Frank C. Pape. 320pp. 5⅜ x 8½.   23670-6 Pa. $4.00

ALICE'S ADVENTURES UNDER GROUND, Lewis Carroll. Facsimile of ms. Carroll gave Alice Liddell in 1864. Different in many ways from final Alice. Handlettered, illustrated by Carroll. Introduction by Martin Gardner. 128pp. 5⅜ x 8½.   21482-6 Pa. $2.00

FAVORITE ANDREW LANG FAIRY TALE BOOKS IN MANY COLORS, Andrew Lang. The four Lang favorites in a boxed set—the complete *Red, Green, Yellow* and *Blue* Fairy Books. 164 stories; 439 illustrations by Lancelot Speed, Henry Ford and G. P. Jacomb Hood. Total of about 1500pp. 5⅜ x 8½.   23407-X Boxed set, Pa. $14.95

HOUSEHOLD STORIES BY THE BROTHERS GRIMM. All the great Grimm stories: "Rumpelstiltskin," "Snow White," "Hansel and Gretel," etc., with 114 illustrations by Walter Crane. 269pp. 5⅜ x 8½.
21080-4 Pa. $3.50

SLEEPING BEAUTY, illustrated by Arthur Rackham. Perhaps the fullest, most delightful version ever, told by C. S. Evans. Rackham's best work. 49 illustrations. 110pp. 7⅞ x 10¾. 22756-1 Pa. $2.50

AMERICAN FAIRY TALES, L. Frank Baum. Young cowboy lassoes Father Time; dummy in Mr. Floman's department store window comes to life; and 10 other fairy tales. 41 illustrations by N. P. Hall, Harry Kennedy, Ike Morgan, and Ralph Gardner. 209pp. 5⅜ x 8½. 23643-9 Pa. $3.00

THE WONDERFUL WIZARD OF OZ, L. Frank Baum. Facsimile in full color of America's finest children's classic. Introduction by Martin Gardner. 143 illustrations by W. W. Denslow. 267pp. 5⅜ x 8½.
20691-2 Pa. $3.50

THE TALE OF PETER RABBIT, Beatrix Potter. The inimitable Peter's terrifying adventure in Mr. McGregor's garden, with all 27 wonderful, full-color Potter illustrations. 55pp. 4¼ x 5½. (Available in U.S. only)
22827-4 Pa. $1.25

THE STORY OF KING ARTHUR AND HIS KNIGHTS, Howard Pyle. Finest children's version of life of King Arthur. 48 illustrations by Pyle. 131pp. 6⅛ x 9¼. 21445-1 Pa. $4.95

CARUSO'S CARICATURES, Enrico Caruso. Great tenor's remarkable caricatures of self, fellow musicians, composers, others. Toscanini, Puccini, Farrar, etc. Impish, cutting, insightful. 473 illustrations. Preface by M. Sisca. 217pp. 8⅜ x 11¼. 23528-9 Pa. $6.95

PERSONAL NARRATIVE OF A PILGRIMAGE TO ALMADINAH AND MECCAH, Richard Burton. Great travel classic by remarkably colorful personality. Burton, disguised as a Moroccan, visited sacred shrines of Islam, narrowly escaping death. Wonderful observations of Islamic life, customs, personalities. 47 illustrations. Total of 959pp. 5⅜ x 8½.
21217-3, 21218-1 Pa., Two-vol. set $12.00

INCIDENTS OF TRAVEL IN YUCATAN, John L. Stephens. Classic (1843) exploration of jungles of Yucatan, looking for evidences of Maya civilization. Travel adventures, Mexican and Indian culture, etc. Total of 669pp. 5⅜ x 8½. 20926-1, 20927-X Pa., Two-vol. set $7.90

AMERICAN LITERARY AUTOGRAPHS FROM WASHINGTON IRVING TO HENRY JAMES, Herbert Cahoon, et al. Letters, poems, manuscripts of Hawthorne, Thoreau, Twain, Alcott, Whitman, 67 other prominent American authors. Reproductions, full transcripts and commentary. Plus checklist of all American Literary Autographs in The Pierpont Morgan Library. Printed on exceptionally high-quality paper. 136 illustrations. 212pp. 9⅛ x 12¼. 23548-3 Pa. $12.50

AN AUTOBIOGRAPHY, Margaret Sanger. Exciting personal account of hard-fought battle for woman's right to birth control, against prejudice, church, law. Foremost feminist document. 504pp. 5⅜ x 8½.
20470-7 Pa. $5.50

MY BONDAGE AND MY FREEDOM, Frederick Douglass. Born as a slave, Douglass became outspoken force in antislavery movement. The best of Douglass's autobiographies. Graphic description of slave life. Introduction by P. Foner. 464pp. 5⅜ x 8½.
22457-0 Pa. $5.50

LIVING MY LIFE, Emma Goldman. Candid, no holds barred account by foremost American anarchist: her own life, anarchist movement, famous contemporaries, ideas and their impact. Struggles and confrontations in America, plus deportation to U.S.S.R. Shocking inside account of persecution of anarchists under Lenin. 13 plates. Total of 944pp. 5⅜ x 8½.
22543-7, 22544-5 Pa., Two-vol. set $12.00

LETTERS AND NOTES ON THE MANNERS, CUSTOMS AND CONDITIONS OF THE NORTH AMERICAN INDIANS, George Catlin. Classic account of life among Plains Indians: ceremonies, hunt, warfare, etc. Dover edition reproduces for first time all original paintings. 312 plates. 572pp. of text. 6⅛ x 9¼.
22118-0, 22119-9 Pa.. Two-vol. set $12.00

THE MAYA AND THEIR NEIGHBORS, edited by Clarence L. Hay, others. Synoptic view of Maya civilization in broadest sense, together with Northern, Southern neighbors. Integrates much background, valuable detail not elsewhere. Prepared by greatest scholars: Kroeber, Morley, Thompson, Spinden, Vaillant, many others. Sometimes called Tozzer Memorial Volume. 60 illustrations, linguistic map. 634pp. 5⅜ x 8½.
23510-6 Pa. $7.50

HANDBOOK OF THE INDIANS OF CALIFORNIA, A. L. Kroeber. Foremost American anthropologist offers complete ethnographic study of each group. Monumental classic. 459 illustrations, maps. 995pp. 5⅜ x 8½.
23368-5 Pa. $13.00

SHAKTI AND SHAKTA, Arthur Avalon. First book to give clear, cohesive analysis of Shakta doctrine, Shakta ritual and Kundalini Shakti (yoga). Important work by one of world's foremost students of Shaktic and Tantric thought. 732pp. 5⅜ x 8½. (Available in U.S. only)
23645-5 Pa. $7.95

AN INTRODUCTION TO THE STUDY OF THE MAYA HIEROGLYPHS, Syvanus Griswold Morley. Classic study by one of the truly great figures in hieroglyph research. Still the best introduction for the student for reading Maya hieroglyphs. New introduction by J. Eric S. Thompson. 117 illustrations. 284pp. 5⅜ x 8½.
23108-9 Pa. $4.00

A STUDY OF MAYA ART, Herbert J. Spinden. Landmark classic interprets Maya symbolism, estimates styles, covers ceramics, architecture, murals, stone carvings as artforms. Still a basic book in area. New introduction by J. Eric Thompson. Over 750 illustrations. 341pp. 8⅜ x 11¼.
21235-1 Pa. $6.95

GEOMETRY, RELATIVITY AND THE FOURTH DIMENSION, Rudolf Rucker. Exposition of fourth dimension, means of visualization, concepts of relativity as Flatland characters continue adventures. Popular, easily followed yet accurate, profound. 141 illustrations. 133pp. 5⅜ x 8½.
23400-2 Pa. $2.75

THE ORIGIN OF LIFE, A. I. Oparin. Modern classic in biochemistry, the first rigorous examination of possible evolution of life from nitrocarbon compounds. Non-technical, easily followed. Total of 295pp. 5⅜ x 8½.
60213-3 Pa. $4.00

PLANETS, STARS AND GALAXIES, A. E. Fanning. Comprehensive introductory survey: the sun, solar system, stars, galaxies, universe, cosmology; quasars, radio stars, etc. 24pp. of photographs. 189pp. 5⅜ x 8½. (Available in U.S. only)
21680-2 Pa. $3.75

THE THIRTEEN BOOKS OF EUCLID'S ELEMENTS, translated with introduction and commentary by Sir Thomas L. Heath. Definitive edition. Textual and linguistic notes, mathematical analysis, 2500 years of critical commentary. Do not confuse with abridged school editions. Total of 1414pp. 5⅜ x 8½.   60088-2, 60089-0, 60090-4 Pa., Three-vol. set $18.50

Prices subject to change without notice.

Available at your book dealer or write for free catalogue to Dept. GI, Dover Publications, Inc., 180 Varick St., N.Y., N.Y. 10014. Dover publishes more than 175 books each year on science, elementary and advanced mathematics, biology, music, art, literary history, social sciences and other areas.